My Times

My

Praise they that will times past,
I joy to see
My self now live: this age best
pleaseth me.
— *Robert Herrick*

The times, they are a-changing.
— *Bob Dylan*

Living with history
1947-1995

Times

By Pierre Berton

Doubleday Canada Limited

Some of the material in this book has appeared in considerably different form in several Canadian newspapers and periodicals.

Canadian Cataloguing in Publication Data

Berton, Pierre, 1920–
    My times: living with history, 1947–1995

Includes index.
ISBN 0-385-25528-4

I. Berton, Pierre, 1920–   2. Historians – Canada –
Biography. I. Title

FC151.B4A3 1995 971'.007202 C95-930995-0
F1024.6.B4A3 1995

I am grateful to these people for their useful comments on the manuscript: my editor, Janice Tyrwhitt; my copy editor, Janet Craig; John Pearce of Doubleday; my agent, Elsa Franklin; my wife, Janet Berton; and to Emily Bradshaw, who prepared the typescript efficiently, in all its myriad forms. Photographs come mainly from my own collection with help from the *Toronto Star, Maclean's,* National Archives of Canada, the late Bernard Cowan, James Ramsay, Boris Spremo, and Susan Gaby-Trotz.

Published in Canada by
Doubleday Canada Limited
105 Bond Street
Toronto, Ontario
M5B 1Y3

*This book
is for Janet,
without whom…*

Books by Pierre Berton

The Royal Family
The Mysterious North
Klondike
Just Add Water and Stir
Adventures of a Columnist
Fast, Fast, Fast Relief
The Big Sell
The Comfortable Pew
The Cool, Crazy, Committed
    World of the Sixties
The Smug Minority
The National Dream
The Last Spike
Drifting Home
Hollywood's Canada
My Country
The Dionne Years
The Wild Frontier
The Invasion of Canada
Flames Across the Border
Why We Act Like Canadians
The Promised Land
Vimy
Starting Out
The Arctic Grail
The Great Depression
Niagara
My Times

PICTURE BOOKS
The New City (with Henri Rossier)
Remember Yesterday
The Great Railway
The Klondike Quest
Pierre Berton's Picture Book of
    Niagara Falls
Winter

ANTHOLOGIES
Great Canadians
Pierre and Janet Berton's
    Centennial Food Guide
Historic Headlines

FOR YOUNG READERS
The Golden Trail
The Secret World of Og
Adventures in Canadian History
    (21 volumes)

FICTION
Masquerade (pseudonym, Lisa
    Kroniuk)

Contents

Photographic albums follow pages 120, 216, 312

Prologue

When this book is published I will be seventy-five years old – a ripe old age, as they said in the days before medical science began lengthening the life span. In my youth, men of seventy-five were old, bent, and grizzled. Women were white haired and bespectacled; they still are, on the Mother's Day cards that haven't kept up with an era of contact lenses and Clairol. Thanks to medical advances during my lifetime, I do not feel old as my father did at the same age – old, infirm, and no longer in love with life. The times have kept me young in spirit, for they have been remarkable times – exciting, alarming, often brutal, sometimes baffling, but always stimulating enough to keep a writer's juices flowing and to hold the years at bay.

As a historian I have been a recorder of other people's times. As a journalist I have been witness to my own – privileged, or perhaps condemned, to live through this most extraordinary century. I have watched history roll breathlessly by at an ever-increasing speed, for this is the first century in which acceleration of change has become the norm.

This speeding up of history has made my times unpredictable.

How could I have known, in my university years, that a new invention, television, would change my life and turn me into a celebrity? In my days at *Maclean's* in the 1950s, we ran several articles about the new computers and how they worked, but we had no understanding of their potential. How could I have foreseen the microchip age, which is now turning society on its ear? I knew a good deal about nineteenth-century rail travel but nothing about a coming information highway. In 1983, I owed my life to a new drug that hadn't existed a few years before. Without it I would have been long gone. Nine additional books owe their existence to streptokinase.

My times have been the most exciting of all times, and also the most alarming – the best of times and the worst, to paraphrase Dickens. Because of the transportation revolution I have been able to visit every one of the seven continents, including Antarctica. I have seen enough

1

of the world not to want to see any more. But I am grateful for having been given a box seat to watch the parade of twentieth-century events in all their dazzling variety. I have seen the Berlin Wall rising, block by block, and have heard the nightly rattle of gunfire in the abandoned streets of Seoul. I have seen John Kennedy in his moment of triumph in Los Angeles, Vyshinsky in full cry in New York, and Lenin mummified in his Moscow tomb. I have talked to many of the movers and shakers of my time: William Zeckendorf, Harold Wilson, Jane Jacobs, César Chávez, Germaine Greer, Abby Hoffman, Daniel Cohn-Bendit, Jerry Rubin, Malcolm X, René Lévesque. I have seen enough of the remains of past civilizations – Machu Picchu, the Great Pyramid, the Parthenon, the Forbidden City – to know that ours cannot endure forever.

I have seen my own country transformed. In my time half a dozen political parties have been born and brought down. A new respect for the arts has been accompanied by a renaissance in national feeling. For all my life Canadians have argued about the future of the country. But who, when I joined *Maclean's* in 1947, would have predicted a separatist party in Quebec – and a separatist Opposition in Ottawa? Certainly not I, then or later. (I have tried to stay out of the prediction business ever since I read that H.G. Wells had forecast at the turn of the century that the next war would be fought on bicycles.)

When I was born there were fewer than nine million people in Canada. Now there are three times that many. This increase has generally been hailed by businessmen and politicians as a good thing. Until recently, it was called progress. Now, with the farmland covered by asphalt, with forests levelled to supply timber for more and more buildings, with the air and the water polluted by the effluent of the population explosion, and with garbage piling up in the burgeoning suburbs, people are having second thoughts. I was brought up to believe that growth meant happiness and prosperity. When, thirty years ago, I among others suggested that this might be a fallacy, we were attacked as either starry-eyed idealists or dangerous radicals. Now growth has become the great concern of my times.

For these have been revolutionary times. Old concepts have been turned topsy-turvy. Thirty-odd years ago it was worth one's job to attack the royal family, as the CBC's Joyce Davidson discovered. To suggest that sex before marriage might be acceptable was to court similar punishment, as I found out. Established religion was about to crumble,

2

but the old guard failed to notice that the pews were becoming too comfortable.

In my youth there was no such thing as a "teenager." I became an adult when I went to work on my seventeenth birthday at seventy hours a week. Today, the youth culture has its own liturgy, its own rituals, and its own hymns. In no other period has music played such an important role as it has in the last half of this century. Rock and roll united people all over the world, as I discovered in the youth panels that I hosted on television from Lebanon and Israel to Czechoslovakia and West Germany.

My times have seen the rise and the fall of the Cult of Personality from Moscow to Beijing, where gigantic photographs of Mao Tse-tung once stared down at me from a hundred billboards. "Personality" has become one of the buzzwords of the century. Individuals are publicized today not for what they do, but for what they are. For years I was introduced at various functions as a "well-known personality." Only recently have I been identified as a writer.

Fame, in my times, has been fleeting. How many baby boomers today would recognize the names of Oscar Brand, Bergen Evans, Tony Galento, Ralph Ginzburg, Hildegaard Knef, Barbara Feldon, Jim Moran, Jo Anne Pflug, Stan Freberg, George Lazenby, Webley Edwards, Sheila Scott, Louis Nizer, Fleur Cowles, or Marjoe? Few if any; yet I once thought them all worth a half hour of television time. They had the fifteen minutes that Andy Warhol allotted them and faded from the scene.

This has been a century of unpredictable upheaval. When I visited Chile in 1949, democracy seemed secure; it wasn't. When I rode the Moscow subway in 1959 and looked up at the portraits of the Marxist pantheon, communism seemed entrenched forever, yet Khrushchev was already writing finis to the Stalinist epoch and sowing the seeds of future chaos. In Prague in 1967, the intellectuals talked of a political thaw; the next year Russian tanks made a mockery of that wistful hope. And how could I have known, as I bought a bracelet for my wife in the famous Gold Street of Beirut, that the whole city would be reduced to rubble within a few years?

For that matter, how could I know when, at the age of twenty-seven, I left beautiful Vancouver for the dubious fleshpots of the East what the future would bring? How could I know that fame and fortune awaited me not in the land of the free and the home of the brave, as so many Canadians believed, but lurked closer to home in the most anally retentive

3

town in the country? Opportunity had tapped only lightly on my door when my wife and I set off for Toronto. I opened the door a notch, hoping to catch a glimpse of a shining future, but all I saw was a series of murky tomorrows, endured in an uptight collection of villages that the rest of the country sneered at and dismissed as Hogtown.

Chapter One

1

Hogtown Toronto! *Oh Good Lord, not Toronto!* It was as if we were leaving for Outer Mongolia. Our friends acted as if we had joined the Legion of the Damned. "Why would anyone want to leave Vancouver?" I had asked Scott Young, as I stared smugly out the window of the hotel at the blue mountains and the dazzling inlet.

"Too bad," Scott said. "I was going to offer you a job in Toronto – on *Maclean's.*"

"I'll take it," I said, without drawing a breath.

Of course, we had no intention of remaining in Hogtown. It was merely a tedious way point on the rocky road of my ambitions. Two years of serfdom at the very most – that was my plan. Surely by then one of the editors of *Life* or the *Saturday Evening Post* would notice my brilliant work for *Maclean's* and extend a beckoning finger.

Even today the image of Hogtown remains, though Toronto has changed out of all recognition. But in 1947 the city was regarded with fear and loathing by every loyal Vancouverite – including me. Those who accepted a job in Toronto were thought of either as traitors, and reviled, or as victims, and pitied. Lister Sinclair had said it all with wit and perception when he wrote *We All Hate Toronto* for Andrew Allan's "Stage" series on CBC radio.

My first impressions of Toronto that June were of almost unbearable heat. Neither Janet nor I had known such heat in our part of the West, where balmy breezes blow off the Pacific and broad beaches beckon. We had managed to sublet, through friends, an airless bachelor flat looking on the inside court on the second floor of an ancient building at the northwest corner of Bloor and Spadina. The environment was rendered even more cheerless by the decor. An interior decorator from Eaton's had decreed that the walls and ceiling be painted battleship grey. How *very* Toronto, I thought, with my Vancouver smugness. Air conditioning was in its infancy, so there we sprawled in our underwear, gasping and sweating with the rest of the city.

Getting to work by streetcar was a living hell. In those days heavy jackets, long-sleeved shirts, and ties were mandatory. Anybody entering the McLean-Hunter building with an open collar would have been spoken to firmly, so nobody dared to do it. We were a buttoned-up crew. On Bloor and on Yonge, specially trained bullies were employed by the

6

Toronto Transportation Commission to crowbar the perspiring commuters onto the clanging streetcars. Forcing oneself in was a considerable feat, for it meant squeezing, pushing, and even belabouring the passengers near the doors. Getting out was even worse, for it meant battering one's way through what W.C. Fields would have called "a living wall of human flesh."

The entire city seemed to me to be suffocating in every way, and not just because of the heat. The population was noticeably uptight. "You must be from the West," said the cashier at the neighbourhood grocery store to Janet.

"How did you know?" she asked.

"Because you always smile and say good morning," came the reply.

It was a tribute, I think, as much to Janet as to Western Canada, for she is always cheerful and open. She has the rare quality of being genuinely interested in everybody she encounters and of really caring about them. She talks to everybody, including cashiers in grocery stores. She remembers anniversaries and birthdays. Most of all she remembers people's names as well as those of their spouses, romantic companions, children, and in-laws. It is sometimes hard to get her off the phone, and even harder to get her to leave any social gathering because she insists on saying goodbye to everybody and getting the latest scoop on their aspirations, ailments, jobs, and social life.

She is also a good cook, and an imaginative one. That meant a lot in those early days in Toronto, where the food in the restaurants was execrable. But then it was execrable everywhere in Canada, save Montreal. The WASPs ate no fish, which meant that there was only one seafood restaurant in town: George's, on Yonge Street. This was a meat-and-potatoes community. At social gatherings beef Stroganoff was the rage. You piled your tossed salad on top of it and ate the unlikely mélange while trying to balance the plate on your knee. The accepted drink in journalistic circles was rye and ginger ale. Wine was the stuff that rubby-dubs in Cabbagetown drank. Occasionally, in a daring move, a hostess might put out a flask-shaped bottle of Bright's Manor St. David Red, at eighty-five cents a jug. Italian food? Spaghetti and meatballs at Old Angelo's, or, as a refreshing change, spaghetti with meat sauce. Fortunately, nobody had heard of pizza, the all-Canadian fodder of the future.

It seems to me, in retrospect, that we had arrived at the beginning of a new era, one that over the next generation would see the end of the traditional Hogtown. Toronto had just become the first English-speaking city in Canada to allow hard liquor in bars and dining lounges. Only five had been licensed, and the town had been assured that there would be no more for a while, if ever: this was Toronto, not Sodom. Never mind; the population had gone bonkers over this gentle loosening of traditional strictures. Down we went on Saturday night to the Silver Rail on Yonge Street, which had won a coveted licence. The place was jammed with tipplers guzzling gin fizzes, pink ladies, Manhattans, and brandy Alexanders – anything sweet and potent to unpractised tastes. The temperance faction, which included Bill Temple, the CCFer who had actually defeated Premier George Drew, cried doom; but their days were numbered.

The notorious Toronto Sunday was on its way out, too – but not yet. There was, literally, nothing to do except go to church. Sporting events, movies, and all forms of popular entertainment were banned. You couldn't even window-shop at Eaton's; in tribute to its Methodist founder, the curtains were tightly drawn. There were no newspapers. The local morning radio seemed to consist almost entirely of church services. You could take the ferry to Centre Island and wander around, or ride the streetcar to High Park and gaze disconsolately at the equally disconsolate animals in their cages. That was about it.

The McLean-Hunter (later Maclean Hunter) complex – two or three buildings of varying age pasted together – stood at the corner of Dundas Street and University Avenue. The latter was rendered antiseptic by the presence of hospitals and insurance offices; the city fathers had decreed that no vulgar places of entertainment – cafés, shops, theatres – should sully the pristine display of wall-to-wall concrete that ran from Front Street to Queen's Park. You could shoot a cannon up that pretentious boulevard any day after 5 p.m. and hit no one. Toronto, apparently, wanted it that way.

Here, on my first day, I was ushered into the austere presence of W. Arthur Irwin, the editor who was single-handedly transforming *Maclean's* from a boring periodical into a national institution. Irwin was already a legendary figure among the young staffers who had recently joined the magazine. His father was a Methodist minister, and though the younger Irwin had long since divorced himself from organized religion, there was always something of the Methodist in him. He was a near teetotaller, which he ascribed to a recurring ulcer but which, I think,

was also the product of his upbringing. He was at the same time a small
l Canadian Liberal (and also a large *l* Liberal) in the tradition of such
great Canadian Methodists such as Walter Massey, Joseph Atkinson,
and yes, Timothy Eaton. The Great War had shaped him (he had been
a young gunner), and so had Victoria College, the Methodist institution
at the University of Toronto. After a stint of book selling, he joined the
Mail and Empire as a reporter. He moved to the *Globe*, became parliamentary correspondent, rose to editorial writer, and resigned in 1925 on
a point of political principle. That same year he joined *Maclean's* as
associate editor. He was twenty-eight years old at the time. When I first
met him he had just turned forty-nine.

Since I myself did not expect to live past forty-five (any further existence, I believed, would be inexpressibly boring) I thought of him as
an old party. Nobody on the staff called him by his first name; he was
"Mr. Irwin" to all. A smallish man, pale and pudgy, he spoke in something close to a whisper. He had absolutely no small talk. He could
scarcely be called convivial, although I think he tried to be. He was a
master of the blunt query and the terse memo. Once, Scott Young told
me, he received a memorandum from Irwin containing a single question: "What is a lobster?" Irwin's curiosity was always scientific, though
I cannot remember whether anyone was assigned to write a probing
article about crustaceans.

Now, after a minimum of grooming talk, Irwin, who had been staring out of the window, turned, looked at me owlishly over his spectacles, and asked, "What do you think of this man Corwin?"

I was a little taken aback. He must mean Norman Corwin, the darling of the avant-garde radiophiles. I said that I thought Corwin was
brilliant, a pioneer of the radio documentary. Irwin chewed that over
for a moment and then slew Corwin with a single sentence. "A bit
pretentious, I think; superficial." After some months and considerable
reflection about my radio hero, I came to believe that Irwin was right.

He has not changed. As I write these words, he is ninety-six years
old, and still driving his own car. I visit him annually in Victoria where
he lives with his second wife, the poet P.K. Page. The last time I knocked
on his door he opened it with a terse greeting and immediately fired off
a trenchant query: "What's happening to the country, Pierre? What do
you think of this man Bouchard?"

Irwin's vision of Canada was being transmitted by osmosis to his

9

young staff. He was a Mackenzie King liberal in the best sense: he saw the country as an independent nation, able to stand on its own feet – free of the colonialism of the British and resistant to the magnetism of the United States. After fifteen years of depression and war, it was time for Canada and Canadians to look to the future invigorated by a sense of pride and confidence. Irwin intended to give them that in the pages of his magazine. He was slightly ahead of his time, but the growing influence of *Maclean's* was certainly one of the factors that contributed to the wave of nationalism that would sweep the country a generation later.

Maclean Hunter in those days was a journalistic anthill, crawling with writers and editors from every field, all crammed into small cubicles, desperately churning away for the five "consumer" publications – *Maclean's, Chatelaine, Mayfair, Canadian Homes and Gardens,* and the *Financial Post* – and more than forty trade publications. The last, which provided the company with the bulk of its profit, ranged from the *Canadian Grocer* to *Canadian Printer and Publisher.* There were so many that the youths who peddled some of them from door to door often had no idea what it was they were selling. My irreverent cartoonist friend, George Feyer, asked one of these youths if he had *Canadian Pederast* on his list. The boy took the request seriously but said he couldn't find any Maclean Hunter publication that covered cycling.

In this eclectic mixture of journalistic expertise Irwin stood out as the only intellectual in the firm. It was obvious that the executives of Maclean Hunter were in awe of him – as a piece of company mythology made clear. Years before, so the story went, when every businessman in Toronto wore a hat, usually a Homburg, Irwin turned up at the office in a cap. *A cap!* Great Heavens, only the lower classes wore *caps!* There were huddles, conferences, meetings, all discussing Irwin's cap. But nobody really wanted to introduce that delicate question to the glacial associate editor. Finally the problem was laid before the company's founder, Colonel John Bayne MacLean, who agreed, reluctantly, to draw it to Irwin's attention. After a handsome lunch at the University Club, MacLean tentatively broached the subject of the cap. Nobody recalls how the conversation went, but the next day Irwin turned up at the office bare-headed. He never wore the cap again, but neither did he, on any occasion, wear a hat. This issue was revived years later when Ralph Edwards, the exquisitely groomed editor of M-H's *Style* magazine, tried to persuade the editorial staff of *Maclean's* to wear hats. In the elevator he would freeze us bare-headed journalists with a chilly stare. I believe he tried to emphasize the importance of hats at higher levels, possibly with Irwin himself, but Irwin didn't give a damn what his people wore, so long as they could write. A generation separated him from us young Turks. He was our father figure, our teacher, our mentor, but he was never one of the boys.

When I joined the magazine, Colonel MacLean was still alive – a small, pink-faced man with a white moustache who turned up at the annual staff Christmas party. I remember his buttonholing Irwin and asking, very tentatively, if he might look in on one of the Friday staff meetings where future issues were planned. Irwin said he'd be happy to have the colonel present. After all, it was his company.

The following Friday, halfway through our regular session, a timid knock came at the door. Irwin's secretary stuck her head in. "I think it's Colonel MacLean at the other door," she said.

Irwin put his finger to his lips. "Keep him out!" he said.

The knocking continued. Nobody budged; finally it ended. I was awestruck. True, it was the colonel's company; but it was Irwin's magazine now, and he intended to shape it to his own design without any interference, even from its mild-mannered owner.

If anyone had earned the right to mould the magazine to his personal exacting standards it was Arthur Irwin. Whatever status the magazine had in the twenties, thirties, and early forties was due almost entirely to him. But he was not given command until late in 1945. For almost twenty years as associate editor and managing editor he had suffered under a silly-ass Englishman, H. Napier Moore, who took all the credit but did little of the hard work. The contrast between the two men was startling, as I soon discovered. Moore, the extrovert, who had at last been shoved upstairs to the post of editorial director when I arrived, was a frustrated music-hall entertainer in the British style. He loved to appear on the stage at the annual Arts and Letters Club revues. He was a good speaker and travelled the country addressing meetings of the Canadian Authors' Association, whose members doted on him.

As far as the country was concerned, Moore *was Maclean's;* few had heard of his brilliant but taciturn colleague. Napier Moore was a British imperialist to his boots; Arthur Irwin was a Canadian nationalist to his fingertips. Moore was a British Tory, Irwin a Canadian Liberal, boring from within like a subversive, trying to sneak his vision of

Canada as an independent country past Moore's indifference. Beverley Baxter, the magazine's most popular columnist, had been Moore's choice. Toronto-born, Baxter had for years been editor of Beaverbrook's jingoistic *Daily Express*. Now, as a Tory backbencher, he wrote his widely read Canadian column with all the insights of David Low's cartoon figure, Colonel Blimp.

Moore was now, fortunately, reduced to a figurehead. I remember lunching that summer with Lister Sinclair, a college classmate and at that time one of the most brilliant members of Andrew Allan's radio repertory group as both an actor and a writer. I thought Lister might make a good profile for *Maclean's*, and we discussed it briefly. That same afternoon Moore walked into the office and said he'd heard the magazine was planning a piece on Lister. His smug, pipe-smoking assistant, Ralph Magee, who had been lunching at the same restaurant (the Rosticceria, on Yonge Street), had listened in on the conversation and scurried back to report the details to Moore.

"I don't think we should be encouraging this kind of thing," Moore told Scott Young and me. "The man's a pinko." At the next staff meeting the matter was broached and Moore's demurral mentioned. Irwin responded by immediately assigning me the article.

The titles of our articles in those days were not cunningly designed to make people want to read the contents. This one was called "Patriarch with a Beard." A much better title would have been "The Arab's Armpit," which was Lister's nickname around the CBC. I mentioned his scraggly beard, of course, in my piece, but magazines in those days were never irreverent.

2

The best   Arthur Irwin's ambition was to hire the best staff to put out the best
of staffs   magazine ever published in Canada. In this I think he succeeded. More than anybody else he was responsible for the era that followed – the so-called Golden Age of *Maclean's* – when every writer in the country wanted it to carry his or her byline.

When I arrived, that age was just beginning. The magazine still had a stuffy, old-fashioned look compared to the slick American periodicals, many of which, like the *Saturday Evening Post,* had had a face lift. Our presentation – layouts, photographs, artwork, titles – was old hat. The presses conspired against both good reproduction and topicality. In fact, Maclean Hunter was a fusty company, well behind the times. Its stock, hugely undervalued, was held by a tight family group that took no chances. Until Floyd Chalmers was raised from editor of the *Financial Post* to a vice-presidency, the owners preferred to sit tight, making as few changes as possible. Under Chalmers things began to change. A new building went up in what were then the wilds of North Yonge Street, and *Maclean's* got the modern presses it deserved. The company was so flush that it built the entire plant with its accumulated cash. Chalmers knew the stock was a bargain and set about sometime later to buy up as much of it as he could. Irwin, who had a few shares, refused to sell. "Someday," I remember his saying after he had left *Maclean's,* "someday they're going to cut the melon." After 1965, when the stock was listed, it split six times. A single share issued at $18 was worth $1,536 in 1988, the basis for Chalmers's huge fortune, much of which he lavished on the arts.

The fiction *Maclean's* carried, much of it written by American hacks, was generally second rate, although there were some notable exceptions such as the stories by W.O. Mitchell and Ernest Buckler. For the most part, these formula tales could have been published anywhere, and sometimes had been. One day, de Maupassant's "Le Bout de ficelle" (The piece of string) was detected in what we called the slush pile of unsolicited manuscripts.

Irwin had set about building a staff well before I arrived. He was cautious when it came to selecting new blood. He did his research carefully before making his move. In my case he had phoned, among others, F.H. Soward, my history professor at UBC, and asked his opinion. "Berton?" said Soward. "Well, he would have been a brilliant student if he hadn't spent all his time on the university paper." That got me the job.

Irwin had snatched the country's most evocative war correspondent, Ralph Allen, from the *Globe and Mail*. Two other newspapermen joined the staff, the slow-spoken Scott Young as articles editor, and the burly and sardonic John Clare as a staff writer. (Once, when Clyde Gilmour arrived at the Clares' for dinner and asked where the john was, Clare shot back that "in this house, Gilmour, we call it 'the clyde.'") All three were prairie bred, from Oxbow, Regina, and Winnipeg, respectively. Irwin had brought in Adam Marshall from the Montreal *Gazette* as copy editor and also Blair Fraser, who became *Maclean's* Ottawa correspondent and author of our regular column from the capital. Fraser was Irwin's kind of Liberal, unlike his predecessor, Grattan O'Leary, who was an unregenerate Tory. There were only two holdovers from the pre-war days – Norval Bonisteel, an immensely dedicated photo editor, and Gerald Anglin, cheerful and garrulous, in charge of production.

Allen quickly became Irwin's alter ego. He had, among his other qualities, an unerring ability to spot bullshit. He had the same toughness of mind that Irwin displayed, and he quickly learned how an article should be structured. His interests were wider than Irwin's; he had, after all, started out as a sportswriter. As a war correspondent he had also been an executive – half the job entailed finding ways to get his copy back, intact, to Canada. He had just been made associate editor. Soon he would become managing editor. He and Irwin complemented one another. A good deal of Irwin's nationalism rubbed off on Ralph – especially his insistence that *Maclean's* be not a pale copy of English or American publications but a truly Canadian periodical with articles written by Canadians about Canadian subjects that foreign magazines could not and would not tackle. On the other hand, Allen, the roistering sportswriter and warco, was a different kind of bird from his soft-spoken, reticent chief. Ralph was not an easy man to know. I worked with him intimately for eleven years; we partied together, drank together, and shared acquired tastes – the love of good food and good whisky among others – but I never felt I really knew him. Perhaps nobody did. In the end, I came to know Arthur Irwin better.

Allen had the newsman's hard shell. That, I guess, applied to all of us. We did not wear our hearts on our sleeves, and our writing showed it. The pieces we all produced were never passionate. Objectivity was drilled into us. We kept our personalities out of our articles. The New Journalism, with all its strengths and all its indulgent flaws, was a generation in the future.

Irwin and Allen taught me the value of solid research. I could not have written any of my works of popular history without that long apprenticeship at *Maclean's*. The experience turned me – as it turned each of us on the staff – into a Canadian nationalist. My ambitions to become a big-time American writer were beginning to fade.

In fact, we were a cocky bunch in those days. We knew we could not compete with the big American magazines on their turf, but we were convinced we could beat them on ours. We were all a little arrogant, a very un-Canadian quality that I have never attempted to play down. Years later I was asked, in a *Globe* interview with Blaik Kirby, why I was so damned arrogant. I replied that it was about time Canadians learned to be a little arrogant about themselves. I was simply trying to teach them not to be so goddamn modest, I said. This statement was considered so remarkable that it was picked up by Canadian Press and carried in dozens of newspapers across the land. An arrogant Canadian! It was like discovering a new species of marmot.

At staff meetings, held in Irwin's office (the only one large enough to accommodate us all), we fought for our ideas loudly and abrasively. I, a new boy from the West, was among the loudest and most abrasive. "We've never heard of that in B.C!" I shouted when somebody suggested some institution that needed airing in the magazine. "Nevertheless, Pierre," said John Clare drily, "it does exist."

One day Irwin caught me in the hall. "I wonder if you've considered putting your disagreements in the form of a question?" he asked me. "It's a softer approach you might think about." It was good advice, and I did my best to follow it.

Our battles were fought without a trace of bitterness. My colleagues were a tolerant and good-humoured gang, indulgent with me and with each other. None ever felt belittled by what was said at staff meetings, nor was there any hint of office politics. We were all determined to put out the best magazine in Canada; that was our bond.

Still, the bluntness of our attacks was poor training for anybody who might go into show business. The world of film and television, as I discovered a decade later, was a world in which backs were patted and psyches soothed to a degree unknown to us rough-and-tumble journalists. "We just love your script," the TV people say. "We *love* it!" They add that there might be a few minor changes needed – nothing basic, you understand, we really respect the way you've handled it, but, well, perhaps... And only then, having smoothed the way, do they insinuate, little by little, that the entire opus needs a complete rewrite. Contrast that with Ralph Allen's remark to his friend Max Braithwaite, as he hurled Braithwaite's article back at him: "Braithwaite, you've written this with your foot!"

Every article I wrote for the magazine before I myself became articles editor had to be revised, sometimes more than once. One major piece, an inquiry into why houses cost so much, was so bad it was never printed. Irwin had, perhaps, the toughest mind I've ever encountered in an editor. He would spot a weak sentence or an unqualified generalization and pounce on it like an owl on a rodent. You couldn't put anything past him. He wanted evidence for every statement you made and the background of every person you wrote about. "Evidence!" he used to scribble in the margins of my pieces, and "Who he?" He could tear an article apart and show you how to put it together to make better sense. I learned about structure as well as research from Irwin. If you didn't do your homework, he treated you kindly, but forcefully, as an errant schoolchild.

I used to fight like a mad dog against editorial strictures at *Maclean's* but in the end surrendered, sometimes with bad grace. The *Maclean's* editorial system became legendary. Those freelancers who finally made it through the labyrinth of editorial queries must have felt that they had triumphed over the most difficult obstacle course in journalism. There were many who felt the *Maclean's* editors were *too* tough, that the system of rewrites was producing an uptight style so that every article read like every other article. There is something in this, but the fact is that we were all new to the game and needed editorial discipline before we could sprout our literary wings. Irwin had launched nothing less than a school of magazine writing. None of us, when we started out, knew how to write a major article of, say, five thousand words. We had to learn structure, we had to learn the value of revealing anecdotes, we had to learn to get things right, to dig deeply, and to prove every point we made. When we began, most of us, certainly including myself, were sloppy, verbose, and fuzzy. Some of us tried to copy, with dreadful results, the deceptively languid style of the *New Yorker;* others, the frantic pace of *Time*. "Hi-ya, Luce!" Ralph Allen wrote against one of my paragraphs that mimicked, subconsciously, the Homeric-epithet style that Brit Hadden had adopted for the newsmagazine. Shamefacedly, I rewrote it.

After my first staff article for the magazine – about how Windsor's citizens had rallied round to help the victims of a tornado – Irwin encountered me in the hall. "A good job," he told me. I beamed and thanked him. "A bit Pollyanna, perhaps," he added and walked on. Having no idea what that meant I looked up the word in the dictionary. "*Blindly optimistic!*" My spirits fell; I saw what he meant.

The staff was small, the quarters cramped. Allen shared an office with Scott Young; I was squeezed into another with John Clare and Eva-Lis Wuorio, an attractive blonde who had made her name covering the Royal Tour for the *Globe and Mail* and whom Irwin had lured to *Maclean's*. Eva-Lis was the only writer on the magazine who put herself into her articles. As the sole woman on staff she was indulged and even encouraged; what she lacked in research she made up in vivid writing. A Finnish-born aristocrat, she moved easily among upper-class Torontonians. Signy Eaton was a close friend. We argued, politely, over our differing political philosophies. I believed in a shorter workweek for the labouring man. (At *Maclean's* we still worked a half day on Saturday.) She was opposed. "They'd only spend their spare time drinking beer in taverns," she'd say. I thought that a weak argument since she was usually consuming her third martini at that point. She could hold her liquor better than most men and was treated as an equal by the otherwise male staff at a time when even the *Toronto Star* was exiling its female reporters in the women's departments.

We were all poor in those days, even though prices were still close to what they had been before the war. That fall, Janet and I found a one-bedroom apartment above a hardware store in East York. The rent was sixty-five dollars a month. Lunch at Mary John's, around the corner from the office, cost as little as forty-five cents. Nobody could afford to entertain lavishly. The Bring-Your-Own-Bottle party was the standard. Few of the freelancers who sold articles to *Maclean's* could have stayed alive unless they had another job. They were paid somewhere between $125 and $200 an article, which meant that the staff writers got the toughest assignments – the ones the freelancers couldn't afford to take. Irwin had one custom, however, that fostered loyalty among the freelancers. "We may not be able to pay well," he told me, "but we can pay fast." Any writer whose work was accepted could get an immediate chit from our editorial secretary, Dorothy Hodgins, take it down to the cash cage, and get paid.

I had heard about Dorothy from Scott Young before arriving in Toronto. She was legendary, a treasure, practically indispensable; the whole staff thought so. She loved her work so much, I was told, that she was reluctant to take holidays and then no more than three or four days at a time. When she came down with appendicitis, her despair at being unable to work at the magazine for at least a fortnight evoked sympathy and praise.

Nobody up to that time had bothered to look at the ledger, but now in Dorothy's absence both Irwin and Allen went over it and, to their dismay, found some remarkable discrepancies. Writers they had never heard of had been paid for articles that had never been assigned. Slowly the truth began to dawn. For years Dorothy had been milking the company by cashing chits in various amounts. No wonder her daughters had been able to attend a private school in spite of her minuscule salary. No doubt she felt (I think rightly) that she was being underpaid by a company that had a treasury full of cash.

She went to prison for fraud, and the chit system was changed. After she was paroled, she wrote a gripping description of her life behind bars and sold it – not to our sister magazine, *Chatelaine,* but to its hated rival, the *Canadian Home Journal.*

3

The world of tomorrow The weather in New York that September was almost unendurable – hotter even than it had been in Toronto when we had arrived in June. My shirt was already clinging to me when I rode the subway to Flushing Meadow. I paid no heed, for I was taking on my first big assignment. The General Assembly of the United Nations was holding its first full session here on the site of the 1939 World's Fair, and I was one of the six hundred and fifty correspondents accredited to cover it. I was simultaneously awed, elated, breathless, and a little nervous as I entered the Assembly Hall. I didn't want to muff it.

Here, eight years before, enthusiastic visitors were introduced, via General Motors, to the World of Tomorrow. Now the real tomorrow was about to be debated. The brave new postwar world we had all been promised had at last arrived. New words were coming into daily use and appearing in various *Maclean's* articles: "plastic," "detergent," "polyester." Now you could get a limp shirt laundered in a day, and soon you could wash and dry it yourself by the "drip-dry" process that du Pont invented. The world, like the women's dresses, had acquired a New Look. The "Free World" was now in business, and so was the Red Menace. I felt like an eyewitness reporting the history of my times, which, in a minor sense, I was. The old League, with its petty squabbles and its craven backslides, was no more. In its place was a new

18

world parliament whose fifty-odd member flags stood in a proud circle, drooping only a little in the oppressive heat.

Those flags had been carefully spaced so that no country's emblem would eclipse any other. Tiny countries, monstrous empires – each had an equal vote. There was only one problem, as I quickly discovered. Several new nations had joined the United Nations since the flagpoles were placed. Unless the entire circle were torn up, some flags would seem more prominent than others. That would never do, and so a compromise was reached: after all, compromise was to be the United Nations' guiding principle. The extra flagpoles were lined up in the centre. Every day, somebody went through the tedious process of hauling all the flags down and raising them one step counter-clockwise until they rotated back to the centre once more. This preserved, at considerable expense and trouble, the fiction of an equality of nations that vanished when the Assembly got down to business.

Thus began my disillusionment. All the fine rhetoric to which we had been subjected during the war began to dissolve as I watched the jockeying on the floor. What I was witnessing, I soon discovered, was a theatrical performance that was often reduced to farce. Designed to play well to the public, it was devoid of any real meaning. This press agentry was set against a background as colourful as any Broadway production: the hawk-nosed Arabs in their galabias, the Indian women in their saris, the Russians in their ill-fitting double-breasted suits, a swirling montage of national colours and styles. One world under one roof.

But the Cold War jargon, emphasized in the press, had already cast a chill over the proceedings. The United States had manoeuvred itself into a first-day address. This gambit was referred to in the press as "taking the offensive," a phrase significantly left over from an earlier war. Everybody, indeed, was manoeuvring. Canada manoeuvred so that the leader of its delegation, Louis St. Laurent, would not have to speak on the same day as George Marshall, the U.S. secretary of state, and thus be overshadowed in the press. Britain was manoeuvring to cancel a Saturday night session to enable its representative, Hector McNeil, to speak on Monday morning, in good time for the home editions. More effort seemed to be spent on the timing of the speeches than on practical methods of securing world peace.

This all seemed silly to me because the speeches meant nothing. I remember asking my colleague Peter Inglis, of Southam's, as we knocked back a double Scotch in the press bar, why there should be such an air of expectancy over George Marshall's speech since everybody knew exactly what he was going to say. Inglis shrugged and smiled. "That's show business," he said.

And, of course, it *was* show business. For a week Peter Inglis and his fellow reporters had been speculating, with considerable accuracy, about this speech. The previous morning the *New York Times* had forecast it perfectly, point by point. Every delegate and every reporter had been given a mimeographed copy of the speech the day before it was delivered. And so, as Marshall walked to the rostrum, looking smaller and greyer than in his photographs, every man jack of us knew what he was going to say, and how he was going to say it.

He read the text carefully – "stonily," in one reporter's words – and I, for one, wondered why he bothered to read it at all. The entire charade had been staged not for the delegates or the newspapers but for the newsreels. When the speech ended, the Free World began to applaud lustily. The Eastern Bloc sat on its collective hands. This, I soon realized, was standard practice. *United* Nations? Hardly.

The reports of the speech in the New York press were embarrassing. According to the *Post*, the Assembly was "stunned, silent, even frightened." Andrey Vyshinsky, the shaggy leader of the Soviet delegation, was, the *Mirror* declared, "visibly shaken." The impression given was that the speech came as a bolt from the blue. That, I told myself, is pure hokum. Is the free press going to conspire in this blatant piece of playacting? Apparently it was. Marshall was described as "tall and silverhaired" and his speech as "bristling," "dramatic," and "hard-hitting." It had been nothing of the sort.

Vyshinsky's speech, which was as bombastic as Marshall's was colourless, offered a contrast because the Soviets refused to issue advance copies. The suspense was thus immeasurably heightened. These were the two stars – indeed, the only stars – at the U.N. Assembly sessions. The remainder of the thirty-eight speeches were so much padding. Few delegates seemed to pay any attention; as each orator spoke, others wandered in and out of the hall, read papers, and chatted among themselves. And yet exhaustive work had gone into these cut-and-dried orations. St. Laurent's people had struggled for a week over his address, writing and rewriting. But when he gave it, most delegates, except the Canadians, did not bother to listen. He was talking not to the United Nations but to his constituents back home.

If the newspapers back home reflected each country's propaganda line it was because these reports were carefully orchestrated – and that was as true of the free press as of the fettered. At the Canadian press conferences held each morning in the Biltmore Hotel, I was introduced to those familiar newspaper creations, the Informed Source, the Official Observer, and the Source Close to the Delegation. These were living, breathing officials who didn't want to be quoted by name but wanted the Canadian press corps to parrot the official line. That allowed the pundits – and everyone at the United Nations was a pundit – to rush breathlessly to their typewriters to report: "I am able to reveal that…" or, "A highly placed source close to the delegation disclosed to me today that…" Different papers; same story.

To me, after a couple of weeks spent at both Flushing Meadow and Lake Success, where the Security Council met, the attempt to achieve a new world government seemed to be all show and little substance. There was something off-kilter in the hollow posturing and clichéd oratory on the Assembly floor, so far removed from the amiability to be found in the delegates' lounge. There one found no bitchy scenes, no cold-shouldering, no recriminations among the very people who had been savaging each other in public.

There, for instance, was Hector McNeil, sitting on the arm of Andrey Vyshinsky's chair, chatting pleasantly with his own arm around the Russian's shoulder. A few moments later he strode into the Assembly Hall to deliver a sulphuric blast at the same man. That, of course, was old stuff to the seasoned observers. But, I reflected, it is public bluster, not idle chitchat, that causes young men to follow the beat of the drum. The Cold War was well under way here on the site of the World of Tomorrow. The first of the hot wars was less than four years away.

4

At the United Nations I had heard a good deal about freedom and *No Jews* human rights, often in speeches given by representatives of countries *need* that weren't very free and where governments jumped, even stamped, *apply* upon human rights. Although nobody mentioned Canada's record, and although Louis St. Laurent's address was full of boasts about freedom and equality, the fact remained that 23,000 Canadians were not free and had, indeed, been stripped of those legal privileges that were the birth-right of their fellow citizens. These were the Canadian-born Japanese, who had been denied both the right to vote and the right to move freely about the country – purely because of the colour of their skins. As a result of the Pacific war, Canada had two sets of laws for these people, all of whom had once lived in the coastal strip of British Columbia. The war had now been over for more than two years, but some four thousand were living in the B.C. interior, unable to move more than fifty miles without RCMP permission. The remainder, who had gone on to Eastern Canada, could not return to the B.C. coast, could not vote in a federal election, could not even take out a commercial fishing licence.

I had lived through the hot wave of anti-Japanese sentiment during my newspaper days in Vancouver and it got my dander up. My first newspaper, the *News-Herald,* had in 1942 protested the forced removal of these Canadians, but the *Sun,* which I joined in 1945, was still viru-lently racist, demanding that the "Japs" – a word it invariably used – never be allowed to return to British Columbia. Yet most were Canadian-born citizens.

This subject seemed to me to be exactly the kind of thing *Maclean's* ought to be examining, and I had no difficulty persuading Irwin and Allen to let me look into it. I spent about six weeks interviewing Nisei who had fled to Toronto. These were emotional interviews. I remember a young girl, Yoshiko Kurita, telling me how on Pearl Harbor day an old man came up to her and spat in her face.

"I ran all the way home up to my room and knelt down on my bed and prayed," she told me. "'Oh, God, we didn't want this war. We aren't a part of Japan now. We are Canadians. Please help us, God.'"

The article appeared in February 1948 under the title "They're Only Japs." Reading it again more than four decades later, I am surprised by the mildness of its tone. In keeping with the magazine journalism of that time I recited the facts, told the stories of the relocation, inter-viewed men and women who had suffered terribly, but gave no hint of my own feelings. The article is obviously written from the point of view of the Japanese Canadians, but without anger. Nor is there any hint that the real villain in the piece was the bigoted minister of defence, Ian Mackenzie of Vancouver, who persuaded Mackenzie King to go along with this outrage for purely political reasons. I would write it differently today.

At the same time I was struck, during my research, by an odd anomaly. Toronto had welcomed the new influx of Orientals, albeit a little grudgingly. They had in fact been given access to the local dance halls that other races were denied – one Japanese Canadian, Bruce Inouye, was at first refused admittance because the manager thought he was a Negro! Maybe, I thought, there is room for only one scapegoat per society. I was wrong: the black population in Toronto, tiny as it was then, wasn't the only victim of racism. The people who suffered most were the Jews. The anti-Semitism was palpable. At the very first party that Janet and I attended – old army buddies from the Royal Military College – the talk was concentrated on "these people."

"Did you ever see a Jew in the infantry?" one of my former colleagues in the Intelligence Corps asked. I had thought him a remarkably tolerant officer, but here he was insisting that the Jews got all the cushy jobs and were afraid to fight. I tried to reason with him – I had trained in the infantry and knew a good many Jews – but I found myself up against a brick wall. Certainly Vancouver was not immune to anti-Semitism, but in the newspaper business it was muted. Besides, British Columbians were so busy hating the Orientals they hadn't much bile left over for others.

I brought up the subject at a staff meeting and was assigned to write about it. The results of my research were far more devastating than I had suspected. All the major professions – engineering, the judiciary, higher education, brokerage, banking – were virtually closed to Jews. The banks, for instance, employed 27,193 men and women, but only 27 were Jewish. In all of Canada there were only eighteen Jewish high-school principals and university professors. Of the 578 Jews in the legal profession, only one had been raised to the bench.

Having dug up these statistics I decided upon a survey. I went down to the Maclean Hunter stenographic pool and asked the director, a Miss Allen, to provide me with two of her people who had similar experience, background, and training. Their task would be to phone in answer to classified ads for typists, stenographers, bookkeepers, and filing clerks; at that time there was a great shortage of experienced help in those fields. One of Miss Allen's pool employees would take the name Greenberg and try to make appointments for job interviews, giving her experience and qualifications. The second woman would take the name Grimes and would follow the Greenberg call a few minutes later.

Miss Allen agreed enthusiastically to find two suitable prospects. Then she dropped a bomb. "Of course, we just don't hire *them*," she said. "It's company policy." She made the remark as if it were the most natural thing in the world, and I was forced to conclude that it hadn't dawned on her what it was I was trying to do. I was shaken. Here I was, preparing a hard-hitting article on anti-Semitism in employment, and my publisher was part of the problem!

I went at once to Irwin and told him bluntly that Maclean Hunter was anti-Semitic. He responded with unaccustomed anger, not because of my revelation, which, I suspect, was not news to him, but because my accusation implied that the magazine was also racist. "*Maclean's,*" he said, "is nothing of the sort." Then he added what he thought was a clincher: "Why, I'd hire Lionel Shapiro today if he'd come on the staff!" Lionel Shapiro was then one of the best-known Canadian foreign correspondents whose byline appeared regularly in the magazine. It did not seem to me that the desire to bring him on board absolved the company, or the magazine, for that matter, of bigotry. Would *Maclean's* have hired an obscure Jewish woman as a researcher? I thought not, but I held my peace; Irwin was in no mood to argue.

Now I had to consult my conscience. As I saw it, I had three options: resign at once; ask to be taken off the story; plunge ahead and do the best I could. I chose the line of least resistance, sensibly I think, and continued my research.

The two employees found by Miss Allen did their job well. We tried the test on the forty-seven employers who were that week advertising in the Help Wanted columns. In forty-one instances "Miss Grimes" was able to make an appointment for a job interview. But "Miss Greenberg" could make only seventeen appointments. In twenty-one cases she was told the job had been filled, even though she'd phoned first.

I should have liked to name the companies involved, as I did in a similar poll for the *Toronto Star* years later, but I could not. First, the magazine wouldn't allow me to name names; second, it would have been hypocritical to mention Procter and Gamble and leave out Maclean Hunter.

I made similar tests in the accommodations field and discovered that more than half the ski and summer resorts habitually refused reservations to Jews. That was scarcely a revelation. The word "RESTRICTED" was on the brochures, and everybody knew what those restrictions were.

My piece was the lead article in the November 1, 1948, issue of the magazine. Although I again kept my opinions out, it was quite clearly a plea for a fair employment practices act, along the lines of one adopted by New York State in 1945. That law made it illegal for any prospective employer to place a query about race or religion on application forms. My article did not sit well with H. Napier Moore. He buttonholed me as I walked out of the Maclean Hunter building and shook his head sadly. "That article!" he said. "Now we'll have every damn Jew in town applying to us for a job!"

The Canadian Jewish Congress immediately ordered a hundred thousand reprints of the piece and distributed them widely as part of its campaign to establish fair employment practices in Ontario. In 1954 the province did adopt such a code, and from then on no applicant was asked to state either religion or race on a job application form. Peter Newman and Vic Koby went to work for the *Financial Post,* and Sidney Katz, among others, joined *Maclean's.* I had been told time and time again by those who wished to support the status quo that "you can't legislate tolerance." But you can legislate against discrimination, and the results proved it. This small but not insignificant movement, in which I played a part, heralded a major change of attitude in Toronto, which in little more than a decade would snub the racist Orange Society and elect the city's first Jewish mayor. As for *Maclean's,* it was praised for its "courage" in running the piece. "That was a gutsy thing to do," Ken Johnstone remarked to a group of us over lunch. Ken worked for the *Montreal Standard,* which would soon change its name to *Weekend.* "Our paper would never dare to print a piece like that," he said. I wondered why.

5

"Don't bother to take your coat off," George McCullagh shouted at me **Wonder** as I entered his office in the *Globe and Mail*'s Art Deco building at **boys** King and York. "You're not staying!" He stood up, tall and handsome in a raw-boned, blue-eyed sort of way, the Boy Wonder of Canadian journalism and finance. McCullagh was so much in the headlines that he had become that rarest of creatures, a Canadian business figure actually noticed by an American magazine – and not just *any* American magazine but the biggest of them all, the *Saturday Evening Post*.

That was why he was about to throw me out of his office. The author of the *Post* piece, a more than competent freelancer named J.C. Furnas, had interviewed McCullagh at expansive length in this very office while his wife, sitting quietly in the corner, wrote it down verbatim in her notebook. McCullagh had loved the piece when it was published until his Bay Street cronies began to rib him and titter at the gaucheries Furnas had revealed by quoting him word for word. Without using a single disparaging adjective, the *Post* writer had made McCullagh sound like a backwoods braggart. Referring to his success on the stock market, McCullagh had unwisely added, "That was the time when big men began to fear me." After that, he didn't want to give any more interviews.

He was certainly big news in Canada. In the mid-thirties he had found, as a young stockbroker, not a gold mine but a man who had found two. William Wright was willing to bankroll his purchase of the venerable *Mail and Empire* and the *Globe*. Wright left McCullagh alone to do as he pleased, interfering only once when his favourite comic strip was dropped (temporarily) from the paper.

Now, McCullagh had just bought the Toronto *Telegram*. As a result, he had more circulation under his wing than any other publisher in Canada – 50,000 more than the five-paper Southam chain. He thought of himself as a political backroom boy. In the thirties he had been a staunch provincial Liberal – the man who, it was said, whispered instructions to the Ontario premier, Mitch Hepburn, from his hiding place in Hepburn's washroom. When Hepburn quit in 1942, McCullagh jumped to the provincial Conservative party, turning the *Globe and Mail* into a right-wing, business-oriented newspaper, a move that must have had its founder, George Brown, spinning in his grave. Obviously, McCullagh was a subject for a *Maclean's* profile, and I, who had already cut my teeth on a piece about the outgoing premier, George Drew, was assigned to tackle him.

Tackle was the right word, as I quickly discovered. "Don't sit down!" McCullagh said. "I'm not giving interviews after that last piece, which was highly unethical." I was amused at these words. Here was the most powerful publisher in Canada claiming that an article was highly unethical because the author had quoted him correctly. McCullagh said he'd talk to me only if I agreed to show him my article before publication so he could check the facts in it. I had heard this before from a variety of interview subjects, and I told him, as I always did, that I did not show my pieces to anybody but the editors.

"We'll see about that," he said, picking up the phone. "Get me Irwin at *Maclean's*."

Irwin refused to let McCullagh see the article in advance but suggested a compromise. Why not agree to have an intermediary check it for facts?

"Who are you suggesting?" McCullagh asked.

Irwin proposed the *Globe*'s managing editor, Bob Farquharson, a longtime personal friend.

McCullagh baulked. "Not him!" he said, knowing the connection between the two. Instead he suggested Oakley Dalgleish, who ran the *Globe*'s editorial page and regularly circulated McCullagh's fancies and prejudices to the *Globe*'s readers.

Irwin agreed. I didn't.

"How can Dalgleish check the facts when he doesn't know all the facts about you?" I asked.

"He'll check them with me," said McCullagh.

I couldn't accept that and told him that I could not allow any outsider to vet my piece.

"Then you're on your own," McCullagh barked. "If you're good enough to get the story without my help, then more power to you."

I knew I had very little time. McCullagh would certainly put out the word that nobody on either paper was to talk to me. I went immediately to the editorial floor and began to interview his intimates, especially the paper's veteran reporter Ken MacTaggart, who cheerfully filled me in with background and anecdotes. I also spent some time in the *Globe*'s morgue, which had a thick file on the publisher. For the next three weeks I interviewed everybody who was willing to talk. After my piece appeared in January 1949, McCullagh sent me a handwritten note of congratulation. I must have done something wrong, I thought.

A manic depressive, McCullagh died by his own hand in August 1952 in his swimming pool. When John Clare came into the office clutching his copy of the *Globe,* I asked him how the paper had handled the obituary.

"They said he really wasn't a shit," John said. "He only *acted* like a shit."

McCullagh had bought the *Telegram* because he hated its evening rival, the *Toronto Star.* "I'm going to knock that pedagogic rag off its pedestal," McCullagh announced. But the *Star* refused to be knocked anywhere, and it was the *Telegram* that eventually failed. Today McCullagh – then one of the best-known names in Canada – is himself largely forgotten. The Boy Wonder doesn't even rate an entry in the *Canadian Encyclopedia*.

This experience taught me that I did not need to interview a big shot in order to write about him. I used that technique when, sometime later, I was assigned to attempt a major article on another boy wonder, Edward Plunkett Taylor. Taylor was then the most publicized capitalist in the country, the *bête noire* of the Left, the darling of the racing crowd, the envy of his fellow capitalists, and a public figure because he controlled, through leverage, so many well-known brand names of the era – Orange Crush, Honeydew, Dominion Stores, O'Keefe Brewery, Windsor Salt, Dominion Tar and Chemical. He was photographed at the racetrack, especially on King's Plate days, wearing his grey morning coat and matching topper, a costume that contributed to the stereotype of a bloated capitalist. Actually, there were men in the financial shadows who could have bought and sold him without blinking a lash, but Taylor had the image.

The public's curiosity about him was unslaked, largely because Taylor refused all interviews. The magazine had twice tried to do a piece about him but had given up because in each case Taylor refused to see the writers. With my McCullagh experience behind me, I decided to interview everybody *except* Taylor – enemies, friends, former colleagues, and relatives, including his brother, Fred, who was both a painter and a left-winger. I even went to McGill University and confronted one of his daughters as she left the classroom. I didn't expect her to talk to me, and she didn't; but I wanted Taylor to know that somebody was on his trail. Sooner or later, I figured, he would come to me.

And he did. After three weeks he phoned with a plaintive query: "When are you going to interview me?" I made a date and he opened up, revealing, among other details, that he had been forced to kite cheques during his early days as proprietor of an Ottawa brewery. I brought along a photographer, and Taylor cheerfully posed behind a desk piled high with his brand-name products. My article ran in two parts, but I doubt that Taylor was happy with the result. "Berton doesn't understand the corporate mind," he later told Peter Newman. There was truth in that.

6

Late in 1948, Scott Young, who had originally hired me, left *Maclean's* on a point of principle. In his spare time Scott was a successful fiction writer; at *Maclean's* he handled the articles desk. He was a good friend and still is. We saw a good deal of him and his volatile first wife, Rassy, and occasionally Janet acted as sitter for his two offspring, Bob and two-year-old Neil, whom I used to dandle on my knee before he became one of the brightest stars in the rock-and-roll firmament.

Scott's departure was touched off when a writer named Ted Allan came into the office with an impassioned proposal for a story on the controversial Canadian surgeon Norman Bethune. Allan and Sydney Gordon had written a book, *The Scalpel and the Sword,* about this Communist doctor who had organized the first mobile blood-transfusion unit while serving at the front in the Spanish Civil War in 1938. He had later gone on to China, where he died of septicemia and became idolized as a hero during the Maoist regime. He was already anathema to North American right-wingers in the forties. I had never heard of Bethune, but Scott, who had attended packed meetings of Spanish Republican sympathizers in Winnipeg during the thirties, knew his story well. Bethune was one of Scott's heroes.

Allan, who had fought on the Republican side in Spain in the thirties and had known Bethune there, proposed to write a three-part article about the little-known but brilliant Canadian surgeon. On the basis of the outline, Scott agreed. He would guarantee Allan six hundred dollars for two articles and another three hundred if the magazine decided to take a third. The subject was presented to the Friday morning editorial conference and greeted with enthusiasm.

When Allan's articles arrived, Scott showed them to me, among others, for comment. I thought the material was absorbing but that the authors had let their enthusiasm for Bethune's Marxist politics obscure much of the story. It would be better if told objectively, I said, and that could easily be achieved through judicious cutting. Certainly the Bethune saga was the perfect piece for *Maclean's,* and we should definitely publish it. Here was a Canadian doctor who was an authentic hero in China, and his story wasn't known.

Scott agreed that the three pieces could be cut to two. Arthur Irwin was at a U.N. freedom of information conference (of all things) in

Switzerland. Scott got Ralph Allen's agreement to put through a chit for six hundred dollars, which, under the new post-Dorothy Hodgins rule, both Ralph and Floyd Chalmers had to initial.

A couple of days later Ralph called Scott and asked if the magazine was committed to two articles. Chalmers, it developed, was objecting on the grounds that Bethune was a communist hero and the act of "publishing two articles about him would give aid and sustenance to people we don't want to support."

It all sounds childish today, but, as they say, those were parlous times. What came to be called McCarthyism was on the upswing in the United States. The Hollywood Ten had gone off to jail. Scores of men and women named in the appalling newsletter "Red Channels" had been deprived of their livelihood. Writers like Ted Allan were leaving the United States and returning home because there was no place for them south of the border.

Scott told Ralph that the magazine was committed and, if necessary, he would pay Ted Allan out of his own pocket. The payment went through, but the articles were never published. This both angered and frustrated me. Again and again I brought the matter up at the Friday planning meetings. What about the Bethune articles? Were we going to publish them? I could never get a straight answer. Irwin, poker-faced, would reply that he hadn't had time to read them. It soon became apparent that he never would.

The stonewalling bothered me, but not as much as it bothered Scott. He was always even tempered, slow to react, slow to anger. I never saw him fly off the handle, as some of the rest of us did. He spoke with con-siderable wit – a wit that was accentuated by the slowness of his speech. Like John Clare and me, he was considerably left of centre – but never extreme. His pride, too, was bruised. He had committed the magazine to a substantial sum, and he felt keenly, I think, that his judgement had been implicitly questioned. He began to suffer asthma attacks. Finally, he resigned quietly. He did not mention the reason; he was not built that way. But there is no doubt that had it not been for the Bethune fiasco he would have stayed with the magazine.

John Clare replaced him as articles editor. Some forty years later, Ted Allan wrote the script for the motion picture about Bethune, in which the Chinese co-operated with the Canadians. We would not have thought that possible in the summer of 1948.

That same summer, the magazine sent me back to the Yukon to write three articles that were later to form part of a book, *The Mysterious North*. There would be plenty to write about, I realized. My home town of Dawson was dying. The little hamlet of Whitehorse, transformed by war, had been turned into a bustling community. The Alaska Highway had been built from the Peace River to Fairbanks, changing forever the dynamics of the territory. I looked forward to this journey back to my roots with excitement and no little trepidation.

As soon as I reached Whitehorse, the memories came flooding back. The ghost of my father stood at my shoulder as I walked over to the White Pass railway station on the river. I had been standing there with him nine years before when a man had come over from the Taylor and Drury store to tell him that war had just been declared in Europe. I saw my father straighten up. He was an old-fashioned patriot who always stood at attention when a military parade marched by. He had seen active service in the Great War even though he was past forty. He had gone back to the Yukon from Victoria in the mid-thirties. Now he knew that his days were numbered, that this would be his last view of Whitehorse, the town where I was born. He had suffered a series of attacks of angina and he was leaving the Yukon forever.

Neither of us then could have realized how the war would change the community. We stood in a dusty street so empty of traffic that husky dogs curled up and slept there. I had half expected to hear the sound of guns booming beyond those rolling hills, but all was silent. Whitehorse on that first day of the new world war was a sleepy hamlet of three hundred souls. Now the war had changed it out of all recognition. The population had surpassed 2,600 and was growing. It nudges 30,000 today.

From Whitehorse I drove in an army transport up the new highway, still not opened to the public and little more than a twisting tote road, assaulted by flash floods each spring and rendered all but impassable by frost heaves. The engineers who built it knew nothing of permafrost. As a result, the bulldozers had removed the insulating blanket of moss, with devastating results. Entire airstrips bulldozed out of the forest had turned into ditches of gruel. The highway, in places, wasn't much better. The real experts on permafrost were the Russians, but we weren't talking to them now and so paid the price of the Cold War in endless fills and patches.

It was impossible that summer to travel close behind another vehicle because of the suffocating clouds of dust that obscured the route. My guide, a Canadian brigadier, and I emerged from our jeep looking like grey ghosts, caked from head to foot in a garment of dried clay, only to be attacked by clouds of mosquitoes that clogged our noses and throats. I was still digging out the dirt and scratching myself when I reached Dawson City a week later.

For nine years I had looked back on my home town with affection and nostalgia, seeing in memory a cosy community sprawled along the tawny Yukon – romantic, unique, and richly textured with the patina of history. What I found, as my taxi rounded the Klondike bluff, was disconcerting. Wolfe's phrase "you can't go home again" rang in my ears. The town was falling apart in front of my eyes, a random collection of old, weather-beaten shacks, crumbling log cabins, and fading Edwardian cottages. The encroaching willows and alders had blurred Dawson at the edges. The wooden sidewalks were rotting. Most buildings leaned at crazy angles, their foundations swimming in a porridge of melted permafrost.

I had never noticed any of this before. As a child I'd known no other town with which to compare it. It was what I was used to. As a teenager in the late thirties, coming in on a rare visit from the drabness and loneliness of the mining camp, to me Dawson had seemed like Paris. Now much of what had once been familiar had gone up in smoke. In a frame community, where the stoves are red hot in winter, fire is inevitable. I realized for the first time, I think, that I had been raised in a ghost town, and the revelation depressed me.

This had been the scene of the most exciting event in Canadian history. The discovery of gold had helped to open up the Northwest of Canada. Dawson *was* its Paris, and the evidence lay all around me. Those dance halls that had not fallen down, burned down, or been torn down stood like aging dowagers on the main street. The most famous saloon in the old days was now a haberdashery. The old Orpheum, where Alexander Pantages, the future theatrical entrepreneur, had kept his tryst with Kitty Rockwell (later known as Klondike Kate), was a movie theatre. The Dominion Saloon and Gambling House, said to have been the setting for Robert Service's "Shooting of Dan McGrew," was now "The Home of Good Eats." Yet Service's own little log cabin still stood, directly across Eighth Avenue from the cottage in which I had been raised.

32

All of this rich heritage was fast disappearing, and nobody seemed to care. The great stampede had focused Canadian eyes on the empty Northwest. This gaudy little town had been its fulcrum. Now it was literally rotting away. What really upset me was the absence of any sense of history. No real attempt had been made to attract visitors whose presence might lead to some form of rehabilitation. Dawson was still dependent on a dwindling source of income. The gold was running out, and the steamboat trade that had helped make it prosperous would soon end. Nobody seemed to realize that the new highway and the burgeoning community at Whitehorse would conspire to rob my home town of its place as capital of the Yukon. Some sort of revival movement was needed, but it would not be launched for another fourteen years.

That August, with three northern articles completed, I plunged into a variety of projects, ranging from the profile of George Drew, now leader of the federal Tories, to a report on the notorious Beanery Gang, whose teenaged members had been making news all that summer. Far more significant was the arrival of our first baby, a daughter, Penny, on August 5. How fragile she looked when we brought her home. There she lay in the centre of our double bed, no bigger, it seemed, than a china doll and even more vulnerable. Naturally, she changed our life. Since we could not afford a babysitter, we took her with us to parties on Saturday nights, laying her on a pile of overcoats in the bedroom. We could not, however, take her to the movies, which played at the Donlands Theatre next door to our apartment in East York. So we went in shifts. I would go to the first showing, leaving Janet with the baby, and she would go to the second and return for feeding time.

When I returned from the Yukon, I found a new man sharing our crowded office. This was W.O. Mitchell, the new fiction editor, hired at last by Irwin after a long period of soul-searching. (Irwin's caution had, however, produced the best staff in the country.) I had never met Mitchell but had certainly heard of him. I remember John Clare remarking to Scott Young, "I think Bill Mitchell has actually produced the Great Canadian Novel." I had not yet read *Who Has Seen the Wind,* but when I did I agreed with John. As for Mitchell, I had thought of him as a man in his late forties or early fifties, perhaps because his byline was "W.O." and not "Bill." Now I was astonished to find he was only six years older than I. And he had already produced the Great Canadian Novel!

There are so many tales about Bill Mitchell – tales told and retold by many who know him, including me – that I find it difficult to separate fact from legend. When I first met him he was wearing a brown jacket that didn't quite match his pants. That was because he bought his clothes second-hand. He had known real want during the Depression, had ridden the rails as a hobo (before taking a job in a carnival, diving from a high platform into the equivalent of a damp sponge), and those times had had a lasting effect.

He was a non-stop conversationalist; "voluble" scarcely does him justice. He could declaim with both passion and humour on any subject, from the *High River Times,* whose robust editor, Mrs. McCorkindale, was one of his mentors, to the idiocies of the Canadian Authors' Association, whose female members he often mimicked in a falsetto voice. He and his wife, Merna, were as inseparable a husband-and-wife team as I have ever encountered. Sometimes, it seemed to me, they bordered on a vaudeville act, continually interrupting one another, correcting old, well-loved anecdotes, shouting, screaming, but clearly very much attached to each other. Their two small boys, on whom they doted, terrified John Clare; one of them once bit him in the ankle and clung like a bulldog. The Mitchells were always screaming at their children, boxing their ears, or squeezing them in ardent embraces.

One of my fondest recollections of Bill Mitchell concerns his brief but satisfying joust with the Canadian Pacific Railway. In one of his *Jake and the Kid* stories (which he later turned into radio scripts), he satirized the flowery wording of the CPR's eloquent travel brochures. Some nameless idiot within that corporation took it upon himself to write Mitchell a pompous letter.

Mitchell replied in his best prose style. He was sorry he'd hurt the CPR's feelings, he said. He would make amends at once. Crocus, Sask., the mythical home town of Jake and the Kid, would immediately be moved off the CPR line and onto the CNR line. Never again in any of his writings would he mention the CPR. Even prunes, colloquially known as CPR strawberries, would henceforth be called CNR strawberries. In vain, the CPR hierarchy pleaded, cajoled, apologized. Mitchell stood firm. Vice-presidents were called in to make amends; it was no use. Crocus remained a CNR town.

He was a superb stylist and did not take kindly to those critics who, he felt, had not bothered to read his books. After he had once taken a critical beating from Gordon Sinclair, nobody was too surprised when a nasty globe-trotting reporter named St. Clair Gordon turned up in one of his scripts. For years he refused to speak to James Bannerman, a suave if sycophantic freelancer, who had once reviewed *Who Has Seen the Wind* unfavourably under one of his pseudonyms. Bannerman would come loping into the office, hand outstretched, and Mitchell would turn and face the wall, often getting slightly crushed in the process.

Finally Bannerman could stand it no longer.

"I have the idea," he said to me, "that Mitchell is a bit piqued. Do you suppose it's because he didn't like my review?"

"He thinks you didn't read the book," I said.

"I shall go home and read it at once!" said Bannerman, and added: "again."

The next morning he lay in wait for Mitchell, and when the author approached he leapt out and delivered a moving encomium of the book. A look of pure bonhomie crossed Mitchell's face. The two departed arm in arm for a cup of tea and didn't re-emerge for three hours.

"Rum chap, Mitchell," Bannerman told me the following day. "He absolutely insisted on driving me home. 'Which way do you go?' he asked – he was in the middle of one of his stories, you know. 'East,' I told him. So he instantly turned west, and when the story came to an end, Mitchell opened the door, and I just got out and took a taxi back."

At one point Bill didn't own a watch, and since there were no clocks, either, in the Mitchell household, he might, and often did, arrive at the office at 6 a.m. or at noon. His boys kept equally odd hours at school. I, who had no sons at the time, thought of those kids as holy terrors. On one memorable occasion they set their house on fire, apparently sticking something into an electrical outlet.

Janet and I had been invited to dinner that night and arrived to find Bill's mother-in-law with her bags packed, determined to leave forever. Richard Needham, the *Globe* writer, who had known the Mitchells out west, was sitting imperturbably on the front steps. The fire was out, he told us, and so were our hosts. They arrived an hour later. Bill, it seemed, had taken Merna to the doctor's office and then forgot where he'd left her. He drove all over town and eventually came upon her quite by accident. Dinner, when it was finally served, was interrupted by the return of several firemen who proceeded to hack into one of the still smouldering walls. At least that is how I remember it, in spite of

Mitchell's insistence that I have made a better tale out of the incident than it warrants.

There was another story put about that the neighbours had got up a petition to have the boys removed from the street because they were peeing on their little friends. Like most Mitchell anecdotes, that one had grown in the telling. The act was usually an assault on the neighbours' grass, not on their offspring.

Later, I was to revise my holier-than-thou opinions. After all, it was at a Maclean Hunter party that my own baby daughter peed all over the lap of Jean Chalmers, wife of the company's vice-president. Years passed, and when I visited Calgary to interview Mitchell for television, a charming and sophisticated young man picked me up at the airport and identified himself as Orme Mitchell, the elder of the two boys. He has since become Professor Mitchell at Trent University. Like his brother and younger sister he is a pillar of the community. It occurs to me now that as parents, the Mitchells had been doing everything right. They may have screamed at their kids as well as cuffing them and embracing them, but they never ignored them. Quite clearly they really cared about their children, and it worked.

Chapter Two

1

BARRANQUILLA, COLOMBIA, January 1, 1949. The things I do for the old mag, I think, as I stand on the airport runway in the blazing sun trying to figure out how to get a Red Poll bull off a DC-4 tramp plane. The bull, which bears the flowery name of Mistleigh Liveryman II, weighs close to a ton; the airport is shut tight because it is New Year's Day; and the only equipment available is a forklift. Nobody has ever disembarked a bull of this size, and nobody wants to try. What if he falls off the forklift and kills himself? What if he jumps off and kills somebody else? Smoky Lee, the Texas pilot, has kept a loaded pistol handy on the flight from Toronto just in case the bull breaks loose and rampages through the plane.

To get an article for Maclean's, *I have signed on as a cattle attendant on a tramp airline, the successor to the tramp steamers that plied the oceans in the days before the jet age. There are twenty-three Holstein-Friesian cattle in the body of the DC-4, all prize milkers from Toronto's Royal Winter Fair, destined to beef up (if that is the right expression) the scrawny dairy herds in Chile and Uruguay. They present no problem; the bull certainly does.*

Somebody builds a rope barrier around the bull, which has just stepped majestically onto the platform of the forklift. The rope is pure window-dressing, of course. We all hold our breaths as the bull is lowered gently to the ground without mishap. He seems to have enjoyed the ride.

That done we take to the air again, landing that night in the muggy town of Guayaquil, Ecuador. We force our way into the hotel through a buzzing barrage of locusts, and the clerk greets us with a gleaming smile. "Ees a good thing you do not arrive in the locust season, Señores," he says. "They eat up your clothes right down to the buttons."

The following day we fly over the green sponge of the Ecuadorian jungle and across the withered brown flanks of the Peruvian desert to land at dusk at Antofagasta on the Chilean coast. There, the residents inform us rather defiantly, it hasn't rained in sixty years; nothing grows that cannot be hand irrigated; some of the people have never tasted fresh milk. Well, we have fresh milk aplenty.

The cattle are parched, having spurned the water at Guayaquil because of the taste. Now we offer to trade milk for water, and a bucket line is quickly organized. The Chileans haul the water up the plane's ladder, and the cows, some of which give thirty-four quarts a day, respond.

At Santiago we drop off two of the prize cows and then head across the Andes to Uruguay, where the bulk of our herd is destined. I can never forget the giddy flight over that ocean of serried peaks.

The four-engined Douglas isn't pressurized. We cross the Andes at 13,000 feet without oxygen, heading for Montevideo. Sometimes we are forced to climb to 17,000 to avoid the highest mountains. The cattle lie down quietly and sleep; the rest of us grow drunk from oxygen deprivation. I look into the cabin mirror and notice idly that my lips have turned blue. We are all gasping for breath. The co-pilot, Johnny Horn, insists on waggling the plane's wings. "Take it easy," says Buzz Baker, the navigator. "You'll run into a mountain."

Replies Johnny, happily, "I couldn't care less."

I should be scared silly, I think to myself. I'm not. I look out the starboard window and notice, vacantly, that the far right engine is on fire. It seems, in my state of inebriation, to be the most natural thing in the world. Below us the lights of Montevideo coruscate. On the runway we can now see other red lights, flashing. "What's all that in aid of?" Buzz asks. We soon find out; it is in aid of us. Out come the trouble cars, sirens howling, as we land. Luckily the fire is extinguished, and so, by midnight, are we.

Our host, Señor Dutra, the cattle baron, insists on wining and dining all of us over the objections of his partner, a stocky German who is all business and wants to get on with the job of moving the prize herd to the pampas. Dutra waves him away. He is determined to show us some Latin American hospitality. We sit down to a Lucullan feast.

"Golly," says Buzz Baker as a gigantic plate of cold meat is set before him. "I didn't expect anything like this."

"Don't eat it all," I tell him. "I have a feeling this is only an appetizer." He can't believe it until a vast steak, still sizzling, arrives.

For several days the fun continues. On Twelfth Night, the Uruguayan Christmas, Dutra invites us all to his seaside villa, where an entire side of beef is turning on an outdoor spit and the wine flows freely. His partner is still plucking at his sleeve, urging that they get down to business, but Dutra laughs him off. I wonder, idly, what the German's politics were before he reached these hospitable shores.

These are golden days. In time I will look back on them ruefully in light of the political disasters that followed. But here in the boulevard cafés of Montevideo, and later Santiago, as Smoky Lee hustles about trying to organize a cargo for the return voyage, there is no hint of the darkness to come.

As we sip our chilled local Riesling, we talk approvingly (and, it turns out, naïvely) about the wonders of democracy in a continent known too often for its juntas and its revolutions. It seems to us that these two hospitable nations are free of any repressive authority.

In later years I will wonder about the fate of Señor Dutra and his bevy of laughing daughters. But I do not concern myself about his partner. He, I know, will survive under any regime.

It is time to leave. Smoky cannot find a cargo and so he flies empty to Miami and drops me there. A day later I hitch a ride from Palm Beach to New York on another tramp plane, this one loaded with nine thousand pounds of gladioli.

What an experience, I think, as I start to type out my story for Maclean's. *I have flown off to South America more or less covered in cow-dung; I've returned in triumph smelling like a bunch of flowers. How lucky can you get?*

2

The Gorilla's Daughter By the time I returned from South America, Ralph Allen was gone, lured to the Toronto *Telegram* with the offer of his own sports column. All of us in those days were torn between the challenge of becoming executives and the deep desire to be writers. Ralph had written one novel, *Home-Made Banners,* and he was now itching to write another. The sports column, he thought, would give him time. John Clare, another frustrated writer, was moved to associate editor. I replaced him on the articles desk. It was a promotion, and in that sense I welcomed it: I was now being paid the enormous sum of $5,500 a year. But I, too, wanted to be a writer – and not just any writer. I wanted to be a *name* writer like Bruce Hutchison, Lionel Shapiro, Hugh MacLennan, Roderick Haig-Brown, Thomas Raddall, and others whose bylines appeared regularly in the magazine. How could I go on writing articles and still handle the articles desk? Stubbornly, I decided to do both.

At first I felt myself drowning under a tidal wave of paper. Everybody, it seemed, wanted to write for *Maclean's,* and would-be writers were sending in everything from brief queries to detailed outlines to entire articles. I had to read and respond to every one. The slush pile of unsolicited manuscripts weighed most heavily on my shoulders. I had to read or at least skim them. We rarely bought an article from the slush pile, but we lived in hope that somewhere in that mountain of dog-eared scripts, each with its stamped, self-addressed envelope in case of return, there glimmered a literary gem that would make us the envy of every periodical on the continent. This was a forlorn hope and we knew it. Today most magazines have eliminated slush piles as an unnecessary expense, making it tougher for new writers to peddle their wares. We didn't then have the fortitude to take that step.

There was also the time-consuming problem of replying gently to those who thought *Maclean's* had stolen their ideas – the lady from Saskatchewan who wanted to write a profile on Foster Hewitt, or the senior citizen from Vancouver Island who was angry because he said we'd appropriated his idea for a piece on the prime minister. These subjects were clearly in the public domain, but I was sometimes hard put to make that point to the amateurs.

It was more rewarding to work with established journalists. Magazine writing of the kind we were looking for was in its infancy in Canada; almost everything we published needed some work before it was accepted. As articles editor, I read each piece first, scribbled notes in the margin, attached a memo about its strengths and weaknesses, and sent it on to John Clare, who did the same thing and sent it to Irwin. After we all agreed on what was needed, I spoke to the writer on behalf of all of us. It was I who had to tell some prominent literary lights that what they'd written for *Maclean's* wasn't yet up to the magazine's standards, and this required the kind of tact that wasn't my strong suit.

There's no doubt that I was overly blunt with some aspiring writers. One day a young editor from *Bus and Truck,* one of Maclean Hunter's profitable trade publications, knocked diffidently on my door. He had written some short humour pieces he hoped to sell to the magazine. I read them and told him, candidly, that he had better go into some other line of business. Such certitude has its pitfalls. The young editor cheerfully accepted my rejection but fortunately did not take my advice. His name was Arthur Hailey. We were to become close friends.

The constant process of examining the flaws of others and making suggestions for improvement helped hone my own craft. My work was no more sacrosanct than anyone else's. In one memorable year I managed to turn out twenty articles for *Maclean's,* but each bore the scars of Clare's scrutiny, and Irwin's. Like everybody else, I learned on the job by the trial-and-error method. But I also learned from the trials and errors of others.

The freelancers who haunted my office were a mixed bunch. Those who did not have the security of a real job teetered on the edge of poverty. Most were in debt. Although our rates were slowly improving – we were now paying as much as three hundred dollars for an article – few could have kept their heads above the financial surf without being incredibly prolific, like John Charles Kirkpatrick McNaught, who churned out a variety of articles under six different pseudonyms. McNaught wrote for *Maclean's* under the byline names of Peter Davidson and James Bannerman. He then assumed the identity of a Czechoslovakian immigrant, Lajos Dohanyi Lahos, for an article attacking Canadian middle-class morality, which he sold to *Mayfair* magazine, a sister publication. He wrote columns on food, books, and music for *Mayfair* under the bylines of Robert Elliott, George Austen, and Mark Carter. There was one memorable *Mayfair* issue in which *all* the articles were written by Jack McNaught under different names. That may have been too much for him; he announced under one of his bylines that his friend and colleague, the music reviewer Mark Carter, had been run over by a truck and killed on the way to a glockenspiel lesson.

I once insisted that for reasons of authenticity, McNaught use his own name for a *Maclean's* piece about the submarine war in the St. Lawrence. After all, he had been an officer in the navy. McNaught resisted strongly, though futilely, perhaps because his father, who had once been a millionaire director of twenty-six companies, had fallen on evil days, and didn't want to see his son associated with what he would have called hack work. Or was the reason that – so it was whispered – McNaught had been cashiered by the navy for an act of insubordination? Sometime later, McNaught, who also wrote for radio, was appointed host of the radio culture program known as "CBC Wednesday Night," a task he performed with wit and urbanity under the name of James Bannerman.

Robert Thomas Allen, another prolific writer, ghosted various articles for us (such as "I Married an Indian"). His forte, however, was humour. He was, quite simply, the funniest writer of his time. His pieces, based on his own experiences ("But I *Like* to Fight with My Wife"), were illustrated by Duncan Macpherson, a young artist of such awe-inspiring ability that I suspected at any moment one of the Toronto newspapers would steal him as a political cartoonist.

The bespectacled Allen was a gypsy, forever moving from Toronto to Florida or California and then back again. He was paid in advance and was always in debt to us for at least two articles. He always paid up, and then went into debt again for two more. He was by no means a social drinker, a phrase he despised, but he told me he drank occasionally to get blotto. It was apparently a carefully thought out decision, for he arranged beforehand for a taxi to pick him up after a bender and dump him at his favourite cheap hotel, where he slept it off.

Frank Hamilton, a plump and prodigious freelancer, sometimes had to be lent an office at *Maclean's* after hours in order to make his deadline. We would schedule one of his articles and then I would have to stand over him and literally force him to complete it. I once locked him in when the office was about to close and told him to stay at his typewriter until the job was done. When I arrived shortly after nine the next morning, he was still there, bleary-eyed, typing manfully away, the office knee-deep in crumpled paper. Hamilton, I came to realize, had an error phobia: if he made a single mistake in his typescript he ripped the page from his machine, crumpled it, flung it on the floor, and started over. The office that morning reminded me of pictures of Broadway after Lindbergh's triumphal homecoming.

Hamilton's overdeveloped imagination had to be curbed by judicious editing, and on one occasion by physical force. On one occasion he called me between the hours of midnight and 4 a.m. from a series of pay phones on the Lake Shore Boulevard claiming that the Roman Catholic mafia was hounding him. He had just completed a marvellous piece about a woman in Orillia who was marked each Easter with the stigmata – actual wounds appearing on her wrists and ankles. "She was bleeding," he cried when he turned it in. "I *saw* her bleeding!" Now he was convinced that the Church was trying to suppress the story and him with it. I spent the small hours looking for him and discovered him at last in a telephone booth in a state of collapse, not as a result of Catholic violence but simply from drink. He eventually quit journalism and transferred his undoubted abilities to the Department of Northern Affairs in Ottawa, where he had a part in promoting the cuddly Inuit owl known as *Ookpik,* a symbol for the department and a popular item on the souvenir shelves.

The most prolific of the bunch, and the most stubborn, was Fred Bodsworth, a self-taught naturalist and one-time newspaper reporter, who had received no fewer than twenty-four straight rejections before *Maclean's* deigned to accept an article from him. Now he could do no wrong and had a dozen pieces published each year, many on natural history ("The Starling: Saint or Sinner?"). A fervent outdoorsman and camper, he eventually turned me into a birder. For more than thirty years we have made the annual trek with our wives to Point Pelee on Lake Erie, in what is called "Canada's Deep South," to observe the spring migration. Bodsworth's novel *The Last of the Curlews,* the first of four, has become an international classic.

The remarkable husband-and-wife team of June Callwood and Trent Frayne probably produced more pieces for *Maclean's* between them than anybody else. They were very much in love, a handsome couple who called each other "Dreamy" with an exuberance that unnerved the less demonstrative members of the staff. June, still in her twenties and stunningly beautiful, was already developing the grace and style that have long distinguished her work. But there was scarcely a hint of a social conscience in the articles she wrote then – certainly no sugges-tion of the activism that has marked her later career. That would not come until the sixties, when her own children helped to politicize her. Bill Frayne (we never called him Trent) was an all-round writer who could and did tackle everything, but his best articles were on some aspect of sports, refreshingly free from the curious jargon that haunts some newspaper sports pages. Somehow he made hockey and football understandable, even to a philistine like myself.

McKenzie Porter, an oddball Englishman who seemed to have stepped directly out of a P.G. Wodehouse novel, had had a long apprenticeship on Fleet Street before coming to Canada and eventually to the staff of *Maclean's.* An elegant writer with considerable wit, he was the master of the low-profile character sketch; he once, indeed, wrote a remark-able story about a member of that vanishing breed, the milkman's horse. We titled it "Goodbye, Barney." Porter claimed he was dropped from the *Daily Mirror* because, as a news editor, he had spiked a story about a woman with two wooden legs who had given birth to twins in an air-plane. It was so typical of that newspaper he simply couldn't stand it.

44

The next day he was told he was due for a tour of European capitals – the traditional kiss of death. Now he was among the colonials, an unregenerate nineteenth-century English imperialist who was also able to laugh at himself. Although a self-declared snob, he was not to the manner born. He grew up in modest circumstances in a village with the unlikely name of Oswaldtwistle, and he wrote about that, too, with wit and nostalgia.

The shrewdest freelancers, such as Bodsworth, developed a specialty. Sidney Katz, who later joined the staff, actually quit working for a year in order to obtain a Master of Social Work degree from the University of Toronto. It stood him in good stead. He once wrote an article for the magazine entitled "Why Jews Don't Get Drunk." About this time, I encountered him at a party when he was well into the sauce. "There's no problem," he burbled. "Jews just don't get drunk. I'm an expert on the subject." He rarely drank to excess except on such social occasions and, a few years later, forswore all alcohol, thus proving, at least to himself, his original treatise.

Ray Gardner, with whom I had worked on two Vancouver newspapers, now began to take assignments in British Columbia. He had briefly been a Kemsley Scholar, an award the Kemsley papers in general and Lord Kemsley in particular later regretted since his first act on arriving in London was to try to organize Kemsley's staff into a union. He was one of the wittiest men I have known, and also a Communist at a time when everybody, including the Communists, took the movement with deadly seriousness. Gardner expended his wit on the capitalistic system, but no hint of his political leanings appeared in the pieces he wrote for us.

The most graceful writer for the magazine was Edna Staebler, who usually wrote about various ethnic groups – Hutterites and Mennonites and the blacks of Nova Scotia. She had an unerring ear for dialogue that I, among others, envied. Later she made her name writing best-selling cookbooks. These are deservedly popular, but I prefer her shrewd and pertinent articles and book about the people of Neils Harbour, N.S., and keep hoping she'll write another book like that. Maybe she will. She's only eighty-nine years old and still going strong.

Gordon Sinclair was in and out of *Maclean's* in those days. I remember our first encounter. He was wearing mustard-coloured trousers, a purple shirt, a green checked jacket, a tie stitched from unborn calf leather, and a cocky yellow fedora. Somebody, probably me, remarked on this get-up. "But I'm in show business!" Sinclair said. "When you're in that business you've got to wear the costume." The best article he ever wrote for us was a searching profile of – who else? – Gordon Sinclair.

The most entertaining of all the freelancers who knocked on my office door was a one-time prizefighter named Thomas P. Kelley, who always seemed to enter in a crouch as if he were going into the fifth round. He had a tough Irish face, a broken nose, and incurable optimism. We bought nothing from him, but he kept trying and was so amusing it was a pleasure to welcome him into the office. He did not submit outlines but acted them out for me, waving his arms, bobbing and weaving, and even, on a couple of occasions, leaping up on my desk to make a point.

Kelley had been writing for the pulps for years – fantasy pieces with titles like "I Found Cleopatra" or "I Found Helen of Troy." His specialty was monster stories. He told me he had an awful time keeping up with his rivals, who were always introducing bigger and better monsters to their readers, until he capped them all by turning the earth into a single sleeping monster, circling round the sun. Kelley was fast and dependable and thus the darling of the pulp editors, one of whom once grabbed him as he passed his office and told him he needed to fill a page immediately. "What do you want me to write?" Kelley asked him.

"Write 'I Was a Love Slave,'" the editor answered. Kelley hammered away at a typewriter until the editor cried, "Enough," seized the manuscript from the machine, and sent it directly to the pressroom.

None of this output was suitable for *Maclean's,* but Kelley's arrival in the office provided a certain relief from some of the run-of-the-mill pieces we were preparing for publication.

"Pee-air!" he said to me once. "This time I've really got it! I tell you, boy, they are slavering for this one. I just came off the phone to them. I said: 'Look, boys, monsters are out. Sex is finished. You got to have an arresting gimmick, and Thomas P. Kelley's got it.'

"Now get this for a cover. We've got an enormous slavering gorilla, see? Oh, a *huge* gorilla, hair all over him, and tiny, red eyes glittering. Over the gorilla's shoulder is draped a beautiful woman, naked, of course, and walking beside him – her tiny, innocent hand in his – is a small, golden-tressed child of some three summers.

"She's perfect in every detail!" cried Thomas P. Kelley. "She's like your own daughter in one of those blue middy things. Dimples in her knees! Lovely golden hair! Only one thing is different: *She's got the face of a gorilla!*"

Six months later I was passing a news-stand at King and Bay, and there was a pocket book entitled *The Gorilla's Daughter,* by Thomas P. Kelley, with the cover illustration exactly as described.

He finally did have a piece accepted by the magazine some time after I left, an excerpt from a book he'd written about an eccentric Ontario snake-oil salesman. It was a subject dear to his heart, and he wrote it well. After all, the snake-oil salesman was his father.

Apart from Eva-Lis Wuorio, all *Maclean's* editors were male; nor did the magazine seek to put its women freelancers on full-time salaries as it had Porter, Katz, and the others. Trent Frayne became an editor; his wife did not. Neither did Dorothy Sangster Katz, who was also a regular contributor. It was the same on most magazines; even some of the women's magazines had male editors. John Clare would soon be seconded to *Chatelaine*. Why should this be? For no reason, I think, but habit. None of us thought in terms of a woman articles editor or a woman managing editor. The inferiority of women – there is no other word for the common perception – was accepted in this field as in others.

Nonetheless, three remarkable women were invading our male preserve through the only route available to them: Miss Allen's steno pool. All three worked their way up to the front desk of *Maclean's,* where they acted as greeters and file clerks, and then, because the front desk could not hold them, moved onward and upward. The first, Barbara Moon, an honours graduate from the University of Toronto, finally became an assistant editor, moved to the CBC, and ended her long and successful career as managing editor of *Saturday Night*. The second, Janice Tyrwhitt, another English graduate, succeeded Bill Mitchell as fiction editor and became an overnight staff writer when the magazine stopped running fiction. Later, after a stint as a researcher on one of my television programs, she worked as a roving editor at *Reader's Digest*. Jan is also a brilliant editor who has worked on twelve of my books, including this one. The third woman, whom I remember as a pudgy jill-of-all-trades during one summer at *Maclean's,* was Christina McCall, who has since had a distinguished career as a political historian.

Barbara Moon was my secretary for a time, in spite of the fact that she couldn't really type – a failing that had unaccountably escaped me when I took her on. I discovered this minor flaw quite by accident when one Sunday I dropped into the empty offices and heard somebody hunting and pecking away on a typewriter. I came upon Barbara in one of the offices, looking a bit sheepish, with a pile of Dictaphone cylinders, frantically trying to type up some fifty letters that I had dictated over the previous fortnight. I could not help but admire her fortitude and so retained her without betraying her secret. By the time she was promoted to assistant editor, her typing had become – well, almost – letter perfect.

The Dictaphone helped me keep on top of the job. In my early months as articles editor I had laboured under the notion that my In-basket always had to be empty before I left the office. As a result I found myself toiling away to past seven in the evening. Soon, however, I learned to budget my work – to put the less important correspondence aside for a slack time and to deal first with essentials. I was nothing if not glib and quickly mastered the bulky dictating machinery, rattling off scores of replies at top speed. In time I found I could handle the job and still make time to write for the magazine.

Arthur Irwin always arrived at the office late in the morning and left an hour or two after everybody else was gone. Sometimes when I was working late, too, he'd drop in for a chat, and it was during these after-hours conversations that I began to absorb Irwin's vision of the magazine and of the country. He was a sometime member of the famous circle of Liberal journalists – John Dafoe, Grant Dexter, George Ferguson, Bruce Hutchison, Blair Fraser – who were on easy terms with prominent Grits and who, often unwittingly, allowed the party line to influence their reporting. After all, they had easy access to Liberal cabinet ministers and high-level civil servants. The party, save for a five-year hiatus, had been in power for more than twenty years, which led to a symbiotic relationship between politicians and press. That was to come to a sudden stop with the advent of John Diefenbaker, who was vastly underrated by many journalists. I remember Blair Fraser dismissing him as a minor figure, going nowhere, and therefore not an interesting subject for a *Maclean's* profile. Later, during the Diefenbaker era, the magazine did not have easy access to politicians in high places.

Irwin realized that just as *Maclean's* could not be the imperial publication it had been under Napier Moore, neither could it be a pale copy of the *Saturday Evening Post* or *Collier's*. "I want to put out the best-edited and best-read Canadian magazine in Canada," Irwin often told me, as he had told others. He did not want to copy anybody else. "You've got to edit from life and not from what the other fellow is doing if you're going to get a dynamic and vital magazine," he once declared.

He ran a tight ship. He listened quietly as we young editors argued with each other. He would let it go on for a while without ever stating his opinion, and then suddenly stop all argument and come to a decision. He tried to run the magazine as if it were a vaudeville show, though he never used that metaphor. But he looked at the contents of each issue carefully to make sure there was plenty of variety: a political profile; a good science article – for Irwin was himself a frustrated scientist; a "you-interest" piece, as he called them; a "stinker," by which he meant an article voicing strong opinions; a light piece; a sports article; and a strong bit of Canadiana. To this smorgasbord John Clare and I added another dish: the *Maclean's* "Flashback," a full-length piece of popular history retelling a true tale just over the hill of memory. These stories attracted a wide following. We asked the writers to try to reconstruct the smell and feel of the period – the fads, fashions, and morals – as a background texture to the story itself. The stories are by now familiar, but in those days few of our readers had heard of them: Blondin's tightrope walk across Niagara's gorge, the sinking of the *Princess Sophia,* the truth about Grey Owl, or the saga of William Van Horne. Canadian history, written almost entirely by academics (Bruce Hutchison was the lone exception), was not a hot subject in those days. Most Canadians thought it was dull. The majority didn't give a hoot about the country's past. The Flashbacks, I think, had a considerable influence. Certainly they influenced me. After editing dozens of these tales from the past I began to learn how history could be written for the ordinary Canadian.

Those after-hours discussions with Arthur Irwin helped shape me, too. I was twenty-nine years old; he was fifty-one, and I still called him "Mister." He not only shaped my idea of what a genuine Canadian magazine should be but he also shaped my own outlook on the country. *Maclean's* was about to enter its golden age, and so was the nation. Irwin was determined to interpret the country to itself. He had got rid of the boring photographic covers and opted instead for paintings of familiar and sometimes unfamiliar Canadian scenes. He used a succession of talented illustrators including William Winter, A.J. Casson of the Group of Seven, Rex Woods, and Oscar Cahen of Painters Eleven. He sent Franklin "Archie" Arbuckle on a three-month tour of the country, his only instructions being to paint Canadian scenes. Archie returned with seventy sketches; most became *Maclean's* covers over the next decade.

Irwin also launched a series profiling Canadian cities and another about Canadian rivers. He insisted on introducing his readers to a wide variety of Canadians who had made their mark, from Garfield Weston, the biscuit tycoon, and Dr. Charles Best, co-discoverer of insulin, to Pacifique Plante, Montreal's racket-busting cop, and Bernie Braden, the Canadian radio star who made it big in London. He wanted foreign articles in the magazine to be written from a Canadian point of view by Canadians on the spot, such as Mollie Lyons Bar-David, a former Saskatchewan writer who joined Haganah and wrote about the uprising in Israel. It was Irwin, more than anyone else, who convinced me – convinced us all – to be a little bit arrogant, to understand that we were just as good as any top-notch American or British writer, and that when we stuck to reporting our own country, we were better.

I realize now that in his subtle way Irwin was trying to get me to stay in Canada. He never came right out and said it; that was not his style. It was all very low key, but it is clear to me in retrospect that the editor of *Maclean's* was trying to persuade me to put down my roots in my own country – a country that had nurtured eight generations of Bertons. It was a decision that, without knowing it, I had already made.

3

Kleinburg It began in the summer of 1948 with Lister Sinclair. He and his wife, Alice, were our closest friends in Toronto. Lister, Janet, and I had written columns for the *Ubyssey,* the campus newspaper at the University of British Columbia, in the late thirties; now he had become one of the leading radio stars in English-speaking Canada. By the time we drove out to Kleinburg that summer he had written seventy plays and documentaries for radio and a couple more for the stage. A gaunt, dishevelled figure, one year my junior, he was respected for his erudition. He was blessed besides with a photographic memory and an ability not only to read anything at impossible speeds but also to retain most of it. He seemed to know every note of any Beethoven or Mozart symphony. He taught maths at the University of Toronto in addition to script writing at Lorne Greene's Academy of Radio Arts. When asked to do an anthropological series for radio, he steeped himself so thoroughly in the subject that an American university tried to hire him. His knowledge of cultural trivia could be maddening. "Do you remember what Mozart said to Haydn that time in Vienna?" he'd ask, knowing, of course, that none of us knew. I sometimes suspected him of looking up these anecdotes the night before. However that may be, they were always told with considerable wit.

In those days Lister dressed abominably, favouring turtleneck sweaters, ancient, patched tweed jackets, and baggy trousers that had seen their best days. His hair was shaggy years before that became fashionable. He wore thick glasses and walked with the help of a cane. Indeed, as the months went on, his limp became so pronounced that his progress was snaillike. Yet he was also a dedicated naturalist, and I began to notice that when he heard one of the rarer species of bird he would leap forward with unexpected agility to try to spot it. Indeed, once in the Holland Marsh he actually captured the most secretive bird of all – a yellow rail, as thin as its name implies. He not only seized the elusive bird but even took it home and kept it in a cage for some time. I know of no other birder who has ever been able to achieve that.

Lister's lameness grew worse. One day in front of the Park Plaza Hotel in midtown Toronto, he became totally paralysed. A wheelchair was found for him and it looked as if he might spend the rest of his life in it. But Lister was nothing if not a scientist. It was a scientific analysis of his lameness that convinced him, sometime later, that his ailment was entirely psychosomatic, a revelation that did not surprise me. Lister became a different person overnight. He threw away his glasses and his cane, got himself measured for a Savile Row suit, bought himself a Lincoln sports car, and appeared as a member of the Hot Stove League on "Hockey Night in Canada."

Lister and Alice had bought a three-acre parcel of land on the Humber River near Kleinburg, a hamlet of about one hundred people some twenty-five miles northwest of Toronto. It was to be part of a co-operative venture – an idealistic community of ten writers and artists and their families living in harmony on forty acres of unserviced land straddling the valley. A friend of Lister's, Bill McCrow, had conceived the plan, buying the property from an evangelical group that had been using the river to dunk the faithful at the moment of baptism. A rustic sign over the entrance read "Happy Valley." That, I thought, is too much; it will have to go.

Lister thought we might be interested in the scheme. I thought not, and told him so. I had no intention of staying put. Own a house? That was for the bourgeoisie! A house was an encumbrance, and I wanted to be free – free to leave the stifling environs of Toronto, to roam the world, perhaps to be a foreign correspondent in the next war, to work for some huge publishing concern (one that had lots of money, gave out generous expense accounts, and turned its writers into stars). I told Lister we would go along for the ride and the picnic he was proposing, but he could forget about tying us down.

We drove north and west through the rolling farmland, following the winding Humber through the little communities of Weston, Thistletown, Humber Summit, Woodbridge, Pine Grove, and finally Kleinburg, a frontier-looking village with its false-fronted stores and its red brick schoolhouse. The countryside at that time was unsullied by strip plazas, shopping centres, or subdivisions. The verdant hills – fields of blue-green oats and golden winter wheat – rolled off in all directions. The Humber meandered through thick groves of birch and white cedar. American elms, tall and vase-shaped, delineated the horizon.

The Sinclairs had a lot on the riverbank next to one owned by Ronald Hambleton, a Toronto writer and poet, and his wife, Jean. We sat on the top of the bank with the brown river gurgling below our feet and the wind caressing the neat clumps of evergreen. There was no hint of civilization save a barn in the next field and the occasional lowing of cattle. Lister explained that there were several more lots available along the ridge above the valley and one on the river. The setting certainly *was* idyllic, but the idea of actually becoming a *landowner* – a word that in those days had many unfortunate connotations for those of us on the Left – repelled me.

"Why don't you two climb up to the ridge and take a look?" Lister suggested. "The view up there is really great, though I prefer to be in the valley."

Off we went, first crossing the Humber by leaping from rock to rock, on a stroll that was to change our lives. We followed a vague pathway, half obliterated by ferns and wild raspberries, through a thicket of white cedar, each tree so neat it seemed to have been carefully pruned by hand. Occasionally a clump of century-old birches rose from the mosses. A long line of elms marched up the hillside like soldiers, separating McCrow's forty-acre purchase from the adjoining farm. Large-leafed may-apples had sprouted beneath them, and here and there we spotted patches of jack-in-the-pulpit.

As the hillside rose we found ourselves in an orchard of wild apple trees mixed with hawthorn. Above, we could see a strip of pastureland, the grass more than ankle high. We reached the top, sat down, and looked due west into the setting sun. The wooded valley stretched off below us for miles, with the tinsel sparkle of the river winking through. On the far ridge we could see a single barn, nothing more. The setting was magnificent, the sunset golden, the stillness all pervading.

We sat there drinking in the view, seduced by the absolute calm. Suddenly I spoke. "I think we should buy it," I said. Just like that.

Janet's cheerful response was almost immediate.

She didn't say: "Where's the money coming from?"

She didn't say: "Maybe we ought to take a few days to think it over."

She didn't say: "Are you out of your cotton-pickin' mind?"

When I said I thought we should buy it, she said promptly, "I think so too."

The price was one thousand dollars – our entire savings in war bonds.

"Everybody will think we're crazy," Janet said.

"We probably are," I answered.

Of course we *were* crazy. The mind boggles at the gamble we were taking: to build a modern home on a three-acre, unserviced property, all on a salary of $5,000 a year!

Looking back on this scene, I continue to be astonished by our audacity or perhaps our naïveté. Here we were, deciding on the spur of the moment to buy a parcel of sore pastureland some thirty miles from the city, and we didn't even own a car. Our war bonds were the total extent of our resources. We had no idea what the house would cost or how we would pay for it. We knew nothing about septic tanks, wells, water mains, roads, driveways, or landscaping. We were babes in the woods, lulled by the sound of the wind sighing in the trees, bathed now in the aureate rays of the dying sun. We didn't give the future a second thought; it would take care of itself. Wasn't this the promise of the postwar world, dangled before us in a score of slick magazine ads, optimistic editorials, and a host of patriotic wartime speeches?

What on earth were we thinking of? Had we been tempted by the idea of a co-operative community of artists, free of racial prejudice? That certainly took the sting out of the word "landowner," but I doubt that it was the reason. We had both been raised in small communities, surrounded by almost unlimited space – Janet in Fernie, B.C., I in the Yukon. Toronto, the uptight community, crowded, noisy, and confined, was really not for us. Janet was heavy with our first child, due in early August. Our tiny flat above the hardware store already seemed cramped.

It was an insane move, but those were heady times. It was an era of high employment. Only 2.5 percent of the workforce – virtually nobody – was jobless. Canadians were commanding top prices for their produce. The national income had soared to the highest point in history. With the war over, a wave of optimism was sweeping the land, and we were caught up in it. *Maclean's* itself was full of articles describing nature's largesse. Oil had been discovered in Alberta, iron in Ungava, uranium at Great Bear Lake. Neither of us had the least idea where the money would come from, but it didn't matter.

I stood up and started pacing out the lines of the house we proposed to build. This would be our living room, I told Janet – facing directly into the sunset. We wanted a West Coast house; not for us the narrow, two-storey brick that defined much of Ontario. Like the others that McCrow was designing, it would have a low roof line and big windows and it would fit snugly into the hillside.

And what about *Life* magazine and the *Saturday Evening Post?* What would I do if I heard that siren call? Well, I thought vaguely, I can always sell out and move, but even as that errant thought crossed my mind, the vision of the Big Time south of the border began to fade and mingle with the blur of the cedar forest. I don't think I quite realized it, but with that one sudden, impulsive action we had cast our lot with Canada.

Without knowing it, we were in the forefront of a movement that had not yet been given a name. We were *exurbanites* – people who had decided to leapfrog the sprawling suburbs, with their monotonous rows of ticky-tacky homes, and opt for the wide-open spaces beyond. In 1955, Alexander Spectorsky, a future managing editor of *Playboy,* would give the movement its name in his best-selling book, *The Exurbanites.* We were well ahead of him.

Except for the Queen Elizabeth Way there were virtually no four-lane highways in Ontario. To reach our property we would have to drive for about an hour and a quarter on narrow roads through the country-side. We didn't own a car; my parents had never been able to afford one in the thirties. My main driving experience had been in the army, when I had managed to operate jeeps, field artillery, and Bren gun carriers. But these were driven during training over broad spaces in southern Alberta. I had never driven a civilian car in heavy traffic, and the only time I had taken a tracked vehicle out on a paved road, I instantly ran into a bank, threw both tracks, and, as a result, failed my course.

We were going to need a car to get to Kleinburg and oversee work on our house. I made a down payment on an Austin, which seemed to operate on a rubber band, then took the obligatory driving course and applied for a licence. I failed my first test dismally, took more lessons, applied again, and squeaked through on the second try. I knew so little about automobiles that I didn't know enough to check the oil periodi-cally. One day at Humber Summit, seven miles out of Kleinburg, I heard a dreadful clanging and banging and was told by a local garage mechanic that I had been running for some time with no oil and had thrown the rods.

Now we plunged into the murky waters of home construction and finance – two mysterious topics about which we knew absolutely nothing. The idyllic vision of a harmonious artists' colony began to fray at the edges and then to rip apart at the seams. Two owners quickly backed out. The others, it turned out, lacked enough money or prospects to fin-ish their houses. These were supposed to be built together and in the same style by workmen under McCrow's direction. McCrow was a good designer of theatrical and TV sets, among other things, but nei-ther an architect nor an engineer. There were long, vociferous meetings that grew bitter, degenerating into recriminations, personal vendettas, and threats. McCrow himself had no real idea of how much our houses would cost. His estimates had been, to put it mildly, on the optimistic side. He hired a building crew for the project, and the houses went up in fits and starts, financed by short-term loans. But there was increas-ing acrimony over who was building what and whether or not each owner was getting his fair share of the workforce. So much for unselfish idealism among artists!

Of the eight remaining owners, we were the most cautious. Our house would be the smallest of all – a mere 1,450 square feet compared with the 3,000-foot monster that McCrow's vision called for and to which the others had agreed. Meanwhile we were faced with the problem of services. Septic tanks could handle the sewage, but we would have to build roads and install our own water supply. My future neighbours wanted to engage the services of a dowser – a man with a mysterious witch-hazel rod who would infallibly find where the water was. I was totally opposed since I considered water-divining a form of superstition. Everybody else, however, seemed to have an anecdote about somebody who knew somebody, who knew somebody else who had, thanks to the dowsing rod, discovered a veritable lake of fresh water just beneath the surface. I scoffed at this. It is all but impossible *not* to find water in Southern Ontario, I protested; all you have to do is drill. But I was overruled. Out came the man with the witch-hazel. To my dismay, the magic rod guided him to the highest point on the property. There, he said, we would find water. On his instructions our well driller went down two hundred feet – at a whopping six dollars a foot. Sure enough, he found water. It was salt.

"Mind if I make a suggestion?" the well driller asked as we stood glumly grimacing at the brackish result. Since we were out twelve hundred bucks we listened. "Let me drill at the lowest point instead of the highest," said this sensible man. He did so and at sixty-five feet produced such a gush of fresh water that it supplied the entire village when the township took the well over from us some years later.

How young we were! How trusting. Here we were – a playwright, an art gallery dealer, a poet, a filmmaker, a magazine editor – trying to create an ideal rural environment with no real idea where the money was coming from. Our deeds were restrictive in the best sense. We could not subdivide our properties; no fences could be built; no trees could be cut down; each single-family dwelling must be designed to complement the whole; a strip of land along the river would be common to all; and so on. We were a private non-profit organization, and we still are; but now the mix is different. Only one family from the original group is left today: that's us. At least three divorces owe their origins to that wild venture. Some houses have been sold and reoccupied four times; many have been changed out of all recognition, including our own, which now has 6,500 feet of floor space. What was once the smallest house on the property is now the largest. And now we own the two lots that were not built on.

Yet our intentions were of the best. One restriction, which was never

56

written down, bothers me in retrospect. Since so many subdivisions were restricted in those days to Gentiles, we decided, as a group, on a reverse process. Anyone who was known to be anti-Semitic or to have made anti-Semitic references or to have told anti-Semitic jokes was to be kept out. We would not sell our own homes or allow McCrow to sell the two vacant lots to anybody we considered racist. Certain friends who wanted to buy at Windrush (as we had renamed Happy Valley) made overtures; in our newfound self-righteousness, we resisted them. Could it be that we ourselves were being smugly intolerant?

We had great difficulty getting a mortgage. For one thing, we were too far from the city; for another, the West Coast design – flat, over-hanging roof, frame construction, big windows – did not sit well with the major lending agencies. At last we secured an $8,000 loan – not from a city firm but from a rural one.

I know that both Lister and Ron had great difficulty writing under the resulting financial pressure. My own reaction was to moonlight in my off-hours, selling my wares to any source available, including the International Service of the CBC, which seemed happy to pay me fifteen dollars for a talk on any subject that popped into my head. I turned my typewriter to anything that would make a buck. I built a cold frame to nurture early seedlings and sold a piece explaining how to do it. When Lister built an experimental swamp behind his house, I wrote a piece about that, too, and sold it for a few dollars. I told stories about the Klondike on a CBC radio series, "Canadian Yarns." I knocked out radio plays at fifty bucks a half hour. And I did a lot of the work on the house myself.

On weekends Janet and I drove out to Kleinburg to do work that did not require much expertise. Our one-year-old daughter, Penny, sat in the orchard below, munching wild apples while we strapped on sheets of fibreglass to insulate the foundations and tacked batts of insulating material to the joists. Often my colleagues from *Maclean's* would lend a hand, as I supplied the beer. "In ten years this property will be a showplace," Gerry Anglin said one afternoon. I could not believe it. Here was a half-finished house sitting on a sea of gumbo clay, sur-rounded by a flat, treeless piece of pasture. I tried, in my mind's eye, to see it as a showplace and failed. What were we doing here, miles from nowhere, trying to scrape together enough cash to buy window panes and outside doors?

At the same time, the idea of having our own home – a modern one, just as portrayed in the slick housing magazines – excited us. We had splurged on a vast fireplace of Credit Valley limestone that gave an illusion of luxury and permanence. It formed the core of our unfinished dwelling. Sometimes on weekends, after a hard day of putting up wallboard, we would cook a meal in that fireplace; it all seemed too good to be true – the fire crackling away, the scent of roasting meat, and the golden rays of the sunset creeping through the huge gap where we intended to place the display window from an old store that we had bought.

We had moved out of the apartment in East York and into a damp and gloomy basement off the Kingsway. We had little choice; Janet was pregnant again, and the apartment had no room for a family of four. The basement was large, if clammy, with a curtained area for one child and enough space available for our second daughter, Pamela, who arrived in May of 1950. The rent was exorbitant: one hundred dollars a month.

By the end of June I was fed up. Every weekend the countryside through which we drove seemed more inviting. To return to that basement was more than I could stand. One night as Janet nursed little Pamela, I made up my mind:

"Let's get the hell out of here," I said.

"You mean – move to Kleinburg?"

"Why not? So the house isn't finished, but it's got a roof and four walls. People are living in Muskoka in worse shacks than ours."

The more we mulled over the idea, the more attractive it seemed. The weather in Toronto was stinking hot, as usual. The basement was dark as a tomb. Why not go out into the light and breathe real air? Suddenly it seemed like an adventure; but then everything is an adventure when you're young.

We moved in July to a shell of a house. There were no interior walls, only black batts of fibreglass insulation. The building was wide open to the elements, without any doors, inside or out, and no glass in the windows. We continued to cook in the fireplace until we bought a stove cheap. Our only luxury was a new refrigerator, which we plugged into one of the naked outlets in the living room. It didn't matter; we were home.

I spent my allotted two weeks' holiday getting the place into some sort of shape. We put up some wallboard and ceiling board to cover the batts. We got the recycled plate-glass window installed in the living room. We had no carpets to cover the dusty concrete floors, no baseboards, and no interior doors, though we managed to hang the outside ones. In those days oranges came in wooden crates, and some of these, except for a couple of wing chairs, made up our only furniture. We covered the bare walls with burlap and sprayed it dark green. Looking down into the crib at the far end of the house, I discovered, to my horror, that little Pamela's nostrils were half filled with green spray.

We lived in this ramshackle way for some years. We finally managed to get telephone service with twenty-two other customers on the party line. Bit by bit, as we could afford it, we had work done on the house. We even installed a bathroom door to replace the curtain because my father-in-law insisted on his privacy when he visited us from British Columbia. It cost eight dollars and he bought it for us.

Our wooden orange crates, which they don't make any more, lasted for several years. I wrote my first books on an Underwood typewriter perched on one of these crates at the foot of our bed. I don't think they were any the worse for it.

4

By the time we moved to Kleinburg, Arthur Irwin had left *Maclean's*. *Changing* The Maclean Hunter company may have been the largest publisher of *the guard* magazines and trade papers in Canada, but its relations with its own people were abysmal. Irwin's biographer, David MacKenzie, has told how, just after Irwin lost his first wife, Jean, to asthma, he received an extraordinary memorandum from the president, Horace T. Hunter, who apparently either hadn't read his own magazine or didn't understand what Irwin had been trying to do. In the memo Hunter had the gall to write: "We are not developing in the minds of our people a sufficient feeling of pride in Canada...could we not make this the keynote of a continuing campaign in Maclean's Magazine...?"

Irwin was crushed. What did Hunter think he'd been doing since he took over the editorship from Moore? He had built up a staff that the company itself had advertised as a group "whose combined knowledge and experience are unsurpassed by that of any other periodical in Canada." He had, as he told Chalmers in a bitter memo, "transformed a tenth-rate American dress into a Canadian dress whose origins are unmistakable." And, in doing so, he had increased the magazine's circulation by 25 percent. Couldn't Hunter see what was going on under his nose? What did he want – a series of patriotic slogans on the front cover? Irwin believed in parables, not slogans.

The heart went out of him as a result of Hunter's silly memo. Now, with his wife gone, he needed a complete change of scene. When the government offered him the commissionership of the National Film Board, he grabbed it and later went into the diplomatic service.

By 1950, we staffers believed that we were turning out the finest magazine in Canada, if not in the world. How cocksure we were! I remember leafing through some back issues and wondering how the hell we could improve on what we were doing. It seemed so, well, so *perfect*. It wasn't, of course. Now, when I look back through those same issues, the magazine seems to be old-fashioned, often irrelevant, and, worst of all, boring. But magazine journalism has changed dramatically in the last half century. By the same token, the ads for nylons, Castoria, Bon Ami, and Lavoris look just as old-fashioned. Aunt Jemima's stereotype black mammy peers out from the back pages along with ads for Spork and Spam, next to an earnest plea to buy an ice refrigerator, "the most efficient and complete refrigeration money can buy."

The writing, it seems to me now, lacked the cutting edge we have come to expect in today's magazine journalism. There was little critical assessment of the people and institutions we wrote about. We took Whipper Billy Watson, the wrestler, as seriously as we took Bob Sanders, the American-born quarterback of the Winnipeg Blue Bombers. We praised frontal lobotomy as "The Cut That Makes Men Sane" (no mention of what it did to women), and we examined a series of social problems uncritically or anonymously, from artificial insemination ("Is It Adultery?") to the backwardness of certain Canadian laws ("How We Faked Our Divorce"). Our profiles of cities and provinces were worthy and informative but not terribly exciting. They not only lacked a strong point of view but were also blind to the real problems of urban sprawl, traffic congestion, and crime that these cities were facing. The articles just lay there, daring the reader to turn the page. A profile of Ottawa was called simply "Capital on a Cliff." Another on the Great Lakes had the title "The Great Lakes." There was no apparent rationale for why we were writing on these subjects.

In fact, however, there *was* a reason. No other Canadian magazine had set out purposely to tell its readers about the country. I had gone north to the Yukon and Eva-Lis Wuorio east to Newfoundland to interpret Canada to Canadians, in Irwin's phrase. That was reason enough in those early days. Our pieces lacked immediacy, but we had no control over that. The magazine's ancient presses, creaking away not far from our editorial offices, made it impossible to get anything topical in print. It took a minimum of six weeks and usually longer for a manuscript to be published. In those days we worshipped the false god of "objectivity," refusing to allow our own personalities full rein. My own pieces lacked fire; I kept myself out of them. I scorned Beverley Baxter's breezy, opinionated London columns from his vantage point on the Tory backbench. I could never understand why they were so popular. How narrow and snobbish I was! Baxter put himself into his columns, establishing himself as a flesh-and-blood character as future writers would do when a new kind of journalism emerged fifteen years later.

Ralph Allen was, of course, the only choice to succeed Irwin and was quite prepared to return to the magazine from the *Telegram*. He was red-haired, freckled, and bespectacled, just seven years older than I – hard-bitten, unsentimental, tough-minded, and, as befitted a former sportswriter, blessed with a dry wit. In many ways he was Irwin's opposite, but when it came to dissecting a magazine article he had the same qualities. John Clare, who now became managing editor, was three years older than Allen, taller and burlier. Adam Marshall, our copy chief, Blair Fraser, and Gerry Anglin were also tall men. I was six foot three. Robert Collins, who joined us fresh out of journalism school, has written that his first encounter with these huge editors had a sobering effect on him, making him feel inferior by comparison. And no doubt we *were* terrifying to those freelance writers whose living depended entirely upon us.

I was elevated to associate editor, and we all worked closely together, often lunching at Old Angelo's or Little Denmark, or drinking at the circular bar at the Town and Country buffet restaurant, especially at World Series time after television arrived in some local bars. Allen, the baseball fan, had to square his conscience with Allen, the editor, but in a tight game it was hard to drag him or any of us back to the office.

John Clare and I were movie buffs; sometimes at lunch we would pick up corned-beef sandwiches from Coleman's delicatessen on Bay Street and take in half a movie – *Broken Arrow,* say, or *When Worlds*

Collide. Our own scruples would not allow us to dip into the company's time by staying through an entire movie, but given the quality of second-run "B" pictures in those days, that didn't seem to matter. We were all Chinese-food addicts at a time when the only Oriental dishes available were Cantonese. At 22A Elizabeth Street, around the corner from the office, with your egg roll and chow mein you could order "cold tea" – Scotch whisky, brought from the closest liquor store by one of the waiters and served in a teapot.

There was a good deal of noon-hour drinking in those days. Liquor licences were scarce, and when a new bar opened it was a cause for celebration. One memorable lunch hour, half a dozen of us trooped down to the brand-new Horseshoe Tavern on Queen Street off Spadina and began to sample the wares. At four o'clock we were still there and well into our cups. At that point somebody suggested we order lunch. "Capital idea," said Clare, "but I think first I'll just have a small aperitif." That was back in December 1947, when Irwin was in charge. He did not share our lunch hours, especially the liquid ones. But when we rolled into the office around closing time he made no comment. He was, I think, baffled but also a little charmed by this show of independence. "My whole staff got drunk today," somebody heard him tell Blair Fraser on the phone. It sounded almost like a boast. I myself did no serious work that legendary afternoon and could only admire Ralph Allen, who was closeted with Irwin for nearly an hour, going over manuscripts. In spite of the heavy tippling, he seemed, to the untutored eye, to be remarkably sober. Just the kind of man needed to take over the editorship of Canada's National Magazine.

Chapter Three

1

ANCHORAGE, ALASKA, March 1951. I am on my way to cover the hot new war in Korea for Maclean's, *flying as a guest of MATS, the Military Air Transport Service, in a four-engine North Star loaded with six tons of tires, machinery, generators, and spare parts destined for vehicles bogged down in the war zone.*

We have stopped briefly to take on fuel and check the weather forecast for the next leg of our flight, which will take us to Shemya, a tiny dot on the map at the farthest tip of the Aleutian chain of islands, a long curved finger pointing at Asia that swings for a thousand miles into the North Pacific.

"See that big island next door to Shemya?" says Dean Broadfoot, our twenty-two-year-old pilot, pointing to the wall map in the pilots' hut. "That's Attu; the Japs held it during the war, remember? I hear they had a hundred-knot gale last month. Blew all the buildings down."

The quick northern night has fallen as we take off. Our ETA at Shemya is set for 3:30 a.m. Below, I can see the tips of volcanic mountains, some of them glowing like embers in the night. I doze off, waking at 3:15 to hear Bud Austin, the navigator, telling me that we cannot land. The winds on the ground at Shemya are sixty-five knots. We must fly back to Adak, a U.S. naval base, at least three hours behind us.

Adak is socked in and we are running short of fuel. The Americans on the ground will have to talk us down to an unseen landing strip. Somewhere below in the murk a man in a yellow truck is staring at a quivering blot made by the image of our aircraft on a gridded radar screen. We are about to experience a GCA (Ground Controlled Approach) landing, about which Bob Hope, after an Aleutian tour, exclaimed: "Greetings!... Congratulations!... Alive!"

"Maintain 180 degrees," the voice from below tells Broadfoot. "Coming in nicely now. You are ten feet below the glide path. Bring her up a little. You are on the glide path; turn left to 172 degrees. You are up fifteen feet above the glide path... twenty feet... come down a little."

I do not know he is guiding us directly between a pair of 4,000-foot cliffs. I breathe in relief as two parallel lines of light loom out of the fog and we are on the tarmac. It is twenty-five hours since we took off from McChord Field in Washington State. "Not a bad day's work," says Broadfoot.

In the grey light of dawn, with the unending Aleutian winds howling like banshees and the temperature standing at one degree above zero Fahrenheit, Adak looks like a forlorn land, its headland black and unbroken by any foliage.

We sleep for twelve hours and then take off once again for Shemya. More than two hours later, a chunk of volcanic rock appears, rising from the chill ocean, treeless and as cheerless as a crypt, half hidden by clinging mists and shifting snow. We hit the asphalt with a forty-knot crosswind threatening to hurl us off the runway. The smashed wreckage of a B-17 thrown over the bank is a clue to what might have been.

"Welcome to Shemya-by-the-sea," says Flying Officer Jack Egan, the commanding officer of the sixteen-man RCAF detachment here. I feel that I have reached the ends of the earth. My familiar Yukon seems almost tropical by contrast. "There's a girl behind every tree in Shemya," the old army saying goes, "but there aren't any trees."

Why is Egan wearing a parka tight around him with the sun shining brightly in the blue? A moment later, as a blizzard springs up and obliterates the surroundings, I understand.

We are quartered with hundreds of Americans in an incredible maze of a building – a series of army huts all linked together under a single roof, dug deep into the ground and banked high with earth as protection against the gales. One hallway is a thousand feet long. Everything an airman needs is here under one roof. Some have spent months in this place without ever venturing outside.

We remain at mandatory rest for thirty-six hours. The crew talks about how much better it will be on the return trip, carrying Korean War casualties home by way of Wake Island and Hawaii. The Canadians transport more wounded than the Americans because the faster North Star cuts two to three hours off the Pacific trip. But it is also the noisiest plane in the sky, and our ears continue to buzz from its engines long after we are on the ground.

We take off at two in the morning. With the sun just tinting the soft ocean of clouds, we head southwest for Japan, eleven and a half hours away. At eleven a lone voice crackles out of nowhere on our radio. The U.N. weather ship Sugar is somewhere beneath the clouds, wheeling in a small, unending circle in the empty sea. The voice gives Broadfoot his position together with a complete weather summary and a forecast.

He wiggles the dial and a Russian voice comes in. We are only sixty miles off the Soviet coast. "That's probably old Joe himself," says Broadfoot. A string quartet begins to play, and he explains that the Russians sometimes beam five-hundred-voice choirs over our frequencies to jam the radar. Once again, as I often do on similar occasions, I feel that I am a witness to history, a bystander in a deadly game being played on a global stage. Broadfoot wiggles the dial again and a new voice intrudes singing "Beautiful Dreamer" in Japanese.

A long line of cumulus clouds looms up ahead, and soon we are tossed about in the turbulence of a cold front. Then the clouds part, and below us I can see the wrinkled old hills and tinted mountains of Japan.

We fly south along the seacoast – the neat, brown land unrolling like a Japanese scroll: brown mountains, brown hills, olive brown rivers, tan-coloured cities, and cocoa brown forests, all roasting in the noon sunlight. What a contrast to the frigid Aleutians!

Yokohama sprawls below us, and a few minutes later we are skipping down the runway at Haneda, in the lee of a blasted Zero factory. I cannot dismiss the irony from my mind. It is less than six years since the last war ended. Now we, the conquerors of that one, are embroiled in a new conflict. The hated Japanese have become our pals; the Chinese, once our comrades-in-arms, have become our bitter foes – a new version of the Yellow Peril. But there will be no new Hiroshimas, no rape of Nanking. This time, neither of the two great Asian nations will be mauled by war. That is to be the fate of the Koreans on both sides of the 38th Parallel.

2

The Leper Colony Tokyo, still under American occupation, was a madhouse. The streets were jammed not only with Japanese, many in traditional dress, but also with soldiers from all nations wearing the blue U.N. patch on their shoulders. Taxis scuttled about, their drivers nodding cheerfully when given an address in a language they could not understand. Most cars had a sack of coal strapped onto the rear; converted into gas, it made a weak substitute for gasoline, then in short supply.

The nightclubs, many of them off-limits to servicemen (but not to war correspondents like me), did a roaring business. Young women in clinging dresses served as hostesses, rubbing suggestively against their dance partners, ordering cheap champagne, and flinging firecrackers at the stage acts as a form of applause. The Kabuki and Noh theatres were attracting hordes of baffled GIs, while *Morgan Oyuki,* a caricature of a Broadway-style musical, was playing to sold-out audiences, even though it ran for more than four hours. On the Ginza you could buy small clockwork animals – bears, lions, panthers – for a few yen. In the Marinouchi Hotel, British officers on leave played with them by the hour. When I entered, I almost tripped over a mechanical polar bear shambling realistically across the carpet.

The high brass, from Douglas MacArthur on down, had commandeered Frank Lloyd Wright's famous Imperial Hotel. I was quartered in the Marinouchi, which had become the British leave centre. Here I paid four dollars a day for a room and three magnificent meals (plus morning tea). In the bar you could get two martinis for a quarter. I had difficulty padding my expense account.

I wanted to get out of Tokyo and into Korea. I was given my accreditation and drew a uniform, part American, part British, with the U.N. shoulder patch. My most important stop, however, was at the Canadian Embassy, where a tax-free bottle of Canadian Club whisky could be had for a dollar. I bought eight and jettisoned half my kit to accommodate them. In Korea, I'd been told, whisky was priceless; one never knew when a bottle might come in handy.

Jock Carroll of the *Montreal Standard* and Bill Herbert of the CBC travelled with me on the MATS aircraft to South Korea. I cannot remember where we landed; I think it was probably Taegu. But I cannot forget that landing. The airstrip was pockmarked with shell craters, and as we hit hard and bounced down the runway, I recalled a grisly statistic: more war correspondents had been killed on landing strips like this than in the actual fighting.

Before I set out for Korea, Ralph Allen had agreed to have my life insured for one hundred thousand dollars. But a few days before I left he asked if I would agree to a policy with a face value of only twenty-five thousand because the two-month premium had been raised to two thousand dollars. Even that sum would stretch the magazine's budget; for that amount we could buy enough freelance pieces to fill an entire issue.

I didn't give a damn about insurance. I would have gone to Korea without any, if necessary. I was desperate for the assignment and didn't want the matter of money to stand in the way. I was convinced, as young men are, that I bore a charmed life. If I had been destined to die in an airplane accident, it would have happened four years earlier when Russ Baker's Junkers almost crashed through the thin ice of the South Nahanni River, or later, when the DC-4's engine caught fire over the Andes. I felt invulnerable.

"Now don't go and do anything rash," Ralph said. He apparently felt it was necessary to repeat the warning. "Be careful! Don't try to be a goddamn hero."

He seemed to think that I would rush into action firing from the hip, but I didn't plan on doing anything of the sort. I had a wife and two little girls, and I was in no mood for heroics. I would observe carefully and safely from the sidelines. I suppose my brashness at the staff conferences had made me sound a bit of a wild man, but I had every intention of staying out of harm's way.

Now, as the plane bumped down on the short airstrip, reversed engines, and shuddered to a stop, I saw why insurance companies were so reluctant to issue policies on the lives of war correspondents.

"Jesus," said Bill Herbert, "it's dangerous here. I'm staying put."

I thought Bill was joking, but he wasn't. One look at Korea decided him. He did not bother to disembark but returned on the same plane to cover the war from Tokyo. My own response was a rush of exhilaration. I could hardly wait to get out of the aircraft and feel the soil of Korea under my feet. I had spent four years in the army during the war and never got closer to the action than Aldershot, England. But now I was a foreign correspondent – like Joel McCrea in the Hitchcock film – complete with portable typewriter! A little too portable, perhaps. I'd carried the same machine – a Hermes Baby – about in my bag during all my army service. I still had it and hated it. It was, without doubt, the smallest typewriter ever made and also the least lovable. When I hammered away with my two index fingers, the words, the sentences, and the lines all tended to jam up or run together, while certain letters popped up above the others, so that each page seemed to have been typed by an inebriate. It had one good point: it weighed only eight pounds, which is why I kept it in my dunnage bag with the Canadian Club.

Jock and I left by jeep for the one Canadian battalion in Korea. The 2nd Princess Patricia's Canadian Light Infantry were in reserve somewhere south of the 38th Parallel that divides the two Koreas. The rest of the brigade, still in training in Washington State, would not arrive until May.

The journey was an ordeal – the first of many I would suffer in South Korea. The roads were atrocious and so was the weather. The damp and bitter winds carried a fine, stinking dust that blew off the rice paddies, which were fertilized with human excrement, euphemistically called night soil. The traffic moved snaillike on roads that were nothing more than rutted trails. As for the Patricias, when we reached their lines the battalion was in a state of disarray. The colonel, Big Jim Stone, had fallen ill and been invalided back to Tokyo. A dozen private soldiers had died from drinking the wrong kind of alcohol. Three more were in the guardroom charged with raping and killing a Korean woman.

In the Officers' Mess tent I ran into several old army friends from the late war. "Have you seen the bold Foulds yet?" asked Rick Constant, whom I'd known at Currie Army Barracks, Calgary, in 1944. Captain Andy Foulds had been a close friend; now it turned out he was the battalion quartermaster. I lost no time in finding his tent and bringing along one of my bottles of Canadian Club.

Foulds hadn't changed – a tall, tough-looking officer with slits for eyes, a bristly moustache, a pugnacious chin, and a mordant sense of humour.

"Hell, I haven't had a drink since I got here," he told me as I produced my precious bottle. "Swore off the stuff for the duration." A pause as I began to pour. "For you, I'll break my own rules," Foulds said at last.

We demolished the bottle, reminiscing about the old days, which weren't all that old. It was just that these had been crowded years. I had last seen Foulds in 1944, when we shared the same bunkhouse at an officers' refresher course at Brockville. He was a former regimental sergeant-major, the most awesome and awe inspiring job in the army, and he still looked it – ramrod straight, hard-muscled, slightly terrifying to anybody who didn't know him well.

At last I staggered off to bed. Next morning at breakfast, I inquired after Foulds and was told that he had suddenly been taken ill with a mysterious disease. I went straight to his tent to find him groaning on his bunk.

He looked up, astonished. "Where did you come from?" he asked.

"You saw me last night, remember?" I told him. "We killed a bottle of rye."

He sat bolt upright. "My God, so we did. All I've got is a hangover!" And he leapt out of bed and into his uniform.

I joined him later in the mess. The only officer not present was the public relations officer, Joe Levison, whose tent I shared. Joe was a likeable but totally unsoldierly subaltern, plump and bespectacled, who clearly felt himself embarrassed in the company of fighting men. I think that was why he so rarely ate in the mess, staying in his tent and living on C rations from the army's emergency packs. Joe was Jewish, but I saw no evidence of bigotry among the officers in the mess. I found it all very strange, but then the whole Korean conflict was strange to me.

This curious war had begun the previous June when the North Koreans invaded the South. It escalated quickly when the Americans, in U.N. guise, sprang to the defence of the South Koreans. Other countries also sent small detachments to swell the U.N. force, but the Chinese, when they entered the war, proved to be tougher adversaries than their North Korean allies. As the Cold War grew hotter, Canada found herself volunteering an infantry brigade to fight on the other side of the globe to preserve freedom and democracy – twin concepts totally foreign to the Asian soldiers who were bent on killing each other in the rice paddies of the Korean peninsula.

I wanted to write about a typical section leader, for this was a section leader's war. A section, no more than ten men, is the smallest unit in the infantry, and this was a war in which there was no room for armies. If it was ever to be won in these cone-shaped hills, blackened by fire and scarred by shovel, it would be won by tiny handfuls of men clawing their way to the high ground. And so Joe found my man for me: Corporal Kerry Dunphy of No. 1 Section, No. 4 Platoon, Baker Company.

The young men of No. 1 Section were all under thirty; only one was married; none save Dunphy had more than high-school education – the cannon fodder of the fifties. They had been blooded in battle and operated as a tight clique within their platoon, calling themselves the Leper Colony, a steal from the Gregory Peck film *Twelve O'Clock High*. Although some had killed Chinese at long range, none, in this curious war, had ever seen his opponent. All were frustrated by an enemy who camouflaged himself into the very soil, then slipped off at night after burying his dead so the advancing forces didn't have the satisfaction of seeing the results of their fire.

70

There was nothing gallant about this war, merely weeks of remorse-less plodding from ridge to ridge, firing into apparently empty hills, struggling up slopes so steep that the padre felt obliged to omit that fine old hymn "Unto the Hills Around Do I Lift Up My Longing Eyes" from the service.

The private soldiers I encountered in Korea had no real understand-ing of why they were there. Enemies and allies alike were "gooks"; the Chinese were "Chinks." For years we had all been fed on a diet of Hollywood war movies when an ordinary soldier near the end makes a speech about fighting to preserve democracy, the right to enjoy Mom's apple pie and boo the Dodgers. There were no such speeches here. The soldiers were volunteers to a man, but all were cynical about the "police action," as the press dubbed it. The phrase was sometimes used as a joke.

Kerry Dunphy told me that he had once thought he knew what he was fighting for. He had joined up intending to write a novel with a Korean background. Now, he said, "it's tough to find anything exciting to write about. I've become too insulated to this whole life."

The enthusiastic press coverage of the war had rendered him cyni-cal. He hated the Americans, as so many Commonwealth troops did – hated them more than the Chinese, whom he called "sporting soldiers." He was under no illusion that the enemy had been beaten and was irritated by Canadian newspaper headlines that read "Pats Hurl Back Reds." He and his fellows in the Leper Colony were convinced that the Chinese could have held the hills of Korea indefinitely if they had want-ed to. Dunphy, who had once thought the so-called police action a good thing, now professed to be as baffled as one of his men, a Maliseet Indian named Bob Perely, who, incredibly, was under the impression he was fighting Chiang Kai-shek's Nationalist troops.

The attitude of the Lepers and that of most of the soldiers I talked to in Korea was undoubtedly conditioned by the stupefying, unending vista of waste and destruction through which they moved. Almost every bridge in the country had been destroyed, locomotives and freight cars wrecked, rails ripped up, buildings gutted, roads reduced to ruts, rice paddies flattened, villages reduced to black and steaming sores. I saw no evidence that this war was in any way benefiting the people on whose land it was being fought. The mass of the Korean peasantry neither knew nor cared what was happening politically in their midst – and why should they? They were being asked to exchange one kind of dictatorship for another. If Syngman Rhee of South Korea differed from the North's Kim Il Sung, it was only by a degree. The troops were not unaware of this. "To them we're not liberators," Dunphy's second-in-command, Bill Denne, told me. "We're just the white race fighting on their ground to save our own face."

War or no war, life went on in South Korea. The farmers, in their loose white clothing, continued to live in their mud-and-straw hovels and till the bean fields, even in the midst of an attack. One of Baker Company's men, spotting movement in a shattered hut in front of the lines, opened fire only to discover that he had wounded a woman and her child, working away, completely unconscious of the war around them.

Looking ahead to the Vietnam War, the parallel between the two actions is clear. "We take a village and they smile at us and put up the Republic of Korea flag, and we know damn well that two days before the same smiles were for the Communists," Dunphy said. "It seems you always got to take somebody's word for it that the Korean people are 'liberty loving.' I haven't met a gook yet who was."

During the Second World War, as a young officer I had given regular lectures with the heading "Why We Fight." In Korea, nobody bothered. Outside of a printed statement by General Matthew Ridgway, there was nothing to inspire the U.N. troops. No doubt the effort would have been fruitless, given the political situation.

In army parlance, the Canadians were cheesed off with Korea. The Pats had been virtually confined to barracks since they left Canada five months before. Here there was none of the sweet that usually accompanies the bitterness of war – no place worth going to and nothing worth looting. Venereal disease was rampant, the villages were riddled with typhus, and the colonel had come down with smallpox. One wag suggested that the country be divided vertically instead of horizontally so the fighting could go that way just for a change.

After I spent a few weeks in Korea, the idea didn't seem all that wacky.

3

On March 25, Easter Sunday, 1951, the entire battalion packed up and *City* moved, in a driving rain, to a bean field northeast of Seoul. Conditions *without* had degenerated so much that it took thirteen hours to travel the thir- *hope* teen miles. I was grateful for Joe Levison's Compo rations, which we heated up, using the jeep's gasoline.

I had reason to think of the trip with Joe in the days following my stint in Korea. I remember at one point how the jeep plunged into a shell crater, and how Joe gunned it almost to the top before it slid back. After I returned to Canada I learned that Joe had again taken his jeep into a crater, not knowing that the Chinese had left a mine concealed in the mud, calibrated to explode when the 100th vehicle crossed it. Joe and a New Zealand correspondent crossed safely – the 99th time the mine had been driven over. But this jeep also failed to reach the crest; it slid back, hit the mine, and blew both men to bits. Joe Levison, the unlucky P.R. man, was the first Canadian officer killed in Korea. I wish he'd spent more time in the mess; he deserved to.

Seoul, the old capital, had been under Chinese occupation for some months, but a week earlier the U.N. forces had retaken it, forcing the enemy out. Although army personnel were forbidden to enter the city, as a war correspondent I was an exception. I needed a jeep. Thank God for Andy Foulds! He not only supplied a vehicle and a trailer full of rations but he also gave me a soldier, Jim Ramsay, to drive the jeep, another, Ron Taylor, to guard it, and a young Korean interpreter, Chai Chung Jyp, whom everybody called Dickie.

Off we went down the broad valley of the Han, the slopes bright with rhododendrons and azaleas and the sky cloudless for once. It was beautiful country, but I was one of the few who could enjoy scenery that had been a horror to the troops.

In just nine months Seoul had been liberated four times, twice by the victorious armies of the People's Republic of North Korea and their allies, the victorious armies of the People's Republic of China (disguised as volunteers), and twice by the victorious armies of the United Nations. As a result, it lay inert along the broad, debris-strewn Han River, a lifeless metropolis without food, without fuel, without power, without water, virtually without people, and almost without hope.

I entered this carcass of a city just ten days after its fourth liberation.

The silence of the grave hung over its shattered buildings as we drove down the empty streets. That emptiness was enhanced by the solitary presence at every intersection of a white-gauntleted South Korean policeman, each of whom made a ritual of ostentatiously waving us on as if there were scores of vehicles rumbling down the pitted roadway.

Seoul was off-limits at night even to war correspondents. But there was a press building – the only one left standing – at the airport. Our arrival caused a considerable stir. Who was this Canadian reporter who travelled with an entourage? As Foulds's three men leapt from the jeep, unpacked my kit, pumped up my air mattress, and awaited orders, I produced one of my bottles of Canadian Club and every correspondent in the shack perked up. We sang lustily late into the night; I led the company in "Alouette" and recited "The Shooting of Dan McGrew," with gestures. They called me the Duke, and I didn't complain.

Jack Thompson, the spade-bearded correspondent for Colonel Bertie McCormick's Anglophobic Chicago *Tribune,* asked if I could supply him with some anti-Brit jokes. His eccentric publisher was demanding at least one anti-British story a day. Thompson got on so well with the British that they cheerfully rustled up a wide range of scurrilous anecdotes for him, many of which, no doubt, appeared in the paper.

His colleague, the correspondent for the New York *Herald Tribune,* smarted under the long and attractive shadow cast by his predecessor, the comely and much publicized Marguerite Higgins, and he decided he must do something heroic to match her journalism. He had persuaded a U.N. conducting officer to take him north to the 38th Parallel. Remembering Ralph Allen's admonition, I declined to go along. That was just as well, for we discovered the next day that his boldness had been rewarded by a bullet in the arm.

The following morning my little cavalcade drove into Seoul. At the city hall we encountered the mayor, a wan figure in an old air force jacket and a faded brown silk scarf, sitting in a bare office behind a borrowed desk. In this little corner of the so-called Free World, the mayor was appointed, not elected, a favour he shared with almost every official in a city known for its political patronage. This was, no doubt, a reward for his faithful service as secretary to the president, Syngman Rhee. The mayor had no real power; an American military adviser, Lieutenant Colonel Joe Verdi, was the real boss.

Seoul, the mayor told us, was 50 percent destroyed as the result of its four liberations. The population, which once stood at more than a million and a half, had been reduced to less than two hundred thousand. It had been systematically looted by the Chinese of every grain of rice, every stick of fuel, every item of value. Its water plant was 90 percent ruined and the people were drinking water from the sewers. The power plant had been wrecked so effectively that it would be at least three months before electricity could be produced. Its citizens had been beaten, hunted, burned out, kidnapped, jailed, starved, and shot by the tens of thousands. The Red World and the Free World had fought their ideological war almost to the last Korean.

"What will the people do to earn money, Mr. Mayor?" I asked him.

"Oh, there will be plenty to do. They will work for the government, rebuilding the city."

"The government will pay them wages?"

"Of course."

"How will you get the money?"

"Why, we will tax the people."

Obviously he was counting not on this Catch-22 solution but on Big Daddy, the United Nations, which, in effect, meant the United States.

What a bizarre city Seoul was on this bright March morning in 1951! The sense of driving through a graveyard was reinforced by an odd spectacle in the shattered gardens of the old Chong Kyongwon Palace, once the seat of the Yi dynasty, later a public park and zoo. Now the hundreds of cages stood vacant. The animals had all been eaten, with one exception. An odd movement at the end of one row caught my eye, and there, picking its way through the debris, was a lone and starving ostrich. I have never in my life seen such a bedraggled creature as this one, its feathers awry, its eyes vacant. It ignored us totally as it continued to peck about in a vain search for food.

But where were the people? In this vast graveyard of a city we had seen only a handful, most of them the Korean policemen waving at non-existent traffic. We found them at last in the old market at the city's East Gate. Here were thousands of wretched citizens, hungry, in rags, filthy, wounded, impoverished by war or orphaned by execution – a human panorama that would become increasingly familiar as the century moved on. Spread out before them on worn mats were all their worldly possessions, from lacquer boxes to small silver flasks and, of course, food.

In this desert of rubble I spotted a small boy wearing a fur hat and a two-piece khaki suit that his mother had fashioned from an army blanket. His name was Song Kank Nyung and he was just thirteen. He told Dickie that his family had fled to a cave in the hills after the Chinese burned his home. Now he had an old desk drawer containing a few packages of chocolate and candy, taken from American K rations. He had bought these items from a boy in the market, paying 400 won for each package of Life Savers, which he was now trying to sell for 500 won. The ember of free enterprise, which was what this was all about, was still flickering here at the East Gate. Not far away, Song's mother was selling hotcakes made from corn at 200 won apiece or about three cents at the current exchange rate.

At the Kootje Hotel, once a fancy Japanese caravanserai, now a headquarters for the U.N. Civilian Assistance Command, I wangled permission to stay overnight. The man in charge, Charles R. Munske, was a big, expansive American with a .45 automatic on his hip and a House of Lords cigar in his mouth. When, at dinner, I told him the story of the lone ostrich, he leapt from his chair with a triumphant shout. "Hey! That's going to be our mascot!" he cried. "We'll feed him up good and use him as a symbol. Get some of the boys together and get down to the zoo right away before dark. An ostrich! Oh, boy!"

We slept that night, but Seoul did not. The retreating army had left behind a number of five-man teams, equipped with grenades and sub-machine guns, to harass the U.N. forces. Only one team had been captured; the rest were out there, creeping through the alleys. Joe Verdi, the "military adviser," had given orders to shoot on sight anybody caught moving after nightfall. From the window of my sleeping quarters, Seoul was an eerie sight. Unlit except for a few flickering candles, silent except for the occasional rattle of gunshots, sinister because of the pockets of enemy hidden in the cellars, the great, dead city was a black ruin at the foot of its twisted purple mountains, where, as many believed, the dragon of the hills still lurked.

The next day I explored the president's fantastically lavish home, now looted of carpets, curtains, and tapestries. Syngman Rhee, the tin-pot dictator whom the United Nations was propping up, had lived like a prince among his impoverished people, and the evidence was all around me: the inlaid floors that had once shone like glass, now scratched raw by Chinese boots; the faded flowers still in their vases; the marble staircase, thick with dust; the panelling and mosaics on walls and ceilings; and the rare blue tiles of the roof, each reputedly worth ten thousand won in the days when that was a month's pay for a labourer. Is this, I asked myself, what we are fighting for? No wonder the troops are cynical.

We had one more call to make. Dickie, our seventeen-year-old interpreter, wanted to visit his old house. We drove down the narrow, cobbled streets to find it intact, but no better than a shell. Except for a few sticks of furniture and some books scattered among the torn paper on the rice matting floor, nothing had been left for Dickie to come home to.

The signs of a furious and deliberate search were all around us – cupboards and drawers ransacked, holes punched in walls and ceiling. On the floor a little lacquer box inlaid with mother-of-pearl lay smashed. Like most Koreans, Dickie was not given to outward emotion. He simply sucked in his breath and said, "The Chinamans come to here, sir. All took!"

He poked through the debris and found a couple of books. "The Chinamans don't take books, sir," he said. "I think they are all ignorance. They do not know anything."

But they did know how to make use of the detritus of war. They had swept through Seoul on a house-to-house search, taking first everything of value – silverware, brass, and jewellery; then every piece of cloth and clothing – carpets, draperies, upholstery, and leather work; and finally, every scrap of food. The only vehicles left belonged to the army. Every private car and taxi had been stripped and gutted.

In spite of this, the resourceful Koreans had somehow managed to save tons of merchandise. I talked to one man who had taken a 1941 Dodge apart, piece by piece, buried each one separately, and later sold a map of the various hiding places to scrape together enough money to buy rice. And I met a young construction engineer named Pak E. Yel who told me how his girlfriend had managed to hide him for two months in one of the big earthenware pots used for storing kimchi, the garlicky spiced cabbage that is a Korean staple. He emerged just before I arrived, his hair and beard thickly matted, his eyes watery, and so weak that before I encountered him he had not been able to speak or walk.

And that was Seoul, the once proud capital of the Land of the Morning Sun, as I saw it in the last days of March. As we headed for the Patricias' lines in our jeep, some of the people were seeping back, and as we drove out of the city, some were already piling broken bricks in neat rows and brushing the ashes from the streets. They were doing it methodically and without hurry, but the pace was steady as they set about building a new city from the carcass of the old.

4

Jim Ramsay had come down with pneumonia, so I drove the jeep out of Seoul. The Pats were on the move again, we were told, somewhere to the northeast of us. But where? Since there was only one road, a rutted trail scarcely the width of the jeep, I figured we would sooner or later reach our objective.

The jeep clung precariously to the mountainside. What I remember most about that long and tortuous journey was the chill that ran down my spine every time we met an oncoming vehicle. Sometimes I was forced to back up as much as a mile to find a spot where we could edge past; otherwise I had to nudge the jeep precariously up the flank of the hill to make room enough for the other vehicle to pass. The road had no guard rail. A single wrong move and we might easily have tumbled hundreds of feet. Not a cheerful prospect for someone who, only a short time ago, had failed his driving test!

We came upon the Pats' convoy eventually, bogged down in the mud, moving by fits and starts towards its objective, a rice paddy some 8,000 yards on the safe side of the 38th Parallel. Here, as everywhere, were the Koreans in their loose, white clothing, the old white-bearded men in black bird-cage hats, the naked children rolling in the mud, the women in scarves and pantaloons, tilling fields that showed the ravages of war.

I felt for these people. In Kleinburg, Janet and I were learning to become gardeners. We had begun to plant trees and shrubs on our naked property and had, with considerable sweat, dug out flower gardens on each side of our driveway. If anyone had trampled on them I would have lashed out in a state of rage. Yet here we were, foreigners, shuffling through rice paddies that had taken centuries to build up. Here was the real beauty of Korea – the sinuous terraces curving down the hillsides, each fashioned to receive its ration of water from the one above, each planted with neat rows of young shoots that needed water to survive. Now we were senselessly clomping through this natural geometry, destroying the dykes, the drains, and the young plants that were intended to feed the very people we had been sent to help. I do not know if any effort was made by those in command to educate the troops to preserve what they could of these exquisite ancient plantations. If so, few paid any heed. When the shells fall, of course, no one gives a hoot about what is underfoot, but no shells were falling here.

As we came to our umpteenth halt, I witnessed an excruciating spectacle on the verandah of a thatched hut. A young Korean sat there shoeless, an expression of distaste on his face that I knew was pain. And no wonder: his feet were being eaten away by gangrene. All we could see were the whitened bones that had once been his toes. Bill Boss of the Canadian Press and I went up immediately to the jeep in which the Medical Officer was riding and asked him to do something for the man. He refused; he wasn't there to help Koreans, he said with a shrug. Bill and I stood there, helpless and humiliated. Then, with a lurch, the convoy moved on, removing the horror from our sight but never from our memories.

5

In the days that followed I saw a good deal more of Korea and a good deal also of the forces of the Free World, whose inspiring task it was to liberate the freedom-loving South Koreans from the communist beasts. As in all wars, there were beasts on both sides. I was waiting for an airplane one day in Pusan, watching a group of Koreans unloading a big C-54. The young GI in charge kept up a torrent of abuse, and when one old man stumbled and almost dropped a packing case, this little pipsqueak, who had clearly never been in charge of anything before, seized him by the shirt front, shook his fist in his face, and shouted, "You sonofabitch, if you do that again, I'll punch you in the nose!" Another time I wanted to get some photographs of a group of soldiers walking past some Korean mud huts. They were very obliging. Before I could stop them, they'd driven out the occupants at bayonet point so they wouldn't clutter up the picture. Later that same day one of our soldiers wanted to empty his Bren gun – and did so into a Korean grave. Once

The forces of the Free World

on a bus, again in Pusan, I listened with embarrassment as a GI shouted to his seatmate about how he hated the "gooks." I cannot forget the look on the face of the Korean bus driver who heard him.

Nor can I forget the crowded streets and the khaki river of soldiers flowing through them, many of them drunk, not a few arrogant, most with too much money to spend – a shifting montage of jeeps driving lickety-split down narrow lanes built for oxcarts, of Western voices cursing those who didn't move quickly out of the way, of faces leering and winking at the women, of hands dispensing the largesse of democracy – a stick of gum here, a package of chocolate there – to the ragged, hungry children begging on the curb. It was, of course, a kind of rehearsal for a later, more brutal war in Vietnam – the one we wisely stayed out of.

Travel around this wounded country continued to be arduous, even for a war correspondent with priority, albeit a low one, on Army air transport. My purpose now was to write something about the captured Chinese. To do that I would have to find my way from the new PPCLI encampment to Eighth Army headquarters at Taegu, two hundred miles down the peninsula. It didn't seem far away, but it took me thirty-six hours to reach it.

I left the Patricias' forward lines one morning at seven. My first stop was divisional headquarters. It was a mere three miles away, but to get there I had to travel fifteen around an intervening mountain range. That took four hours.

At Div, I ran into an artillery FOO (Forward Observation Officer) who offered to wedge me into his one-man Auster aircraft, which was used as a Flying O Pip to spot artillery bursts from the air and radio back to gun crews to alter the range. The Auster wasn't made for two people, especially if one was a 220-pound six-footer with a dunnage bag full of gear and whisky. I knew there were enemy guns somewhere below, but since I was convinced my life was charmed – at least in an airplane – I paid them no heed. Over the mountains we hopped, sideslipping in the downdrafts until we landed on the beat-up runway back at Seoul.

An Eighth Army staff plane was about to leave for Taegu by way of Yoju. I grabbed it. Where was Yoju? I had no idea then and haven't now, since I can't find it on a map. But I remember it well because when we landed, a dozen staff colonels climbed aboard and I, with my low priority, was unceremoniously bumped. There I was with all my gear and no idea of what to do. I stood on the tarmac as darkness fell, seeking some sign or sound of human habitation. Nothing. Yoju was quite clearly off the beaten track, and so was I. I felt an unbearable sense of loneliness. I had no idea where I was, only that I had been abandoned in the dark heart of a foreign country torn by war. I had no idea where to go or how to find transport. I was alone with my dunnage bag and my rapidly dwindling hoard of Canadian Club.

I stood there, trying to figure out which way to proceed. At last, in the distance at the end of the runway, a pinpoint of light showed itself. I hoisted my dunnage bag onto my shoulders, the bottles clinking inside, and headed for it. The light came from the window of a Korean hut, but when I rapped on the door I was greeted not by a native but by an American officer.

"Sorry," he said. "You can't come in."

As he started to shut the door I raised my dunnage bag.

"I've got a couple of bottles of Canadian Club in here," I said.

The effect was magical. He flung the door open, and blessed light poured out into the gloom. Inside, a group of American officers was sitting around a table drinking coffee. They looked startled.

"He's got booze," the man at the door explained, and there was an instantaneous scramble to offer me a seat.

"Just one thing," said my host. "You must never, *never* whisper one word of this. You must never mention our presence. Not a word; got that?"

I told him I'd got it, reached into my dunnage bag, and produced two bottles. To this day I have no idea who those people were. CIA? Perhaps. There was little need to swear me to secrecy, but by the time we had polished off both bottles I had no clear idea of who *I* was. I can remember very little about that night. I believe we sang. I suspect I recited Robert Service. I seem to remember I slept on the floor, fully clothed. The next day I found a truck loaded with Koreans headed for Suwon. After four hours of bone-shaking travel I arrived, at dusk, at the Suwon airport and back into civilization.

I presented my priority pass and waited. I was starving but could find nothing to eat, so I pulled a paperback from my kit and began to read. On that chilly, windblown day in Suwon, I had chosen to pass the time with the coldest of all tales – Apsley Cherry-Garrard's classic story of Scott's Antarctic expedition, *The Worst Journey in the World*. My only consolation was that the surviving members of that two-year travail had been far colder than I.

Eventually I was able to board an Australian aircraft that dropped me at the Taegu runway. Night had fallen. I phoned headquarters, only to learn that the press hut was eight miles away. I thumbed my way by truck and jeep and sometimes used my own legs, and finally reached my destination.

I spent some time with the Americans, studying the Chinese prisoners. The censor passed my piece on to the high command who, to my surprise, asked if they could reproduce it in the form of a training pamphlet for the troops. I was happy to agree.

Off I flew to Pusan, South Korea's great seaport. It looked to me like a city that had never had enough elbow room. It clung to the gummy red clay hills like a sailor to a mast. The grey tile roofs of its houses jostled so close to one another that the narrow streets, cutting between them like ruts, often seemed to vanish in a choppy sea of buildings.

Even before the war, when Pusan housed six hundred thousand souls, it was crowded enough. Now, more than a million were crammed into the town. One family in three had no home at all, only a cave in the hills or a cardboard shack on the ridges above.

The big news when I reached Pusan was that the omnipotent general, Douglas MacArthur, had been fired by Harry Truman. That precipitate action had apparently touched off a violent reaction back home, but I had no sense of it here. The GIs I talked to registered mild surprise, nothing more. MacArthur, after all, had wanted to carry the war into China. All the GIs wanted was for it to end.

My own concern was to find an interpreter. Three South Korean newspapermen were available, all of them acting as stringers for United Press, Reuters, and Agence France-Presse. Since all were accredited war correspondents, each wearing the blue U.N. patch, I invited them to dinner at the American officers' club, where the other correspondents took their meals. They looked embarrassed at my invitation and finally revealed that they were barred from the club because of their nationality.

Our old enemies were welcomed; our newest allies were banned. Japanese war correspondents had no trouble gaining admittance, though their country had kept Korea subjugated for years. How bitterly ironic, I thought, and how dumb. If anything illustrated the stupidity of the U.N. (i.e., the U.S.) policy in Korea, this simple act of exclusion did. We not only went out of our way to insult the very people we were supposed to be liberating but we specifically singled out newspapermen –

the ones who could interpret or misinterpret the Western way of life to their countrymen. In Korea we gave little thought to anything but military expediency, whether that meant the breaking up of a paddy field or the tacit support of a government that was no more democratic than that of Francisco Franco. The Syngman Rhee government had just banned the singing of popular songs because, it said, the war was too serious for such levity. Shades of Marxism!

I took my new friends to a Chinese restaurant and we talked about all this over a superb Cantonese meal. I can still remember one fervent young man, a university graduate, looking at me intently across the remnants of a dinner that had cost the equivalent of two months' wages in Korea and saying, "You Americans are so stupid! You have made prostitutes of our women and beggars of our children. Surely you are not going to make the mistake of thinking the Koreans love you?" To him, all white men were Americans. "I'm not sure I wouldn't trust the Chinese more than the Americans," he added.

I told him I thought that was pretty extreme. "I think in the end you can trust the Americans," I said.

He turned to me. "Sure," he said after a pause, "you can say that. You're *white*."

The next day he took me up to the shack town above Pusan. It was not possible to escape these tragic hovels built of cardboard squares cut from K ration cartons. They straggled along the benchland in long, wretched lines. They clustered by the thousands at the water's edge and along the railway. They hugged the craggy promontories in silent accusation. In one of these shacks, looking down on the grey harbour with its flotilla of merchant ships unloading the paraphernalia of war, I was introduced to a soft-spoken little widow of twenty-seven, Tak Sook Tyun.

Her home was one of the myriad crowding the hills, the cardboard walls supported on a flimsy frame, the roof covered with straw mats. The cracks between were stuffed with old bits of burlap; the mud floor was covered with rice matting. An old board did duty as a shelf; some faded mauve and grey clothing hung from a line strung across a corner. A pot embedded in baked clay served as a stove, an old whisky bottle as a canteen. There was little else.

In this hovel, seven feet long, five feet wide, four and a half feet high, eight members of Mrs. Tak's extended family lived, ate, and slept. They had been living this way for three months, their only income the profits the children made selling Mrs. Tak's rice candy. Yet for her, and thousands like her, this cardboard hut symbolized a happy ending to her appalling story.

She had walked from her home on the Manchurian border in North Korea to Seoul, wearing low rubber slippers and carrying her two-year-old baby in her arms. After a long wait with her hungry children, she had managed to squeeze aboard a refugee train for Pusan. After four days and much walking along the tracks between stops, she reached the seaport with her baby dead in her arms. There she and her family and her sister's family were quartered in a bare, unheated theatre, convinced they would die of cold. The two sisters sold all the rice they had managed to squirrel away and all their spare clothing to buy this cardboard house from a man who was moving out.

The spectre of a smile crossed Mrs. Tak's unlined face as she told me of that magic moment when she stepped through the red mud and swung open the cardboard door, first removing her slippers at the entrance. Her heart sang a little, she told me, for again she had a place of her own.

I thought then of my home in Kleinburg, still unfinished, with the inside doors missing and only orange crates for furniture, and of my friends who asked: "How can you live like this, in an unfinished house?" Later, when the winter winds howled and the fine snow drifted in through the cracks in the uninsulated walls, I had only to think of Tak Sook Tyun to realize how lucky we were.

The members of Mrs. Tak's extended family bade me a solemn goodbye. The following day I said my own goodbye to the battered peninsula, flew off to Japan and then Toronto.

I returned greatly disturbed by what I had seen and experienced in Korea. *Maclean's* had certainly got its money's worth out of my trip, in spite of the hideously expensive insurance premiums. In five major articles I reported what I had seen and heard, but I did not inject my own opinions into the copy. Now I wanted to squirm out of the straitjacket of the "objective" reporter and say, as bluntly as possible, how I felt and what I thought. I wrote a long editorial for the magazine and later expanded it into a radio broadcast following the Sunday night news. In it I recounted some of the tragedies I'd witnessed.

"Have we won the war in Korea?" I asked. "I think the answer is *no*. We've won the military war, which really doesn't matter much, and lost the war that *does* matter – the war for men's minds. The U.N. soldiers are supposed to be the ambassadors of democracy; well, any ambassador who acted that way would be kicked right in the striped pants. And yet let's not blame the soldiers. They've no training in this business of being an ambassador.... Wars are fought with more than guns these days.... They're fought with ideas and concepts, and it's precisely these things that seem to have been forgotten by the people who drew up the army syllabus of training."

These words would still be relevant forty-two years later when Canada sent troops with no briefing to Somalia, whose people were treated just as badly, on occasion, as the Koreans – an unpalatable truth that required several courts-martial and a good deal of press reporting to reveal.

"We are supposed to be saving democracy in South Korea from the dictatorship of the North Koreans," I said. "But anybody with half an eye – and the soldiers all have two eyes – can see that under this infamous man, Syngman Rhee, South Korea is little more than a police state.... It may be necessary, from the point of view of military expediency – there's a word that sends a chill down my spine – to temporarily support the Rhee regime. But why in the name of Heaven must we keep acting and talking as if he and his government were democratic? They aren't...."

The broadcast produced a considerable reaction, most of it favourable. It was reprinted in several newspapers, and for a day or so my phone seldom stopped ringing. The other side of the argument was aired by the Peterborough *Examiner*, whose editor then was Robertson Davies. He pointed out in an editorial that the troops were not in the country "to preserve Korea for Koreans; they are in Korea to keep that peninsula the outpost of the West...the first duty of troops in action is to win the battle, not to be spreading loving kindness. If the natives are in the way... then out the natives must go at the point of a bayonet.... An army is not a democratic organization inculcating gentleness.... The Korean incursion is the operation of harsh politics on the world and not Arthurian chivalry in quest of a Grail."

I couldn't disagree with anything Rob Davies wrote. I simply disagreed with the idea that the game was worth the candle. We had inflicted horror on the Koreans in order to keep their country an outpost of the West. In the long run, was it worth it?

Chapter Four

1

A Canadian television service was more than a year in the future when
I returned from Korea. I had seen TV for the first time in 1949 when I
had gone to New York to report, with some amusement, on what was
called "history's first TV town." My article, "Make Way for the One-Eyed
Monster," read as if it had been written by an alien from some distant
planet observing the quaint folkways of a strange and exotic tribe. "The
visiting fireman," I wrote, "inescapably finds himself like a Wells time
traveller viewing with some awe the picture of our future society."

A TV set was still such a luxury in New York that those who owned
one found themselves inundated with friends and neighbours eager to
experience the thrill of watching blurred black-and-white pictures on a
ten-inch screen. A friend swore to me that he had known his neighbour
intimately for a year but had never seen his face. "He comes into our
room in the dark, sits down in front of the set, stares at it until the show
is finished, gets up, puts on his hat, and leaves before we turn on the
lights." There were TV snobs in New York, too, as there soon would be
in Canada. "The monster will devour us all unless we resist it," one of
these told me.

But TV had already become inescapable. Bars were jammed with
the greatest crowds since the days of the free lunch, all staring at the
screen. People peppered their talk with references to the deities of the
medium – Howdy Doody, Milton Berle, and the Golden Superman – a
puppet, a burlesque comedian, and a wrestler. A big indoor pool advertised "Swimming with Television." And on Sixth Avenue, a fund-raising
organization attracted crowds by building a model home on a vacant lot
and installing a TV set on the walk to the front door.

In Canada, everybody was making predictions about the new medium, both optimistic and dire. In an article about the CBC, I reported
that it was "determined that like radio, TV will be primarily Canadian."
The crystal ball was already clouded. There was talk of running full-
scale dramas to their proper length – two and a quarter hours, say –
instead of fitting them neatly into an hour-by-hour schedule. There was
even talk of running short operas to be produced by the fledgling Royal
Conservatory Opera Company (later the Canadian Opera Company).
How naïve, how innocent we all were! In another article I reported that
Stuart Griffiths, who had been named program director of the coming

TV network, and his top producer, Mavor Moore, had made a pact that they would remain with the corporation "only as long as TV is put to a serious purpose."

"They do not want to follow the American pattern," I assured my readers. "They are also determined that Canadian live talent will not be submerged under a Niagara of kinescope recordings from the U.S. If plans now maturing are carried through, the sponsor will find it as expensive to import foreign films as to employ live talent." O brave new TV world!

My own attitude to the medium was one of bemusement, even bafflement, and more than a little snobbishness. I did not understand its potential, nor did it occur to me that I would ever master it. Griffiths kept announcing (quite wrongly) that nobody over the age of thirty could work in television. Blair Fraser told me that he would never want to own a TV set. Andrew Allan, the reigning king of CBC radio drama, did not deign to join the bright young men then at work creating the CBC's television arm. As a result, he himself became obsolete.

For more and more Canadians, however, television, which came over a forest of aerials from Buffalo and other U.S. border cities, was an obsession. At the beginning it changed social habits. I remember inviting a colleague from *Maclean's* to a dinner party. "I'll have to see what's on television that night before I can give you an answer," he told me. He had sprung for a set; I hadn't. We were still living with our orange crates.

I was, by that time, a seasoned radio performer, appearing as guest on a variety of shows, from "Citizens' Forum" to "Beat the Champs" (Ralph Allen was a regular), as well as writing and reading talks for the network and the CBC's International Service. We needed the money because the kitchen was still unfinished. Janet had laid down an ultimatum: "We won't have any more babies until I have kitchen cupboards." The kitchen was finished at last in good time for Christmas, 1951. Nine months later, almost to the day, our third daughter, Patsy, was born. I think of her as our "Court of Opinion" baby because I had become a regular panellist on that weekly CBC discussion program, which helped pay the bills.

My fellow panellists included Lister Sinclair and the indomitable Kate Aitken, then at the height of her radio popularity. Kate was a mainstay of CFRB, the country's largest radio station. Grey-haired, motherly, well-travelled, hard-working, she was the voice of the status quo majority on a program in which Lister and I often expressed opinions at odds with generally accepted beliefs. Kate would say such things as: "If there was only more love in the world, there'd be no wars," a sentiment that caused Lister to gag. But she was not all Pollyanna (Irwin's word); she kept a small flask of whisky in her purse, which she sampled privately from time to time.

It was on a television version of "Court of Opinion" that I had my first horrible television experience. The date was Tuesday, September 9, 1952. Television in Toronto had begun just four days before. The program was, of course, live; tape had not yet been invented. We sweated under the hot, glaring lights required by the bulky cameras, and we wore the mandatory blue shirt and the heavy pancake make-up that made us all look like cadavers prepared for the casket. Between us and the unseen audience lay a small thicket of cables, cameras, booms and other paraphernalia, and an army of gesticulating men with earphones, talking to some hidden deity.

We were supposed to be expressing instant opinions about various contentious subjects posed to us by our moderator, the lugubrious Neil LeRoy. I had no real grip on what I was saying or what anybody else was saying. I found it impossible to concentrate. We peered into the gloom, awkwardly looking for cues, not sure which camera to talk to, and trying to appear nonchalant. We were painfully conscious that our every gesture, facial expression, and, worse still, fumble were being watched with an intensity that no other mass medium commanded.

The notion was held at the time, quite erroneously, that TV required more than a mere panel of men and women arguing the issues of the day. Everything had to move; everything had to be visual; words were no longer enough. The producers, seduced by this idea, had devised a series of awkward playlets using actors to set up the issue at hand. The scene would show, for example, a wife looking through the Help Wanted ads in front of a protesting husband to illustrate the question: Should wives go to work? After that, Lister, Kate, and I, with a guest, would give our opinions – or try to.

The program was not a success. I, for one, was transfixed. No doubt I babbled away, but I don't think I made much sense. At times I felt like a drowning man in that sea of lights and cables. Nor was the program helped by "that tired old boy, Neil LeRoy" as he called himself in his Saturday morning disc jockey guise. Since he owned the show, he could not be replaced, and it died a quick death on television. Radio was more forgiving. Some time later, a very similar show, *Fighting Words,* had a successful run. It did not use playlets – just talking heads, to use the new expression. And its host, Nathan Cohen, had the personality that Neil LeRoy lacked.

I left the studio that night resolving never again to let myself be put through such an ordeal. The following day, when the power of the medium was brought home to me, I did an about-face. People who had seen the program professed to be in awe of me. "You're Pierre Berton!" a taxi driver said as I stepped into his cab. "I saw you on TV last night." No taxi driver had ever before called me by name. I had written scores of articles for the largest magazine in the country, but nobody knew me. I realized that, in spite of my lofty attitude and my abject terror, I would have to come to terms with the new medium. It was the greatest marketing tool yet devised, and since I was now determined to write best-selling books, I would have to make use of it. Television was not an end in itself, but it would be the means to publicize my real work.

I continued to appear on "Court of Opinion" on radio and to make guest appearances on some of the new television programs such as *Press Conference, Midweek Review,* and even *Musicmakers,* Jack Kane's variety show (I recited "The Shooting of Dan McGrew," of course).

In the fall of 1952 I was raised to associate editor of *Maclean's,* in whose pages the social history of the country was being written. Institutions that we now take for granted, such as the supermarket and the shopping centre, received their editorial baptisms in our pages. We were one of the first publications to ask, as early as 1954, "Can Cigarettes Kill You?" We ran the first articles to appear in any popular magazine on the subject of cholesterol and on the discovery of cortisone. We tried to show Canadians the most fascinating corners of the country, from the Butchart Gardens on Vancouver Island to Louisbourg on Cape Breton Island. We dispatched Bruce Hutchison to "Rediscover the Unknown Country" and sent Yousuf Karsh from sea to sea to explore the face of the nation in photographs. Sidney Katz had joined the staff and was producing a remarkable series of articles, including two pioneering scoops.

Thanks to Sidney, *Maclean's* was the first publication anywhere to report the story of a woman with a multiple personality, a term then as foreign to me as to our readers. I suggested to Sid that a good book could be developed out of his research, but before he got around to it, the story titled "The Three Faces of Eve" was published by another writer and eventually made into a popular movie starring Joanne Woodward.

Katz was also after a hot story about schizophrenia, which some scientists believed was caused by a chemical imbalance. Out in Saskatchewan, Dr. Humphrey Osmond and Dr. Abram Hoffer were experimenting with a new drug that seemed to turn people temporarily into schizophrenics. So off Sid went to Saskatchewan to investigate.

"Don't do anything rash," Ralph Allen told him before he left. "Whatever you do, don't experiment on yourself." But Sid was intent on doing just that. After he'd checked in from Saskatchewan, Ralph called me into his office. "I think that goddamn Katz is going to take that bloody drug," he said. "I told him not to, but my gut tells me he will. Christ, he's probably taking it now. Before we know it, we'll have a corpse on our hands."

Of course Sid took the drug, which was LSD. The name was new to me – new to almost everyone. No other magazine had yet reported on it. Sid didn't expire, but the effect on him, which he described in stunning detail, was such that for weeks he couldn't ride on a train without hallucinating.

By the spring of 1953 I had been elevated to managing editor to replace John Clare, who had, somewhat reluctantly, been promoted to the editorship of *Chatelaine*. The idea of the gruff, sardonic Clare at the helm of a magazine that dealt in recipes, fashion, and glossy fiction tickled my fancy. But he was a brilliant journalist, and it showed in the pages of the magazine. Nobody asked the question then that would be foremost in the minds of the most casual reader today: was there not, in all of Canada, a single woman journalist equipped to edit Canada's most successful woman's magazine?

But this was the fifties; nobody thought that way in those days. *Chatelaine* itself, through its articles and its advertisements, implicitly and sometimes explicitly supported the credo that a woman's place was in the home. I find it significant now (I didn't then) that not a single male editor of *Maclean's* had a wife with a nine-to-five job. Janet had worked briefly doing publicity for the Conservatory Opera Company and the Canadian Arthritis and Rheumatism Society. She had a natural talent for public relations – everybody liked her – and could easily have established herself at the top of that field; but when the babies began to arrive, she abandoned any idea of a career.

As for me, I accepted my new responsibilities with enthusiasm. I loved the job, loved every moment of it, loved working with pictures, layouts, and titles. I liked and admired the people I worked with; they were now among my closest friends. I believed I had reached the height of my ambitions. I did not expect ever to be made editor of *Maclean's* – my conspicuous left-wing leanings conspired against that, as Floyd Chalmers would later admit in his memoirs. Still, my job also allowed me the freedom to write, and I was convinced that I had found my niche in life. Someday I would write a book or two, perhaps based on my *Maclean's* work. Maybe I would make the *New York Times* best-seller list. That was enough for me.

I was more than merely content; I was ecstatic. I felt that I was playing a leading role in the full flowering of magazine journalism in Canada. Every writer, it seemed, wanted to have his or her work in *Maclean's,* even though we still paid relatively poorly. The writers knew, however, that when their article was accepted, they could go down to the cash cage and get their money. That was a powerful incentive.

The best writers in the country were appearing in the magazine: Farley Mowat, W.O. Mitchell, Hugh MacLennan, Bruce Hutchison, Morley Callaghan, Roger Lemelin, Lionel Shapiro, Thomas Costain, Robert Kroetsch, Earle Birney. We ran less fiction, sometimes only one story per issue, but Ralph had established the *Maclean's* $5,000 Novel Award to help make up for that. The novels, of course, had to be Canadian. We serialized Mitchell's "The Alien" and Callaghan's "The Man With the Coat," both of which were later revised and expanded into hardcover works (as *The Vanishing Point* and *The Many Coloured Coat*). To my dismay, however, Ralph refused to give an award to Mordecai Richler's first novel, *Son of a Smaller Hero,* because, he insisted, it was anti-Semitic. I had liked the novel very much and felt we were about to launch a new talent. "How can it be anti-Semitic?" I said. "The author is a Jew." But Ralph was adamant.

Once, when Ralph was on holiday and I was left to run "the old mag," as he called it, I was forced into a drastic decision. Without warning, the advertising department announced it had acquired so much business that the next issue of *Maclean's* would contain thirty more pages than we had planned for. What to do? In any other publication this extra editorial space might have been hailed as a triumph, but for me it was a disaster. At that juncture we did not have enough material on hand to fill the expanded magazine. We always ran very close to the bone: sometimes we had to scramble at the last moment to fix up a late article and squeeze it into the magazine just before deadline, a situation that drove my friend Leslie Hannon, our production manager, to distraction. It was his job to get the magazine out on time, and he took it so seriously that he had the reputation of being a worrier and a nag.

Now, with the hopper empty, we were faced with finding three or four new articles to fill the editorial hole – and with no more than a week to go. There was only one solution. Morley Callaghan's novel had just won the $5,000 prize. There it sat, invitingly, on the copy editor's desk. I took the plunge and decided to run the entire novel in a single issue, complete with a special cover and nine pages of four-colour illustrations.

The only artist fast enough and competent enough to do it all in a week was Oscar Cahen, whose lively covers for *Maclean's* were as well known as his serious gallery work. We locked Oscar up in a hotel, and in one astonishing painting frenzy he produced a brilliant series of illustrations. Thus *Maclean's* was able to trumpet Callaghan's award-winning novel, complete in one issue, in addition to its normal complement of articles and features.

"You did *what?*" said Ralph Allen on his return from Florida. I explained, and he nodded, slowly. "Berton had no other choice," he later explained to his wife, Birdeen, who told me – making it a point to temper my misgivings. Ralph was not a man given to fulsome praise, but happily he was not one to condemn, either. I think this was a turning point in our professional relationship. Ralph now breathed more easily because he realized that in his absence, no matter what disasters threatened, I would somehow be able to cope. More and more he left the nuts and bolts of the magazine to me, and I revelled in this freedom.

I felt constrained in only one area, and that was Ralph's adamant refusal to allow me to take any public positions that might suggest a conflict of interest. The old Canadian Radio League, which had really been responsible for the establishment of public broadcasting back in the thirties, was being reorganized, and I was happy to join and attend meetings. The purpose was simply to improve the quality of public broadcasting in Canada, but Ralph would have none of it. He told me that either I would have to quit the league or quit *Maclean's*. I quit the league, but it rankled.

By this time the magazine had an editorial staff of twenty-one, including Barbara Moon, who was now an assistant editor and staff writer. I once gave her the job of re-researching and revising an article by the noted Canadian novelist Hugh Garner. We had assigned him, foolishly as it turned out, a profile of Toronto's raunchy Jarvis Street. Garner turned in an appallingly bad piece, thinner than stone soup, devoid of any hard information but studded with exclamation marks. He was a good novelist, but he hadn't the remotest idea of how to go about his research.

I suggested to the irascible Garner that he might, for example, want to tell us something about the man for whom the street had been named. He bridled. He had researched the subject thoroughly, he announced, and there simply was no information about this mythical person. Since Sheriff William Jarvis was one of the leading figures in the history of nineteenth-century Toronto, and since the biographical material was available at the nearest library, I simply suggested to Garner that we call it quits. We would, of course, pay him in full. I turned his manuscript over to Barbara, who did the research and rewrote Garner's heated prose. We published the result under the magazine's house byline of Grattan Gray. But Garner was furious. Even though we had paid him in full for a shoddy piece and had not done him the disservice of running something he hadn't written under his byline, he felt hard done by. A quarter of a century later, in his memoirs, he returned to the subject with considerable bile.

By this time some *Maclean's* pieces were acquiring an edge. June Callwood raised a good many hackles with an article we titled "The Not-So-Happy Gang," an examination of the behind-the-scenes tensions that belied the studied cheerfulness of Canada's best-known radio program. This confused and angered some readers (it certainly confused and angered Bert Pearl of "The Happy Gang") who believed that all magazine articles should throw nothing more than sweetness and light on the subject. But journalism was changing everywhere; hagiography was no longer our business. I remember Ralph Allen calling me in to discuss Barbara Moon's less than glowing profile of Joe McCulley, warden of Hart House, who had been chosen, God knows why, to be host of the CBC's live TV interview program, *Graphic*. This was a copy of a successful CBS show, *Person to Person*, hosted by Ed Murrow. But poor McCulley was no Murrow, and Barbara, in her acerb way, made that clear. She had, in fact, neatly sliced him up – a treatment that both delighted and appalled Ralph.

"Look," he said to me, "I've got a proposition for you. We both know that one of us is going to depart the old mag some day for greener fields. If you leave, I'll probably assign a piece about you. If I leave, you may want to assign a piece on me. Let's promise one another right now that neither of us will ever assign such a piece to Moon."

2

Hard covers When I first arrived in Toronto in 1947 I brought with me a sheaf of notes for a book. I had spent a week at Fort St. James, in the heart of British Columbia, interviewing Russ Baker, the bush pilot, whose adventures, I was convinced, would make a lively tale. With eight thousand flying hours to his credit, Baker was the best-known and most experienced mountain pilot in the country. He was also the head of the newly organized Pacific Western Airlines. I already had a title for the book: "Snowball in Hell." In his many hairbreadth adventures, Baker's chances of survival reflected those odds.

I hadn't known, when I flew with Russ Baker to the fabled Headless Valley of the South Nahanni River in 1947, that the trip would mark a turning point in my career. It led me straight to Toronto. I had done a good deal of research into the geography, history, and legends of the South Nahanni country – enough to write a story about the place before actually visiting it. I had never written a magazine article before, but *Maclean's,* to which I sent it on the recommendation of my neighbour, Clyde Gilmour, bought it immediately.

This single piece persuaded Arthur Irwin that I was a likely candidate for a job at *Maclean's.* He later told me that it was the absence of "gee-whiz" in my piece for the magazine that had caught his notice. I had curbed my natural enthusiasm and written it without embroidery. How chancy life is! If I had written a piece in wide-eyed, newspaper feature style, my career would not have taken this ninety-degree turn. The *Maclean's* editors would have considered me just another sensational journalist regurgitating old northern myths. Certainly they would not have brought me to Toronto.

96

So now I wanted to write a book. In the late forties I had spent my weekends and evenings struggling with the Russ Baker story. I have since lost the manuscript, but there's no doubt it was pretty thin stuff. I showed it to John Farrar, one of New York's most prominent publishers whom I had met during a scouting trip to Manhattan. He wrote me a diplomatic letter explaining that it was the sort of book that was once fashionable but no longer acceptable – a gentle way of saying it wasn't good enough. *Once fashionable?* That was a telling phrase. My plans to come up with a best-seller that would knock them dead dissolved with those words. Yet I saw what Farrar meant. I had written the kind of story that might have appeared in *Chums Annual* – the kind I had devoured as a boy. But times and tastes had changed. Actually, I had known, without admitting it to myself, that the book was not publishable.

I did not waste it. I recycled the Nahanni story and Baker's colourful background into a series of CBC radio yarns. Later they made a chapter in *The Mysterious North*. In Canada, a non-fiction writer cannot afford to waste anything. The market is thin, the potential readership less than a tenth of that south of the border. A writer must recycle his research like empty pop bottles.

"Snowball in Hell" was the second manuscript I ditched. The first, "Marching As to War," was a lighthearted and unfinished story of my army career. I didn't actually ditch it; I lost it. Anyway, since it was supposed to end with a stirring account of my experiences under fire and since I didn't have any experiences under fire, it was no great loss. I liked the title, though, so much so that I recycled it twice, as a chapter title in *The Invasion of Canada* and again in *Vimy*.

In those days, eighty thousand words constituted an acceptable length for a book. Since then, books – mine, at least – have got considerably longer. Had anybody told me that I would eventually publish a book of 250,000 words (*The Arctic Grail*), I would not have believed it. A quarter of a million words! The mere suggestion would have knocked the breath out of me. Nonetheless, having served my apprenticeship with two badly flawed works, I wanted to play for keeps.

There was only one problem: I had no idea of what to write about. I thought vaguely of something about religion, the hold it had on people. What was it that made middle-aged men and women stand wanly on street corners holding up copies of the *Watchtower?* Was this the way Christianity was going? Or was religion taking a different tack?

The question absorbed me, but I had no idea of how to go about it. *The Comfortable Pew* lay a dozen years in the future.

The problem solved itself for me. King George VI died in February 1952, and the country was soon abuzz with excitement over his daughter's coronation in June 1953. In those days Canada was solidly royalist. The tour of the princess and Prince Philip in October 1951 had caused an outpouring of fervour that was almost religious. The slightest incident made headlines; a casual remark by one or other of the royal couple was blown out of all proportion. If either deigned to utter a word to any journalist, the comment was flashed around the world.

I especially remember in Winnipeg, I think, an occasion when Philip commented on the flashy tie worn by a *Vancouver Sun* reporter. The reporter did not bother to record what Philip said but was immediately besieged by his comrades, who pleaded for the details. He gave a faithful account of the prince's very matter-of-fact remark, but the story grew in the telling and was featured on the news wires in this fashion:

PHILIP: What newspaper are you from?
REPORTER: The *Vancouver Sun,* sir.
PHILIP: You seem to be wearing the Vancouver Sun on your tie!

This allegedly hilarious riposte, front-paged in the *Sun,* was picked up by the Fleet Street correspondents on the tour and wired to London. There it was seized upon by the *Sun*'s own correspondent in Whitehall and wired back to the *Sun* in Vancouver, where it again appeared on the front page. Meanwhile, nothing would do but that the actual tie be rushed to Vancouver by air and displayed for the enjoyment of the large crowds who flocked to see it in a department store window.

In the face of all this frenzy it behooved Canada's National Magazine to do something special to accompany the inevitable gush of royal sentiment that would attend the upcoming coronation. At our editorial conferences the subject was batted about like a shuttlecock. Beverley Baxter? Ralph Allen winced. Baxter would write something anyway, but Allen didn't want him slobbering over the Royals in a major series. People were already talking about the new Elizabethan era as if, by the magic of an ancient investiture, the imperial nation would rise again in all its glory to smite new armadas. Although this clearly wasn't going to happen, the magazine couldn't ignore the pomp and ceremony that would take place the following year. I had recently written a long article about the Massey family – the nearest thing to royalty in Canada. Why not use the same technique on the House of Windsor? And so we agreed that I should prepare a seven-part series, beginning with Queen Victoria and winding up with the present queen and her consort.

Those were innocent days. A new Elizabeth was on the throne and all was right with the world. The royal marriage was treated, as all royal marriages were, as a made-in-heaven love match. Philip and Elizabeth were mad about each other – that was the party line. No whisper of criticism of the institution or its human symbols could be countenanced. And that was equally true – perhaps even more true – among the Québécois, who had welcomed the royal couple the previous year with wild enthusiasm.

I was already thinking that my series on royalty might make a book and so was especially meticulous in my research, which would include a step-by-step insider's account of the 1951 Royal Tour. I started gathering material in Saint John, N.B., and worked my way across the country to Eaglecrest Lodge on Vancouver Island, not far from Nanaimo, where the then princess and her consort had spent a night.

In Saint John I stayed with the Sclanders family. Ian Sclanders, a dependable freelance writer, had had several pieces published in the magazine. Now, as part of Ralph Allen's attempts to broaden our national coverage, Ian had been named East Coast editor of *Maclean's* (we would soon have editors in Montreal, Edmonton, and Vancouver as well).

This was the beginning of the long friendship Janet and I enjoyed with Ian and his elegant wife, Christina, of which Chris's part was to continue long after Ian's untimely death. I look back now on that first, quite remarkable encounter with considerable astonishment and a certain sense of goofy satisfaction. What better way to cement a friendship than with several quarts of the best lubricant?

Maritimers, I discovered, are hard drinkers. In the three days that I spent under the Sclanders roof, I had difficulty in keeping up with Ian, who showed few outward effects of our marathon carousing. He was a short pudgy man with a thin moustache and glasses that always seemed about to tumble from his nose. Women thought he was cuddly and had trouble suppressing a desire to mother him. An engaging companion, he offered to drive me to Halifax to pursue my royal researches. He himself had been assigned to write a profile on Helen Creighton, the best-known collector of folk music in the Atlantic provinces, who lived there. As he took the wheel, looking slightly glassy-eyed but otherwise dead sober, I remember Chris extracting a pledge that we would not stop on the way except to eat. Sclanders nodded benevolently and off we went.

We lunched in Moncton in a small fish restaurant that had no liquor licence. I remember it with disgust because at the very height of the lobster season they actually served the stuff out of tins. The culinary state of the Atlantic provinces in 1952 left much to be desired.

One hour later, Sclanders suddenly slumped in his seat, took his hands off the wheel, and in a thick voice said, "You drive." He lapsed at once into unconsciousness, leaving me no time to be flabbergasted. The car lurched off the road and, fortunately, came to a dead stop before it could hurtle into a ditch. It was only then that I began to understand Ian Sclanders's special quality. He could drink for days without showing the effects; then, suddenly, a harmless glass of water would catapult him into a state of intoxication.

At five minutes before six that evening, as we drove through a small settlement, Sclanders woke up as if on cue. "The liquor store is on the right after the next intersection," he said. After we stopped to take on supplies, he relapsed again into torpor until we reached Halifax, where a party was under way in our honour.

The following morning, apparently none the worse, Ian ordered a whopping plate of finnan haddie and suggested we talk with Jack Brayley of Canadian Press about the Royal Tour, which Brayley had covered. After that, he explained, he had a luncheon date with Helen Creighton.

Brayley greeted us in the CP office with enthusiasm. "You guys have come at the right time," he told us. "There's a new brewery opened, and they've sent along some samples. Let's see how good the stuff is."

He produced three bottles. We savoured them carefully. "Pretty good, eh?" Jack said, as he drained his.

Ian didn't answer. "Got to see Helen Creighton," he mumbled and lurched toward the exit, banging his head on the door jamb. He staggered off, waving farewell but not daring to speak.

"My God!" cried Brayley. "One bottle! I didn't know it was *that* good." He examined the label with admiration and made a note to order a case.

Later, he and I made our way to the Lord Nelson Hotel to sample a bowl of its famous clam chowder. There, at a table near the door, waving a bottle of wine with one hand and trying to take notes with the other, was Sclanders, his glasses toppling from his nose. The very proper Helen Creighton sat rigidly upright across from him.

I winced. "He's really blown it," I told Brayley.

But he hadn't. He produced a first-rate article on Helen Creighton, who became a lifelong friend of both Ian and Chris. Shortly after this he was transferred to Toronto to take charge of the articles desk, a job made to order for him. More than anyone else on the staff except Bill Mitchell he had a rapport with writers that endeared him to them and inspired them to excel. Ian and Chris became our close friends, and the following summer when the Stratford Festival was launched we began an annual custom that lasted almost to Ian's death. Each July, the four of us drove to Stratford to take in the plays, often stopping en route to visit Edna Staebler at her cottage on Sunfish Lake, near Waterloo. These occasions were made memorable as much by Edna's cooking as by the action on the stage, but Janet has no recollection of one of the early performances. The plays were then produced in a sweltering tent, and she was seven months pregnant with our fourth child, Peter.

Ian rarely lasted for a full performance. He'd slip away during intermission, seek out the nearest tavern, and make friends with several of the customers, often inviting them home for dinner in Toronto the following Sunday. He had no recollection of these events afterwards, and Chris would sometimes open her door to be confronted by a crew of swarthy truck drivers, dressed in their best, ready to dine.

As a result of this kind of contretemps, Ian was persuaded from time to time to eschew hard drink. He always amiably agreed. I remember one day when a group of us was loading up at the liquor store for a weekend conference in Ottawa. Sclanders buttonholed me. "Do you think forty ounces is enough for a man on the wagon?" he asked. He died of a heart attack in 1967 in a hotel room in Saint John while sitting at his typewriter, working on a piece for *Maclean's*. I still mourn his loss.

In late October 1952 I flew to London, rented a small flat off Piccadilly, and continued my research into the Royal Family. I haunted the reading room of the British Museum, drove to Scotland to visit Gordonstoun, the tough school that Philip had attended, and embarked on a marathon series of interviews ranging from one with Lord Hardinge, once private secretary to Edward VIII, to one with the postmaster at Craigie, Scotland, just outside the grounds of Balmoral

Castle. It was not easy to arrange interviews with the close-mouthed British. Lady Brabourne, Philip's cousin, agreed to talk only if the queen's press secretary, Lieutenant-Commander Richard Colville, would give his okay. Colville, who had spent much of his career in the silent service, firmly refused. "I am not what you North Americans call a public relations officer," he explained in his chilly fashion at our first meeting, and when I asked if I might be shown through the public rooms of Buckingham Palace, he raised his eyebrows and seemed to shudder. "It's private!" he exclaimed. "It's a *private home*. Nobody ever sees it."

That was an exaggeration, as I quickly learned after phoning Sir John Wilson, keeper of the Royal Philatelic Collection. I didn't actually tell him I was a stamp collector, but he may have gained that impression. At any rate, he cheerfully gave me permission to view the collection. I had already memorized the plans of the palace while at the British Museum and knew that the route to the stamp collection involved a ride in a little bird-cage elevator and a walk down a succession of corridors rich in paintings and tapestry. I made mental notes as I went, all of which were invaluable when I wrote my articles.

It later occurred to me that Colville was perhaps a better press agent than I had thought. His crusty refusals so maddened the journalists of three countries that they contrived to dig out and publish more stories about the House of Windsor than of any comparable institution in the world. These stories were always reverent. Secure behind its contrived curtain of silence, the monarchy was inviolable. Nobody – not I, certainly – could have conceived of a day when royal personages would lift that curtain, appear on TV, and even discuss such personal matters as divorce and adultery. The Royal Family was sacrosanct, and that was clearly the source of its prestige and its strength.

"The Monarch," I wrote in *Maclean's*, "can be nothing less than perfect. Her appearance must be above reproach.... Her actions...must be suprahuman and this is why she cannot be shown munching an apple or lying on a beach, or riding in a subway."

I had carefully read Frazer's *The Golden Bough* and saw many startling parallels between the British monarchy and the ancient priest-kings on whose well-being the annual harvests depended.

"Her inner being must be God-like," I wrote of the sovereign. "She herself must be pure in heart, she must conform to the accepted standards

102

of her day, and she must follow faithfully in the footsteps of her ancestors as the ancient Irish kings had to do. For if she does not – if she neglects her business, or walks about in the streets like a mortal, or seeks to marry a divorcé – the crops of Empire will fail and the fruits of Commonwealth will wither on the vine."

In the forty-odd years since those words were written, much of the mystery that surrounds the Monarch has been torn away and – to continue the *Golden Bough* analogy – the crops of Empire and Commonwealth have indeed failed. Can the Monarchy survive its next incarnation? In Britain, perhaps. In Canada, where the ties with royalty are fraying badly, I doubt it.

But in the Canada of 1953, the veneration of royalty became a sort of public hysteria as Coronation Day approached. My own series was published in seven issues of the magazine, beginning in mid-March and ending in our June 5 issue, on the very eve of the big event. The previous September I had written a seventeen-page outline of the book I proposed to do and sent it to my agent, Willis Kingsley Wing, who had a stable of Canadian authors that included Ralph Allen, Scott Young, Eva-Lis Wuorio, and John Clare. The first publisher that Willis spoke to was the legendary Alfred Knopf, who had been quietly looking for exactly this kind of book. Some time later Willis told me that the firm was "enormously enthusiastic" about the project. "They asked me to tell you that their enthusiasm has a broader base than this book," Willis added. "They feel and hope that this could be a continuing relationship and there will be much more fine writing…which they will publish." I was ecstatic.

I immediately took a two-week holiday and spent it at home revising and expanding my series from about thirty thousand words to the required eighty thousand. I think this first book contains some of my most polished writing. I was, of course, influenced by the writers I was reading as part of my research – Lytton Strachey, Harold Nicolson, Christopher Sykes, Edith Sitwell, Margot Asquith, and other elegant English stylists – whose cadences were still running through my head when I sat down at my typewriter. "You write like an angel," Alfred Knopf wrote to me in a personal note after he had read the manuscript. From North America's most revered publisher, that was enough to turn any writer's head. Fortunately for my ego, not every critic has been as kind.

The Royal Family was published in the spring of 1954. I was on tenterhooks until my dozen author's copies arrived. *My first book!* I tore open the package, the books tumbled out, and I held one like a new baby, close to my chest. There is nothing to compare with the moment when a writer opens his first work. I fawned over my book, gazing at the type, riffling through the pages, taking off the dust-jacket, examining the case, reading the copy on the jacket flaps: "Everyone will be struck by the astonishing amount of fresh, lively, detailed information Pierre Berton has gathered.... There has never been a book like this.... Berton, a brilliant and engaging writer, neither sensationalizes, nor adulates...." And so on and on, a paean of praise written by Knopf's publicity department and therefore to be taken with a grain of salt. I started to read my book, savouring once again the words in Caslon typeface (even though I had already combed through the galleys and the page proofs), revelling in my portraits of the Royals, "so vivid and intimate one suspects he must have concealed himself somewhere in the corridors of Buckingham Palace...." Now I was more than a mere writer; I was an *author,* with all that word's connotations – the pipe, the smoking jacket, the finger lightly touching the forehead.

The sales figures brought me down to earth. The book was a flop – victim of the media overkill that marked Coronation Year, of which I had been a part. By the time it was published, Canadians had had a belly-ful of royalty. Would I have bought my own book in 1954, after such a deluge of unadulterated praise and saccharine prose? I have my doubts. For almost two years, from the Royal Tour of 1951 to the Coronation of 1953, we had been fed daily doses of Royal Pablum. Rather than strengthening the bonds between the sovereign and her Canadian subjects, it had had a stultifying effect that contributed to a growing indifference, which would remain unspoken until a Toronto television star blurted it out on an American network. In *Maclean's* I had written that the queen, "chosen only by the roulette wheel of birth...was subject to a veneration only slightly less awe inspiring than that accorded to the Deity." That was written at the height of the fervour, when we were all telling ourselves that the institution was immutable and how nice it was to have something the Americans didn't have – and far superior, too! Now, in retrospect, it's obvious that such a peak would never again be reached. The government sensed the coming change when it announced that the new governor general would not be drawn from the queen's aristocracy but would, for the first time, be a Canadian – one whose family background was peddling farm implements.

The publication of *The Royal Family* had one positive result. Quite by happenstance I was drawn into Jack McClelland's stable. I would have preferred to publish with Macmillan of Canada, then the country's leading publishing house, whose authors included Bill Mitchell, Morley Callaghan, and Hugh MacLennan. But McClelland and Stewart was Knopf's Canadian outlet, and I had signed a North American contract.

When I first encountered Jack, he told me he hated the Knopf jacket, a sedate-looking production that showed the Royal Coat of Arms in red on a royal blue background, with a sales blurb in such minuscule type it was virtually unreadable. The design was by Herbert Bayer, one of the great figures of the ground-breaking Bauhaus School of Design in Germany. Alas, in spite of his awesome reputation, Bayer hadn't the foggiest idea of how to design dust-jackets. He did covers for my first three books, all terrible. Jack scrapped two of them for the Canadian edition, Bauhaus or no Bauhaus. A book's jacket may look distinguished, but it must be more than that; it has to be a poster, easily spotted in the stores, and intriguing enough to make a prospective buyer leaf through the book. Jack put people on the cover – royal personages – and launched a lively publicity campaign. That time it did no good.

The annual authors' tour, which has since become an autumn ritual, with writers of every size and shape traipsing through TV studios and bookstores, was then in its infancy. One day, I remember, Farley Mowat and I were summoned to Morgan's department store in Montreal to do a tandem autographing in the book department. We arrived, eyes glittering at the prospect of being lionized by eager buyers, and were perfunctorily greeted by the manager, who sat us down behind a small table with a backdrop of shelves containing our works and then left us to our own devices. We sat there and waited, pens at the ready. Nothing happened. People passed us by without so much as a glance. At last one man arrived with a book and asked us to sign it for him. We were happy to comply, even though it had been written by someone else. Finally I turned to Mowat. "Let's leave," I said. "But before we do, I'll sign all your books and you sign mine." He cheerfully agreed. I autographed his with the words, "To Farley Mowat, without whose help this book would never have been written," and appended my autograph. He did the same for me. When we left I cannot recall that anybody bade us goodbye.

In the United States, *The Royal Family* did better, thanks to favourable reviews in the leading papers ("… unsurpassed in our day for its grave and gay stories of the lives of kings" – *Times*; "…the most entertaining book about Royalty since Lytton Strachey wrote his *Queen Victoria* thirty-odd years ago" – *Herald Tribune*). In Canada it was treated, sometimes with glee, sometimes with acerbity, as a case of *lèse-majesté*. Basil Dean, editor of the *Calgary Herald*, expressed his outrage that I had referred to the queen merely as "Elizabeth" throughout.

The book was also published in Germany but not in Great Britain. It was, however, serialized in the *Sunday Empire News*, which hailed it as "the frankest Royal story ever told." The slogan amused me because, through a friend, I had earlier gained access to the paper's considerable royalty files. The paper's editors did not know this but managed to cut out almost all the "frank" material in the book, retaining mainly the copy I had already scalped from their own library.

3

River of If I was able to write *The Royal Family* at breakneck speed, it was part-
death ly because I had a singular advantage that I hadn't foreseen when we moved to Kleinburg. As an exurbanite, I was faced with a long drive to and from home, and that gave me, as a writer, time to think. "How can you stand it?" friends would ask. "All that driving!" I stood it very well. With nothing to distract me, I was able to concentrate on my work, sometimes at the expense of my driving skills. For two and a half hours each workday I was alone in the secondhand Ford that had replaced the Austin. At this time I composed entire openings, whole paragraphs and sentences in my head. I thought up turns of phrase, figures of speech, descriptions of people. I figured out how each piece should begin and end. I worked on style, pace, point of view. If I became a fast writer, it was partly the result of these moments of solitude.

Sometimes I shared a two-man car pool into the city with Robert McMichael, a portrait photographer who had moved to Kleinburg in 1952 and had roamed the countryside in his spare time searching out old barns, whose logs would form the structure of the house he intended to build. McMichael and his wife, Signe, were hooked on Canadiana. They bought an ancient bellows and turned it into a coffee table; they hung old maple-syrup kettles above their fireplace; they had made a frieze out of nineteenth-century wrought iron objects with which they decorated their log walls. This hobby kindled an interest in Canadian landscape painters, or more specifically, the Group of Seven. I remember Bob's enthusiasm when, driving to town, he revealed that he'd acquired his first Tom Thomson for $1,200, an enormous sum in those days. It would form the nucleus of the now famous McMichael Canadian Art Collection. Later McMichael picked up seven oil sketches by Lismer, Carmichael, and Varley.

"I can't afford this many," he told me. "Could you take a couple off my hands?" I couldn't really afford the investment either. Our house was by no means complete. The slab floor had no carpets. I was still writing on orange crates. But I liked the two Lismers and, in a moment of madness, bought them for about one hundred dollars apiece. It meant putting off certain improvements, but what the hell! I wanted Canadian paintings on my walls. I still have them.

One of my trips home turned out to be a horror. The date, October 15, 1954, will always be engraved on my memory. I waited at the office on tenterhooks for Janet, who was buying overshoes for the children and had the car. She had no radio and so did not realize the disaster that was impending. All that afternoon reports had been broadcast of an approaching storm. We set off an hour late, at 6 p.m. – four adults and three children, all squeezed into our secondhand Ford – my seventy-six-year-old mother, Ethel Post, a house guest from Vancouver, Patsy, who had just turned two, and her sisters, aged four and six, besides Janet and me. The weather was dreadful. It had been raining in sheets for days, and now as we drove north, splashing through hub-deep pools, the downpour seemed to increase in fury. In fact, though we did not realize it, we were driving through the very heart of Hurricane Hazel, which was then devastating the environs of Toronto.

Until this night I had known the Humber as a pleasant pastoral stream, leisurely winding for seventy miles through the elm-shaded farmland that stretched north from Toronto. Below our house it was so narrow a child could wade, or an adult leap, across it. It bore no relation to the rivers of my childhood. In the Yukon we would have called it a "pup."

But that night the Humber became a torrent of terror, a tearing, frothing monster that tore out entire city blocks, ripped viaducts to shreds, destroyed houses and automobiles, murdered little children, and changed the face of the countryside. For three spine-tingling hours, at the peak of the great storm that dropped 300 million tons of water on greater

Toronto, we struggled to get home. Our route took us past pleasant little valley communities that were wasted by wreckage and death that night: Islington, where twenty-four were drowned; Etobicoke, where twenty-six from a single block perished; Thistletown, where two died and twelve lost their homes; Woodbridge, whose toll was six dead and seven hundred homeless.

When we left Toronto we had no inkling of what we were in for. We crawled slowly west, locked in a monumental traffic tie-up that all but paralysed the city. Even when the water had risen to the hub caps, rendering the brakes useless, we did not realize the immensity of the disaster that was striking.

By the time we reached Highway 27, which would take us north to Kleinburg, we realized that we were in the grip of a storm of unparalleled fury. The road was awash. Cars lay stranded, abandoned, or up-ended for its entire length. Farmers' fields had become lakes. Gullies were rivers. That was only the beginning. Soon our car became an amphibious machine fording a perpetual torrent. All traffic vanished. Ahead of us, out of the lashing rain and into the headlights, a shadowy figure loomed, waving a flashlight.

We stopped just in time. The highway dipped under a railway bridge here, but the depression had become a lake, its waves lapping almost to the railway ties. In its midst the top of a car was barely visible. Beside it, turned on its end, was a tow truck.

I suppose we all should have been frightened. I know my mother was. But, in fact, we didn't really know what was happening. To me it was just another big rainstorm. I had no idea that we were driving through a hurricane. That fact would not come home to me until the following morning. I had experienced summer storms before; this was just another – a little more powerful, perhaps, but nothing to get concerned about.

We turned about and sought the alternative route through the villages of Weston and Thistletown on the banks of the Humber. They had yet to feel the full force of the river, the floodtide of which was gathering several miles upstream. But as we crawled steadily north, the roar of the waters began to drum louder and louder in our ears. Up ahead, bridges were breaking up one by one. We drove through Humber Summit, not far from the village of Woodbridge, and as we came over the crest a macabre sight met our eyes. The road had vanished, and in

108

the unblinking glare of the headlights we could see nothing but angry water pouring from the bank above and roaring down what had once been a road.

In the foreground, like black puppets, danced tiny figures of men. Hazy in the rain, the hulks of automobiles teetered at various angles. We turned back again and moved off through the network of country roads that interlaces the Humber country, now resembling canals. We passed a motel, and my mother at last spoke up. "For God's sake, stop here," she said. "We'll never get home, and at least this is a place to stay."

I stubbornly refused. I didn't want to stop; I wanted to press on home to my own surroundings and my own bed. In situations like this, my immediate instinct was to keep moving. And that was just as well because next morning the motel was under eight feet of water.

It was after nine o'clock when we finally reached our village. We could take the car no farther. Our home was half a mile away on the far side of the valley, and the road had been closed after a cliffside collapsed and blocked it. Down we trudged in the lashing rain, past the rubble that had blocked the right of way. A few yards farther on a fourteen-foot pit had opened up. I was told later that a station wagon had plunged into it, breaking the driver's nose and fracturing his skull. We trudged on as the rain increased, carrying little Patsy. "My God," said Ethel Post, "and I didn't even think to bring a raincoat."

Fortunately we had built high above the river, which now lapped within a few feet of the three houses in the valley. But we were isolated. The water mains we had built co-operatively had been torn away where the bank had slipped into the river. Telephone poles had been ripped up. Dangling wires hung everywhere. We were without phone, light, power, heat, or water. We went to bed with the sound of the roaring waters, the snapping of trees, and the roar of landslides in our ears.

Only when the tales of horror began to filter in next day from Woodbridge, five miles downriver, did we realize how lucky we were – luckier than Don Reid and his family, for one. Little Dallas Reid had taken dancing lessons with Penny. While we were crawling past Woodbridge, Don, his wife, and Dallas were trying to reach his brother's home. They came to a dip in the highway where the trickle of Plunkett Creek normally ran through a culvert. The road was flooded, and somebody shouted to Don not to attempt to go on. He decided to try it anyway. At that moment, a breaker thirty feet high rolled over the road, caught the fender of his Studebaker, tossed it off the road like a cork, and swept it into the Humber. The horrified people on shore could see its headlights bobbing along with the torrent until they winked out. The car and the bodies were found next day a mile away.

The tragedy hit home to us a second time when we heard the story of Don Radley, who ploughed our garden twice a year and usually brought his kids along to play with ours. Don lived on Clarence Street, at a bend of the Humber in Woodbridge. That night it became part of the river. Firemen struggled to get the five Radley children from the marooned house to higher ground. Two of them, Bobby, aged four, and Dan, aged ten, were hustled into a rescue boat. Don stayed behind to wait for the next craft, only to see a wall of water seize the boat when it was a few feet from the house. The bodies of the two children were found the next morning, buried in a four-foot blanket of silt.

Now we realized that we had been blessed with extraordinary luck. For the amount of damage it did, this was probably the briefest flood on record. It lasted only a few hours, but its scars took a generation to heal. Nothing was ever quite the same again along the Humber, except the river itself. The meadow on the riverbank where we used to picnic was now covered with a thick layer of sand and silt. The cascading water had torn a wide gash through the cedars and birches below the house. The approaches to the bridge that our group had built in common to join the lots on both sides of the river had been torn away, and there the span stood, marooned in a lake that hadn't existed the night before. With my neighbours I took a week of holidays to help put the bridge back into service, hauling in huge, house-sized boulders to anchor the new approaches that no other flood could shake free. We slaved like tarriers because Ruth Hogg, who lived on the far side of the river, was awaiting the birth of her fifth child and could not hope to breast the torrent when the call came. Even so, she had to leave for the hospital by crossing a rope bridge hastily flung across the river. Shortly after that our bridge was open again, and the Humber was already lapsing back into what it had been a few days before – a quiet, pleasant, little stream, meandering lazily through the rolling farm country on the outskirts of Toronto.

4

My mother published her memoir of life in the Yukon in the autumn of *A new* 1954. She had been working on it for years, and it had already gone *kind of* through two drafts when she asked me for some help and advice. The *gold rush* book was marred, I thought, by her naïve belief that I, whom she thought of, for no good reason then, as a celebrity, should be front and centre in it. But it was she, and not I, who should be the centrepiece, and I told her so. Her working title was "It's a Boy!" and she wrote lovingly about little Pierre, the apple of her eye, with somewhat less space devoted to little Lucy, my sister. With some difficulty I talked her into removing all references to me by name and sticking to her own remarkable story – that of a young kindergarten teacher who travels to the all-male Klondike a decade after the gold rush and watches the decline of the country's gaudiest ghost town.

I knew her story well but found that she had glossed over much of it. And so we sat down together to rework it. I questioned her extensively, treating her proposed book as I would any other manuscript, cutting and editing out the dross, expanding the interesting parts with more detail, and adding lively material she had not thought to include. I put the manuscript through two more drafts of my own and suggested a new title. I could remember Osa Johnson's book about her explorations with her husband, written in the thirties and titled *I Married Adventure*. I shamelessly stole it and persuaded my mother to call the book *I Married the Klondike*. I retained as much of her own writing as I could, and when that wasn't possible tried to imitate her style, which was quite different from my own. To my delight, after the book was published, many readers declared that my mother "is a better writer than you are."

They still say that, on occasion, for in the forty years since the book was published it has become a minor classic. How my mother enjoyed her celebrity! She came from a literary family: her father was one of the best-known journalists in Toronto in the nineteenth century; she herself had long been a member of the Canadian Authors' Association. In her Yukon days, she had written for *Saturday Night* and the *Family Herald and Weekly Star*. Now she was a real author, unlike many of her friends in the CAA, which had entry requirements so loose that anyone who wrote a Letter to the Editor could claim admittance.

She was in her element, appearing on radio and television, speaking to women's clubs, answering fan mail, and being buttonholed by admirers. "It's just my little book," she'd say modestly; but she wasn't modest. She was proud and delighted by all the attention. She lived another fifteen years to enjoy her book's continued success. It was published in England and the United States and is still in print in a new edition in Canada. The CBC eventually produced it as a miniseries, but she did not live to see it, which was, perhaps, just as well.

Meanwhile, John Gray, the suave and sophisticated president of Macmillan of Canada, had approached me with an idea for a juvenile book for his series *Great Stories of Canada*. He had heard some of my tales of the gold rush on the CBC and suggested I write a book on the subject for teenagers. "You can do it from library research," he told me over lunch. I was startled. Did he really believe there was a lot of material available in previously published books? I flinch now at my naïveté. The Klondike stampede is perhaps the most thoroughly documented event in Canadian history. It had been given blanket coverage in contemporary newspapers and magazines, and in addition there is (as I well know now) a treasure trove of letters, diaries, government documents, and published personal accounts. The bibliography of the adult book that I wrote later lists 158 hardcover works, apart from the pamphlets, essays, articles, news stories, and other documents.

The Golden Trail was published the same year as *I Married the Klondike*. Indeed, my mother and I sometimes found ourselves on the same television programs, promoting our separate works. My juvenile was highly successful, selling more than 100,000 copies for Macmillan, thanks partly to a growing interest in the North, fed by a natural resources boom – a new gold rush at Yellowknife, uranium at Great Bear Lake, nickel on Rankin Inlet, lead and zinc at Pine Point. But few Canadians knew much about it yet. The North was to the 1950s what the West had been in the 1860s and 1870s – an unknown realm, rich in potential, mysterious and haunting.

In a later work I described that attitude:

"It must be wonderful to see it! Oh, if only one *could* see it, but it was so remote, so hard to reach! Something ought to be done about developing it; they said parts of it were very rich. But why would anyone want to *live* there, so far away from everything, in that dreadful climate? One day, of course, millions would live there – that was certain. One day...."

112

I was then writing, actually, about the public's vision of the prairie country in 1871, before the building of the railway, but those words could easily have fitted the general attitude to the North in 1954. Within three years, John Diefenbaker's political antennae would sense this explosion of interest in an almost unknown realm, and he would roar into power proclaiming his Vision of the North, a vague and muddied notion that he was never able to delineate. It served him well, however, at the polls. *Maclean's* was a bit ahead of Diefenbaker. In 1954 we decided to publish an entire issue devoted to the Canadian North.

Ralph agreed that I should write the lead article – a fifteen-thousand-word overview of the Mysterious North, as I called it. That summer I set off on a twenty-thousand-mile odyssey that took me from the tip of Baffin Island in June to the Mackenzie Delta in August. In Aklavik I ran into the young minister of northern affairs, Jean Lesage. It was a measure of the Liberal government's new interest in the North that Lesage was the first cabinet minister to visit the delta in a decade. Knowing from long experience the northern propensity to dress up on public occasions, I'd brought along a suit, tie, and fresh shirt, which got me into the cocktail party in the minister's honour. The rest of the press, having nothing to wear but blue jeans, parkas, and high boots, which they considered appropriate wear for a backwoods community in midsummer, was shut out. Lesage asked me to join his group, and so I roamed the North with them in a single-engine Otter owned by its curly-headed young pilot, Max Ward. He would shortly found his own charter company, Wardair.

The line that separated editorial content from advertising in *Maclean's* in those days was a firm one. I remember at the regular planning meeting for executives, which I attended, how the advertising manager perked up when Ralph Allen outlined our special issue. His salesmen would set out immediately, he said, to get special ads from companies with a stake in the North.

"No," said Ralph. "*Maclean's* doesn't put out special issues to get advertising, and we don't want our readers to think we do. If there's a single ad sold connecting the advertiser with the North, I'll cancel the issue." Later editors have not always been so circumspect.

Our special issue, boldly identified on the cover as MACLEAN'S REPORT ON THE NORTH, enjoyed the largest news-stand sales the magazine had known since Beverley Baxter wrote his famous inside story of the abdication ("Why Edward Quit") in 1937. Clearly I had the material for a new book – or thought I had. For the next several months I rose at six each morning and before going to work went about putting together a personal account of my travels through northern Canada, combining the material previously gathered on the Alaska Highway and the Yukon, my research on the Nahanni, and the recent journey for *Maclean's*. I called the book *The Mysterious North* and sent it off to New York.

The reaction at Knopf hit me like a cold shower. Harold Strauss, my editor there, was never one to mince words, and in a return letter, he didn't. The manuscript, he wrote, "lacks positive attractiveness…surely a writer of your gifts can make his style much more inviting…[it] needs a thorough stylistic polishing…" and so on. He showed me no mercy. He pointed out that the manuscript was full of errors, misspelled names, geographical offences, and ungrammatical sentences.

I gulped. Here I thought I had written a masterpiece, only to find that the whole effort was indescribably shoddy! I had churned it out – that was the right verb – at top speed, as I would a news story. I was a victim of the Curse of Journalism: "Don't get it right, get it first." It has haunted me all my life.

Harold Strauss mentioned another discrepancy: I had neglected Northern Quebec and the Eastern Arctic. As a result, I spent my next vacation travelling, first by the little narrow-gauge railway that ran from Sept-Iles to the iron mines in Ungava, and then by cargo plane to Frobisher Bay, at the southern tip of Baffin Island.

I still needed a practised eye to go over my original manuscript, paragraph by paragraph. I offered the job to Barbara Moon, who turned in a first-rate report on the book's many failings. I rewrote it almost entirely. It was published in 1956 by Knopf in the United States, and in Canada through McClelland and Stewart. Somewhat to my astonishment, it won a Governor General's Award.

It was not a moneymaker. I had spent the better part of a year rising early each morning, and typing away on weekends, working, in effect, for nothing. By the time I had paid my expenses and a fee to the mapmaker, I about broke even. Whatever profit there was came from spin-offs: a series of talks on the CBC about the North and a piece for one company's annual report for a handsome fee.

More important, I now had a cachet. To appear on a panel program or in public, one needs an identifying tag. All authors who appear on TV are invariably introduced as best-selling authors, no matter what the sales figures show. "Expert" is another useful tag; it carries a kind of spurious authority and answers the viewer's unvoiced question: "Why is *he* on the program?" Producers could now identify me as a "best-selling author" or a "Northern expert" or even an "award-winning author." "Best-selling" I think worked best since it suggested I had my feet firmly planted on the financial ground.

My juvenile for Macmillan, *The Golden Trail,* meanwhile astonished me by outselling *The Mysterious North*. At Knopf's request, I expanded it by two chapters for the U.S. market and retitled it *Stampede for Gold.* I now realized there was material for an adult book on the subject, even though my mother was highly sceptical. "Why would you want to write about the gold rush?" she asked me. "*Everybody* knows about that."

Fortunately, everybody did *not* know. The great stampede had taken place some sixty years before – just over the hill of memory, as in our "Flashback" series. There were men and women still alive who had taken part in it. I would have to hurry if I was to interview them. My own father, who would have been of immeasurable help, had been in his grave for a decade. I cursed myself for neglecting his experience.

The story was by far the most complicated and daunting piece of research I had yet attempted, but it was also the most enjoyable. There was a mountain of material available, yet, I was surprised to learn, no contemporary writer had prospected this latter-day gold mine. Nobody had looked at the Klondike experience as a whole. The one who had come closest was Kathryn Winslow, whose book *The Big Panout* concentrated almost entirely on the Chilkoot and White passes, leaving out the other routes to the gold fields. I decided that if my book were to be successful, it would have to be as definitive as I could make it.

This was my first venture into popular history, a genre that scarcely existed then in Canada. There was a good deal of excellent scholarly work, but at this juncture in our literary development nobody had ventured to do what the British and Americans were doing. Nobody except Bruce Hutchison was casting a romantic eye over the follies, triumphs, and adventures of the past. Our historians in Canada were good at sober analysis, but few knew how to tell a story.

I was fortunate in my choice of subject. Had I tried to tell a tale such as the building of the CPR, I suspect it would have been too much for me. The Klondike story was easier because I not only knew the geography, which many writers get wrong, but also understood the essence of the tale – the geology of placer gold, the psychology of the prospector. And there would be no dull spots: everything about the gold rush is fascinating – or it was to me. Yet without Janet's help I doubt that I would ever have finished the book. As a former journalist, and a good one, she was an expert on the care and feeding of authors. She also understood the kind of research I needed (I had no other research assistant in those days). Janet haunted the University of Toronto library, searching out personal accounts, background information, and social histories of the era. Then, in the summer of 1956, we decided to cross the country by car and interview the last of the pioneers, most of whom were living along the Pacific coast between Vancouver and San Francisco.

I will not forget the exhausting last day in Seattle, poring over the yellowing pages of the *Times* and the *Post-Intelligencer* and bound copies of Dawson's first newspaper, the *Klondike Nugget.* By the end of the day I was tired and hungry, but I still had one thing to check. Lulu Fairbanks of the Sourdough Association had told me that Belinda Mulroney, one of the great figures of the stampede, was still alive and, she thought, living on the outskirts of town. I caught my breath. Belinda had run a saloon, the Magnet, at Grand Forks, where the two richest creeks in the world – Bonanza and Eldorado – are joined. Later she had launched Dawson's ritziest hotel, the Fairview, on dance-hall row. A legend in her time, she had known everyone of importance. And her own story was the stuff of which Victorian novels are constructed. She had married the Count de Carbonneau, and the pair had travelled the world on Belinda's fortune, riding up and down the Champs-Elysées in a coach-and-four and getting red-carpet treatment everywhere they went. It did not matter to Belinda that Charles Carbonneau was not a count but the son of a Quebec City barber, who eked out a living peddling champagne to the Kings of Eldorado. Belinda, a plain-faced, plain-spoken washerwoman's daughter, had loved him and lived with him in a legendary castle in Washington State. I had thought her long dead; the knowledge that she might be alive was exciting, even if it wasn't true.

Now Janet acted as a goad. "Let's eat," I told her. "I want a steak in the worst way." Janet, however, insisted I look up Belinda in the phone book under her married name. I looked, but there was no Carbonneau listed.

"She's dead," I said. "I figured that. Let's eat."

Janet wouldn't give up. She had always been a stubborn and meticulous reporter. She insisted we find a drugstore that had a city directory and check the name in its pages. There was one C. Carbonneau a long way out past the city limits. "It's not her," I said. "Let's eat."

Then Janet found a number for a next-door neighbour, phoned, and was told that a little old lady lived next door who *had* said something once about having lived in the Yukon. "It's all pretty skimpy," I said. "Let's eat."

By then Janet was adamant. She insisted I take a long and expensive taxi ride to the outskirts, just in case it might be Belinda.

Forty-five minutes later, I rapped on the door of a small frame cottage. A small, wizened person peered out at me.

"Are you by any chance Belinda Mulroney Carbonneau?" I asked her.

Her reply caused my heart to hammer. "C'mon in, m' friend!" she said, in a throaty voice. "We got a lot to talk about."

Researching a book is rather like seeking the clues to a murder: the writer becomes a detective. And when he finds the smoking gun – *Wow!* I cannot now begin to describe the thrill that went through me when I realized I was in the presence of a living legend, one with a knife-sharp memory who was clearly possessed of all her faculties. Well over half a century had passed since the day Belinda had reached Dawson and thrown her last silver dollar into the Yukon River, crying, "I won't be needing this. There's plenty waiting for me here!"

She remembered everything. As we talked, all my pangs of hunger, all my fatigue vanished. I managed to interview some fifty old-timers for the book, but Belinda was worth all the rest put together. I cannot remember now whether or not Janet and I finally had the steak dinner. I suspect we simply tumbled into bed, exhausted but fulfilled.

Chapter Five

1

There is a scene engraved indelibly upon my memory that I retrieve occasionally from the filing cabinets of my mind and caress as I would a favourite pet. I had come home from work to find my two eldest daughters seated side by side on small chairs directly in front of the Bendix washer, a look of rapt concentration on their faces. I see them now, with their bangs and their pigtails, Penny, aged seven, and Pamela, five, staring at the laundry spinning behind the Bendix window.

"What's up?" I asked.

"We're watching television," said Penny.

It was, in a way, an oddly endearing spectacle, but even as she spoke I felt a pang. Every kid in the Kleinburg school had television except these from the one home that thrived on the medium. I had been appearing on TV with fair regularity for three years, but Janet had not been able to see me in action unless she walked across the field to a neighbour's and asked her to switch on the set. My little girls were reduced to staring into the Bendix in order to keep up with their schoolmates! And so, with the profits from my recent appearances on the home screen, I finally joined the twentieth century.

It would be nice to report that having been exposed to the other side of the set, I was able to approach the new device with some discrimination. But like everybody else, I was obsessed by it in those early years. I find it hard to believe now that I even gave *The Bob Cummings Show* my fascinated attention.

By the following year we had more or less finished our house, though we still had no baseboards. A desk had replaced the orange crates at the foot of our bed and we had finished the hallway in plywood. But our newest baby, Peter, was already too big for his crib, and so I knew we would have to enlarge the house.

I was spending my evenings and weekends freelancing, not only appearing on radio and television but also writing articles for some of our sister magazines. Every year I contributed songs, skits, and blackouts to the hugely successful satirical revue *Spring Thaw*, which Mavor Moore had first cobbled together in 1948 at the last moment to replace a production that wasn't working. At that time the New Play Society, launched by Mavor's mother, the indomitable Dora Mavor Moore, was the only home-grown theatre in Toronto. Canada was on the verge

120

A 1949 publicity photograph of me at my desk at
Maclean's, *taken to illustrate an advertisement*
boasting that we now had the best editorial staff
in Canada, thus fulfilling Arthur Irwin's dream.

One of the several raucous parties that helped bond the Maclean's staff.
John Clare looms large at the centre. The drunk on the right is me.

W. Arthur Irwin

Ralph Allen

Lister Sinclair (right) *introduced us to Kleinburg where, in the summer of 1949 the foundation for our house was dug in the midst of a barren landscape. Forty years later* (below), *the vista was unrecognizable.*

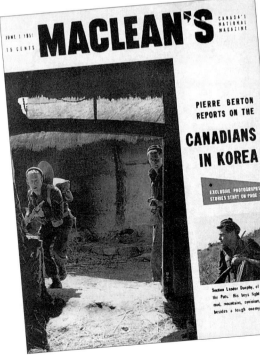

JUNE 1 1951
15 CENTS
MACLEAN'S
CANADA'S
NATIONAL
MAGAZINE

PIERRE BERTON
REPORTS ON THE

CANADIANS
IN KOREA

EXCLUSIVE PHOTOGRAPHS,
STORIES START ON PAGE 7

With my entourage in Seoul, spring 1951. Ron Taylor, guard, Chai Chung Jyp, ("Dickie"), interpreter, and Jim Ramsay (right). Everything, including the jeep, was supplied by an old army buddy, Captain Andy Foulds. American correspondents, astonished at this lavishness, called me "the Duke." My photographs of the troops made a Maclean's cover, but the one of the lone, bedraggled ostrich I found wandering about the zoo wasn't published.

*I had to learn to use a
Rolleiflex because the
magazine couldn't afford to
send a photographer with
me. Above is Tak Sook
Tyun, the 27-year-old
North Korean refugee
who managed to bring her
extended family down the
peninsula to Pusan. To
her, this shack made from
cardboard ration boxes,
was a luxury home.*
Left: *Song Kank Nyung, 13,
ekes out a living selling
packages of lifesavers and
candy that he liberated
from American K rations.*

SOUVENIR OF CBC - TV'S -- *Front Page Challen*

An early promotional photograph for Front Page Challenge, *circa 1958, showing the original panel members with the effervescent Toby Robins. Toby was replaced in 1962 by Betty Kennedy, a superb journalist and broadcaster who helped take some of the rough edges off Gordon Sinclair and me.*

In the spring of 1958, Pat Watson and I flew to Europe for Close-Up *to interview Robert Service, the Bard of the Yukon, who many people thought was dead. Here he is in his villa in Monaco. When I asked why he didn't return to the Canadian North, he said it was too damn cold. So much for the spell of the Yukon.*

Ross McLean, the CBC's wunderkind, who produced both Tabloid *and* Close-Up *and later helped launch* The Pierre Berton Hour.

The Toronto Star *ran this promotional photograph when I joined the paper in* October, 1958. *It shows Janet and the kids allegedly waving good-bye as I head for work with my new briefcase. Actually I spent the first week in bed—with the mumps.*

Beland Honderich,
Editorial Director

Ennis Halliday,
my long-time secretary

Marilyn Craig,
Operative 67

of a cultural flowering, but it hadn't happened yet.

It was Mavor who was responsible for *Spring Thaw'*s success. Satire is, after all, peculiarly suited to the Canadian style and has been since the days of Sam Slick. In the theatre, Canadians tend to be derivative; hence the success of both Shakespeare and Shaw each summer. But satire is where we shine, and *Spring Thaw,* in its gentle and occasionally wicked fashion, poked fun – Canadian style – at our most cherished institutions. I myself made sport of everybody from E.P. Taylor to Vincent Massey.

The revue became the longest-running and most successful theatrical production of its kind in Canada, staying alive for almost a quarter of a century. I contributed to it for about half that time. It was most successful when Mavor himself was in charge, an arrangement that was sometimes rendered difficult by his mother, whom he revered but with whom he did not always agree. There were whispers of phenomenal battles between the iconoclastic son and the tradition-steeped matron. I remember one edition that featured a short blackout starring Andrew McMillan, a consummate operatic baritone, who strode to the front of the stage dressed as an immigrant and sang to the audience that the handful of soil he held "might mean nothing to you, but it's America to me!" We began to shift uncomfortably in our seats. What was Mavor doing, inserting a piece of pro-American schmaltz in a satirical revue? But we were quickly disabused when McMillan continued:

America! America!

America is dirt to me!

Mrs. Moore was appalled by this spoof and ordered it removed from the show. That sort of interference led to Mavor's resignation in 1957. Three years later he bought the rights from his mother, and *Spring Thaw* was revived in its original irreverent format. Years afterwards I presided at a tribute to Mrs. Moore in which many of the old skits were revived. It was no more than her due. Almost single-handedly she had given Toronto live theatre, making stars of such actors as Don Harron and Dave Broadfoot, whose alter egos – Charlie Farquharson, and the Member for Kicking Horse Pass – had their birth on the cramped stage of the little Royal Ontario Museum Theatre, which was *Spring Thaw'*s home in those early years.

Of all the writing I did in the mid-fifties, *Spring Thaw* was by far the most fun. I would have worked on it for free, and I very nearly did. Its small royalties didn't pay the bills. My salary had increased with my promotion at *Maclean's,* but that wasn't enough to pay for an addition to our house. And so I hustled. My God, how I hustled! I look back on those years with awe. I had become a jack-of-all-writing-trades, and it seems to me now that I spent every waking moment – evenings and weekends – at my typewriter: a pamphlet for the government, a film for Budge Crawley, a record for Folkways in New York, radio plays for the CBC, the lead piece for the *Britannica Book of the Year,* articles for *Cavalier* magazine based on my Klondike research, a CBC documentary about the gold rush, and, last but certainly not least, the National Film Board's award-winning documentary *City of Gold.*

Because I wrote, and read, the narration for this ground-breaking film, it has often been referred to as "Pierre Berton's *City of Gold,*" a phrase I find embarrassing. The guiding geniuses were Tom Daly, Colin Low, Roman Kroiter, and Wolf Koenig of the NFB's animation department, who had been putting the documentary together for two years before I was called in. Most of the film consists of still pictures of the gold rush – so carefully edited and shot that the audience tends to forget they aren't moving. Most were made from old glass plates recycled to construct a greenhouse in Dawson. I knew that greenhouse well – used to pass it every day on the way to school. How could I have known that a fortune in rare photographs was being used to ripen tomatoes in those brief northern summers?

I was paid three hundred dollars for my work on the film on the grounds that it would probably be shown only in church basements. But after its release, *City of Gold* won more awards than anything the NFB had yet done – nineteen in all, including an Oscar nomination and the Grand Prix at Cannes. The demand for prints exceeded anything the NFB had ever experienced, and more people have now seen the film than any other documentary the board has made. My own connection with it opened doors for me when, some years later, I took my TV show to Hollywood. I remember when we tried to book Lucille Ball for one of our programs. Ball, who did not agree to many interviews, asked what I'd done, and so we arranged for her to see *City of Gold.* As soon as the screening ended, Ball agreed to appear with me.

My experience with the animation department was in sharp contrast with my work on *Women on the March,* a three-part history of female progress that I was asked to write and narrate by another branch of the

122

NFB. The third part was never produced because I insisted on dealing with the changes in morals that were, inevitably, altering the role of women in society. It was too much for Ellen Fairclough, the strait-laced Tory minister in charge of the board. In those days before the rise of the women's movement, any forthright discussion of morals was taboo. My experience was so unhappy and the results, in my view, were so tepid and confused that I asked to have my name taken off the two parts that survived. Later, I learned that one had actually won an award in New York.

My work on *City of Gold* had a positive effect on my unfinished manuscript for *Klondike*. Roman Kroiter saw the documentary as something more than a mere visual rendition of the story of the stampede. It was the old tale of man's eternal quest – not so much for gold as for himself. I had reached the same conclusion as a result of my research.

My father was one of the tens of thousands who had made their way to the Klondike, ostensibly to search for gold. But that, I began to see, was a mere excuse. He had really gone to test himself – to see if he could backpack a ton of goods over the frozen steps of the Chilkoot, cobble together a raft, tempt the Yukon River for more than five hundred miles, and then build a cabin of green logs sturdy enough to shelter him from the winter gales. He had suffered during the depression of the nineties, but it wasn't security he sought, or even a job; it was adventure. When he turned up at the post office at Dyea at the foot of the Chilkoot Trail, a letter was waiting for him offering him a job on the staff of Queen's University. That would have set him up for life, for he was clearly cut out for the academic world. He did not take it because he was curious to see what lay on the far side of the mountain barrier. And so he pressed on, and in doing so changed his life.

My research told me that thousands of would-be prospectors, after reaching their goal, didn't even bother to search for treasure; they had found it in themselves. The film underlined this by showing the throngs of shabby men shuffling back and forth along Front Street, ignoring the famous creeks that lay a few miles away. *City of Gold* treated the great stampede as an allegory, and it was as an allegory that I decided to write it.

By then I had a first draft, albeit a very bad one. I had resolved to dictate the entire book (a foolish conceit), which I managed in thirteen weekends. I never used this technique again, for it took as long to

123

correct and rewrite the manuscript as it would have had I begun it on my typewriter. Every author has a style. Analysed by a computer, it is as unmistakable as a fingerprint. *Klondike* is a little different in cadence from some of my other books because I wanted to write it as the allegory it was. I had been poring over a great many badly written but useful books, and I knew I had to cleanse my mind of turgid prose. I chose *Pilgrim's Progress* as the most suitable catharsis, and with those biblical phrases running through my head, addressed myself to a final draft.

Klondike taught me a lot about writing narrative history. The style would be that of a novel, not an essay. I knew what the narrative *purported* to be about; but what was it *really* about? The answer to that question – man's quest for himself – shaped the book. I didn't want the underlying theme to surface explicitly. What I needed was a quotation for the title page that would give a clue to the reader – something that I hoped to find in Bartlett. Here is what I used:

> *"All my life," he said, "I have searched for the treasure. I have sought it in the high places, and in the narrow. I have sought it in deep jungles, and at the ends of rivers, and in dark caverns – and yet have not found it.*
>
> *"Instead, at the end of every trail, I have found you awaiting me. And now you have become familiar to me, though I cannot say I know you well. Who are you?"*
>
> *And the stranger answered: "Thyself."*
>
> – From an old tale.

From an old tale? What old tale? Whose old tale? Where did I find it? In Bartlett? No such luck. There was nothing remotely suitable in any of the compendia I consulted. So I simply made it up.

My researches confirmed a growing conviction that, contrary to accepted belief, Canadians were a distinct breed in North America, not better, not worse, than their American neighbours, but different. The gold rush provided a unique opportunity to observe men and women from the two neighbouring countries struggling side by side toward the Klondike Mecca. In the course of that travail they demonstrated starkly differing attitudes to law and order, freedom, authority, democracy, and morality. There were scores of examples. The Americans discovered, to their chagrin, that nobody but a policeman could carry a handgun in the Yukon. Soapy Smith, the confidence man, could easily make

124

himself dictator of Skagway, Alaska, but didn't dare face the Mounted Police on the Canadian side of the border. The hoochy-koochy dance, a hit at Chicago's Columbian Exposition in 1893, was banned from Dawson's stages as immoral. My firm belief that, in spite of superficial similarities, we are not Americans became a sub-theme in many of my subsequent books of history. Two decades later I returned to it in *Why We Act Like Canadians*.

In our crowded home I hammered away at *Klondike* while workmen hammered away building an addition to the house. Small children – we had four by then – interrupted me from time to time to show me drawings they'd made or books they wanted me to read to them. That didn't bother me; I found it a welcome respite from my work. But I couldn't stand any adult fussing about, especially with a vacuum cleaner, and Janet learned to leave me alone at such times.

It is not easy to live with a writer. On evenings and weekends I existed in a kind of cocoon, obsessed with the story of the gold rush, shutting myself off from the world around me. I did not hear Janet when she called me to lunch or dinner, did not listen when she imparted the latest gossip. I was back in 1898, climbing the passes. Our social life suffered. I had no time for movies or for drop-in visits from friends seeking a pleasant afternoon in the country. I steeled myself to ignore television, save for the *Ed Sullivan Show,* which had become a family custom. I went to few parties, and when I did I was very bad company, staring glassy-eyed and uncomprehending as groups of friends chatted around me. I was a pill, no doubt about that. No witty repartee from this scrivener, no bright sayings, nothing. How could I explain that on these occasions I was actually *writing?* Only Janet, bless her, understood.

The office still consumed at least eight hours of the day and sometimes more, as I put my own manuscript aside in order to read the work of others. The *Maclean's* staff continued to grow, although our man in British Columbia, Ray Gardner, was forced out. Ralph said that he could not have anybody officially representing *Maclean's* who was a Communist or a Communist sympathizer. Ray could still write for us, but he could not write as a staff editor. I found that line of reasoning pretty flimsy, but Ralph was adamant. He had a strange obsession about the Red Menace that conflicted with his usually liberal-minded attitude. He himself had written two articles, one on James G. Endicott, the fellow-travelling United Church minister, and another on Tim Buck, the

Communist Party leader. They were far tougher than most of the articles we were publishing on other prominent Canadians, but in the atmosphere of those times anything less than a trenchant attack would have left the magazine open to charges of being "soft on communism."

The separatist movement in Quebec was then no more than a wisp of a cloud on the national horizon. Ralph's plan was eventually to start a truly national magazine in both official languages, accepting articles in both tongues and publishing them in both magazines in translation. He even hired a teacher to try to make us all bilingual. Alas, those two-hour sessions after a day's work found us wanting a drink, not a lesson. When at last Maclean Hunter did launch a French-language magazine, it bore no relation to the one Ralph had envisaged.

We were riding high in those days. The new presses allowed us to publish up-to-the-minute pages on yellow paper at the front and back of the magazine, giving a stronger sense of immediacy. Peter Newman, who had come to us from the *Financial Post,* was put in charge of these last-minute sections – a task that sometimes required an iron nerve.

One day Peter came into my office looking shamefaced. "I have to tell you I'm not in very good condition," he told me. "I thought I was taking a couple of Benzedrines to keep going, but I got mixed up and took a couple of sleeping pills instead."

"Well, he better goddamn well stay awake," Ralph remarked when I reported the problem.

Some months later Ralph called me into his office looking baffled and not a little irritated.

"Do you know what's going on out there?" he asked.

"Peter Newman is leaving his wife in order to marry Chris McCall," I told him.

"Christ!" said Ralph. "How do you know these things? Nobody tells me anything."

I told him it had been obvious ever since the last staff party. Peter had gone home that night in such a state that he had actually driven a stick through one of his favourite drums. Eventually he divorced his wife and married Chris.

Ralph was never at ease with the women on the staff. He was, as they say, a man's man, who liked to go fishing with old cronies from his warco days. He did not quite know how to deal with women writers, whom he saw as a separate species. He was always afraid, I think, that they might break down and cry in his office or throw a temper tantrum. They never did, but sometimes they dropped into mine next door to shed a tear.

Ralph had been absent from home for much of the war when his elder son, Glen, was growing up. The relationship between the two had never been smooth. Ralph was also unaccountably jealous of his vivacious wife, Birdeen, and if anyone paid too much attention to her at a party, he'd put on his coat at once and drag her away.

But he was an absolutely first-rate editor and an innovative one, a strong Canadian nationalist whose magazine, more than any other, mirrored the triumphs and concerns of the time. The rise of rock and roll, the problems of the burgeoning suburbs, the revolt from religion in Quebec, the birth-control pill, tranquillizers, bird watching, the Fowler Royal Commission on Broadcasting, the Athabasca tar sands – all these were subjects of *Maclean's* articles in the fifties. The titles tell the story: "Toronto – The Fastest Growing City in the World"; "How Long Can the Boom Last?"; "What the Machine Has Done to Quebec"; "Let's Stop Building $15,000 Shacks"; "Is Wheat Obsolete?" How far off they seem now – those heady days when the only Quebec problem was the Duplessis political machine, when you could buy a new house for $15,000 and the boom went on and on.

Television was having its effect, making the slick, formula magazine fiction obsolete. *Maclean's* success in these postwar years had been based on non-fiction; our readers clearly wanted reality, not fluff. We began to run panels, à la TV, on such subjects as church union and the perennial problems of the CBC.

We had moved into the Diefenbaker era. The Tory prime minister had won a minority government and was now jousting with Lester Pearson, who had replaced the aging and ineffective Louis St. Laurent. The new, shorter deadlines provided by the yellow pages had not been enough, however, to protect Ralph Allen, who in June 1957 had written an editorial assuming a St. Laurent victory. Since the editorial would run *after* the election, there was some danger in this assumption, which I recall mentioning, mildly, to Ralph. "There's nothing to worry about," he said. "Liberals are a shoo-in." That was apparently Blair Fraser's opinion as well.

Two days after Diefenbaker won with 112 seats to the Liberals' 105, *Maclean's* appeared declaring that "for better or for worse Canadians have once more elected one of the most powerful governments ever created by the free will of the electors." Except that they hadn't. Ralph took it all with wry humour and accepted the blame. In a *mea culpa* in the following issue, he wrote that the editorial represented "an almost unexampled case of editorial fatheadedness." It was, he wrote, "an altogether pessimistic guess about the temper of the Canadian people in this prosperous year of 1957."

In the spring of 1958, the country faced another election. This time there would be no editorials. In their place we offered in-depth interviews with the two leaders – television-style. A panel of three, Barbara Moon, James Bannerman, and Hugh MacLennan, would, under my chairmanship, try to learn as much as possible about the two disparate personalities – their hobbies, reading tastes, philosophy. These questions would be largely non-political and, we hoped, highly revealing. For me, the contrast between Diefenbaker, the testy prairie populist, and Pearson, the amiable ex-diplomat, was stark. It did not quite come out that way in print. On television it would have been much more devastating to Diefenbaker.

I found the new prime minister touchy and imperious. He refused to allow us to bring any new-fangled recording device into Sussex Drive, insisting instead that we use two Hansard shorthand reporters. But it was his opening encounter with Barbara Moon that threw the interview off balance. She wanted to know about his father: was he, in any sense, a strict parent? Diefenbaker instantly bridled. He did not answer the question directly. His father, he declared, was a dedicated man, a great student, and an accomplished musician who had "an unusually strong and abiding sense of history."

> MOON: But in the home, how was he?
> DIEFENBAKER: My father was a great student.
> MOON: A disciplinarian?
> DIEFENBAKER: *No!*...

Later:

> MOON: Did your father encourage you to go into law or go into politics?
> DIEFENBAKER: That is as far as I will go in that direction...

What's this all about? I asked myself. The Prime Minister was clearly angry and from that moment on did his best to ignore Barbara Moon. Yet he kept returning to her question.

BANNERMAN: Used you to hear your father talking about the opening of the West?

DIEFENBAKER: No... he hadn't been out there before. Everyone who travelled through the country seemed to make it a point to stay with us, for we had a nice home. That is why [*turning to Barbara*] I took strong objection to your suggestion that my father was stern in any way whatsoever.

MOON: It was just a question.

DIEFENBAKER: My father was the kindest of men, far too kind for his own welfare, and when you said he was a forbidding person you touched something that cannot be touched. My father helped out every single solitary person that came along, and when I heard that story about being forbidding – it may only have been a question. But it was a mighty poor analysis.

Of course, Barbara had never used the word "forbidding," nor had she suggested that she was analysing Diefenbaker's parent. Nonetheless, he was sensitive to the point of fury about any questions in that area, and that suggested an odd relationship with his father – one that we were obviously unable to probe further.

When the interview ended and the prime minister left, I looked at Hugh MacLennan, who was clearly badly shaken by the encounter. "The idea of that man being prime minister..." he kept saying. Suddenly he hurried to the washroom and threw up.

Our encounter with Pearson a few days later was in total contrast. Pearson was so relaxed that he greeted us in dressing-gown and pyjamas, having forgotten all about the interview. He was, as always, cheerful, boyish, and accommodating. But he was no political match for his prickly opponent, who beat him hands down, 208 seats to 49, in a landslide of epic proportions.

2

I did not realize it at the time, but 1957 was a pivotal year for me. At the age of thirty-seven, as much by happenstance as by design, I became a television star. That was the year the Canadian Broadcasting Corporation launched its two most popular and influential programs: *Close-Up,* its flagship public-affairs show, seen live on Sunday nights, and *Front Page Challenge,* its enormously popular panel show, broadcast live the next evening. I was a regular on both. By the spring of 1958 I was a familiar face in the living rooms of the nation and a recognized name in most households.

Ross McLean, the boy wonder of Canadian television, was responsible for *Close-Up.* It was the first public-affairs show on television in North America and the most influential of all the magazine-style formats then being seen on the small screen. This ground-breaking half hour set the pattern for all the similar programs that followed, from *The Journal* to *Sixty Minutes.* Ross had learned the technique early, especially with his highly popular early evening program *Tabloid,* a Toronto chatter-and-interview show, new for its time, that turned Joyce Davidson and Percy Saltzman, among others, into celebrities.

While he was planning *Close-Up,* Ross tried out his future stars on *Tabloid* and used me as an occasional interviewer. I had no charisma and little small talk, but I did know how to conduct a hard-hitting interview. That was what he wanted for his upcoming yeasty brew of live encounters, edited film, fast-paced panel discussions, and pithy documentaries. Ross was determined to cram in as many items as he could in the half hour at his command, a technique adopted thirty years later by *Entertainment Tonight* and similar programs. But *Close-Up* was live, not edited.

I found myself operating like a whirling dervish, trying, for instance, to squeeze three or four experts on the Soviets' newly launched sputnik into a panel discussion that lasted no more than five minutes! Nor was I allowed to say, as so many did, "Sorry, we're out of time." To Ross that was a cop-out; he didn't want to worry the viewers. Somehow I had to find a graceful way to end the discussion without any breathless sense of urgency. That was like driving a chariot behind four spirited steeds and attempting to bring them to a graceful stop.

I started off in television sporting an unfashionable bow tie. In fact, I think I was the only performer who wore one. The tie was the result of a zany encounter with Hal Straight, my old managing editor in Vancouver. As I have written elsewhere, Straight was a reincarnation of Walter Burns, the hard-driving editor in Hecht and MacArthur's famous play, *The Front Page*. Some time in the early fifties, when Straight was still drinking (he claimed he had spilled more hooch than most people consume in a lifetime), I was on assignment on the West Coast and I looked in on him at his office at the *Vancouver Sun*. Nothing would do but that we repeat our old practice of driving to Stanley Park for a bracer or two.

As we drove off down Georgia, I commented on the fact that Straight was wearing a bow tie.

"You should have one, too," he said, and, being a man of sudden impulse, screeched to a stop in front of George Straith's haberdashery. Straight, who owned the town in those days (or thought he did), thought nothing of double parking in the midst of heavy traffic and rushing into Straith's to pull a tie off the rack for me. "Charge it!" he shouted imperiously and was back in the car in an instant. En route to the park he showed me how to tie it.

From that moment I was hooked on bow ties. What was good enough for Franklin Roosevelt, Winston Churchill, and Harry Truman was, I thought, good enough for me. I became a bow tie collector. Indeed, to this day I cannot pass a haberdashery without examining the merchandise. I own about two hundred bow ties and wear them on and off television. Even if I wanted to, I could not switch back. The press now refers to my "trademark bow tie." Once, and only once, I turned up on *Front Page Challenge* with a four-in-hand.

"You're different," said Fred Davis. "What's happened? Have you lost weight?"

It threatened to become a matter of embarrassing public comment, and I returned to the butterfly bows. As for Straight, he never wore a bow tie again. It didn't really matter. When we went fishing for coho on the Sunshine Coast every summer, our shirts were always open at the throat.

My bow tie was, I suppose, an attempt to be different. Television had its own clichés. The chief one was that host and guest should be perched awkwardly on tall stools – uncomfortable enough for a man, positively embarrassing for a woman. We also used large and ungainly microphones in those days, but no attempt was made to conceal them. Women would arrive, resplendent in evening dress, only to have a metal phallic tube draped across their décolletage to tangle with their neck ornaments.

131

In my early days on *Close-Up,* I was amused to discover that the *shadow* of a boom microphone was considered a no-no while the real thing worried nobody. People were always changing the lighting to make sure the shadow didn't show; nobody seemed to care about the mike itself. But then, in a sense, all of TV is shadow play.

I didn't always shine on *Close-Up,* but Ross stuck with me and with his other regular interviewer, an ex-evangelist named Charles Templeton, whom I first encountered in Studio A before a rehearsal. "I guess all this is pretty new to you," I remarked by way of greeting – the old pro dealing kindly with the neophyte.

He looked at me with something approaching scorn. "I've been doing religious TV in New York for years," he told me. "Had two shows of my own." I was about to retort that religious TV didn't count but thought better of it.

The day I met Templeton I was interviewing Joseph Salsberg – an unsuccessful exchange because that old and dedicated Communist had just left the party that had been his life and wasn't sure now exactly who he was. I thought there was a parallel here with Templeton, who'd been second only to Billy Graham in the Youth for Christ movement but had for some time been harbouring doubts. These were exacerbated when, in spite of his Grade 10 education, he managed to break through the academic barriers to study philosophy at the Princeton Theological Seminary. He emerged as an ordained Presbyterian minister, unsatisfied by the blacks and whites of his earlier faith and exasperated by the need to distort and simplify his message at the great evangelistic rallies in order to make it clear to somebody seated a block away. He felt, as he later told me, "like an ecclesiastical mountain goat leaping from obvious truth to obvious truth."

Speaking about something in which he no longer believed as often as five times a day and to thousands of people a week caused coronary pains to shoot through his arms and upper chest – a symptom of his inner unhappiness. "Evangelism is not for me," he told his wife. "I'm quitting." They were shortly divorced. Now here he was, at forty-two, plucked out of New York by Ross McLean, who liked to people his program with new and unaccustomed faces.

Ross may not have fitted the stereotype of a TV producer – he was tall, pink-cheeked, curly-haired, and bespectacled – but he had his finger on the pulse of the country and especially on the pulse of show

132

business. He knew instinctively who the comers were. Both Mort Sahl and Brigitte Bardot appeared on *Close-Up* before they were widely known. In fact, Ross was totally instinctive. He was in the communications business, but he couldn't communicate very well. If he didn't like my performance, he sulked and often fled the studio, but he could not explain what was wrong. And so we had to learn by our mistakes. It took me a while to understand that on that tight program there was no time for opening pleasantries. In New York I was assigned to do a five-minute spot with Henry Morgan, the wry radio comedian. I started out with one of those long, convoluted questions that now make me squirm. Morgan stared at me for a few seconds after I'd finished. Then, "What was the question again?" he asked mildly. I couldn't repeat it.

In the spring of 1958, Ross decided I was the ideal man to travel to Monte Carlo to interview Robert Service, the "Bard of the Yukon." Uncharacteristically, he decided to devote the entire program to this one interview. Off we went – Pat Watson to direct and Bob Crone to film in Service's winter home. This was one show I'd spent my life researching. The bard's log cabin in Dawson had become a national shrine and a Mecca for the tourists who poured off the steamboats each summer. Special editions of his books, bound in caribou hide with real nuggets on the cover, were in our library. In my mother's single days, Service had occasionally squired her to a dance. He had also written the preface to *I Married the Klondike*. I knew many of his verses by heart and recited them without encouragement.

He met us at the door of his villa, a spare and feisty little man with lively blue eyes and sharp features that belied the plump cheeks of his youthful photos. He wasted no time. "I've got the scripts right here," he said, as we walked into his living room. "I've planned two programs. My part, of course, is bigger than yours. After all, this is *my* show!"

He handed us a thick sheaf of typewritten pages, which, he told us, he had been working on ever since he had received Ross's invitation. "I suggest you go back to your hotel and study your parts," he said. "I already know mine."

I gave Watson a bleak look. Service had written his own interview and had apparently memorized his own role. And he clearly expected me to follow his script!

"What are we going to do?" I asked Pat as we reached the hotel.

"Maybe we should look at what he's written," he said. That seemed a sensible idea, so we read Service's scripts carefully.

"You know, they aren't half bad," I said.

"They're damn good," said Pat.

Why shouldn't they be? Service was one of the highest-paid writers in the world – for prose as well as for verse. One of his books had stayed on the *New York Times* best-seller list for two years. Several movies had been based on his work. He knew his business.

We decided not to discuss the script with the poet or tell him what we intended to do, which was to sit down with him in his living room and conduct a typical *Close-Up* interview as the camera rolled. I would ask some of my own questions but also some of Service's. He responded amiably, and when I used one of the questions that he had put into his script, I noticed his answer was word for word as he had written it. But it didn't sound stilted. With his soft Scottish accent, he had "got it off the paper," to use an industry term.

His villa, Service told me with some relish, had once been a bordello. He was no stranger to the ancient profession, remarking matter-of-factly that as a young bank clerk in Dawson he had been used to "going down the line" in the days when the painted ladies occupied cribs in Klondike City, better known as Lousetown. We did not get those remarks on film. What would have been the point? Those were strait-laced times. *Close-Up* had already been the centre of a controversy over a reference to homosexuality in a program that a Moncton station had cut from its schedule. And when Ross sent Charles Templeton to Sweden on an expensive trip to produce a major documentary on the new morality, the CBC killed the result.

Service remained exuberant. At the age of eighty-four he confessed he was suffering from what he called "a conky heart." Then he brightened. "Say, wouldn't it be a gorgeous thing if I was to pop out in the middle of television?" he asked. "It would be a great sensation." It sounded like a spontaneous remark, one that many Canadian newspapers carried. But it had been there all the time in the script he had given us.

We asked him to recite some of his favourite poems for the record, and he did so with great enjoyment except for "Dan McGrew," his most popular work, which he hated. "It makes me squirm," he said. "It's not exactly tripe, but there's no real poetry in it, to my mind. Of course, I don't write poetry anyway, so there's no use talking like that. Newspaper verse, if you like, but I think I've written better stuff. And here I am, crucified on the cross of McGrew."

We spent four days filming the interview with Service, his French wife, and two little granddaughters, who tripped cheerfully in and out of the room. Before we took our leave, Service brought out a bottle of champagne and we toasted each other. "I hate it to end," he said. "Must it end? Can't we do more? I've lots more I could give you."

At those wistful words, my mind went back to a lonely telegrapher's cabin on the banks of the Yukon River where our family – I was six at the time – had spent an hour enjoying a lunch of porcupine stew. The operator, briefly abandoning his key when we departed, ran down the bank to see us off, crying, like Service, "Must you go? It's been such a short visit! Please stay!" I was reminded again, as I often am, of a phrase from Service's own poem "The Telegraph Operator": *Oh, God, it's hell to be alone... alone... alone...!*

The program ran on the CBC in July. Three months later the Richest Poet in the World died quietly at his villa. Ross had asked me to shoot extra footage so the CBC would have good material when Service died. I turned on the CBC news expectantly – *nothing!* Not a single foot from the "outs," nothing of Service reciting his own work. I phoned next day to see what had happened. Why hadn't they used some of the material we had gone such a long way to get? I asked.

The answer depressed me. They couldn't find it, I was told.

3

HOLLYWOOD, December 10, 1958. Ross McLean and I are standing around in NBC's Studio 4 talking about the Legend of Milton Berle and waiting, not without considerable curiosity, for the Legend himself to appear. At last he arrives, greets us without brashness, his mien passive, his voice a muted chord, his manner unobtrusive.

We feel a little cheated as he stands there, listening attentively to Ross like a small, well-scrubbed Boy Scout on his best behaviour. Is this the Berle we'd heard so much about? The Great Worrier, the frantic last-minute scene switcher, the man who habitually carries a policeman's whistle to command attention – insistent on having his own way, noted for his rough-and-tumble battles with the crew?

*Mr.
Television*

135

Here he is, standing quietly with Ross – Mr. Television, nodding cheer-fully at instructions and puffing on an enormous two-dollar cigar.

"I wonder if you'd mind if I make one small suggestion," Berle asks, and he says it so quietly, so courteously, that we feel grateful. "I use the word 'suggestion,'" Berle goes on, "because I have an unearned reputation for interference. So I wish to make it very clear that this is merely a suggestion on my part."

Ross and I feel warmed by the humility of the man.

Berle makes his suggestion. We nod. In the next sixty seconds he makes six more. In the hour that follows he makes about a hundred. They cover the placing of the lights, staging of the interview, changes in the script, positioning of all three cameras, handling of opening shots, possible use of music, and even the type of microphone we intend to use.

Many are sensible suggestions. One or two are brilliant. Most are put into effect. After all, this is the man who, after forty-five years in show business, has forgotten more than most entertainers have learned.

By this time Berle has ceased to make suggestions. He is telling people what to do and how to do it. The Legend is in action.

"Please! Please!" he cries at the slightest breath of sotto voce con-versation. "Can't we have a little quiet here?" The obsession with utter silence increases in intensity until the studio is alive with people hissing "Sh-h-h!" at each other.

A sort of built-in retinue has arrived with him – a valet, a make-up man, and two brothers, Jack and Phil, who carry a script containing some promotional messages for Berle to okay. Most of the time Phil stays in the control room. Jack does anything he's asked. When Berle calls for his coat, Jack has it. When he wants to test a knee bend for a camera trick, Jack stands in front of the camera and bends his knees.

When the interview is over and the lights go down, an enthusiastic knot of people surrounds Berle, like parents after a school concert.

"You were great, Miltie... you were really wonderful.... Wonderfully human and warm-hearted, Milton.... It showed a new side of you.... Beautifully low key...."

"Was it really all right?" Berle asks anxiously. "Do you think it went all right?"

"It was wonderful, Milton."

But it has not been wonderful, and Berle and I both know it. It has been flashy, disjointed, pointless, and dull. None of this is the fault of

136

Milton Berle, who has tried to wisecrack through the show. I realize that I'm not really a good straight man.

He comes back from the make-up room and, with the crowd gone, becomes himself, quite relaxed, once again the polite little boy, courteously and warmly expressing his thanks. He's about to leave when I think of a question I meant to ask in the interview and didn't – a question that had been asked earlier that day.

"Would you say you had a normal childhood, Milton?"

And Berle answers slowly, "No, I guess I never had any real childhood at all."

He thinks for a moment and then comes up with a gag, spoken only half in jest.

"I was too busy fighting with the drummer," says Milton Berle.

4

The great panel show craze reached its apogee in the late fifties. Panel shows and game shows were cheap to produce and they garnered high ratings. Millions tuned in weekly to watch *What's My Line?*, the daddy of them all, as well as *To Tell the Truth* and *I've Got a Secret.* All were half-hour shows involving a celebrity host, three celebrity panellists, a celebrity guest panellist, and two or three mystery guests. Not to be outdone, the CBC in 1957 launched its own panel show with a similar format. Instead of determining the line or the lie or the secret, the panel's job was to go after a news headline from the past with which the mystery guest had some connection. Most of the big panel shows finally folded, as did the CBC's *Live a Borrowed Life* and *Flashback,* but *Front Page Challenge* endured. As I write these words it has entered its thirty-eighth season. Why? The chief reason is that *Front Page Challenge* has been the only program in which the panellists were journalists and acted like journalists. All the other programs featured "celebrities."

The success of *Front Page Challenge* says something about Canadian tastes and attitudes and how they differ from those to the south. Unlike the United States, we lack a strong show business tradition. Our popular entertainment tends to be rooted in reality. That explains why the National Film Board's reputation is based largely on its award-winning

Front page challenges

137

documentaries and not on its rare fictional films. Few of our cultural pooh-bahs have risen up from the ranks of show business. The CBC hierarchy has always been dominated by Ottawa mandarins, former weathermen, and journalists. Mike Wallace, an early guest panellist on *Front Page Challenge,* was so taken with the show that he wanted to produce a version of it in the United States, but the American networks thought it too highbrow for their audiences. And when Wallace tried to recruit a panel of stand-up comedians for the American counterpart, the CBC, to its credit, wouldn't give him the rights.

Another reason is that *Challenge* adapted to the times. In those early days the emphasis was on the game. The interviews with the mystery guests were perfunctory and short – a quick question from each panel member and then on to the next four-minute quiz. As time went by, the game was shortened to two minutes and the number of games from three to two. The emphasis now was placed on the interview section of the show, and the questions, which had never been sycophantic, began to cause controversy because they were often hard-hitting. *Front Page Challenge,* in its later years, has become a news program dealing with up-to-the-minute stories rather than events from the past.

It did not begin that way. In the spring of 1957, the word was all over town that the CBC was holding auditions for a new panel show. Everybody, it seemed, was being tested – everybody, that is, except me. That season the show was a summer replacement, and few gave it any chance of permanence. The panellists consisted of the veteran news-man Gordon Sinclair, the effervescent actress Toby Robins, the Toronto *Telegram*'s entertainment columnist, Alex Barris, and one guest. The "managing editor," as the host was then called, was Winston Barron, known as the voice of Movietone News.

It was those *Maclean's* "Flashbacks" that eventually got me a job on the panel. I appeared twice that summer as a guest and thanks to my knowledge of the past, gleaned almost entirely from the magazine pieces, acquitted myself well. The producers were then looking not for incisive interviewers but for people who knew something about popu-lar history – who could make a stab at guessing the Halifax Explosion, the birth of the Dionne Quints, the Regina Cyclone of 1912, or the Abdication of Edward VIII.

These were the kinds of news stories the program featured that first summer. Nobody expected it to last past the fall. Win Barron was nervous and obviously ill at ease, and the show dragged horribly. But someone, probably Harvey Hart, the first producer, felt it had something. There was nostalgia in the old stories and the film that accompanied them. There was also real chemistry between the hard-bitten, icono-clastic Sinclair and the lively ingenue, Toby Robins. A new moderator was needed, and the obvious choice – or so it seems in hindsight – was Fred Davis, the apparently unflappable host of the CBC's afternoon program *Open House*. I say "apparently" because, at least at the beginning, Fred was a bundle of nerves before each show. No hint of that, however, was evident on the screen. Since I had appeared to know something about past headlines, I was engaged for three weeks out of four, at $150 a show, to round out the panel in Alex Barris's spot.

The program, which was originally a replacement for the musical *Denny Vaughan Show,* is a prime example of Berton's First Law of Television: *Any new show that starts out with visual gimmickry will grow simpler and simpler as the years roll by.* The show began that summer with an ornate and unnecessarily elaborate set and a format cluttered with extraneous gimmickry. For example, a pair of beautifully dressed models escorted the mystery guests to a seat after their identity was disclosed, while a hysterical succession of bells, buzzers, sirens, and flashing lights punctuated the action.

In those days the CBC had plenty of money with which to indulge itself. The three guests were paid fancy sums for their brief appearances. One of them, Lady Docker, the controversial wife of a British peer, was paid a fee of $2,500 – an enormous sum then – and provided with first-class travel from England for herself, her husband, and her son. A special greeter was hired to meet the flights of mystery guests, drive them to the Park Plaza, wine and dine them, and bring them to the studio. In addition, the program paid three actors to play the role of plausible guests with plausible headlines in the camera rehearsal that preceded the real show. These rehearsals were timed to the second; after video-tape came in, they were recorded. I doubt if anybody ever watched the results, but they were on a full half hour of tape that went to some stations on a delayed basis, sitting right next to the real program.

We did not take rehearsals seriously. They were used to check the lighting and sound. We asked outrageous and often raunchy questions of the fake mystery guests, and, of course, the inevitable happened: a CBC menial erred and sent out the wrong tape. It ran on the Prince

George affiliate and nobody, apparently, phoned in to complain. The show went on for twenty minutes before the station manager realized something was terribly wrong. It didn't matter. TV audiences will accept anything.

I may have got most of the answers, but Toby and Gordon made the show. Toby was, without doubt, the most beautiful woman on television and possibly the most beautiful in Canada. She looked as if she'd stepped out of an Arabian Nights tale, glowing with an incandescence that lit up any room, sparkling with good humour, and sometimes exhibiting a charming naïveté in contrast to the hard-nosed journalist who sat on her right. Her name had been picked off a list of TV union members – she was one of the stars of *The Big Show,* an early extravaganza of the kind now obsolete – and one of seven comely actresses chosen to audition because the CBC knew that one of the panel members would have to be female.

"I know it's ridiculous," Toby told her husband, the stage producer Bill Freedman, "but I have nothing to lose by trying." Anyway, it was only a summer replacement job that could not possibly conflict with the arrival of her baby in January.

The first rehearsal was held at Harvey Hart's house, and there Toby astounded everybody by guessing two news stories out of three. She claimed she had never read a front page in her life yet identified the grisly story of the Coconut Grove fire in Boston because her family had a friend who played piano in that nightclub and had spent an entire day trying to find out if she was all right. Toby had been eight years old at the time.

I admired her immensely because she took her task seriously, going to the library every day, reading the back files of newspapers, and writing down all the major headlines in a small notebook. Four years later she moved with her husband to a theatrical career in London. She was replaced by Betty Kennedy, a one-time model and working journalist who ran her own daily interview program on CFRB.

Betty bore a child, lost a husband to cancer, and remarried – all without missing a program. Her second husband was Allan Burton, who had also lost his spouse to cancer. Their friendship was an open secret that caused me some embarrassment because certain viewers confused my name with Allan's. One woman wrote me an angry letter accusing me of leaving my wife and children for my television

140

colleague. I said nothing to Betty, but when nuptials were finally announced I wrote her a note expressing both my congratulations and my relief at the news.

I suppose "gracious" is the best word to describe Betty. She brought a serene quality to a program noted for the overbearing pressure of us rough-hewn males. But she also had a retentive mind, a long apprenticeship, and a journalist's curiosity. Like Toby's, her presence worked to soften the effect of Gordon Sinclair's often belligerent attack.

Sinclair, of course, was the driving force behind *Front Page Challenge*. I learned a lot from him. He taught me that the question can be just as interesting as the answer. It was never possible to predict what he was going to do. Sometimes he was affable, almost humble; sometimes he was a holy terror, especially around income tax time. At the outset he was both good guy and bad guy, though the image of villain died away in his declining years. He often riled the guests by asking them how much money they were worth; almost without exception they became embarrassed and refused to answer. Once during a *Close-Up* interview, I turned the tables on him, knowing he couldn't duck the question. He gave me the figure – $400,000 – a statement that produced a surprisingly vitriolic uproar. Ultimately, the audience grew old along with Gordon; he became the eccentric uncle that everybody loved.

Gordon was proud that he had risen from his Cabbagetown beginnings to become the best-known and richest journalist in Canada, a man who loved to drive a Rolls-Royce and who appreciated the plaudits of members of the old neighbourhood – "one of our boys made it." The critics, of course, tended to sneer. As Bob Shiels wrote in the *Calgary Herald*, "I find his arrogant attitude as a TV performer increasingly unpalatable. The guest must feel like he's being attacked by vultures." But after all, the guests were well paid and had been told exactly what to expect. Who said TV interviews had to be namby-pamby? Why couldn't a newspaperman act on a TV panel the same way he would act during a press conference?

Surprisingly, the real bad hat in the early panels wasn't Gordon; it was me. "He's a marvellous villain," John Aylesworth, the creator of the show, told the newspapers. "The panel became much better when they started using Pierre." One critic said I had "mastered the art of upsetting people." Another chided me for "cynical remarks and caustic comment." I was called "stubborn, opinionated, arrogant," all of which was probably true. Paul King, in the *Vancouver Sun,* referred to me as "Hack the Knife," and criticized me as "overbearing and brutal."

The truth is that the public was not used to a panel show in which journalists asked journalistic questions. All the other shows treated their guests with kid gloves. In the United States, especially, the panellists were witty and superficial, never probing. Our use of the term "mystery guests" was also confusing. A number of viewers wrote in to say that by asking tough questions I was abusing the rules of hospitality; the "guest" ought to be treated as I would treat a guest in my own home. When, sometime later, I went after Angus McLean, the premier of Prince Edward Island, for declaring that he was an Islander first, a Maritimer second, and a Canadian third, there was an outcry from P.E.I. But I had simply told him he'd got his priorities wrong. McLean's exemplary war record was trotted out in the local press. How could I attack a war hero? That, of course, was beside the point.

Some years ago, Ray McConnell, a later producer of the show, went through some of those early kinescopes to put together a retrospective and was surprised by what he found. "It's really interesting," he told me after looking at the programs of the late fifties. "*You* haven't changed. You're asking the exact same kind of questions that you asked then. But the audience has changed. They accept tough questions now."

The fact that the program was live meant that the men and women who ran the CBC couldn't put their sticky fingers on it. They were then, as they are now, petrified by the possibility of public controversy. When Gordon asked the champion swimmer Elaine Tanner if her menstrual period affected her athletic ability (she told him calmly that it didn't) there was an awful foofaraw. The wave of outrage caused George Davidson, the CBC's craven president, to issue a public apology, denouncing Sinclair and declaring that he had been guilty of "a deplorable lapse of good taste." "I deplore it," Davidson declared, "I regret it," and he promised that the CBC would do everything it could to make sure such a thing didn't happen again.

As long as the show was live, the nervous Nellies had no control over it. But when we switched to videotape it was another matter. In 1977, a segment of the program dealing with mercury poisoning among the native peoples of Northern Ontario, with Warner Troyer as the mystery guest, was hoisted by the corporation until after the provincial election. It was just too political, we were told. Ye Gods, I thought, it has come to this! We cannot discuss the known facts about river pollution and the damaging effect it's had on the native peoples because it might either help or hurt one of the political parties. As the *Toronto Star* editorialized, it was "an exercise in censorship rather than political fairness." But then, the CBC has rarely wanted to rock the boat.

Gordon was deliberately controversial whenever he felt the program needed a goosing. He'd come up with a zinger, often to his own detriment. He was a team player, cared about the show, and was prepared to take his lumps if necessary.

Once when a mystery guest turned out to be a missionary nun who had survived a massacre in Africa, Gordon whispered to the panel, "Don't let me at her. I don't need the grief." After a couple of questions, I turned the interview over to him, with devastating results. Gordon picked up the sister's remark that she had fallen to her knees and thanked God for her deliverance. "Ah," he said, "is that the God who controls everything that happens? Did he then sit back and allow your friends to be murdered? Did you thank him for that? Did you praise him for that?" The CBC switchboard would light up on these occasions with angry calls, but Gordon persisted. In an interview with the radical priest Daniel Berrigan, he pointed out that the cross was predominantly a symbol of torture, not love.

It isn't fair to say, as some have said, that the resultant furore failed to bother Gordon. It bothered him greatly, but he didn't veer from his own beliefs or stop expressing them in public. That was a secret of his own success as well as the program's. He told it, as the saying goes, like it was.

The strength of *Front Page Challenge* in its early years lay in its glittering array of international guests, from Eleanor Roosevelt to Mary Pickford, from Jacques Cousteau to Aleksandr Kerensky. Every provincial premier and five prime ministers occupied the guest panellist's chair (only Brian Mulroney declined). William F. Buckley, who believed in keeping appointments, turned up at the last moment, bedraggled and unshaven, delayed by storms that forced him to change his flight schedule again and again. He had been travelling for twenty-four hours when he finally reached the studio, but to him a commitment was a commitment. "Bring me a six-pack of beer," he begged. He got it, and the show went on.

Randolph Churchill was one of our most difficult guests. He demanded a bottle of whisky and berated the staff when they had difficulty getting him one. He was unconscionably rude, but the viewers didn't see that side of him. When the camera's red light winked on, signifying that the show had begun, a beatific smile crossed that craggy and forbidding face, and he became a pussycat.

His sister, the divine Sarah, was even more of a problem. We were warned that she was a heavy imbiber, and so Lorraine Thomson, our program organizer, was assigned the task of keeping the booze from her. Lorraine sat guard all afternoon in Churchill's suite at the Park Plaza until finally, and regrettably, she was forced to visit the washroom. In that short interval, Sarah Churchill managed to call room service, order, and consume three double Scotches. En route to the studio she somehow escaped and was discovered trying to direct traffic on Yonge Street. She appeared on the show, clearly the worse for wear, to the bafflement of the audience and to the detriment of the program.

Sally Rand, the legendary fan dancer, turned up in Halifax where we were taping two shows at a school auditorium for one of the several charities we were then supporting across the country. She had just concluded, at the age of seventy, a week of disrobing in a Winnipeg nightclub, and the members of staff were chewing their fingernails. Would she make it through an Atlantic blizzard? She arrived at the last moment, hoisting up her skirts as she ploughed through a snowdrift. Gary Lautens, the witty *Toronto Star* columnist who was also scripting the program at that time, thought that our producer, Don Brown, was perhaps a little too rapturous as he greeted her. "What a marvellous trouper you are," he gushed, "to come through a dreadful storm like this so that the show can go on. Bless you!" Then he noticed that she was *Turning* clutching her famous ostrich plumes. "And you've brought your fans," *point* he burbled. "What a wonderful touch of nostalgia!"

"Fuck nostalgia," said Sally Rand. "Where's the dressing room?"

5

By the spring of 1958 I was well launched as a home-grown celebrity, subject to the fierce light now thrown on those of us captured by the new medium.

> *We're doing a roundup about what celebrities eat for breakfast, Mr. Berton; could you spare a few minutes?*

We're doing a piece about what celebrities want for
Christmas. Can you help us out?
We're doing a survey for the Saturday page about what
celebrities read. Can you tell us the last book you bought?

It was a remarkable transformation. In the summer of 1957, in spite of a hundred articles for *Maclean's,* in spite of my regular appearances on "Court of Opinion," in spite of an award-winning book, in spite of sporadic appearances on television, I was not instantly recognized by the general public. One year later I was a name in bold face in the newspaper columns, the subject of searching magazine articles (many feeding on one another), and a perceived source of opinion on any human problem *(what's your view on capital punishment?... euthanasia? ... immigration?... violence on TV?... etc., etc., etc.),* invited to judge beauty contests, to appear on learned panels, to endorse other people's books, to act as an honorary member of the honorary executive for a dozen honorary causes. Strangers on the street wrung my hand, sometimes mistaking me for somebody they knew. Soon I had to stop riding the Toronto subway because there was too much comment, some of it derogatory. "What are *you* doing on the subway?" one man asked me accusingly, as if I had invaded his washroom. On the other hand, I did not have to wait for a table in a fancy restaurant or a room at a hotel.

For a journalist, there are advantages in being well known. People returned my phone calls. I no longer needed to explain who I was. Big wheels who would once have given me the cold shoulder now *wanted* to be interviewed. Shortly after the 1958 election I was sent out to British Columbia to do the lead article and prepare for a special issue *Maclean's* was planning on the province. That required me to beard some of the biggest names in the province in their dens, including H.R. MacMillan, the lumber baron, and Dal Grauer, the head of the B.C. Electric Company. With my newfound celebrity status I had no difficulty in seeing them all on short notice.

Parenthetically, it was during this journey that I first came to realize what devastation the large corporations were wreaking on the wilderness. The Canadian boom mentality was savaging the environment, though "environment" was not a word one heard in the fifties. Few people cared about the rape of the forests, the destruction of the wild rivers, the overfishing on both coasts, or the wrecking of our national parks. In our Northern issue in 1954 I had written an article entitled "The Yukon's Coming Alive Again," under a pseudonym. In it I reported, without a hint of criticism, the plans (fortunately aborted) to dam the Yukon River and flood most of the Trail of '98 for a hydroelectric development. Now, flying across northern British Columbia with my old friend Russ Baker, and gazing down on what was left of Tweedsmuir Park, I was appalled.

In order to provide power for the aluminum plant at Kitimat on the Douglas Channel, the park had been destroyed; its white sand beaches were eroded, and the margin of its largest lake was defaced by a ragged line of decaying trees. Nobody had had the gumption or guts to remove the forest growth before the lake was backed up. Now, for hundreds of yards, and in some places for two miles, a rotting jungle of fallen timber, gnarled roots, deadfalls, broken branches, floating snags, and gaunt spars stretched far into the water. The moose on their annual migrations could no longer reach the shore. Nor could the sportsmen. A few naturalists had opposed the rape of Tweedsmuir Park's lakes, pleading in vain that, at the very least, the area should first be logged and cleared before the water backed up into the forest. But the boom was on; the clean-up, they were told, would delay the great adventure of Kitimat. With a stroke of the pen the park was reduced by a third, the flooded area listed as "unsuitable for park purposes." I reported all this, but again with a dead-pan objectivity that was the approved *Maclean's* style. It would take a later generation to summon up the anger needed to alert the public to the downside of the Great Canadian Boom.

I did not know it at the time, but this was the last article I would write for *Maclean's*. Three months later I was forced to choose between continuing as managing editor of Canada's national magazine and pursuing a second career in broadcasting.

It began when Sidney Katz insisted on sending a memo to Floyd Chalmers explaining that he was thinking of going into commercial television and asking what the rules were for such a move by a company employee.

Rules? What rules? There weren't any. No one had thought about rules, and I tried to explain to Sid that when there are no rules you don't rock the boat by asking for them. A good many Maclean Hunter employees – Blair Fraser, for one, and Ken Wilson of the *Financial Post*

146

– were appearing in various CBC public-affairs programs. They hadn't asked for rules. Sid had no specific program in mind, and, in fact, never did appear on commercial TV. But he was adamant.

I'm sure that my own high profile on the CBC's two most popular programs was a factor. I seemed to be popping up on the tube almost as if I lived at the CBC headquarters on Jarvis Street. I had been scrupulous in keeping my TV chores from interfering with my work for *Maclean's*. *Close-Up* was produced on the weekend. I studied my research on Saturday, turned up at the studio early Sunday evening, and was home by ten. I couldn't tackle the out-of-town junkets, to which Charles Templeton was assigned, unless, as was the case with the Service interview, I took my holidays. *Front Page Challenge* was produced live on Monday nights after the dinner hour. It took no more than two hours of my time. The half-hour radio program "Court of Opinion" was recorded at the Thursday lunch hour.

I'm not sure the powers-that-were at *Maclean's* understood this. No doubt they thought my TV performances were eating into their time. I could understand this because when I first got a television set I wondered how Bennett Cerf could possibly appear on *What's My Line?* and still have time to edit books. Of course, Cerf simply walked into the studio, did his half-hour bit, and walked out. Although TV and radio took no more than five hours of my week, such was the power of the new medium that the Maclean Hunter hierarchy, I believe, thought they were my major preoccupation.

There were meetings at the executive level as a result of Sid's memo. Finally the company issued a set of rules. No employee could appear on any television program without being clearly identified with the magazine for which he or she worked. And no employee could appear on any commercial program unless the sponsor also advertised in the magazine for which he or she worked.

There was only one member of the great Maclean Hunter family who was affected by these rules. I was always clearly identified as managing editor of *Maclean's* on two of my three programs: "Court of Opinion" and *Front Page Challenge*. But Ross McLean felt that was enough; the CBC was even getting a bit antsy at giving Maclean Hunter employees so many free mentions – baulking at having to publicize Fraser, Wilson, and others as employees in another medium. Ross did not want to plug *Maclean's* on a third program, and I felt that two out of three wasn't bad. I tried to explain that to Chalmers in a memo I sent through Ralph. The company's various publications were getting a small fortune in free advertising that other publications would kill for. I also pointed out that *Front Page Challenge* was sponsored by Lever Brothers, whose products were advertised in *Chatelaine* – a far better target audience for laundry soap and shampoo than *Maclean's*. Couldn't he see that?

He couldn't. Rules were rules, and these had to be inflexible. I think Chalmers expected me to knuckle under, give up my broadcasting commitments, and remain exclusively with the company. He was a pretty good publisher as publishers go, but there was also an authoritarian streak in him. I remember that when John Clare was tabbed for *Chatelaine,* Ralph had told Chalmers that John didn't want the job. "He'll go where we send him," said Chalmers shortly.

I have one rule that I've always stuck to: *Never make threats about quitting.* So I had never so much as hinted in my memos to management that I would quit if the rules weren't changed. I didn't want to quit. I loved my job, loved its creativity – laying out pages, choosing pictures, thinking up subjects for articles, shaping the copy, and, on occasion, writing major pieces myself. Two or three months earlier, Beland Honderich, editor of the *Toronto Star,* had made an attractive approach to me about a job, but I told him I was content where I was. I would have been happy to stay on as managing editor forever, but now I had no intention of bowing to Chalmers's dictum. The company had a good piece of me, but it didn't own me twenty-four hours a day.

And so, early in August 1958, with Janet already in labour with the baby who proved to be Paul, our fifth child, I walked into Ralph's office and told him I was quitting. I still remember his reaction, and the startled look on his face.

"Oh, shit!" he said.

After the baby was born I went over to Wellesley Hospital and broke the news to Janet.

One of her great strengths is that she doesn't panic. She may worry about her children and her grandchildren, but she never worries about her own situation. She moves easily through life, taking the good with the bad, her equanimity undisturbed. Unlike me, she is not a Type A personality. She will never suffer from high blood pressure or nervous prostration.

Now she looked up at me from her hospital bed and remarked, with a giggle, that it wasn't the best time for me to be jobless.

But I have another rule, which I had already invoked: *Never walk off a job unless you have a fallback position.*

I had called Beland Honderich at the *Star* to tell him that if he still wanted me, I was available. He wanted me. *Maclean's* at that time was paying me $14,000 a year; Honderich offered me $15,000. It did not occur to me to haggle. Honderich wanted me as an "adviser," with the title of associate editor. I think what he was really looking for was a managing editor, but he wanted to test me first. For all of his brilliant career, Bee Honderich had searched vainly for the perfect second banana – one who could remove the heavy burden from his shoulders and run the paper for him. There was no such paragon, though Ralph Allen, who eventually left the magazine and took the job, came close.

Honderich, who would soon become both publisher and president of the company, was a hands-on executive who often sat on the rim of the copy desk, editing stories and writing headlines in order to keep in touch. A succession of managing editors came and went through the *Star*'s revolving door. I had no intention of letting myself in for that kind of grief, but, of course, I did not tell Honderich. I craved a simpler boon. Could I please write a daily column? Honderich readily agreed. I think he was trying to humour me, treating my request as a minor issue that could easily be shunted aside when and if the big moment came. It never came, of course.

I had no idea what I would put in my column, which was scheduled to begin September 16. I had a free month to think about it. I took the family, baby and all, to Ogopogo Lodge in the Haliburton Highlands, and there, as we frolicked, I began to think up ideas and to list them all in a small notebook. By the end of our two-week vacation I had forty of these, and in the months that followed I used every one.

Unlike Chalmers, Honderich was delighted that the paper would be plugged every Monday night to the two million viewers of *Front Page Challenge*. I was introduced now as "associate editor and columnist for the *Toronto Daily Star*," and he saw the advantage in publicity that Maclean Hunter, in its obtuseness, had ignored.

A short time later, when I turned up as usual at Studio Four, the old Pierce-Arrow showroom on Yonge Street that was *Front Page Challenge*'s television home, I was astonished to find Sid Katz in the make-up room.

"What're you doing here?" I asked.

"I'm a guest panellist," he told me.

I was flabbergasted. "What about the rules?" I asked him. "Lever Brothers doesn't advertise in *Maclean's*."

"Oh, *those* rules," said Sidney. "They changed those rules some time ago."

Chapter Six

1

Like the previous year, 1958 marked another turning point for me. We were approaching the end of the smuggest decade of my time – the fifties – and were about to enter the swinging sixties. The trivia of those times are largely forgotten. Who remembers the Purple People Eater or the Witch Doctor mumbo-jumbo *(ding-dang, wallah-wallah, bing-bang)*? Who dances the cha-cha today? How quickly fads and fashions die. Back in 1958 we said things like "Take me to your leader" and complained about the number of Westerns on TV (now we wish there were more). If you wanted to be thought an intellectual you pretended to read *Dr. Zhivago,* but you also kept a copy of *Lolita,* with the jacket removed, under your pillow. Is it really possible that the great Vladimir Nabokov was once thought of as a pornographer, his best-known work barred from the Toronto Public Library? No wonder the world was sick, sick, sick, to use the phrase of that day. Subliminal TV, Teen Age Monster pictures, tail fins on cars, and the Sack dress (along with the Flounce and the Trapeze) were all extinct by the time the sixties arrived – as dead as Debbie and Eddie's much publicized marriage, as ephemeral as Liz's grief over Mike Todd. Nothing lasted very long in those years of Planned Obsolescence. The country and, indeed, much of the world were about to enter an era when traditional values also would be seen as archaic. I couldn't have begun a newspaper column at a better time.

The *Toronto Star,* when I arrived, was going through a sea change. Under Joseph (Holy Joe) Atkinson and his son-in-law, the formidable H.C. Hindmarsh, it had established itself as the wildest, most brilliant, most infuriating, most readable, most successful, and most biased newspaper in Canada. It covered the world by sheer force of numbers, shooting platoons of reporters off to the scene of a disaster or major crime, even hiring, on one occasion, an entire train to get its reporters' copy back to the desk. There were times when the number of *Star* reporters in the United States equalled or even exceeded the entire staff of the *New York Times.* The paper's expense accounts were as legendary as the men who invented them. The *Star* had made celebrities of Gordon Sinclair and Gregory Clark, both of whom had left it before my arrival. Since the days of Morley Callaghan and Ernest Hemingway, it had been the launching pad for most of the working journalists in the country.

The *Star* made no pretensions to objective journalism, especially where politics was concerned. Left of centre between elections, it became slavishly Liberal after the writ was dropped. That started with Atkinson but reached its peak when Hindmarsh, in an attempt to smear the provincial Tories and their leader, George Drew, during the 1948 Ontario election campaign, had composed the most astonishing headline in journalistic history:

KEEP CANADA BRITISH
DESTROY DREW'S HOUDE
GOD SAVE THE KING

Hindmarsh's blatant attempt to tie the Tories to Camillien Houde, the mayor of Montreal – unpopular in Ontario because of his wartime opposition to conscription and consequent internment – flopped. Nevertheless Drew, who became federal Tory leader, remained the paper's *bête noire*. His party's retroactive legislation had made it impossible for the Atkinson Charitable Foundation, set up as a trust under the founder's will, to continue to own the paper. But Drew's attempt to destroy the *Star*, which he hated with a virulence rare in politics, didn't work.

Beland Honderich, with the help of the younger Joseph Atkinson and members of the Hindmarsh family, easily raised the $25 million necessary to buy the paper, and the foundation became a separate entity. When I arrived at the *Star*'s King Street skyscraper, Holy Joe's son was the paper's titular head, and Honderich, as editor and future publisher, controlled the news side.

I had earlier written a two-part article about the *Star* for *Maclean's* and had heard that young Joe hadn't much liked the profile of his father, although Hindmarsh had liked it well enough to engage me to write his obituary. Thus, it was with a certain trepidation that I entered Atkinson's office on the building's fourth floor.

He told me flatly, but without acrimony, that he did not agree with my assessment of his parent, after which he welcomed me warmly to the paper. Honderich disappeared and we indulged in some small talk. I found Atkinson a quiet, decent man, with none of the flamboyance associated with the newspaper. "It's nice to have you with us," he said, as he reached out to shake my hand on leaving.

"Thank you, Mr. Atkinson," I responded.

"Joe," he said genially. "It's Joe. Everybody calls me Joe."

"Okay, Joe," I said cheerily, just as Honderich returned.

"I'll take him up to the editorial floor, Mr. Atkinson," Honderich said. *Mister?*

In my four years and two months at the *Toronto Star* I would sometimes encounter Atkinson when I entered the sacred precincts of the executive floor. "Hi-ya, Joe!" I would say. But I was the only one in the building, from Honderich down, who called him by his first name.

Honderich was determined to turn the wild and woolly *Star* into a responsible and objective paper. He had hired me as an adviser, and now he actually asked my advice. He desperately needed an editorial page cartoonist. At that time, except for the *Vancouver Sun* (whose publisher, Don Cromie, had hired Len Norris on my recommendation), no paper in the country had a political cartoonist of stature. One of the *Star*'s cartoonists was so inept at drawing the human form that he put all his male figures into bulky overcoats, winter and summer. I had been terrified for years that some smart editor would snatch Duncan Macpherson from *Maclean's*. Now I suggested that the *Star* lure him away. Honderich asked me to approach him, and we met for a drink at the neighbouring Lord Simcoe Hotel. He was interested until I told him the paper wanted to see some samples. Macpherson bridled. Why was he, a professional artist, being asked to audition? Honderich was insisting on a trial week. Duncan said he couldn't work in a vacuum. Finally he agreed and arrived with his drawings a few days later.

I wish now I had preserved the comments of the members of the editorial board, none of whom, it seemed to me, knew much about either draughtsmanship or political humour. Macpherson was a superb artist who could work in any medium, from woodcut to wash, yet here were people scribbling marginal notes saying the themes were witty but it was too bad he couldn't draw, and others announcing that the drawings were okay but the subject matter was weak.

"What am I going to do?" Honderich asked me. "These reports are terribly conflicting."

"You hired me as an adviser," I reminded him. "I'm advising you to grab Macpherson before he gets away." And he did.

Macpherson, of course, went on to become the greatest political cartoonist in North America, his work praised and sometimes plagiarized by his peers. He stunned the country early in his career, when the prime minister ditched the Avro Arrow project, by depicting Diefenbaker as Marie Antoinette, crying, "Let them eat cake!" The cartoon's power

154

was enhanced by Macpherson's meticulous draughtsmanship; a lesser artist could not have pulled it off. That was the beginning, I think, of the country's disillusionment with the Diefenbaker government. Until then scarcely anybody had taken a crack at the prime minister. We have forgotten now the reverence that reflected his stunning victory at the polls. Anything harsh said about him in the long honeymoon that followed would be considered *lèse-majesté*. With a few strokes of his pen Macpherson demolished the image.

The cartoonist was himself a Jekyll-and-Hyde character – a mild-mannered and gentle companion when sober, a raging bull in his cups. Who else could have been rejected for life by the Toronto Press Club not once, but three times? One day, I remember, he told me of his plan for slowly changing the sacrosanct oil portrait of Holy Joe that graced the executive floor. He proposed to creep down in the dark of the night and, bit by bit, change the mouth slowly until a sneer spread across the face of the founder. This admirable jape, which I encouraged, never reached fruition; but one night, after a bout of drinks at the Press Club, he actually stole the sacred portrait and walked down King Street trying to sell it. I don't know which bothered the executives most – that Macpherson had made off with an icon, or that nobody would pay two cents for it.

In February 1959 I took a brief holiday and returned to discover, to my horror, that Macpherson's daily cartoon wasn't in the paper. Ralph Allen had crossed his palm with silver and persuaded him to return to *Maclean's*.

Actually, Macpherson had walked boldly into Honderich's office, proffering a box of cigars.

"Ah," said Bee, "I presume congratulations are in order."

"They are, indeed," said Macpherson.

"Is it a boy or a girl?" Honderich asked.

"Neither, I've quit. Have a cigar!"

Bee explained to me that Duncan (*a*) wanted to draw only three cartoons a week instead of five, and (*b*) wanted to be sent to Castro's Cuba to do some sketches for the paper.

"Why not let him?" I said. "Three Macpherson cartoons a week are better than no Macpherson cartoons. And a couple of his Cuban drawings would be a far greater asset than photographs."

Honderich agreed. I called the lost sheep and returned him to the fold. His brilliant drawings from Cuba, to which the *Star* devoted a full page, were widely praised.

155

Honderich needed a good theatre critic and again asked my advice. I recommended Nathan Cohen, whom I thought the best critic in town. His commentaries were enlivening the CBC and enraging half the actors in Toronto. Somewhat to my surprise, Cohen jumped at the offer I made him and began writing a regular theatre column for the paper. He was, of course, reviled. He was the one critic who told it as he saw it and refused to pull any punches. At that time the acting community thought that the job of a critic was to publicize whatever production was on the boards. Cohen, on the other hand, didn't consider himself a press agent for the theatrical companies. Toronto was beginning to warm to live, locally produced theatre, but Cohen was in no mood to molly-coddle. He saw no reason why Canadian theatre couldn't compete with the best in the world, and if it didn't, he said so. The general feeling among actors was that he wasn't being fair, that he was writing out of a sense of spite, or merely to advance his own ambitions; in fact, he was saddened when a performance didn't meet his expectations. But he would not compromise. Today, he is a legend. Time and again his name is invoked as one of the giants in the business. It was not always thus.

In addition to Cohen and Macpherson, Honderich enticed two other regular columnists – Ron Haggart of the *Globe,* who was soon writing the best city hall column in town, and Robert Fulford, who launched a daily book column, a task that often required him to read and report on five books a week. He performed it with a clarity of style uncommon to the genre. Today most newspaper commentators write no more than two or three columns a week, each only eight hundred words in length. But Cohen, Haggart, Fulford, and I wrote twelve hundred words every day. I often wonder how we did it.

As if that weren't enough, I joined radio station CHUM that fall to write and read not one but eleven capsule comments every weekday, a total of fifty-five a week, each about a minute in length. I was paid $125 a week and again didn't haggle. I realize now that I could have been, and should have been, better paid. But in those days, in spite of a rep-utation for immodesty, I was still uncertain of my strengths. Could I pull it off? CHUM made it as easy as possible by lending me a tape recorder on which I voiced my comments each evening. The tape went into our mailbox at the end of the driveway and was picked up by a CHUM car before dawn. By the time I rose to work on my column, I was already being heard on the air.

I don't quite know how I accomplished all this. For the *Star* alone I was writing close to 300,000 words a year, far more than I had put into *Klondike,* which was published that fall. In my time at the *Star* I knocked out a million and a quarter words – enough for six *Klondike*s. And, of course, there was the usual author's publicity tour to work into a crowded schedule. The long drive to town and back still helped, even though the new four-lane highways were cutting the time by at least fifteen minutes. Nevertheless I was able to compose many of my columns in my head during these intervals, as well as to think up capsule comments for radio.

Thanks to all this activity my income was three times what it had been at *Maclean's,* which meant we could again afford to enlarge our house at Kleinburg. By this time we had both become fanatical gardeners and landscape nuts. (I handled the flowers, Janet the vegetables.) The land, which had been as bald as the tundra when we acquired it, was now sprouting young trees and shrubs, many of which we found we had put in the wrong places. I moved them about, using a shovel and a wheelbarrow, and planted more each spring and fall, supporting a local nursery almost single-handed, or so it seemed to me. Landscape architecture is the only four-dimensional art we have; it moves through time as well as through space. I tried to envisage how the property would look in ten, twenty, thirty years. A painting is flat and unchanging, and even a piece of sculpture, though you can view it from every angle, is static. But a garden moves with time. It is never the same from day to day, from season to season, from year to year. Its very impermanence conspires against its enshrinement. You cannot hang a garden in a picture gallery – even capture it properly in a photograph – and only a few famous gardeners are honoured in legend and gardens of the past preserved.

The work taught Janet and me the value of patience. Many people I knew insisted on buying big, expensive trees and monstrous shrubs for instant effect. We bought little ones and watched them grow over the years. Sometimes, in a burst of enthusiasm, we planted them too close together, and I was forced to rip out every other golden philadelphus or Eva Rathke weigela and replant them elsewhere. We had plenty of space thanks to the owners of the two adjoining lots, who had thought better of their initial enthusiasm. We obliged them by purchasing both properties on the instalment plan. We now had nine acres to look after, and were, in the best sense of the phrase, property poor.

157

2

Beholden My first column purported to be a memorandum of agreement between
to nobody myself and the editor. It was, of course, entirely spurious, since
Honderich and I had concluded our business with nothing more than a
handshake. But many readers, including some journalists, believe to
this day that I had an iron-clad contract with the paper unlike any other.

Why anyone took this so-called contract seriously is beyond me. It
contained such clauses as:

1. The Columnist's opinions shall be his own and not those
   of the Editor or the Editor's wife or the Editor's bridge
   partner. On occasion, the Columnist may even dissent
   from the published opinion of the Editor. At such times
   the Editor will refrain from punching the Columnist in the
   nose, at least during office hours.
2. The Editor shall not censor the Columnist's work even
   when it appears to him to be excessively foolish.... Should
   the Columnist be so lacking in convention that he runs
   counter to the cherished views of the directors of this
   newspaper (or their wives or bridge partners), the Editor
   will merely grit his teeth and stare glumly out of the window. Should the Columnist be so heretical as to raise his
   tiny voice against Certain Interests who are also advertisers (such as the Quislings who push "instant" coffee or
   the brigands who manufacture bread that tastes like library
   paste) the Editor will grin and bear it.

The so-called agreement also promised that the Columnist would
not make fun of his wife and family in his column and that he would
not interview talking animals, real or fancied, or "render into quotations
the alleged words of any animal." This last clause was an unnecessarily bitchy reference to the column of one of my predecessors, Dennis
Braithwaite, who appeared to own a talking cat that he quoted period-
ically. Braithwaite moved to the *Globe* to become a television columnist,
where he quickly got his own back.

I was given an office, but for the first week I could not use it. I was
forced to work at home and send my column in by courier because I

158

had developed a bad case of the mumps (in my neck glands, fortunately). In the Yukon we had all been spared most childhood diseases, from chicken pox to measles. The major ailments there were flu and pneumonia, perhaps because (so it was claimed) it was too cold for any other kind of microbe. Now my photograph was appearing in the paper with my neck looking like a balloon; hailed as the *Star's* hot new columnist, I was apparently badly malformed. I suppose I could have held off for a week until the swelling subsided and I could show my face in the newsroom, but that didn't occur to me. My column had been trumpeted to begin on September 16, and I had no intention of stalling. Janet would gather up the three youngest kids (she was nursing baby Paul at the time) and drive me to the *Star* building. I skulked in the car, averting my swollen face from passersby while she took the column up to the editorial floor. On one of these forays the car broke down on the highway. We sat there while Janet fed the baby. Then she set off on foot down the road, leaving the invalid columnist to guard the children until she located a garage.

On joining the paper, I had asked Honderich what the taboos were. There were but two: you couldn't mention liquor by brand name, in deference to the ghost of Holy Joe, and Honderich reserved the right to kill a column if he thought it was in bad taste. That meant, really, that he could kill any column he chose to, but he used that privilege sparingly. Once he killed a column of mine supporting some striking workers and attacking the scabs who had been hired to replace them. Honderich, who was facing a strike at the paper and was planning to import strikebreakers to keep the *Star* publishing, invoked the bad-taste clause. Another time I took issue with a *Maclean's* article that claimed all prostitutes were unhappy. I found a happy prostitute and wrote about her, but Honderich said that was in bad taste, too. No other paper in Canada was quite so strait-laced.

On one memorable occasion during a federal election, I tried to present a slate of Greater Toronto candidates from all three parties – men and women I thought would adorn the House no matter what their affiliations. I did considerable research on this project, even sending out a questionnaire on matters of public interest to see where each one stood. Since our editorial board regularly presented *Star* readers with its own political slate for city council, I saw no reason why I shouldn't use the same technique for federal MPs. Honderich would have none of it. He said I wasn't equipped to know enough about each candidate. A party, yes; an individual candidate, no. I suspect his reasoning was clouded by the painful knowledge that one of the candidates I supported was John Bassett, the publisher of the rival *Telegram,* who was running as a Tory. I thought the ebullient and often maverick Bassett would be an ornament to any parliament.

I scrapped that column and wrote one titled "Why I intend to vote for the NDP." Having already said I could support a political party, Bee could scarcely kill that one. The NDP, without my permission, immediately published it in a pamphlet. Apparently my piece helped split the vote in Eglinton, where Mitchell Sharp, the Liberal standard bearer, went down to defeat at the hands of the Tories. Keith Davey, the Liberal trouble-shooter, credited my column with Sharp's loss. On the rare occasion when I encountered Sharp, he always referred to me as "my socialist friend."

The liquor taboo rarely bothered me because I was able to revert to some subterfuge. Once I wanted to refer to "a case of Mumm's." I put *mumm's* in lower case, and just before the presses rolled went to the composing room and had an upper case "M" substituted. Nobody on the desk seemed to know the difference.

One of the clauses in the fictitious contract, to which I clung like a small boy to his pet puppy, advised:

> 4. The Columnist will be beholden to nobody. He will accept no gifts of any kind, be they vicuna coats or bottles of cheap booze. He will accept no free trips to luxury hotels in the Caribbean, no free junkets to Europe, no free enter-tainment of any kind, no matter how exotic, except in those instances where a large section of the press corps has also been invited and no special privilege is indicated.

I think now that I was unnecessarily rigid and more than a little pre-tentious in my strict adherence to this principle. Once, I recall, the female clerks in one of the departments at Simpson's sent me a box of chocolates as a kind of thank-you for something I'd written. I am ashamed to admit that I sent the candy back. Were they trying to bribe me? Of course not, and it was an insult to suggest it in this clumsy way.

On the other hand, there was the instance of Oscar Berceller, the much-publicized owner of the tony Winston's restaurant. I didn't care

160

much for Berceller; any man who serves caviar on steak has taken surf and turf to impossible extremes. Nor did I like the snobbism of Winston's famous key, provided to special customers to allow them entrance to the hallowed dining room, safe from the keyless rabble on the outside. One day, on a CHUM broadcast, I had taken a mild crack at the wife of Hans Freed who had made some public statement about the province's liquor policy that I thought in bad taste. Freed was another successful restaurateur and Berceller's hated rival. Berceller sent a thank-you note to my home, congratulating me on taking Freed's wife to task. When I opened the envelope, five crumpled and rather dirty twenty-dollar bills tumbled out.

This clumsy bit of payola got under my skin. I thought I had long since established my independence from advertisers, restaurateurs, public relations men, and politicians. Berceller obviously thought I could be bought, and that was a blow to my pride. If he believed it of me, he must think all newspaper writers were venal. Worse, he might have had experiences that suggested some were.

I was in a quandary. If I wrote a column on the subject it could be seen as an attack on my profession. Yet I couldn't let Berceller get away with this blatant attempt at baksheesh. I called Beland, told him what had happened, and asked his advice. "Write the column," he said, and I did, in the form of an open letter to Berceller, which included these comments:

"... To what depths has the noble calling of journalism sunk when the town's leading restaurateur blandly assumes that a columnist – any columnist – will cheerfully pocket $100 in cash?

"... you have been in the restaurant business for many years. Is it possible I am the first to be favoured in this manner? Am I, above all others, past and present, chosen as the One Most Likely to Accept? If so, it is a heavy blow to my pride...."

These words produced a tidal wave of rage from my colleagues, who thought it pretentious of me to make a public issue of Berceller's foibles (several told me that they had been on the receiving end of his largesse but had always sent it back without making it public). It brought an equal wave of anger from the upper levels of the cultural community who ate at Winston's. Berceller's restaurant wasn't far from the Royal Alexandra Theatre, and he had made a good thing of reproducing on certain tables the autographs of theatrical luminaries, local and international, in return for free or discounted meals. One society matron wrote me a scathing letter about my attack on this patron of the arts. He was merely offering me a little tip, she explained; what was wrong with that? The whole episode left me feeling humiliated.

When I first broached the idea of a column to Honderich I had no idea what kind of column I would write. I was terrified that I wouldn't have enough ideas to fill my space five times a week. What would happen if I ran out of juice? During my whole stint as a *Star* columnist this problem haunted me, which explains why I always kept at least three columns ahead of the game against the day when I would dry up. But that never happened, largely because the column itself was self-perpetuating. People wrote in with ideas, tips, and experiences of their own, which I put into print. I began to refer to these correspondents as "Operatives," thus creating the impression that I had a formidable staff of researchers at my beck and call.

I doubt that I could have written a successful daily column had it not been for two influences. The first was my close friend Jack Scott, who wrote the best column in Canada for the *Vancouver Sun*. We had worked together in the early days when he was managing editor of the *News-Herald* and I was city editor. His column, "Our Town," was a model of graceful writing, wit, and trenchant opinions. My second influence, of course, was *Maclean's*. I remembered how we struggled over our editorial menu – a piece of punditry here, a profile there – to create a lively mix of human interest, humour, popular history, and even fashion. I organized a week of columns on a similar principle – a strong opinion piece followed by a bit of satire, then an exposé of crooked car dealers or TV repairmen, and then a look at the changing city – a drive through the new suburbs, maybe – or a prose poem about a ride in the country. I wanted to achieve a sense of surprise, to put my readers off balance, so that they would be asking what that son-of-a-bitch was going to do next. That was the Gordon Sinclair formula for *Front Page Challenge*. From time to time I published satirical verse, drew cartoons, even published photographs and drawings. Once, I was able to get the plans for a million-dollar trade centre, which the Toronto Harbour Commissioners had hailed as brilliant and original. I published them to show graphically that they had been snitched from various British architectural trade journals without a change.

I began at a propitious time in Toronto's development. My own

162

pieces, which were, in effect, miniature magazine articles, reflected the social revolution that was under way when I arrived at the *Star*. The old WASP mix was being turned topsy-turvy. I spent a week in the new Italian district and wrote a series about these immigrants who were changing the face of the community. The Yorkville area had become a hippie haven, and I wrote several articles about the new coffee-houses and the folkniks, as they were called. I even recited poetry and sang satirical songs at the iconoclastic Inn on the Parking Lot. I applauded the opening of the first shop in town devoted entirely to cheese. Is it possible that there was a time when you couldn't buy a wedge of Port Salut or Brie in that meat-and-potatoes city? And I heralded the opening of the Fujimatsu restaurant on Elm Street – the first time Torontonians were introduced to sukiyaki. But the old morality died hard. The Fujimatsu had to close because the Liquor Licensing Board wouldn't allow it to serve sake – a devil's brew in their minds, no doubt – while handing out licences to Yonge Street bars no more than a block away that catered blatantly to prostitutes and their customers.

Nothing, however, reflected the change in Toronto more than the public's attitude to its city hall. The city needed a new one, and the press enthusiastically published pictures of a proposed plan. It looked like a gigantic version of the Royal York Hotel, and the ratepayers, to their credit, turned it down flat. The new mayor, Nathan Phillips, significantly the first Jew to hold the position of chief magistrate, then launched an architectural contest to adopt a new design. Four of the five judges split evenly and the winner was decided by the vote of the fifth, my friend Ned Pratt, a Vancouver architect whom I had once hailed in *Maclean's* as the New Elizabethan. Pratt, who had an eye for beauty in both women and public buildings, chose the sinuous curves designed by Vilju Revell, a noted Finnish architect, because, he said, his design was the sexiest among the finalists. The results were announced only a few days after I launched my column in the *Star*. To my astonishment, nobody had bothered to call Frank Lloyd Wright in New York for his opinion. I took it upon myself to redress that oversight.

3

NEW YORK, September 28, 1958. He is waiting for me as I enter his suite in the venerable Plaza Hotel, where the walls are of gold and old rose and the scent of incense sweetens the air. There he stands, an erect, towering figure in an ill-fitting blue serge suit and a floppy tie of sky blue, his white hair framing his pink cherub's face in a sort of halo. It is hard to realize he is eighty-nine and still at it.

I have with me a set of photographs showing the designs of the eight finalists in our city hall contest. I spread them across his desk and he groans aloud, muttering such phrases as "brazen effrontery," "totally lacking in imagination," and "really fantastic." He sweeps them into a heap and turns to me with a look of mild exasperation.

"Why," says Frank Lloyd Wright, "these are all nineteenth century. There isn't a twentieth-century building in the bunch. They're all tarred with the same stick – the cliché of the International Style. That's what you get for holding a competition." He speaks with the air of a man who's saying I told you so. "No self-respecting architect would enter it."

I remark that one very famous architect, Walter Gropius, had entered.

"That old rascal!" says Wright. "He's done more harm to North American architecture than any of them."

I show him the winning design and the Greatest Architect in the World groans aloud once more.

"Oh no! Do you know what this will do? This will advertise to posterity that Toronto is without a soul and knows no better than to follow the blind leader of a stupid fashion that is already badly overworked. He's used no feature except the box.

"Every graveyard, if it could speak, would say 'amen' to the slab. Well, that's what this building says for Toronto. You've got a head marker for a grave, and future generations will look at it and say, 'This marks the spot where Toronto fell…'"

I tell him the man on the street seems to like the design.

"If the man on the street is going to get what he likes then goodbye to any future for us," says Wright. "He's what you call the Common Man, isn't he? Well, he's without vision, and that's what makes him common. In our country he's beginning to dislike the thought of the uncommon man. He's trying to make the uncommon man unconstitutional, and he's pretty well succeeded in doing it.

"What the common man likes is size: imposing mass. It's what he calls 'monumental,' but a truly monumental building is organic – it springs out of nature. It's what is inside that counts. A building ought to be built and designed from the inside. That's how you're built. That's how a tree is built. That's nature's principle, and in this century we can do it because we've got structural steel.

"The trouble is that man was seduced by the lumberyards in the eighteenth century, and he never understood the nature of steel. So they rolled the steel into lumber for him, and he's been using it like lumber ever since, building boxes."

On and on he goes as I scribble away. Everything he says is, as usual, quotable: "A tall building is really only an upended street, invented by Otis, the elevator man. It dumps its human freight at its foot every morning, noon, and night, causing an unholy traffic congestion."

I show him the design the ratepayers rejected. "Really, it's the same building you're getting now, but in more modest terms," he says. "The soul of man has said nothing more in the new building than in this old one. And the new one is really worse, because it represents such a betrayal – such a waste – of opportunity."

My God, I think, he's telling me that the new design for Toronto's city hall isn't too radical – it's too conservative!

"Well," he says sadly, "I guess I've insulted Toronto and I've insulted this young architect. But I've always said what I thought." He shows me blueprints of the new Guggenheim Museum, which he calls "the first twentieth-century building in New York."

"Have you seen my new museum?" he asks. I tell him I've spotted it from the taxi driving down Park Avenue.

"You must see it," he says, and he produces a card on which he writes: "Please show this young man around my museum. Frank Lloyd Wright."

I bid him goodbye, and as he walks me toward the door of his oddly old-fashioned suite he says, "People ask me the secret of my long life, but there's no secret. I love my work. I love my wife. And I always tell the truth," which is what he has been doing, after his fashion.

I head for the airport with a stop at the half-finished Guggenheim, its awesome bulk silhouetted against the brownstones of Park Avenue. There is no work on Sunday, so I approach a caretaker seated by a fire in a small hut, and tell him I want to see over the museum. He tells me that is forbidden.

165

"Ah," I tell him importantly. "But you see, I have written permission from the architect himself, Mr. Frank Lloyd Wright."

"That old man?" the caretaker says. "He's always sending people up here to look at 'his' museum, as he calls it. Well, I never let any of them in."

4

If Toronto was changing, so was Canada, but not fast enough, in my view. I did my best to hurry it along. It is hard to believe now that mental defectives in Kingston Penitentiary in 1958 were stripped, tied down, and beaten black and blue with a perforated leather strap known euphemistically as the Paddle. This sadism was not only legal and approved by the authorities but it was even reported in the press without an outcry. After I revealed the details in a column, this instrument of torture was finally banned.

It is even harder, looking back, to realize that there was a statute on the books that allowed this country to hang children. Indeed, we actually sentenced one to hang – a fourteen-year-old named Stephen Truscott, found guilty of the sex murder of a young girl. I had no idea whether or not the verdict was just; what sickened me was that he had been told in open court that he would hang by the neck until he was dead. The fact that the authorities had no intention of carrying out this grisly sentence made it worse. They didn't intend to kill him, only to torture him by pretending. In a black fury I rapped out a bitter piece of verse:

> *It's true enough*
> *That we cannot brag*
> *Of a national anthem*
> *Or national flag*
> *Although our Vision*
> *Is still in doubt*
> *At last we've something*
> *To boast about;*
> *We've a national law*
> *In the name of the Queen*
> *To hang a child*
> *Who is just fourteen.*

166

The full poem, which took up an entire column, touched off the most violent reaction I'd yet known. The mayor of Goderich, where the boy was sentenced, phoned about the affront, as he called it, to his city. One caller said she hoped my daughter would be raped by a sex fiend. Another wrote that the boy should be whipped before he died. And I had besmirched the queen's name! – dragged it through the mud! I was accused of "coddling sex fiends." Mothers of small children phoned in tears. One of them shouted over the phone that the Bible called for an eye for an eye, ignoring the precepts of the New Testament.

My columns attacking the teaching of main-street Protestant religious tenets in the schools brought another wave of protest. It did not seem to bother some people that an eight-year-old child attending Fallsview Public School in the Niagara District had been given a long row of black marks – the longest in the class – because, during the compulsory (i.e., Protestant Christian) instruction period, she admitted that she had not attended Sunday school the previous day. Her parents were Unitarians. I documented scores of similar cases in Ontario.

The country was slowly emerging from its nineteenth-century shell, but it had a long way to go. I was appalled to find, for instance, that it was against the law to discuss or comment on birth control on the air without first submitting the script to the Board of Broadcast Governors. I learned that only after discovering that none of my various radio comments on this subject had been used because it wasn't possible to send them to Ottawa in advance. Here I was, talking about the population explosion or about a recent court case in which a man was fined for distributing birth-control information; here I was, predicting that the Roman Catholic Church would have to change its inflexible stand on the subject, pointing out that large numbers of Catholics were already disobeying their priests by going beyond the rhythm method; protesting that our Northern native population was ill-equipped to shoulder the burden of large families – only to find that these comments were never aired. In fact, CHUM radio had specifically been warned by the BBG that my scripts, especially, must be carefully vetted.

Any discussion, mention, report of, or expression of opinion about venereal disease was also subject to BBG approval. The press was not hemmed in by this kind of control and could say what it wished. Why not radio? "The answer," I wrote in my column, "is that the people who frame the broadcasting regulations in this country are scared to death of Quebec and the Roman Catholic church. For this is where the opposition comes from and there is no use shutting our eyes to it. This is censorship and there's no other word for it."

Soon I was getting an average of 180 letters each week, some adulatory, some carping, some infuriated. Not long after I joined the paper I was given a secretary – a man of great reticence, extreme efficiency, and retiring habit. His name was Lee Rathlou, and I had no idea how old he was. His mien was deferential. He called me "sir," which embarrassed me. When, on occasion, I asked him to do something out of the ordinary, he looked worried. I once sent him to a used-car lot to see if the advertised prices were the same as the real ones. When he returned, I realized, with some remorse, that it had been a torture to him. He was certainly timid when people telephoned me in moments of high emotion. He would come into the office with a worried look: "I'm afraid there's a rather angry gentleman on the phone, sir. He seems to be in quite a state, and I just can't reason with him."

He liked, he said, to take his holidays in the winter and planned to go down to Mexico.

"First trip?"

"Well, no sir, I've been down before." And then, a little hesitantly, "I take movies."

He added, apologetically, that he hoped to get them on TV.

"Well, well," I said expansively. "I know a few people in TV. Maybe I can help you get your films shown" (I thought, perhaps, an interview with Joyce Davidson on *Tabloid,* and a few feet of "My Trip to Mexico").

He looked embarrassed. "Thank you very much, but I'm afraid I've already signed up with the ABC network."

I gulped.

"They used the last footage as a half hour on *Bold Journey.* It was done mainly in the jungles of Yucatan. Of course, I can't be sure to get another like it. The natives aren't too friendly sometimes."

Off he went on his holiday, leaving me without a riposte. And back he came three weeks later, tanned almost black, his hair shaved to his scalp. I was anxious to know how he made out.

"Not so good, I'm afraid," he said sadly. "I mean, it was all right at first. We did get in to see the native puberty ceremony, which was quite interesting, and, of course, no white man had seen it before. But when they started throwing those stones and poison darts, well, I just had to

168

stop shooting. There's just no holding those people when they drink that brew of theirs."

"How many of you were there?" I asked.

"How many? Oh, you mean white. Oh, just myself. I had native carriers along, of course."

The phone rang, and the worried look appeared on his face, for I had written a controversial column the previous day.

Later I went off to Mexico with Janet, and on my return mentioned to Lee that I'd visited the museum in Mexico City.

"How fortunate," he said. "You know, I've never had the opportunity."

"Too bad," I said – glad to be one up on him. "They've got a copy of a tomb there that's really worth seeing."

"Oh, you mean the mortuary crypt from Palenque," he said. "No, I haven't seen the copy. The original is very fine, though. I saw it in the jungle just after it was discovered."

He didn't stay with me much longer. The angry phone calls were too much for him. He told me he intended to make a career of taking movies in the remote jungles of Yucatan.

The last letter he sent brought me up to date.

"I'm just out of the jungle after thirteen of the most interesting days I've ever known, and I'm unstoned, though the people of Tusic got a little belligerent again. I gather some of them believed that I had arrived in fulfillment of a prophecy in their sacred book. In a couple of days I'm off to Tehuantepec, where the Amazon-like women rule their menfolk, and around the middle of March hope to head into the Chiapas jungle to photograph another group of Lacandón Indians. Can't say I'm missing the Toronto winter..."

Or the angry phone calls either, I thought.

I advertised for a replacement, received thirty replies, and interviewed them all, deciding at last on a tall woman of considerable experience named Ennis Halliday.

"I should tell you," she said, "that I'm thirty-nine. Maybe that's too old."

"Nothing wrong with being thirty-nine," I told her. "I'm thirty-nine."

She remained with me for almost a quarter of a century until her retirement, as I moved from job to job. She had all the right qualifications: a fast typing speed, an efficient executive ability, and she looked after me like a sister. She kept her lip buttoned at all times, refusing to be interviewed about my work; nor did she tell her friends whom she worked for. Several of my colleagues tried to spirit her away, but she resisted those temptations. Nothing fazed her. I did not realize until years later that when she went to work for me her first marriage was breaking up and she was plunging into a soul-searing divorce. She didn't give a hint of that as she went about her duties, and I didn't cotton on – a tribute to her own grace under pressure and a comment on my myopia.

And she didn't turn a hair when the angry phone calls poured in. I suspect she rather enjoyed them. No doubt they were to her what the people of Tusic were to Lee Rathlou.

I also persuaded the paper to let me have a part-time research assistant, who later worked full time. Her name was Marilyn Craig, and she had several strengths. One was a dogged determination to get to the heart of whatever investigation I assigned to her. Another was a chameleon-like ability to look dowdy one day and glamorous the next. A third was her unshakeable belief in the cupidity of almost everybody; she was convinced that the entire world was populated by crooks and con men, a useful attitude for any investigative reporter. I sent her to the Arthur Murray Dance Studio and told her to step all over the instructor's feet. He insisted she had the makings of a ballerina and tried to sign her to a lifetime contract. I printed his patter verbatim. When a vacuum cleaner company offered a machine for twenty dollars – the old bait-and-switch ploy – I told her to insist on buying the cheapie. Before she was through, the salesman was down on his knees pleading with her not to take it; he'd lose his job, he said. Door-to-door magazine peddlers, crooked TV repairmen, dishonest used-car salesmen, sewing-machine fakers – all these met their match when Marilyn played the role of an innocent housewife. Innocent? She was about as innocent as the Boston Strangler. She looked the perfect mark as she pretended to swallow the bait. Only when they read my column did they realize she was on to them. Partly as a result of this investigative barrage, the province changed the law at last, giving the suckers forty-eight hours to reconsider what had been, to that time, an iron-clad contract.

Marilyn had been brought up in the right atmosphere; her father was a longtime and well-loved magistrate in Chatham, Ontario. She herself soon built up a network of informants, ranging from the Better Business Bureau to the Fraud Squad of the Ontario Provincial Police, who once tried to hire her. She had no qualms about walking boldly into the library of the rival *Telegram* to check their files. The man in charge simply assumed that she worked for that paper.

Without her I could not have published this kind of exposé, since I was too well known to make the rounds myself; my newfound celebrity worked against me. Marilyn proved her worth when we exposed, in a memorable series of columns, suspicious land deals in York Township. This led to a royal commission and the defeat at the polls of the reeve, Chris Tonks, who we showed was working hand in hand with the developers. (His son, Allan, later became supermayor of Metro Toronto.) Later we went after the Mimico council for another highly suspicious series of land deals. That forced a judicial inquiry and the humiliation of the building inspector. "We will meet Mr. Berton in court," his lawyers declared after I pointed out that this public official had been able to build an $18,000 home, buy property, own a summer cottage, drive a late-model car, support five children, and visit Florida with his real estate friends – all on a salary of $4,500 a year. He did not see me in court; instead, the court sent him to the penitentiary.

During my time at the *Star,* I received four libel notices, each for a million dollars. When the first landed on my desk, I turned pale. *A million dollars! Migawd – these people mean business!* I felt my stomach heave as I contemplated bankruptcy. Enter the *Star*'s lawyer, Alex MacIntosh, a tough, stocky libel expert. He strode into my office, took the libel notice from my trembling hands, glanced at it, crumpled it, and tossed it into the wastebasket. I felt a little better.

I soon learned that people who threatened court action did so because it gave them an excuse when inquiring friends asked about the dreadful things I was saying. None of these suits ever came to an examination for discovery. In fact, one pair of mortgage sharks who claimed to be suing me left the country when I revealed how they were milking widows and other innocents with unconscionable mortgage rates. MacIntosh dealt summarily with them all. He was that rarity in the newspaper business, a good libel lawyer. So many find it easier to say, "Don't print it!" MacIntosh, however, after he vetted my column, sometimes told me I could be even tougher. Thus, when he did say not to publish a piece he considered actionable, I believed him. Honderich, of course, wanted to make him managing editor; he refused but did become director of the parent company, Torstar.

One man who went to jail because of a column was the feared Mafia enforcer in Hamilton, Johnny Papalia, known as "Johnny Pops." It began when I noticed a two-inch item, buried in the back of the paper, reporting that a Max Bluestein had suffered a bad beating in the Town Tavern on Yonge Street. The press made it sound like a drunken brawl, but a few days later I received a call from Bluestein asking to see me. I went straight to his home in Forest Hill and found a man with a face like raw meat who had been beaten almost to death by hoodlums swinging iron bars. And all this in front of a hundred people!

The Town Tavern was a well-known hangout for gangsters but in spite of that had no trouble getting a liquor licence, unlike the Japanese restaurant a few blocks away. Bluestein, a.k.a. Maxie Baker, was a gambler who controlled the Toronto territory. The Hamilton Mafia was determined to muscle in and when Bluestein stood up to them decided to teach him a lesson. Bluestein was clearly apprehensive when I talked to him. He wouldn't let me photograph his battered features, wouldn't even use the term "Mafia," but his description of the incident was crystal clear.

I went at once to the Town, whose employees did their best to avoid me and kept insisting they had seen nothing. All were terrified. The beating had taken place a few steps from the hat-check concession, but the hat-check girl turned pale and literally shook with fear when I approached her. She had seen nothing. Freddie Black, a prominent football player who was also present, had seen nothing. *Nobody* had seen anything. I described it in my column as perhaps the greatest case of mass blindness in medical history, worthy of a learned article in the *Lancet*.

This column produced a public outcry. The revelation that organized crime was gaining a toehold in Toronto aroused the citizenry. The police, who had done nothing about the events at the Town, were goaded into action and organized a special "Bluestein squad" to bring the attackers to justice. In the end, Papalia and two others were charged, found guilty, and sent to Kingston Penitentiary for brief terms. Once released, they resumed their activities in Hamilton. Bluestein never recovered from the attack. He suffered physically and mentally for the rest of his life. He survived an attempt to bomb his car but later shot and killed his best friend and business partner, Leonard Stillman, in the paranoid belief that Stillman was trying to murder him. He was found not guilty by reason of insanity and was committed to the Clarke Institute of Psychiatry on a lieutenant-governor's warrant that was later eased to allow him to spend some time at home. At the age of seventy-two he was found dead in his own garage.

There is an odd coda to this tale. In 1994 I was invited to speak to the Real Estate Board of Metro Toronto. The man who introduced me, a member of the executive, sat next to me at the head table. He remarked that he had been fifteen years old the last time he met me.

"Where was that?" I asked.

"At home," he said.

I had forgotten his name, so I looked at the tag on his lapel. It read: "Ron Bluestein."

"You were the only man my father would talk to that time," he said. "He told me you were the only one he trusted."

It was these tough columns for which I was best known, but they were not my favourites. I preferred to write about the Ontario countryside in October, to spoof the crassest programs on television, to write nostalgically about the popular culture of the past, to publish profiles of people who typified my times, such as Harvey Kurtzman, the editor of *Mad*, or Hugh Hefner of *Playboy*.

It was a relief to be able to do and say what I wanted and to join, or even help found, a series of organizations that at *Maclean's* would have been outside the rules. I appeared on the stage of Massey Hall as a member of the Committee of Concern for South Africa. I helped reorganize the moribund Canadian Civil Liberties Association. As a result, Al Borovoy of the Labour Committee on Human Rights, who had worked with me to expose those summer resorts that discriminated against Jews and blacks, became general counsel, a post he still holds. I wrote about Harold King, the furniture auctioneer whose home had become a private halfway house for convicts released from prison. With others, I helped found the Harold King Farm at Keswick, where he and his wife became surrogate parents to scores of released convicts. And I publicized and helped raise money for Dr. Norman Z. Alcock, the nuclear scientist who had quit his job to found the Canadian Peace Research Institute.

All these were worthy causes. They were also controversial. My columns on the dreadful conditions in Canadian prisons had connected me with Harold King, but they brought a chorus of protests that we were "coddling criminals." My support of the Peace Research Institute caused some readers to label me a Communist; the Reds had corrupted

173

the word "peace." One writer even suggested that the institute's initials, CPRI, had a communist taint, because Lenin had once lived on the Isle of Capri! The Red Menace had made the whole country paranoid. As for my revelations of discrimination in Ontario resorts, they brought howls from resort owners in Muskoka and Haliburton, who claimed my column had ruined their business.

But the column that produced the greatest reaction – and all of it positive – came from a piece that I had written in desperation. Unable to come up with a single bright idea, I copped out and wrote a rueful essay about my vain attempts to make Big Money in my spare time raising Siamese cats. Alas, my purebred female refused to co-operate, preferring to carry on with the disreputable alley cats down the road and producing quantities of cute, but worthless, mongrel felines. I despised myself for knocking out this trivial bit, but I brightened up when the mail and phone calls arrived. I had been devoting a good deal of time and space that month trying to make sense for my readers of a series of mortgage scams, but nobody wrote in to praise me for this fine example of investigative journalism. It was my sad tale of the wayward Siamese that got the kudos.

5

"Must the dog watch television?" With the column well launched, I now entered a new and mysterious realm – that of children's fiction. I had already written a history for twelve-year-olds; now I decided to write for a younger age group, the one to which most of my own children belonged. This was *The Secret World of Og,* my favourite of all my books and by all odds my most successful.

At the time I knew nothing about the curious business of publishing books for small children. I did not realize, for instance, that such books were really written not for kids but for librarians and were often edited by spinsters who had no children of their own. I had five by 1960 and was convinced that I knew what they liked to read. I also thought I knew what fathers liked to read, and it certainly wasn't pallid little tales about goody-goody moppets named Dick and Jane, or their dreadful cat, Puff. Children like crazy things. They like mystery. They like to be scared a bit – but not too much. They like jokes. And, above all, they like stories

174

about real children with whom they can identify, and who do real things, such as reading comics or watching TV.

I was soon to discover that the women who were running the libraries and the children's departments of the publishing houses in those days were dead set against this kind of book. Children's literature was a mare's nest of taboos. At Boys and Girls House, a division of the Toronto Public Library, I found to my dismay that *The Wizard of Oz* was kept under the counter, like a pornographic novel, because it was part of a series, and "series books" were a no-no. The same was true of *Anne of Green Gables.*

The Secret World of Og, which stars five of my children by name and temperament, is about role playing or, to use the children's term, "dress up." Everybody in it plays "let's pretend." They also read series books. Penny, the eldest, has read dozens of books in the Lucy Lawless series and models herself on her heroine. Her sister Pamela dotes on comic books: the *Mad Monster* is her favourite. And all five watch television, as does the dog, Yukon King, who identifies himself with a dog of the same name in a Northern adventure serial. All that was anathema to the librarians who bought 85 percent of the children's books published. Since children didn't buy books, they didn't count.

I was convinced that this Establishment was engaged in a vast conspiracy to take the guts out of juveniles. Grimms' fairy tales could not have been launched at the time I wrote *The Secret World of Og,* nor could *Alice in Wonderland.* In addition, writers were discouraged from making adult comments in a book for children.

I didn't know that. One reason I wrote the book was to give fathers a few jokes to enjoy when they read aloud to their kids. I suppose I ought to make the usual disclaimer that this conspiracy to water down juveniles, if it existed, was not entirely effective, and that a good many dedicated librarians, teachers, and publishers deviated from this attitude. But an attempt was clearly being made to protect children from the world around them. How this could be done in the television era I found difficult to understand.

I wrote the book during two vacations in Mexico. The childless woman editor at Knopf gave it a cool reception. She hemmed and hawed a bit and then revealed the problem. "It's this emphasis on comic books, series books, and TV programs," she finally admitted. "That's really not the kind of thing we're trying to show." I was stunned. *Not the kind of thing we're trying to show?* What was she running – a propaganda factory? I talked to Jack McClelland and asked for a second opinion. He told me that a personal friend of his was one of the most experienced and very best children's editors in New York. "I'll send the manuscript to her," he said, "and ask her for a private and honest opinion."

Some of his own people were also squeamish. The baby in the book, who is one year old, hates baby food. I wrote that he liked "gum drops, steak, licorice cigarettes, and Dr. Kleeb's pet food, but he could not stand Pablum." On this one of the editors commented: "This will certainly not endear us to the manufacturers of Pablum and, after all, it is *the* accepted baby food, and we are told infants' taste buds do not develop until they are past the Pablum stage." Ye Gods, I thought, spare me from humourless editors!

Another passage caused trouble. In the book, Pamela was presented as a child with a vivid imagination who sees things nobody else does. "One day during a Social Studies examination, she had looked out the window and seen an old man in the sky looking down at her. The old man had a long white beard and his face was inexpressibly sad. He was the saddest man Pamela had ever seen and she fell to wondering who he was and why he was so sad and whether, up in the sky, he was allowed to drink chocolate milk and other things like that." The key editor thought some people might think this sacrilegious – not the children, but the adults.

Now the distinguished New York editor checked in. She found "a real problem with the manuscript." The reader would be prejudiced by the "utter absorption of the children with comic books, series stories, and melodrama on television.... Is it possible the author is spoofing the attitude of teachers and librarians? If so, it is in very bad taste and, too, very unrealistic, for after all, *this is our main market"* (emphasis mine).

There it was in black and white. "Must the dog have to watch television too?" she asked. She could not recommend the manuscript. "You are sure to have repercussions." But if I would remove the "offensive material," then it was worth consideration. She even offered to mark the passages that must come out: the sections about Penny reading *Lucy Lawless, Girl Pirate,* for one; the section where Pamela laughed uncontrollably at a comic book called *Larry the Ghoul* because it was labelled "comic"; the section that described the baby, Pollywog, as a jelly-bean thief and "a master safecracker with a brain as sharp as a

176

cold chisel"; the section in which Patsy crossed her eyes at old gentlemen who tried to pat her on the head. All this had to come out.

Her memo went on and on, neatly emasculating my manuscript. In the book, young Peter paints himself green in order to spy on the green people who live in the world of Og. *Consternation!* Every boy who read it would want to paint himself green! (I believed that every boy should – at least once in his life.) The baby, confined to playpen or highchair, always contrives to escape and "head for the Mexican border." The female editors who had never seen a Western movie didn't know what to make of that, but the kids who eventually read the book wrote to me that they loved it. That vied with the green paint as the most popular passage.

Of course I ignored all this, and Jack McClelland went along with my refusal to toe the Establishment line. The book was picked up by Little, Brown in the United States and also by a German publisher. The results have been refreshing. *The Secret World of Og,* in its several editions, has sold more than two hundred thousand copies and is still selling. The children who originally read it and loved it now have children of their own reading it. It is a standard work in many schools, and I get more mail about this book than any other, most of it from young children. It's also been made into a three-part animated feature for the American Broadcasting Company. School after school has turned it into a play, a pageant, or a musical. A short time before writing these words, I was invited to a school in Toronto, as I often am, to read from the book, and was greeted at the classroom door by the teacher and a small band of cheering pupils.

To my delight, every last one, including the teacher, had painted their faces green!

Chapter Seven

1

CAIRO, April 20, 1959. We have been sitting around for four days, a CBC crew of four – Daryl Duke, producer, Erik Durschmied and Bob Crone, cameramen, and I – waiting vainly for our promised interview with Colonel Gamal Abdel Nasser for Close-Up. *I have only a week of holidays to devote to this. The government officials have promised faithfully to produce the Egyptian president. They counsel patience, but we are impatient. What if we are forced to return to Canada with no film and a hefty expense account? How will that sound when some backbencher rises in the House with the figures?*

It is not that the Egyptians are unfriendly; far from it. I have an impression from reading Western papers and newsmagazines that they are violently anti-Western. Nasser is represented as a fire-eater, exhorting his people against the English and Americans. I expect the curled lip, the stony glance, the muttered imprecation "Infidel dog!... Yankee butcher!" On the contrary, they seem overjoyed to welcome us. Everywhere a Westerner goes in Cairo he gets courteous, even enthusiastic treatment. This, I begin to realize, is an Egyptian trait.

We can wait no longer; we must bring something back on film. In the brief time at our disposal we decide to do our best to produce a one-hour documentary on Nasserland – without Nasser.

Off we go into the hinterland to film the fellahin in the fields and to interview doctors desperately trying to combat the effects of the dreaded bilharzia, the snail-borne worms that attack the barefoot peasants and sap their energy. We film the Suez Canal, blocked by the wreckage of the Suez War, and we travel to Alexandria, talking to shopkeepers and bureaucrats. "Who is the enemy?" we ask them; unanimously they reply, "Israel." This will be a standard CBC documentary. I'm writing the script as we go along, but I don't much like it: doubtless a worthy effort, yet lacking in pizazz.

Some pizazz is supplied at last by a ragged man in a faded galabia who greets us in the shadow of the Sphinx and boasts that he is "the Champ of the Pyramids." The scene here astonishes me. I had not expected such bedlam. Obviously I have seen too many movies in which the three great piles stand alone like sentinels on the silent desert (Claude Rains and Vivien Leigh as Caesar and Cleopatra). Actually, we're on the outskirts of Cairo, a cheap taxi ride from our hotel, surrounded by throngs of tourists and guides and scores of get-rich-quick Egyptians, offering everything from a camel ride to a piece of pottery. The Champ of the Pyramids is one of these: if we will pay the requisite amount of baksheesh, he promises to scamper all the way to the pinnacle of the Great Pyramid of Khufu and down again – all within seven minutes. Otherwise we don't have to pay.

This is what we've been searching for – a crazy interval in the midst of our otherwise earnest documentary. It will not be easy shooting in the brilliant sun. Bob Crone must climb to the very top and look down on the Champ while Durschmied will try to keep pace with him on his upward climb. I will hold a stopwatch and try to cover the story with a Foster Hewitt-style commentary.

The Champ removes his beat-up galabia to reveal a new T-shirt and pair of pressed shorts of dazzling white. He is wearing expensive running shoes and no fewer than six gold watches on his right arm. I look at his legs, knotted like tree trunks, and have no doubt he'll make it, which he does. Now we have a centrepiece for our documentary.

That night we celebrate. We have been told of a fabulous nightclub beyond the pyramids. At eleven, after the velvet mantle of night has fallen over the desert, we head out for it. This is more like it, I think. This is the Egypt of antiquity – and also of the movies. Ahead of us, a dark mass cuts the rich blue of the sky. The Great Pyramid is silent now. To the left the Sphinx rises mysteriously from the sands.

We veer right, passing the lesser pyramids of Khafre and Menkure, their triangular silhouettes limned against the spangled heavens. At last we are alone with sand and sky, skimming across Giza. From ahead comes the faint sound of restless camels. Another bulk looms up – a tent that would make the Ringling Brothers envious. Hooded figures in white galabias drift by. Six-foot Nubians in brocaded Turkish dress and crimson fezzes slide through the flaps bearing trays of kebabs. Ragged Arab children open the canvas and bid us salaam. Faintly, the sound of music comes to our ears, and we enter the tent, each of us alive to the romance of it all. What are these strange instruments? What is this weird music?

They are saxophones, and they are playing "Deep in the Heart of Texas."

But the belly-dancing is entirely authentic. We order kebabs and drink quantities of arrack, the local drink, flavoured with anise. Two *plumpish Egyptian girls wriggle resolutely and with considerable artistry for forty-five minutes until the sweat rolls down their faces. One bears the delicious name of Titti Mohammed. Later they are joined by two half-naked, seven-foot Watusi, their ebony skins shining in the half-light. The music, now strictly Egyptian, rises to a crescendo, the room whirls about, the arrack flows. The two belly dancers have put on white terry cloth housecoats, and they, the Watusi, and most of the crowd are leaping up and down to the frantic music.*

"How do you like this arrack?" I ask Daryl.

"It's great," he replies. "It isn't like any Western drink. It's more like, well, pop or something. It's had no effect on me."

"Then why," I ask him, "are we dancing on the table?"

2

Black market, Moscow-style A month after Cairo, I found myself aboard a British European Airways inaugural flight to the Soviet Union. A thaw had set in, hence the BEA franchise. Khrushchev was in power; the Cult of Personality was fading. The new leader was highly visible – I saw him twice in the course of a week – but I did not see a single photograph of him in any public place.

A voice on the loudspeaker told us to put away our cameras. We would be landing soon, and because this was a military airport, as were all Soviet airports, taking photographs of any kind was strictly forbidden. Then what was Erik Durschmied doing at the foot of the stairs with his camera on a tripod as we landed? "Hold it!" he shouted to me. "Okay, now come down the steps slowly. That's it. Good! Now stop and wave. Okay, now go back up and we'll try it again. This time I want a closer shot." For *Close-Up,* of course. Ross McLean had decided to piggyback on my *Star* assignment and had sent Durschmied on ahead to film me in Moscow.

The crowd stayed back as Durschmied completed his filming. In the background I could see a policeman, keeping order. But how had Durschmied been able to shoot film in forbidden territory? "Easy," he said. "I didn't ask. Here you never ask what the rules are. If you do, they tell you *nyet.*" A lesson, I thought, that Sid Katz hadn't learned.

I checked into the Ukraine Hotel, which, I was astonished to learn, was only three years old. It looked like an ancient Canadian railway hotel,

182

only bigger. If you took the lobby of the Château Laurier, made it three times as ornate and twice as draughty, then stuffed it inside the Royal York's shell and covered the roof with spikes, steeples, and battlements, you'd have a rough idea of the Ukraine. Put it on a grander version of University Avenue and you've got Moscow. Stalin's approach to architecture didn't differ greatly from that of Fred Gardiner, the first Metro Toronto supermayor, whose vision of a city hall the ratepayers had rejected.

The sexless public buildings in this sexless city reminded me of the ones we used to put up in Canada thirty or more years before. One American woman told me that when she was first taken to her hotel she thought they had put her in the post office by mistake. The USSR was clearly going through a stage common to many countries seeking architectural grandeur. It was the same kind of thinking that had caused Americans to build classical domes on their state capitols and Canadians to erect railway stations that looked like cathedrals.

Durschmied suggested we meet for dinner that night in an elegant Moscow café where, he said, they might rustle up a decent meal. He was there waiting for me, drinking vodka and chatting with the most beautiful woman I would see in all my time in Moscow. She was young, dark, alluring, and animated.

"Where on earth did you find her?" I asked him.

"Easy," he said. "In any city the prettiest girls work at the perfume counter of any large department store. I went to the one in GUM, and there she was." Being Durschmied, he had simply walked up and asked, "How's about a date, baby?" A bespectacled, round-faced youth with a slight German accent, he had a bravado that belied the innocence of his features.

"Sh-h-h!" she had whispered. "Meet me at the front door in five minutes."

"Why the whispers?" Durschmied asked her when she arrived. "You afraid of the KGB?"

"No, no," she said. "I just don't want my girl friends gossiping and laughing at me."

So there we were, the girl softly humming American popular songs she'd heard on the Voice of America. "I wish Sarah Vaughan would come to Moscow," she said. "Sarah Vaughan is the very best." She was also familiar with Perry Como, Louis Armstrong, Bing Crosby, and Frank Sinatra.

We had red caviar, borscht, baked sturgeon, and scalloped potatoes, washed down with Georgian wine. The girl, who was from Azerbaijan, ordered a filet, sang "Sugah in the Mawnin" with a Southern accent, and told me regretfully that she had never tasted Coca-Cola.

She was starting to sing "Rock Around the Clock" when the hotel orchestra arrived – four saxes, two trumpets, a bass fiddle, drums, and a piano – drowning her out. A stoutish woman in a red dress stood up and sang, in a shrill voice, something in Russian. She did not sound like Sarah Vaughan. The dancers faced each other at arm's length and moved slowly and almost ritualistically to the music. They provided a shabby contrast to this magnificent room with its polished marble and its vaulted ceilings, three storeys high, decorated with enormous murals and supported by clusters of pillars of green and blue marble. Only the girl from the perfume counter was dressed in anything approaching style – a soft, white wool sweater and a flaring ballerina skirt in pastel hues that must have cost her a month's pay.

We dined and chatted beneath immense gilt chandeliers, our table set with the finest linen and sterling, sipping our red wine from goblets of blue crystal that rang like a bell when struck. What a contrast these surroundings made to the men in their rumpled double-breasted suits and sports shirts and the women in dark blue wool that bulged in the wrong places. Lounging nonchalantly against the pillars, the young *stilyagi,* the so-called Golden Youth of Moscow, presented another contrast in their excessively long jackets, white shirts open at the throat, and tight corduroy trousers. They did not need to work, these teenaged sons of prominent party members.

"I am trying to learn the hula hoop," said the girl from the perfume counter as we drove her home in a taxi. She asked us to stop some distance from her apartment block. We dropped her and bade her goodnight as she strolled away, singing "Blue Moon" softly to herself.

It occurred to me then, as it was to occur to me again in other foreign climes, from Tokyo to Budapest, that no political system, no ruthless dictatorship could withstand for long the creeping tide of American pop culture. Wendell Willkie's original high-minded concept of One World was taking shape in a way the Republican standard-bearer had not envisaged. Some would see it as a dream come true; others might view it as a nightmare.

In the days that followed we filmed all over Moscow without asking permission and without any fuss. Policemen automatically helped us trundle our equipment around and held back the gathering crowds in the belief that we were privileged foreigners. There was only one problem: most Muscovites spoke only Russian. I suggested to Durschmied that we film the activity in the GUM department store and try to interview a salesclerk who could speak English.

"Easy," he said. "I got a guy in the tourist bureau who wants to go to Paris and needs hard currency. I been exchanging for him on the black market. He'll fix it up."

He phoned his friend and told him we wanted to interview an English-speaking saleswoman at GUM. A careful little charade followed. Durschmied's friend phoned his superior. "I've got a couple of Canadian tourists here who want to take some snaps in GUM," he explained. "Is that okay?"

Snaps? Of course it was okay, he was told. The Soviet Union welcomed tourists.

Durschmied's contact then phoned the manager of the department store. "I've got permission for a Canadian television crew to film in your store," he announced, "and they'd like somebody who can speak English."

The manager was all smiles when we arrived. A sophisticated middle-aged woman appeared and cheerfully agreed to be interviewed. After it was over we chatted briefly about life in the USSR. "The troubles we have getting servants you wouldn't believe," she told me. "Why, the first thing they ask is, 'Have you got TV?' and then they wish to know what kind of TV it is. Then they ask, 'How much do I get? How long do I have to stay?' I tell you, it's a real problem here to get somebody to look after your children. It has become the source of many anecdotes here. There is one comedian on TV, especially, who makes jokes about it." So much, I thought, for the classless society.

John Chilwell, a South African reporter, and I encountered another class when we were approached by a twenty-one-year-old student, pink-cheeked and curly-haired, who offered to sell us some illegal icons.

How did he know we were British? "The slits in the back of your coats," he explained. "I like British clothes. When you wear them you don't look like you came off a collective farm. You got any jazz records?"

We hadn't, but since I was interested in reporting on the Moscow black market, he offered to introduce me to his boss, a man of thirty with a sharp, agile face, a gold tooth, and a tattoo on his left arm. He'd been working the black market for fifteen years, he told me, beginning in Odessa with cigarettes and girls. We met at a corner bus-stop, where he introduced me to another "businessman," a nineteen-year-old with a suitcase full of icons. I asked where these came from and he revealed that his grandfather owned a church, thus conjuring up in my mind the spectacle of a bearded old party methodically stripping the sacred walls in the interests of a forbidden trade.

We climbed into a taxi, where he produced, furtively, the wares in his suitcase. But these businessmen as they called themselves – a swear-word in the USSR – were even more interested in changing money for American dollars, at three times the going rate.

As we pulled up at a stoplight, another car with four men in it stopped beside us. "This is interesting for you," one of the youths remarked casually. "Those are the police." He meant, of course, the secret police. I asked him, a little apprehensively, how he knew.

"First, because of the special number on the licence. Secondly, when-ever four men travel together in a car they are likely to be police; thirdly, well, just look at them! How could they be anything else?"

I held my breath, but the car full of police drove off. I had brought with me an American hundred-dollar bill secreted between the pages of a book, thus making myself a co-conspirator. They agreed to complete the transaction the following night in the Ararat Café in the Hotel Europa.

Chilwell and I ordered dinner in the Ararat, and a very good dinner it was, contrary to what I had been told about Russian cuisine. Unable to communicate or make sense of the Cyrillic print on the menu, we simply pointed to the most expensive items to indicate what we want-ed. A deep earthenware pot arrived containing a wonderful soup in which floated a quarter of a chicken, black cherries, green olives, and lemon slices. Then a bottle of Georgian wine appeared, along with an omelette in a copper skillet, full of meatballs sizzling away. A bottle of Georgian champagne and a wooden platter loaded with slices of fresh pineapple made up the meal.

The businessmen arrived as we were demolishing this repast. "You got the green?" one asked. His colleague darted off, signalled us, and the two of us repaired to the washroom. I produced the C-note and he handed me a wad of paper rubles. I tried to count them. "Not here!" he hissed, and popped the American bill into his mouth.

186

Back at the table they talked of the crowded housing situation, which meant that in winter there was no place to take a girl. In summer, of course, there were parks. Thirty years of Soviet indoctrination had not erased the competitive spirit. They told me they would use the money to buy hard-to-get items they would then sell at a profit. They were as cynical as Western teenagers, refusing to believe their country's propaganda, but were well informed about the West. They read Western magazines and newspapers bought from tourists, and they listened to American jazz on bootleg records. When I asked about the Khrushchev regime, they shrugged. "I am just a small man," one said. "With government I can do nothing. With government I have no interest. My interest is to make money."

The bill arrived and one of the businessmen snatched it away. "Please!" he said. "It is the Russian hospitality," and he casually tossed the waiter a few notes. The meal must have cost about two hundred rubles, and though I did not see the bill, I have reason to be sure it did. For when I returned to the hotel and counted my illegal cash, it was short by exactly that amount.

3

In July 1960 I went off to see how television had changed presidential *Crowning* politics south of the border. The setting was the Democratic Convention *J.F.K.* in Los Angeles – the one that nominated Jack Kennedy. The city was a madhouse. Every hotel had been booked for months, and we country cousins of the Canadian press were relegated to the suburbs, miles from the heart of the action.

Duncan Macpherson had preceded me, and when I arrived late in the afternoon of July 9, I found him ensconced in our single room breathing enthusiasm, good nature, and a whiff of something stronger. He was preparing to wire the *Star* for funds; as usual, he had already overspent his advance.

"The Los Angeles press club is holding a shindig downtown to welcome the out-of-town newspaper guys," Macpherson told me enthusiastically. "Let's go!"

I pointed out that the invitation said the party was from five to seven and that it was now well past the deadline.

"Give it no thought!" cried Duncan. "There'll still be some people around and the bar will still be open."

The party, when we finally made it, was clearly over. Half-eaten sandwiches and soggy canapés littered the tables, together with the remnants of various drinks in which cigarettes had been doused. A few remaining guests clung to the bar, mumbling to one another. From this group a personable young man detached himself, strode over, and extended his hand in greeting. A lapel label identified him as FRED.

"Hi-ya, fellas," he said. "Glad to have you aboard. Where are you guys from, anyway?"

Macpherson fixed his eyes on the name card.

"Fred, eh?" he said.

"That's right," said the cheerful young man.

"Well, Fred, I have some advice for you."

"Sure, you bet. What is it?"

"Fuck off, Fred," said Mr. Hyde.

Several free drinks later we rolled onto the street and tried to find a taxi. But in that fevered environment there were none.

"No problem," said Macpherson. He walked into a corner bar, produced a twenty-dollar bill (his last), and waved it.

"Twenty bucks to anybody who will drive us to our hotel," he cried.

"I'll take that!" a customer shouted. Half an hour later we were home.

On Sunday afternoon – and a sticky, steamy afternoon it was – Macpherson and I found ourselves pinned to the wall of the Biltmore Hotel lobby in the swirling crush of people. We were trying to fight our way toward the reception room allotted to supporters of Adlai Stevenson. It was slow going and so we caught our breath and let the sweating crowd rustle past: old men in shapeless seersucker carrying FAUBUS FOR PRESIDENT signs; young couples in shorts, pushing prams; veterans with medals; a ventriloquist with a dummy; five IRA sympathizers in paddy green; Alaskans in parkas; housewives in specially fashioned dresses of red, white, and blue; Democratic "Golden Girls," honey-haired and sun-kissed; and hundreds of rubbernecks, souvenir-laden, be-badged and be-ribboned, all indulging in the American passion for funny hats and odd costumes, all dressed up for the first television convention in living colour. As Macpherson remarked, it was exactly like the crowd leaving the Food Products Building at the Canadian National Exhibition. I thought of our own mild political process and

188

wondered how long it would take us to mimic the American pizazz, as, in the end, we mimicked everything American.

Why was I there? I kept asking myself. What was there to do, what to write that hadn't already been written? Radio had changed politics below the border; television was totally transforming it. I felt like a tiny cog in a gigantic machine, one of 950 members of the working press all struggling for a story, not to mention 4,560 others connected in some way with the gathering of news – taking pictures, making sketches, scribbling in notebooks, jockeying bulky TV cameras, hollering into telephones, lurking in hotel corridors, and all endlessly interviewing each other. There was nothing any of us could write about – speculation, hard facts, gossip, lies, rumours, jokes, or plain opinions – that hadn't already been written or voiced over and over again to the last fresh figure of speech or the final tired cliché.

I ran into Mike Wallace. "There are just too many of us," he said, shaking his head. "There's blood in the Congo, Khrushchev's eyeing Cuba, Eisenhower's on the links at Newport, and here we are, five thousand of us, rewriting each other."

He bustled off on his own quest and I took a stroll through the two floors of the Biltmore set aside for the working press. In one curtained area, forty-two toilers for AP crouched over their typewriters. In another, forty-two more clacked away for UPI. Every medium, from the *Wichita Journal* to the *Norddeutscher Rundfunk,* was represented. Tass had two reporters, the Voice of America ten. The Los Angeles *Times* ran photographs of its convention staff – so many that they encircled the front page, forty-six in all. The *Star* had a staff of five, in addition to its syndicated coverage. Western Union was transmitting twelve million words a day. The day the convention opened I counted seventy columns in the *Times* dealing with the subject. Cuba that day got slightly less than one column, the crisis in the Congo slightly more than three.

The real effort here was the care and feeding of the media. The combination of tradition, circus showmanship, and skilful public relations ensured that the thinnest public debate, the most hackneyed political speech, was somehow front-page news or the lead item on television. The reports on Senator Frank Church's keynote speech gave me a bad case of déjà vu, taking me back to that early session of the United Nations more than a dozen years before. Had this flabby piece of political propaganda landed on the city desks of America at any other time, it would have been tossed in the wastebasket. Yet this week it was hot news. There are times when I weep for my profession, and as I studied the background mechanics of this piece of play acting, I wept again.

The day before the speech (Sunday) the newspapers speculated on what Church would say. One even expressed the hope that he would not fall into the errors of his predecessor, whatever those were. In fact, the writer of that editorial already knew the contents of the speech, word for word; the full text was available thirty hours in advance – one of forty-six press releases handed out that day by the convention's staff of forty public relations experts. By noon on Sunday the floor of the press headquarters was ankle deep in worthless paper. Once again, the world's greatest reporters were playing the old game of let's pretend. Under the unspoken rules of that game, the news hawks and the TV pundits declined to let their audiences in on the secret. If the people knew in advance, what would happen to circulation? Where would the ratings go?

Before Church got a word out, the L.A. *Times,* hungry for a scoop that wasn't a scoop, jumped the gun and pretended the speech had already been given. A copy of the paper reached me just as he strode to the rostrum. The front-page story burbled that the senator from Idaho spoke to "a great crowd" who "gave their emotions free rein" and that "he lifted the delegates from their seats near the conclusion." That, of course, was bullshit (a word no daily newspaper would have dared print in those uptight times). The truth was that the crowd was sparse and listless, only half the seats were occupied, and those delegates who did turn up, having no need to listen, dozed in their chairs, read newspapers, or walked about the floor, buttonholing friends or having their pictures taken. What we were watching was a piece of contrived theatre for the TV audience, as phony as a fixed wrestling match.

There were so few dramatic moments that the press tended to overplay them. The first piece of real entertainment was the so-called debate between Lyndon Johnson and John Kennedy. Even before it began it became clear that Johnson had lost, for it was Kennedy who carried the aura of success like a halo and who could sense the rustle of excitement in the hall when he walked in. Suddenly, he had achieved star status. In the duel between the young pretender and the old pro, it was the old pro who had his back to the wall. At one point, I remember, Johnson made some remark about love of country. "I don't need Senator Johnson to lecture me on patriotism," said Kennedy evenly. He didn't have to mention his war record.

It was no contest after this set-to. The real contest would be between Kennedy and Adlai Stevenson, and so the pundits, who had very little to chew on, began to speculate on the possibility of a Stevenson miracle.

It didn't happen, in spite of a last minute attempt to seize the convention by a group of young amateurs – girls with the scent of the campus about them, youths in corduroys and sneakers. They disguised themselves as Kennedy supporters and moved like ferrets through the aisles, filling the seats like an army creeping to the start line for a dawn attack. The delegates looked nervously up at the galleries where the youth army was exchanging phony Kennedy hats for Stevenson hats. They had seized the high ground, and this was the only moment of real excitement the convention produced. As Eugene McCarthy finished his nomination speech for the reluctant candidate, I saw the block leaders of the Stevenson organization half rising from their seats while others with megaphones slid into position. As the speech ended, a roar shook the convention hall and a rhythmic beat began, *"We want Stevenson! We want Stevenson!"*

A mass demonstration was under way, and it was impossible not to be caught up in it. Here was the new youth generation feeling its oats at the start of the sixties. I was standing directly behind the box occupied by the Kennedy family and saw two small Kennedys begin to wave their flags in time to the insistent chorus. One of the well-groomed Kennedy women, her face devoid of expression, reached forward quietly and plucked the flags from their hands. Like the relatives, all the Kennedy supporters sat quietly through the demonstration unmoved – pleasant, self-possessed people for the most part, in contrast to the zealous Stevensonites, whose hearts were always on their sleeves.

At last the pulsating galleries quieted, and the convention went about its business, almost as if the demonstration had not occurred. There had been no voting delegates among the fresh-faced chanters, and as the balloting began, the Stevenson people crept out of the arena as quietly as they had entered.

I turned on my transistor radio, which could pick up ABC's television broadcast from the booth including the walkie-talkie calls from the director to his outposts. I caught the beginnings of a statement from Adlai Stevenson himself, but even as he talked I heard an insistent voice order: "Get him off! Get him off! Kennedy's on his way." Off went the old, in the middle of a well-turned phrase, and in came the new. Kennedy's style seemed to reflect that of the convention – no emotion in his thank-you speech, no catch in the throat, no tear in the eye. He spoke crisply, with the air of a man who had had it in the bag from the beginning, who wanted to get on with the job as quickly as possible, and who had known all along that the sound and the fury were so much wasted window dressing.

4

With the convention winding down, it was time for me to attend to other business. Hollywood was only a taxi ride away, and there *Klondike* was being turned into a TV series. I had been hired and paid as a consultant and thought I had better earn my pay, even if no one seemed to want to consult me.

I had had a dispiriting experience in New York the previous fall when I walked into the office of Joe Bailey, executive producer of the series, to see what was cooking. What was cooking, I discovered, was just another American TV Western about cowboys shooting at each other. The key character, Bailey told me, would be a U.S. marshal who brings law and order to the unruly denizens of Dawson.

When I explained that Dawson was in Canada, not Alaska, Bailey seemed baffled. Had I checked? I reminded him that I wrote the book. Well, he said, that's okay, we'll bring in a U.S. marshal *type* who'll be elected by the miners to bring law and order to Dawson. But, I told him, there were forty members of the North West Mounted Police in Dawson at the time, not to mention 202 soldiers from the Yukon Field Force sent to prevent the Americans from grabbing the Yukon. Dawson was never a lawless town; a typical "crime" was chopping wood on the Lord's Day.

"There were no murders in Dawson in 1898," I said. "And no major crime, unless you count that terrible lawbreaker Freda Maloof, the Turkish Whirlwind Danseuse, who dared to wear tights on the stage while performing the hoochy-koochy dance before it was banned."

He seemed depressed at that but brightened suddenly. "I've got it," he said. "We'll move the whole story to Alaska!"

So here I was, technical adviser to Ziv Television's hot new series, *Klondike,* for which the pilot script had already been written by a man I'd never heard of – Sam Peckinpah.

I was received with opens arms by the production group – young, intelligent men, hungry for information about the Klondike. I'd been told by Bailey that nobody would have time to read my book. "They have to turn out a script every five days, and the book is too long for that. Maybe somebody – story editor, perhaps, or director – will read it."

As far as I could discover, nobody had. I felt more than a little deflated. All the legends I had heard about Hollywood were turning out to be true.

The director, William Conrad, a burly man with a dark moustache, I would later recognize as the star of another TV series, *Cannon.* He was eager to learn about my home town. One of his production assistants produced a notebook, and they all began firing questions at me.

"What's the foliage like up there?"

It was boreal forest, I told them. Birches, aspens, and spruce.

"Any pines or oaks?" Conrad asked.

It was too far north for those, I explained.

"Too bad," he said. "All we've got here in Southern California are pines and oaks, so I guess they'll have to do."

Another member of the team asked me about sunshine in the north. He said the lighting conditions were very important. I told him that for six weeks the sun didn't shine. I told them how, as a child, I remembered the moonlight glistening on the snow.

"We won't be using snow," one of the young men said. "Snow's too expensive."

I explained that one of the distinguishing things about the Yukon was the presence of large amounts of snow, which arrive in early October and lie around until April.

"Well, we start production July 26 and we got to have thirteen episodes in the can before fall and this is Southern California and we just haven't *got* any snow," one of them said.

"How'd you like the mud we used in the pilot?" I was asked.

I said I liked it fine. It gave the film an authentic feel because when there wasn't any snow in the North there was usually plenty of mud, especially in the spring. I said I hoped they would use of plenty of mud.

"You know what mud costs?" Conrad asked. "It costs seven thousand dollars just for one episode. We had to bring it in to the ranch, wet it down during the night, and have it out by Monday morning. We can't afford any more mud."

Well, I said, at least they could save money on electric lights and things, since it was light all night during the summer. They could shoot night sequences in the daytime because it never got dark.

Conrad looked sad. "Nobody's going to believe that," he said. "I mean, if you say it happens, I go along with you, but how're you going to explain it to twenty million viewers? How can you arrange a midnight rendezvous in a back alley that's blazing with sunlight? And suppose a couple of sharpies want to sneak out of town under cover of darkness? How do you handle that, if there *isn't* any darkness?"

"Am I correct in assuming that the only tailor-made cigarette at the time was the Sweet Caporal?" somebody asked, to change the subject.

The stampeders actually smoked pipes, I told him, and when they struck it rich, they smoked big cigars.

There was gloom.

"I'm afraid cigars and pipes are pretty well out," Conrad said. "The sponsor is a cigarette company. We had a smoke-filled dance hall in the pilot, and they weren't too happy about that. Too *much* smoke."

We got talking about little background touches that might enhance the production. It was a polyglot stampede, I reminded them, with men and women of every race involved. There were Kanakas from Hawaii and even Maoris from New Zealand, who built huts of wattle along the trail – a nice exotic touch.

Conrad squirmed. He was a sensitive man who, I think, really wanted to make an authentic series, and it hurt him to have to tell me they couldn't use Maoris. "The sponsor was very firm," he said. "No coloured people at all. I'm afraid that lets the Maoris out."

To cheer him up, I told him I'd liked the pilot. The costumes, especially, were authentic. I had one small suggestion: everybody in those days sported a handlebar moustache. It would add authenticity if the extras were moustached.

"I'm afraid not," he said. "If we put handlebars on everybody the viewers will think it's a comedy."

And that was the end of my technical advice. Conrad and his colleagues told me that I'd been absolutely invaluable and they'd like to have me back in the near future for another shirtsleeve session.

194

But they didn't ask me back. That fall I watched the first episode of *Klondike* and then gave up. The star was Ralph Taeger, billed as a "combination Clark Gable and Jack Kennedy, who speaks and acts a little like Humphrey Bogart." He failed to live up to that billing and was never heard from again. Two vapid actresses with typically Hollywood names – Joi Lansing and Mari Blanchard – provided the romantic interest. The only actor who seemed to have any quality was a new-comer, James Coburn, who played the villain, modelled on Jefferson Randolph "Soapy" Smith, the dictator of Skagway. Coburn went on to greater roles.

The series was not a hit. Joe Bailey claimed the viewers were depressed by all that mud. But what really turned them off, I believe, was the col-lection of tired clichés that did duty as a script. *Klondike* could as eas-ily have been set in Dodge City. In an era when more than a dozen Westerns were featured on the tube – including such long-running hits as *Gunsmoke* and *Bonanza* – *Klondike* was a spent fuse. It ran for only twenty of the contracted twenty-six weeks, after which the location was suddenly transferred to Acapulco, of all places. Telly Savalas replaced James Coburn as the villain. Coburn was turned into a nice guy. After six episodes the show expired.

Years later I discussed the demise of the series with Joe Hyams, president of Screen Gems, then the television wing of Columbia Pictures, which was producing my nightly talk show in Canada.

"Snow pitchas don't go," Hyams cried in his best Brooklynese. "They just don't go!"

He turned to me. "I'll tell ya what goes!" he said.

"What goes?" I asked.

"Tits and sand!" shouted the ebullient Hyams. "Tits and sand! *That's what goes!*"

Chapter Eight

1

When I joined the *Star,* Beland Honderich agreed to my request for an
annual five-week holiday. He asked only that in the interests of staff
morale the extra two weeks be disguised as an assignment. In September
1960 Janet and I flew off to Tokyo for our extra fortnight at the *Star's*
expense and checked into Frank Lloyd Wright's famous Imperial Hotel,
where each room, designed by the architect himself, right down to the
furniture, was unique.

Our adventures began with my vain attempt to order a crab sandwich
from room service. Japan is known for its seafood, especially crab,
which, in those days, was so cheap and so readily available that no one
had thought of inventing the fake variety that is standard fare today in
the sushi bars of North America. When the order arrived, we found they'd
brought *club* sandwiches. "Next time, order two club sandwiches and
hope for the best," Janet said.

That night, in the Tennessee coffee-house, we watched a group of
seven Japanese youths snapping their fingers and singing rock and roll
with a genuine Southern accent upon which was superimposed a genuine Japanese accent. "Rove you!" they carolled. "Rearry, rearry rove
you!" Obviously Janet had figured out the language. Back at the hotel
for a late-night snack, I took her advice, ordered two club sandwiches,
and got the crab I craved.

The presence of thousands of late-night coffee-houses, such as the
Tennessee, was to me an indication of how much Tokyo had changed
after the Occupation. It was so startlingly different that it was hard to
remember what it had been like when I'd first seen it ten years before.
Japan was a beaten nation in those days. MacArthur was Regent; the
streets were jammed with GIs, their pockets stuffed with Occupation
scrip; and great blank spaces marked the spots where the firebombs
had fallen. The people were dazed, demoralized, and subjugated; they
weren't even allowed to own a car less than ten years old because the
newer ones were reserved for the victors. It was not a happy city.

I did not feel compassion for these people. After all, during the war
I had lectured at the Royal Military College in Kingston on the fanaticism of Japanese soldiers; they got what they deserved. But I could not
hate the citizens: they seemed to me rather like errant children. Now,
after ten years, there was no reason for either compassion or hate. When

198

Janet and I tried to get a drink in a bar, we were turned away. "Japanese only," we were told. For the first time, I felt like a member of a visible minority – especially because of my height. At six-foot-three, I towered over the average person. In a perfume shop, I remember, the sales-girls gathered around me, chattering, pointing, and giggling as if I were the Cape Breton Giant.

But there were other bars, thousands of them quite happy to accept our custom. The streets reverberated with life and passion. Three million more people had crowded in, making Tokyo the world's largest city. The scars of war had been obliterated, not only physically but psychologically. The taxi drivers demonstrated all the *élan* of the new Japan. They scared us silly, actually popping into the oncoming lane or climbing onto the sidewalks to get past traffic line-ups. The police looked the other way, trying to erase their wartime reputation as bullies.

Yosh Kawakita took us to lunch and talked about the sudden enthusiasms that regularly swept the country. Born in Canada, Yosh had a foot in each culture. After he graduated from Parkdale Collegiate in Toronto, his father sent him to Japan to visit his relatives. Unfortunately, he arrived on December 7, 1941, of all days, and found himself conscripted at once into the Japanese navy, even though he could not speak a word of the language. He adapted, and in 1960 he was head of public relations for Canadian Pacific Airlines; soon he would be a vice-president of the parent CPR in Japan.

The country was still caught up in a post-Occupation spree, and there seemed to be no end to it. Every season brought a new fad that the Japanese seized on with an enthusiasm exceeding anything we'd known in the West. The latest fashion involved chocolate make-up, chocolate face powder, and chocolate lipstick, a tribute, apparently, to black entertainers – Harry Belafonte, the Mills Brothers who had recently received a tumultuous reception in Tokyo. For the first time in history, Japanese girls were actually going to the beaches to get a tan.

The country was also on an extended Latin-American kick, if the bands in the nightclubs were any evidence. The year before it had been rockabilly. The Japanese latched onto any new craze, squeezed it dry, and just as quickly discarded it. Their closets, Yosh told us, were all jammed with Italian pointed shoes, popular the year before but already out of fashion. The late-night coffee-houses featured hot jazz and French chansons. "Parlez-moi d'Amour" was almost as big a hit in Tokyo as "Swanee River." One Japanese businessman told me, "Every time I hear 'Auld Lang Syne,' tears come into my eyes."

The greatest phenomenon of all that season was an inflatable black doll with eyes that winked and arms that clung. These Winkie dolls were selling in the hundreds of thousands and were in such demand that people lined up for them, prepared to pay double the going rate of fifty cents.

Did this mean the country was going Western? Hardly. Yosh reminded me that the sukiyaki we were enjoying was actually a Japanese version of the Irish stew introduced by Matthew Perry only a century before and now one of the country's great festive dishes. The Japanese have a habit of taking foreign ideas and things and making them their own.

"We arouse easily," Yosh explained. "We forget easily, too. After all, that's how it was with the war." It was a shrewd assessment, for the Japanese were once as enthusiastic over war as they now were over Winkie dolls. But they had put the war behind them, like the discarded Italian shoes. They weren't bitter or obsessed about the war as some Germans were. They were just sorry it happened. "Such a stupid war," a man from Kyoto remarked, shaking his head sadly.

The new buzzword was peace, especially among the students, 300,000 of whom belonged to the radical Zengakuren. They had rioted the previous spring on the occasion of Dwight Eisenhower's proposed visit to Japan because they thought the Japanese government was trying to ram a security pact down the public's throat. These students didn't want anything that hinted at foreign entanglement. Their executive director, Ondo Nore, in his fourth year of teacher's training, spoke with all the idealism of students everywhere when he told me the Zengakuren didn't even want Japan to have a standing army.

Was this enthusiasm for peace, I wondered, simply another manifestation of the Japanese fanaticism, like the craze for chocolate make-up or the fashion for "round eyes" that was enriching the plastic surgeons?

The following day we were conducted around a Japanese factory by a neatly briefcased young P.R. man who seemed to be the very antithesis of the young students I'd met the day before. "The Zengakuren?" he remarked. "Why, I was its president ten years ago." What an adaptable people they are, I thought, able to switch attitudes as easily as they switch from *yukata* to business suit. Everything changes, yet nothing changes.

200

One of the most revealing sights we saw in Tokyo was a labourer squatting on his haunches in the time-honoured manner, dressed in loose white garments with a band around his head and a stubble of beard on his chin. Here was a figure straight out of a Hiroshige woodblock. But there was a difference: first of all, he was eating a pink popsicle; second, he was watching an outdoor TV set on whose screen a young Japanese was strumming a guitar and singing, in English, the latest Pat Boone hit about putting your sweet lips closer to the phone.

It came to me that these were a slippery kind of people – slippery, to me, at least, because I could never quite grasp the way they thought. They seemed to operate on two levels. There were, for instance, thousands of bar girls in the city, euphemistically known as "hostesses." As Janet and I sat at a bar in the Ginza district, I felt a soft pressure on my hand; a beautiful girl in a kimono had slipped in beside me. "Nice," she said, squeezing my hand tenderly once more. I introduced her to Janet. "Beautiful," she said, meaning Janet, and suddenly the pressure became sisterly. It was only eleven o'clock, but the bar had to close because the law said it must. The reason? Because these innocent young women must not be out alone on the streets after midnight – an hour when their Western sisters in sin were just beginning to ply their trade. And so the neon signs that made Tokyo's night brighter than any day winked out, the laughing crowd poured singing into the streets homeward bound, and suddenly Tokyo and its alleys was silent, gloomy, mysterious, and very Oriental.

We went the next night to a vaudeville show in a large theatre and were placed, over my protestations, in the front row because we were foreigners. Two sad-faced comedians, wearing Western fedoras, ambled onto the stage, chattering to each other and the audience in Japanese and laughing, rather spiritlessly, at their own jokes. Suddenly one spotted me. "Hey, Poppa!" he cried in English. "How many kids you got?"

"Five," I told him.

"Have six!" he said, and tossed a squirming baby into my lap. The "baby" turned out to be a wizened midget, who quickly made his escape. So did we. I have tried to avoid front row seating ever since.

Now nothing would do but that we should try to live like Japanese, as far from Western influence as it was possible to get. We ignored the official Japanese travel agency, which puts people in phony tatami rooms with Western conveniences. We wanted to live in a real Japanese inn – a *ryokan*.

An American travel agent, Joe Grace, agreed to send us to something authentic. "You won't like it," he told us bluntly. Yes we will, I insisted. "Well, don't come back and complain you had to sleep on the floor," he replied. He sent us off to Kinagawa, a spa in the mountains generally unknown to foreigners, "where the Japanese businessmen take their mistresses." It sounded authentic, and it was: two rows of rambling Japanese hotels, facing each other across a dizzy gorge.

We found ourselves in a hotel where English was unknown, occupying a delicate little room overlooking a perfect little garden. It turned out that we were the only white couple in town and thus the object of much curiosity. We decided to go native, to bathe communally, naked as jaybirds, to sleep on the floor, and to eat a Japanese breakfast, complete with rice and pickled seaweed (the ham and eggs our waitress insisted on bringing we left untouched).

That night we decided to go cormorant fishing on the roiling river. Hordes of Japanese tourists were pouring off the big buses, travelling light because the hotels supplied everything from toothbrushes to flowered cotton *yukatas*. As we headed out, I peered into the banquet rooms, where long, low tables had been set for the evening banquet. Here cushions, chopsticks, sake flasks, rice bowls, and teacups were arranged in such geometric harmony that they seemed to have been laid out with a set square. Such neat, orderly people, I told myself.

But when we returned two hours later, we were met with a scene of unmitigated chaos. The lacquer tables in their neat rows had been overturned. Chopsticks, teacups, and rice bowls littered the floor. A few disoriented guests were still staggering around, bombed out of their skulls. Here was proof that in Japan drunks as well as children and old men were permitted to throw off the strict code of behaviour that acted as a social strait-jacket.

These tourists never seemed to sleep. About 4 a.m. Janet nudged me and pointed out of the big window that faced the glass-fronted hotels on the far side of the gorge. The baths were on the main floors, and there we witnessed a Rabelaisian spectacle: men and women frolicking in the water, splashing away at each other as they cavorted in the altogether. How long will it be, I wondered, before this particular form of unisex invades our own puritan shores?

The following day, surfeited by sake, I began to long for a real drink. To my delight, I found that the hotel's brochure carried a colour photograph of what appeared to be a North American bar. We made our way through a labyrinth of polished staircases and lacquered doorways and at last we found it, just as advertised: a curved bar complete with a white-coated bartender, a tiny dance floor, a jukebox, and an array of familiar brand-name bottles on the shelves.

The bartender, divining that we were Canadians, proudly gestured at the jukebox, from which Paul Anka's voice was oozing. I indicated a bottle of Canadian Club, and the bartender poured me a tot, splashing in the requisite amount of ice and mixer. Rye and ginger – the all-Canadian drink! Home at last, I said to Janet, here in the wilds of Kinagawa.

I raised my glass. Down the hatch! *A-a-a-argh!* Up the hatch again. What was this – turpentine, kerosene, fusel oil? If that is C.C., I thought, then I'm a Magyar.

I checked out the label and reeled back. Canadial Club. *Canadial?* Next to it was a bottle that looked like Caruba rum, except they'd spelled it with an *l* – *Caluba*. Janet was already gagging on it.

And that was our final impression of the authentic Japanese spa – the taste of ersatz booze and the voice of Paul Anka, raving about Diana.

2

In the Casablanca nightclub, a farmer from the rice country in high, Hiroshima
*muddy rubber boots is trying to dance the mambo with a slightly
unwilling young woman. Across the street in the Grand Palace, an almost
totally naked girl is completing the final formalities of a striptease. Out
in the narrow alleys, lit by Japanese lanterns and neon tubing, groups
of young men go by, arm in arm, singing.*

*The city is alive and vibrant like any other large industrial city in
Japan on a Saturday night. But this is not just any city. This is Hiroshima.*

*We have come by fast express from the ancient town of Kyoto, with its
1,029 Buddhist temples, all untouched by war. We have passed through
green rice paddies veined by irrigation canals, under conical hills dotted
by twisted pines, past clusters of houses with roofs of smoky, blackened
tile or thatched cypress bark, and through mountain passes shadowy
with mist, as in a Hokusai print.*

*We have come to Hiroshima in the rain – not the strange, black,
radioactive rain that fell on the smoking city that day in 1945 but a soft,*

warm rain that gently blurs the terraced slopes and puts a sheen on the temple roofs. And when at last we arrive, Hiroshima looks almost like any other city in Japan.

Later, we drive up the steep hillside through the thick underbrush of Hijiyama Park to get a good look at the town. Hijiyama means "pine hill," but there are no pines left. They, and everything else that was green, were burned to a crisp when the bomb exploded. Yet the hillside is once again thick with new foliage.

From the top we look down over the city, split by seven river channels. The eye commands a huge, 10,000-metre semicircle. It is hard to realize that within this 180-degree segment only twenty-six buildings are more than fifteen years old. Everything else – houses, factories, streets, foliage, yes, and people, too – is brand new. Only the extreme width of some of the main streets, the presence of a green park in the town's heart, and the shattered skeleton of the Industrial Promotion Hall – a monument to the blast – remind us that fifteen years ago, everything below was a radioactive desert.

This is a new town. Except for the river channels, it might bear a new name. Half a million people live here, but only eighty thousand old-time residents remain. The rest of the survivors couldn't bear to stay.

The stores and shops carry the names of strangers. The people who poured in here after the war got the land for a song because nobody really wanted it. Some got it for nothing by squatting on it because the records had been vaporized. Now every inch of property has been bought up, and Hiroshima, once a quiet country town, has become a great industrial city.

In the Peace Memorial Museum, a shuffling line of sightseers moves past the exhibits, which, for sheer horror, outdo everything save the relics of Belsen and Auschwitz. As a Westerner I do not find it a pleasant experience to walk past these frightful photographs of screaming women and infants covered with blisters; past scraps of tattered and charred children's clothing, plucked from the smoking ruins; past pieces of shattered granite, exfoliated like a peeled onion by the heat of the blast.

I cannot escape the feeling that Japanese eyes are boring into my back as I stare at those terrible pictures of heaped and peeling human bodies. The Germans, we are told, were stunned by motion pictures showing the horrors of the extermination camps. No sensitive Westerner can escape the same sense of guilt in this museum of horrors. We roasted

204

people to death over a slow fire – soldiers and civilians, men, women, and children alike – and there is no getting away from it. We tortured them as surely as the Nazis tortured the Jews, and it took some of them months to die. Few Japanese museums carry English translations with their exhibits, but this one is an exception. Our crime is there, described in meticulous detail, for all of us to read.

In a small glass case is a photograph of a young smiling boy. Next to it is a heap of small, curled objects, not immediately identifiable. I stop to read the inscription:

A junior high-school boy of 14, working outdoors at Zatoba-Cho, 1,200 metres from the epicentre, received severe burns that proved fatal. Shown here with his picture are pieces of finger nail and skin which he tore off in his agony as he struggled in vain for five days and nights before death finally relieved him.

There were 240,000 like him, killed by the bomb. Some died instantly and mercifully; others lingered for days, months, years. As I read these words I know that some are still dying, and that the instances of leukemia among the survivors suggests that the tally of victims is not complete.

The Japanese are remarkably resilient. They have not only restored their blasted city, they have even restored its art treasures. That great pre-war sightseeing attraction, Hiroshima Castle, which vanished with the blast, has been faithfully copied to the last roof joist.

From the hills above, Hiroshima looks like a town untouched by any war. The morning after our visit to the museum, we make a pilgrimage back up the hillside to look down once again in wonder at the reborn city. Directly below, not far from the hypocentre of the blast, is a new school, and here, in the yard, several hundred small boys and girls are lining up in neat rows to enter classes.

I look at my watch. It is shortly after 8 a.m. Fifteen years before, at almost the same moment, another group of children had also been lining up in just this manner when the sky suddenly turned yellow and shrivelled them all to ash.

3

On August 17, 1961, the East Germans began to build the Berlin Wall, a twelve-foot-high barricade of hastily mortared cinder blocks topped with barbed wire and broken glass, effectively splitting the city in two. It was still under construction when Janet and I took a plane to Hamburg, rented a car, and drove to West Berlin via the autobahn that ran through East German territory. It was a spooky trip. The Communists were not anxious to have people living too close to the entry and exit points. Save for two government gas stations, each identified by a single blue light, there was nothing to see along the route – no villages, no farmhouses, no sign of human habitation other than the freshly harvested fields. When darkness fell, ours appeared to be the only car travelling this ghostly highway. For an hour and a half we saw no other vehicle until we reached the Berlin checkpoint and entered the old capital, warmed by the neon glow on the Kurfürstendamm, where the West Berliners lounged in sidewalk cafés.

In spite of all we had heard, no words had been able to convey the sobering impact the wall would have when we came upon it. We encountered it first on Bernauer Strasse, where the tenements of the Soviet sector faced the Western sidewalk. It ran right through buildings. A second glance was needed to realize that the ground floors had been evacuated and that behind the windows was a wall of solid concrete. Yet in the upper stories, East Berliners, living under communist rule, were actually leaning out and talking to their West Berlin neighbours and were accepting pails of provisions hauled up on long ropes.

We drove on to a church that lay in East Berlin but fronted on a Western street. The wall ran through the vestibule, denying the former West Berlin congregation access. Not far away a group of East Berlin workmen was still working on the barrier.

On a side street we encountered a ragged knot of people standing on stools and waving handkerchiefs at their former neighbours. A man was waving to his sister, who occupied a flat half a block away. He did not expect to see her again unless the wall came down. "First it's Berlin!" he cried to us. "Next, England! Then America!" The tears began to stream down his cheeks.

At two that afternoon – the end of the school day – we drove to the northwest limit of the city, a few paces from East Germany, to view a strange spectacle. A twelve-year-old schoolboy, Erwin Kruger, came pedalling along on his bicycle, a bag of books on his shoulder, escorted by no fewer than seven British soldiers in two armoured cars and a jeep-load of West German policemen. We watched the little procession as it moved off down a narrow road flanked on both sides by a forest. The road was part of West Berlin, but the whole forest belonged to East Germany; that was why a schoolboy needed an armed guard to reach his classes and return. We had been warned not to put so much as a foot on the shoulder of the road, let alone a tire. Just two days before, two British military policemen, eating their lunch by the roadside, had been captured by East German police.

Erwin Kruger lived in the odd community of Eiskellar, a remote island of West Berlin lying far out in communist territory like an oasis in the desert and linked only by the thin umbilical cord of this road. It was, indeed, an ice cellar – an enclave chilled by the gathering frost of the Cold War.

We followed the road to the village – a 165-acre patch of woods and meadow, surrounded by a barrier of stakes and barbed wire and patrolled by green-uniformed policemen with guns, dogs, and binoculars. I borrowed a pair of binoculars from our interpreter and looked across the border. "My God," I told Janet, "look at this." For there, in the grass, was another set of binoculars looking back at me.

Now we made an even weirder discovery. Within this strange West German island was another island, a few acres in size, held by East Germany. Until a few days before our arrival this inner island had been occupied by a family living under communist rule. The family had been hustled away on one day's notice, with tears in their eyes and taking only their portable belongings. Was there ever a more ironic illustration of international politics gone mad? East Germans surrounded by West Germans, surrounded by East Germans! All had been neighbours and friends for more than twenty-five years, speaking the same language and springing from the same culture, even if ruled by opposite philosophies. But the people of Eiskellar (six farm families) told us they had no intention of moving. "After all," they said, "this is our home."

Later that day we came upon the strangest sight of all. Here was a handsome farmhouse separated from its barn and outbuildings by the now familiar line of bricks and wire. The wall ran up to the side of the house, then right through the house, dividing the living quarters. The owner continued to live in the part of the house that lay in West Berlin. But he could not live in the rest, nor could he farm his land because that lay in East Germany. He had been forced to take a job as a gardener in West Berlin.

A day or so later we obtained a visa and drove our Volkswagen through Check Point Charley and into the East. Our first impression was that it wasn't as bad as depicted. But then, as the hours rolled by and we drove methodically through the streets, a sense of gloom crept over us, perhaps because there was no point of contact with the West – no popular songs, no gaudy electric signs for Shell or Kodak, no Italian shoes on sale, no gin fizzes in the bars. In this most Stalinesque of cities, sullen with the puritan strictures of the Red religion, there was almost nothing we were accustomed to, except the puritanical air itself.

The brooding presence of that implacable barrier of concrete blocks added to the general spookiness. I felt detached from the real world in a way I had not felt in Moscow. We were walled off, quite literally, from the West. On the other side was the glittering, artificial metropolis of the new Germany, supported almost entirely by American cash; on this side was an eerie void. At the climax of the James Bond craze it was hard not to feel like a spy, risking exposure. I had read enough and seen enough movies about innocent tourists accidentally enmeshed in a web of espionage not to feel a small shiver of apprehension as we drove past the Hitler bunker and what was left of the famous Adlon Hotel. What if some stranger sneaked a compromising document into our car, or a pack of unlawful currency, or a message addressed to a friend in the West written in invisible ink? What if we were detained because we had the wrong papers – or simply because we looked suspicious?

I think our general discomfort in East Berlin was as much the product of the utter cheerlessness as anything else. The absence of sidewalk cafés, which add a carnival air to every European city, was as noticeable here as it was in, well, Toronto. The restaurants we visited had the look and feel of Child's or Bowles Lunch, *circa* 1943. The Bukarest, supposedly a communist showplace, reminded me of a Canadian beverage room, devoid of music, empty of joy. The meaning of the word "atmosphere" was as unknown there as it was, in those days, in the Royal York.

We drove off down Stalin Allee, East Berlin's showpiece boulevard, and found it as cheerless as University Avenue in its architectural sterility. If you took the Shell Oil building, Maclean Hunter, and the Bell Telephone headquarters, made them four times larger, and plastered them over with white tile, you'd get an approximation of Stalin Allee, except that it seemed to go on forever. Not far away, on Unter den Linden, various versions of Toronto's Union Station were strung out for half a mile or so. The absence of people became oppressive. As Janet remarked, "It's like Bay Street on Sunday."

The old city, once the throbbing heart of Berlin, was silent as the tomb – for it *was* a tomb, and spooky enough to make us shiver. Here were shattered cathedrals, gutted department stores, smashed government buildings, and courtyards still heaped with mossy rubble after sixteen years of peace – block upon block of age and decay, mould and desolation, spectral in the gathering dusk. Why, I asked myself, does this ravaged section have for me a chilling familiarity? And then the memory came back to me of a ghost town on the banks of the Yukon, where the main street was also mouldering to dust.

It was pouring rain now, adding to our sense of depression. We drove again to the wall to view the section we had seen from the other side a few days before, something only a foreign visitor could do. There, fifty yards away, was a row of West German faces craning to look at us. The buildings that fronted onto the West Berlin streets were alive with policemen posted in pairs at the back entrances, checking the identity of every soul who entered and left. That had not prevented some East Berliners from leaping out of the upper-storey windows to freedom, or to their deaths.

Here was the same group of sad people with their binoculars, waving their handkerchiefs. We watched one elderly couple approach as close as they could. A rope barrier, fifty feet from the wall, kept the public back. The man produced a handkerchief tied to a walking stick and waved it furtively. From the other side came an answering wave. Then a policeman walked over and spoke a few words. The old man removed the handkerchief and took his wife by the arm. Together they walked slowly and sadly away, occasionally looking back at their children, so near and yet so far from them.

We emerged from East Berlin as from a cave into a community where the night was aglow, the sidewalks were alive with people, and snatches of music could be heard amidst street chatter. We felt relieved to return, like visitors from another planet. And yet, in another sense...

"Tell me truly," I said to Janet. "Which of these two Berlins most resembles the average Canadian town?"

She answered without hesitation, "The one we just left."

4

On Dominion Day, 1961, my wife and I and our family – six children, including a six-week-old baby, and a Siamese cat and her kitten – set off from Honey Harbour on Georgian Bay on a family adventure. We proposed to navigate the Trent-Severn waterway – 240 miles of twisting lakes and canals with two marine railways and forty-three locks. My friends thought I was crazy. I've been told that before and since, but I never listen.

We travelled aboard a rented houseboat built like a trailer on pontoons, thirty-six feet long and ten feet wide, powered by twin forty-five-horsepower outboards, capable of travelling at fifteen knots and drawing only nine inches of water – a behemoth, if ever there was one. It was a foolhardy but also an eminently satisfying adventure, and it was followed, as we soon discovered, by most of the *Star*'s half-million readers.

At Big Chute we pulled into the first marine railway, a submerged narrow-gauge track on which we were first hauled up and then back down in order to circumvent a hydro dam. A second railway followed, after which we entered the limpid waters of the Severn. The beginning was not propitious. Here, on the busiest day of the year, with the river alive with pleasure craft, we snapped a steering cable and drifted helplessly in to shore – marooned on our first day. Happily, the houseboat rental company came to our rescue. It sent us one of its young employees with a stronger set of cables. With the help of the two eldest children, who swam under the boat like eels, we replaced them.

But there was a problem; we had reversed the cables, making the steering even more complicated than intended. It was bad enough to operate this monster under the best of conditions. The wheel was thirty-six feet forward of the rudder, which took some time to respond. Thus, I always had to be two turns ahead of myself. When I swung the tiller to starboard, the boat would continue to move to port – straight at a stump or another boat. *Panic!* Only at the last minute did the rudder respond, so that the boat turned slowly out of harm's way – and kept turning and turning as I worked the wheel madly in the opposite direction. I learned in the end to keep a step or two ahead, but now I faced a more complicated problem. Because the lines were reversed, I had to go through the entire operation backwards. We were not able to reorganize the steering until we reached Lake Couchiching.

"Don't worry, Dad. It all makes a good story," said Pamela, and she was right. My column would chronicle our adventures; if there were *no* adventures, what would I write about?

When we awoke that first Sunday, Janet remarked that the boat resembled a miniature immigrant ship crowded with humanity, each traveller surrounded by his or her worldly possessions. At night, of course, the scene was positively claustrophobic. The best traveller was tiny Peggy Anne, our newest daughter, lying in the buggy on the rear deck, staring solemnly at the shifting sky with her large blue eyes, saying little, and causing no problems.

"You're taking that child on that trip?" one neighbour had asked, aghast.

"Why wouldn't we?" Janet replied. "Do you think we should leave her alone at home?"

"Great heavens!" people would say as they pulled up beside us in their motorboats. "Is that really a baby in that buggy? How on earth do you manage?" But we managed very well. Babies are the easiest to manage, especially if they're breast-fed.

Our Siamese cat, Sari, was more of a problem. We left Big Chief Island in Lake Couchiching in a violent storm, our underpowered craft rolling wickedly in the trough of the waves, tossing the smaller children off their bunks and bringing in the lake through the cracks under the doors. Only when we reached Orillia did we realize the cat was missing. Janet borrowed a motorboat and headed back, bringing Sari's kitten in a plastic bag in case some bait was needed to lure the mother out of the forest. But there she was, sitting bolt upright on the beach in the rain, looking like a piece of marble sculpture, expecting to be picked up.

My next problem was to manoeuvre this oversized houseboat through the narrow locks of the Trent Canal. When we reached the first lock, eight boats lay moored ahead of us. That meant I had to squeeze my ungainly craft into a space not much bigger than the houseboat itself. The gates closed and there we were: houseboat, yachts, cabin cruiser, speedboat, all tossing about, a foot apart, as in a giant bathtub. From the concrete walls that towered over us long chains were loosely suspended. The older children learned to cling to these to prevent our boat from being thrown about in the rising water as the lock filled. A heavy boat smashing against its neighbour could do thousands of dollars' worth of damage.

Entering a lock was rather like threading a needle. The lock keepers rarely opened both halves of the gate, which meant I had to slide through a narrow entrance, turning off the motor well in advance so I wouldn't slam into the far side. By the time we reached the great lift lock at Kirkfield, I felt myself an old hand.

This monster was advertised as "the only steel hydraulic lift lock on earth." Imagine a swimming pool big enough to hold six yachts, each weighing 2,100 tons, rising like a barber's chair on a single piston, seven feet in diameter. Imagine a second swimming pool, the same size, being lowered on a second piston. There we were on our tossing houseboat, bobbing about in one of these tanks, hoisted fifty feet above the surrounding countryside. Nowhere in North America except on this canal could we experience such a sensation. Looking back, we could see the great ditch, dug more than a century before, running straight as a ruler toward Lake Simcoe. Ahead, at eye level, we could see it stretching forward to Balsam Lake.

We had approached this mechanical wonder through five small locks and an even stretch of water bordered by willow and brier roses. From the shrubbery there had emerged, suddenly, a pale young man in a chauffeur's uniform and cap. He hailed us and announced that he had been tracking us for miles on orders from his employer, a Mrs. James Adams, who we later discovered was also his mother-in-law. She wanted us to tie up at her dock when we reached Balsam Lake and spend a night in what she described as her "cottage."

The cottage turned out to be the most fantastic summer home in Ontario, if not in Canada – a two-storey rambling structure, three hundred feet long, containing more than forty rooms, ten bathrooms, and five fireplaces. It had once received the ministrations of ten servants but was now in sad condition. We had stumbled on a footnote to Canadian history, for Mrs. Adams, a widow in her late seventies, turned out to be the daughter of Sir William Mackenzie, a historical figure of some prominence who would eventually turn up in four of my books of narrative history. He could have well afforded this so-called cottage because he was one of the most prominent of the nineteenth-century tycoons, having built the Canadian Northern Railway with his partner, Sir Donald Mann, and involved himself in a variety of entrepreneurial ventures ranging from the Toronto streetcar system to Brazilian Traction. Mrs. Adams had read about our trip in the *Star* and, unable to resist a look at the houseboat, had driven up from Toronto to greet us on our arrival.

But Sir William's cottage was now crumbling away. "There were nine of us in the family," Mrs. Adams told us. "We all drew lots for it when my father died, and it went to me. Now I'm going to have to sell it." The children ran up and down the decaying hallways but refused to sleep in the "spook house," preferring the familiar claustrophobia of the houseboat.

By now my travel diary was appearing in the paper. Janet described the rest of the trip as being "like a royal tour, only less organized." Crowds began to follow or lie in wait for us in the various communities through which the canal system passed. At Fenelon Falls, a throng stood on the top of the lock gate and called down to us as we passed under. "Show us the baby!" they cried. "Show us the cat!"

We needed all our wits to keep the cats aboard since Sari had developed a craving for dry land and leapt ashore at every opportunity. Two of the children were detailed to chase her down at each lock. Near Rice Lake, the kitten fell into the drink and was rescued. A little later, Paul, aged three, having just been helped out of his life-jacket, tumbled overboard between the houseboat and the dock. The wash from a passing speedboat could have crushed him, but Pamela fished him out so quickly that he didn't have time to be frightened.

As we moved toward our destination the crowds increased. At Hastings we were overwhelmed by people bringing baskets of flowers, samples of local industry, and pieces of local quilting. I was signing autographs at the rate of six a minute, almost overwhelmed by the sea of outstretched hands proffering everything from little books to ragged scraps of paper. At one point, after signing a note, I looked up to find that had been being pushed at me by my nine-year-old daughter, Patsy.

"*Why?*" I asked.

"Well, everybody else was getting one," she explained.

On the way into town we were accosted by a hurrying citizen. "Get your kids down to see the houseboat!" he shouted. "Everybody's going!" I said we'd already seen the boat. "What's so special about it?" he asked. "Is it some sort of Walt Disney contraption?" I told him it was some crazy publicity stunt, ignoring the small, baffled children tugging at my shirt.

The kids were getting irritated by all this public fuss. "Can't we find a quiet spot where we can have a skinny dip without being bothered?"

they asked. I found a small, isolated cove where, in the calm waters, we briefly disported ourselves. I knew it couldn't last because I'd been receiving messages from the mayor of Campbellford about welcoming us with a brass band. And sure enough, as we splashed about, a group of Campbellfordians popped out of the bushes and, in spite of their good suits, waded knee-deep out to the houseboat. There they identified themselves as members of the Campbellford Chamber of Commerce. Would we be their guests for lunch when we arrived? We cheerfully agreed, only to find ourselves in the centre of a local political battle. The next day the mayor himself and the city treasurer were lying in wait for us. Would we be his guests at dinner? the mayor asked.

"But we've already agreed to lunch," I told him. The mayor looked mystified; the city treasurer looked perturbed. They asked for descriptions of our erstwhile hosts, like police demanding descriptions of a criminal gang. I gave them, and the mayor said darkly that he would have to look into the matter. An hour later he returned. "It's a political trick," he said. "The Chamber of Commerce is run by Conservatives. They're trying to shut out us Liberals. Why, did you know that not a single council member has been asked to that lunch? They've been plotting behind my back to steal you before we could get you into town." I felt as if I'd stumbled into a scene from Leacock's *Sunshine Sketches*.

Sure enough, lurking two full locks before Campbellford were the leaders of the chamber, complete with fast cars to spirit us all away. The lunch was refreshingly free of politics, but enough, finally, was enough. We wanted to get away from all of it. Just before sundown on our last night on the water we turned the boat's nose into a small island far from settlement. Janet put some lamb chops on the barbecue on the rear deck. There we sat, facing the reddest sunset of our journey. In the reeds we could hear the frogs croaking. Two of the younger children paddled out on air mattresses and came back with a yellow water lily. As it happened, it was my birthday and this was their present – as nice a one as I have ever had.

As we sat there in the dusk, my mind went back to earlier family trips with my sister and our parents. My mother and I still talked about them whenever she visited us; they were, in fact, among the high points of childhood. Years from now, I thought, when my children, grown, and perhaps scattered, and with children of their own, are reunited for feast

214

days and weddings, I hope they will remember this voyage and talk about it: about the great storm on Buckhorn Lake; the time the air mattress fell overboard, and we fished it out with a boat hook; about the first fish Patsy caught, and how she insisted on cooking and eating it, even though it was only six inches long; how little Paul kept claiming he saw Indians in the woods; about the time the steering wheel broke; and about the family games of Careers and the readings from *Ozma of Oz*. Would we remember what it was like on the Trent waterway back in 1961? Of course we would. How could we ever forget?

5

Broadway on the Yukon

A year later we made a second family trip, this time by station wagon and tent trailer up the Alaska Highway to Dawson, where Tom Patterson, who had created the Stratford Festival, was trying to repeat his triumph in the most unlikely town in Canada. But then, the whole country had caught the festival spirit. Every community wanted one, perhaps to match the ice carnivals that were also becoming part of the social fabric. When Tom Patterson walked into my office to describe what he was planning, I thought he was crazy. Of course, everybody had thought he was crazy when he suggested the Stratford Festival. Tom had got the idea of a Klondike Gold Rush Festival as a result of reading my book. Now he wanted to import a Broadway-style musical all the way to Dawson. How could I resist? In spite of many qualms, I joined his board of directors.

Tom had persuaded Robert Whitehead, the Canadian-born Broadway producer, to commission a musical version of Ben Jonson's *Volpone*, to be called *Foxy*, starring Bert Lahr, the rubber-faced lion of *The Wizard of Oz*, and an up-and-coming Broadway star, Larry Blyden. That would mean restoring Arizona Charlie's famous Palace Grand Theatre and bringing the entire cast to the Yukon. Somehow, with the help of government and private industry, he pulled it off.

On June 20, Janet and I and our six offspring flew to Edmonton, where I rented a nine-passenger station wagon and a two-wheel trailer that miraculously transformed itself into a nine-by-twelve tent each night. It would be a fairly formidable undertaking. We would cross five mountain ranges, 120 majestic rivers, and 8,000 mountain torrents. We would gaze

215

on some of the most beautiful alpine lakes in the world and experience extremes of heat and cold – from blue glaciers, sparkling in the sunlight, to hot springs where the water was 95 degrees Fahrenheit.

For the children it would be a long but lively school lesson – a little bit of science, geography, nature study, and history rolled into one. There were a few problems: Peggy Anne was crawling now, and that meant we had to bring along a stroller and a playpen. Janet had purchased a big Coleman lamp to light the way to the latrines at midnight, she said. I could not convince her it would be light all night. I also insisted that everybody bring big-brimmed hats with mosquito nets attached. Nobody believed we'd need them until we reached Teslin Lake, where the insects were so thick our mouths and nostrils became clogged.

We realized that we were driving through North America's last frontier. There was no other road like this one on the continent. The first hundred miles were paved, but when the pavement ended we entered an enormous wilderness area of unbroken forests, rivers, lakes, and mountains. Except for the thin wriggle of the dusty highway, it looked just as it had when the first fur traders arrived. Just how unspoiled this country remained was brought home to us when we reached Toad River. The smaller children spotted a brown mouse on a sandbar and toddled after him. The mouse made no attempt to flee. In fact, he allowed himself to be petted, and when Patsy handed him an arrowroot biscuit, the rodent, which had never known humankind, ate it greedily. We all sat down and watched him, there in the shadow of the Rockies, far from the hoots and catcalls of the settled world.

There were other small adventures. We camped near the Liard in order to enjoy the hot springs. One great pool, fringed with violets as big as pansies, was fed from two sources – a glacial stream at one end and a steaming sulphur brook at the other. I took Peggy Anne in with me but had to bounce her up and down so that the hot surface water wouldn't burn her neck.

At Whitehorse, I took the children to the local museum to see some relics of the old days. Outside, a strange little vehicle was on display – an eight-passenger open stage on sled runners. I told the kids that this was almost certainly the same sleigh in which, in 1910, their grandmother had travelled for the best part of a week between Dawson and Whitehorse with no protection from the biting cold save a fur coat and muffler and the human warmth of the other closely packed bodies.

216

My first weekly television show, in 1961, was just five minutes long. Titled By Pierre Berton, *it was an extension of my* Star *column. I sat at the desk and talked glibly into the camera.*

In those days I was a jack-of-all-media. Here I am, daring to read my own poetry and sing my own songs at a Yorkville coffee-house, the Inn on the Parking Lot.

In 1962 the Star *sent me and my family on a long odyssey up the Alaska Highway to the Gold Rush Festival in Dawson. I insisted on taking mosquito nets. Nobody understood why until we reached Teslin Lake and found we couldn't eat dinner without this protection. Our baby daughter, Peggy Anne, enjoyed the trip but kept waiting for it to get dark thus signalling her bedtime. Of course it never did.*

In 1963 my mother was a guest
along with Robert Goulet on my
television show. "Will it never
end?" she asked sotto voce just
before the wind-up. The sensitive
microphones caught it all.

Elsa Franklin joined the show in
its third year as a program
organizer. She quickly took over
in spite of resistance from the
all-male hierarchy at Screen
Gems, who didn't want a woman
producer. They soon changed
their minds. Since then she has
produced all my TV shows.

Lenny Bruce did his last television interview with me in Hollywood in 1967. Everybody was terrified he'd say a dirty word on the show, but actually he was a pussycat. (Below) *Throughout the sixties I concentrated on the issues of the day. Everywhere we travelled I interviewed groups of young people. This is Yorkville, Toronto's hippie haven.*

A dinner at the Park Plaza, Toronto, in 1967, marking our one-thousandth show. Jack McClelland at the microphone with Elsa Franklin, vice-president Lloyd Burns, and me. (Below) *In Hollywood, guests included the stripper Gypsy Rose Lee, whom I interviewed on the roof of Hollywood's Hyatt Hotel.*

Nathaniel Branden, just before he walked off the set of Under Attack.

Below: *Pierre Elliott Trudeau under attack by students at Carleton University. Some of the questions were, to put it mildly, unexpected.*

In The Great Debate,
*Peter Ustinov opted for the
negative in the resolution:
"That TV is a destructive
force in our society."
McKenzie Porter (left)
took the positive.*

Left: *"Two-Ton" Tessie
O'Shea disagreed that "the
stage is no place for a lady."
One-third of the program
involved questions and
comments from the audience.*

Here's the houseboat we took to Expo 67 the week before it threatened to sink in the Eisenhower Lock. (Below) With cartoonist George Feyer in Budapest, summer 1963. Born a Hungarian, he couldn't stand the gypsy violins, but they played in spite of him.

"Why wouldn't she drive, like us?" Peter asked. It was difficult to explain how much life had changed in the North since those days.

As we drove about town I began to spot, here and there, the occasional cabin from my parents' era. One looked oddly familiar – a small green bungalow on a side street. I remembered that I had seen it long ago in a photograph, and there was also a baby, squinting from a perambulator. The memory eluded me until I ran into an old resident who identified it. This was the very house in which my parents had lived in 1920 before moving to Dawson. I was the baby in the perambulator.

North of Whitehorse, the highway became a horror. Huge dust clouds from other vehicles blotted out the view ahead. Our clothes were caked with it, our mouths and nostrils thick with it. We kept the windows tightly shut – so tightly that the difference in pressure caused the rear window to shatter into hundreds of pieces, all the size of sugar cubes. "Take it easy!" Janet kept telling me. "Slow down!" But because of the need to phone in my column from various points, we had to allow time for me to find a terminal. Even as Janet warned me, there was a great crash and we lumbered to a stop. In my haste I'd gone off the highway and broken the trailer axle. Fortunately, I'd brought along a spare.

"Oh, well," said Pamela, once again, "it will make a great story for Dad to write."

Seven-year-old Peter was laboriously writing out a postcard to his friend Cameron Allan in Kleinburg. I was curious to know what had impressed him most on this journey through the wilderness. Would he describe the snow-capped peaks, or the mint-green lakes, or the dark little streams gurgling through the mosses? Had he been impressed by the relics in the museum? More likely, I thought, he'd write about swimming in the hot springs. I peeked over his shoulder to find out.

"Deer Cam," he had written, "I seen a old smashed up truck in a ditch on the side of the road near here. Yr friend, Pete."

Our last night was both miserable and memorable. We camped on the Canadian side of the Alaska border in pouring rain. I stripped the inner bark from some big trees and with some difficulty got a fire going. The Indians at Kluane Lake had sold us a salmon, which Janet cut into chunks, wrapped in foil, and roasted in the coals. Nobody slept in the station wagon that night. We all crammed into the tent, playpen and all, and ate the hot salmon with our fingers.

Next day we crossed into Alaska and turned off onto the Top of the

World Highway, one of the most spectacular roads on the continent. There we teetered for sixty miles on the edge of blue ridges drifting off into the haze above a bald tundra decorated with alpine flowers, the vistas stretching for one hundred miles or more in every direction. Suddenly we rattled downhill and burst out of the woods to find the grey Yukon boiling and hissing past us. There, on the far bank, rising out of the weeds and willows, was Dawson City.

"Why, it's like an old-fashioned town," Patsy cried in delight. The "pilgrims," as the invading throngs were known to the old-timers, had never seen anything like it – an Edwardian village falling into decay in the wilds of northern Canada. Here were street after street of houses where I had played as a boy, all reeling at crazy angles in the tall grass. Even more bizarre was the spectacle of those familiar wooden sidewalks alive with Broadway habitués – Bert Lahr and Robert Whitehead, the song writer Johnny Mercer, the ragtime pianist Bob Darch, even the great comedienne Beatrice Lillie, who came in from London and landed by helicopter in the local park. There were fifty newspapermen here, including a *Life* photographer and a man from *Reader's Digest*. There were four CBC crews and one CTV crew. Broadcasts were going out to three continents in five languages, including Russian.

Half of Broadway, it seemed, wanted to go to the Klondike. Ring Lardner, Jr., who had written the script for *Foxy,* was here; so was Willy Nolan, one of the country's top set designers, who shut up his Manhattan studio at considerable personal expense and set off for the North with a truckload of sets. Every one of Dawson's seven hundred available rooms had been booked, and the vacant lots were filled with campers and trailers. A number of authentically bearded men walked the wooden sidewalks – not pioneers at all but members of the chorus, who had travelled five thousand miles to be part of Tom Patterson's spectacle.

It was like the gold rush all over again, and I could not quite grasp it. Deep in the cellars of the Occidental Hotel, which I had known as the Bucket of Blood, Bob Darch found a cache of vintage champagne. We drank it all in one long continuous party. That night, Bob played ragtime piano and Johnny Mercer sang his own songs, including "Moon River." The Americans treated me as the fount of all knowledge and even asked me to find them the best fishing hole along the Klondike. I am no angler, but I did remember that in my boyhood the family had sometimes gone out to Rock Creek for Arctic grayling. So off to Rock

218

Creek we went, my guests eager to try their luck. I had not seen it for thirty years, but now the memories of those times came back – the fish in their cornmeal batter sizzling in the pan, the smell of wood smoke, and my father with his arm around my mother. "You try first," somebody said, and so, for the first time in three decades I awkwardly flung my line into the rippling waters. Almost instantly a fat grayling struck, and I landed him to the plaudits of the mob. Everybody was eager now to repeat my performance. Nobody succeeded. Before we packed up, a grizzled figure happened by and looked at us all in astonishment. "Hasn't been a fish found in this creek for twenty years," he said. I responded with a shrug, indicating smugly that some of us had the knack, others hadn't.

The Yukon Order of Pioneers held a dinner for me. I had known most of the members from childhood and gone to school with several. Walter Troberg, who had been my foreman at Middle Dominion Creek when I worked there in my teens, spoke of the miracle that had once again put the community on the map. I was asked to speak and rose, prepared to say a few words and tell two or three witty anecdotes. I talked about the old days, especially about my father, who had been a member of this lodge in his prime, proudly wearing the purple and gold sash of the Pioneers on Discovery Day, which celebrated George Carmack's famous find.

"How proud he would have been had he lived to see this day," I said. "I see his ghost everywhere...he walks the wooden sidewalks still, as he did in those days so long ago when..."

I found I could not go on. My throat would not speak the words, and the tears were streaming down my face. There wasn't a sound as, slowly, I took my seat, unable to finish. I looked across the table and saw the mistiness in the eyes of my former schoolmate Axel Nordling. "Geez," he said, "you got me doing it."

This was the beginning of Dawson's rehabilitation. The government had paid to restore the Palace Grand. The *Keno,* last of the sternwheel steamboats, had been saved from destruction and propped up on the riverbank as a tourist attraction. By all the laws of geography, history, economics, and common sense, my old home town ought to have been dead and gone. Instead, it was seething with a new vitality, a vitality that would continue long after the festival ended and would spark the restoration of the town's most historic buildings to help turn it once again into a bustling community. And all because Tom Patterson read my book about the gold rush! I have written many books since then, some of which have been praised and others damned. But this is the only time a work of mine can be said to have had some influence. *Klondike* helped preserve one of the most important heritage sites in the country. What writer could wish for more? My father would indeed have been proud.

Chapter Nine

1

"This is Pierre Berton's town," the *Vancouver Sun's* front-page colum-nist, Barry Mather, reported after a visit to the wilds of far-off Toronto. He was bemused to find that it was not possible to move a block through the city without being aware of my presence, thanks to streetcar ads, newspaper box placards, billboards, and the photograph that appeared at the head of my column, five days a week. My phone at home and at the office never seemed to stop ringing with requests, comments, news tips, and angry attacks. I listed both my numbers in the phone book, a decision that cost me a good deal of sleep but provided me with more than one column. If it was a nuisance sometimes, there was real satis-faction in the instant reactions each column provided. In the old days at *Maclean's,* at least six weeks would elapse before my pieces saw print and evoked comment. The response to my books took even longer. *Klondike* was finished in January 1958; the reviews didn't start to appear until the following October. With the column I could get an opinion into print at noon, and the phone would start ringing that night.

At the office, Ennis fielded my calls; at home, Janet usually answered the phone. She was better at it than I – polite, sympathetic, helpful. Sometimes, I thought, she spent too much time on the phone, commis-erating with callers who were suffering from injustice, discrimination, family troubles, or various maladies, mental as well as physical. But that was her nature. She would have made a wonderful politician's wife, but I was not a politician.

"You have to learn to hang up," I told her on more than one occasion.

"Oh, the poor soul," she'd say, "I just couldn't cut her off. She had to have someone to talk to." More than once, on her own, she searched about and found help for those who needed it.

I had less patience, especially with those who disturbed her sleep and mine for trivial reasons. One evening we returned home late from a party to find our eldest daughter, Penny, in tears. She had been harassed all evening by a caller who insisted that I was home and she was shield-ing me from him. He had awakened her time after time, belabouring her and refusing to take no for an answer. The following night I set my alarm for 3 a.m., phoned her tormenter, and got his wife.

"Is it really important?" she asked, blearily.

"It's a matter of life and death," I replied. She gasped, and her husband finally answered. I gave him both barrels. "I intend to call the police and have you charged with harassing a teenaged girl," I told him.

His voice shook as he pleaded with me not to carry out the threat. "I guess I had a couple of drinks and got carried away," he said. I let him stew for a while, and then took him and the phone off the hook.

A good many readers called me when they were drunk. Most were lonely and wanted to talk, usually on Sunday morning. "I'm just sitting here having a coupla beers," one regular caller used to say. "The wife and kids are at Sunday school and I got no one to talk to." So I'd talk to him. I was less enthusiastic about the calls that came after midnight from the West, usually from people at parties who forgot the three-hour time difference. Some wanted to settle a bet; if I was in a bad mood I gave them the wrong answer. Sometimes, out-of-town friends moved mountains trying to find my phone number. They never thought of looking for it in the book.

One day in June 1959, I kept count of the number of calls to my office at the *Star.* Between nine that morning and four that afternoon, thirty-seven people phoned me – a woman who wanted to expose the government, a pharmacist's wife to upbraid me for applauding the sale of generic drugs, a man complaining about the high cost of pills for diabetics, a Czech immigrant who said he couldn't get a job, a woman to say her son had been beaten up in the Don Jail, a woman who said a death threat against Toby Robins was only a publicity stunt, someone who said a recent column had made her laugh, and so on. The phone continued to ring. It rang that night at 2:30 a.m., waking me from a sound sleep. My wife picked it up. "Why won't he answer it himself?" a woman's voice, slightly slurred, demanded. "Is he a coward or something? Why won't he answer his own phone?" Janet hung up and I rolled over. Yes, I was a coward. Yet I enjoyed the give-and-take with my readers; there was no better way of estimating the quality of my audience and also the reaction that certain columns provoked. I felt a bond between us.

I did not like to waste a column by publishing letters. I thought my readers deserved better. The "mailbag" type of column is a lazy man's device. I persuaded Honderich to let me run a sixth column on Saturday – "Pierre Berton's Mailbag" – in which my readers could let off steam. I printed an occasional eulogy, but preferred this kind of letter, from one Harry Crawford:

"After reading your junk trash, I am like the English writer who wrote about Liberace. You are a purveyor of dirt. You make people vomit. Nothing nice to say about anything or anybody. You think that because you have a newspaper to hide behind you can say what you like but some day your big mouth will get you and your Paper in a lot of trouble. They ought to put you in a cage in the Riverdale Zoo now summer is here and let the kids throw peanuts at you. I am sure the city will make money out of the act...."

Since I had recently exposed the phony sales pitch invented by a "Hollywood Sales Consultant" for used-car dealers, I had a pretty good idea who Mr. Crawford was. For people like him I devised two alternative replies:

1. "Dear _____: I was absolutely delighted to receive your lively letter this morning. What a master of invective you are! I stand in awe of your use of the language. You have taken the art of insult to new heights and I salute you for it. Believe me, this is a worthy addition to my enviable collection of angry mail. In fact I may even frame it along with the bomb threats my children occasionally receive... [etc. etc.]"

2. "Dear _____: I think you should know that somebody has been using your name in the libellous mail recently received by me. I attach a copy in case you should want to take legal action. I realized at once that the signature was a forgery, since I am certain you would never stoop to writing such filth. With all good wishes, I am... [etc. etc.]"

Soon some of my readers – ex-convicts, confidence men, press agents, politicians, and ordinary people who had been victimized – began to send me tips. An aluminum-siding salesman, working the door-to-door scam, took me out for drinks and gave me the entire phony spiel that the so-called tin men used to push their product at exorbitant prices to innocent housewives. I was astonished. "Why are you telling me this?" I asked. "I'm going to give away all of your secrets in my column."

He turned to me with a smirk. "That's what I want," he said. "I'm going to use that column to sell more tin. I'll simply say, 'Look what Pierre Berton says about these phony salesmen. Isn't it awful? Thank God there are a few honest men like me still left in the business!'"

The Irish linen scam was operating in those days, and my friend Buddy Abrams, then at the *Encyclopaedia Britannica,* told me how it worked. A little old Irish lady was employed to knock on doors with a cheap piece of linen that had been soaked in coffee to make it seem ancient and valuable. She was given a story to tell and at the end instructed to say: "It's a family heirloom, do ye see, and it's been in my family these ninety-two years. But I'd rather have food on the table for me children than this beautiful bit o' linen." That night Janet greeted me with triumphant news. "This dear little Irish lady came to the door with this marvellous piece of linen," she told me, "but she said she'd rather have food on the table for her children than keep a family heirloom."

"You gave her money?"

"Oh yes, a little more than she asked for. She was so sweet and so poor."

"So will we be," I told her, "unless you start reading my column."

I gave my informants "Operative" numbers. But Marilyn Craig, known as Operative 67, was my sole professional support. It was Marilyn who checked the automobile records to find which used cars had their odometers tampered with. We also discovered that many new-car salesmen had microphones planted in their closing offices. When the salesman left a husband and wife alone he could listen in to see what they were prepared to pay. One dealer, who called himself the Mayor of Motor City, applauded me for this and made news by announcing that he was spearheading a campaign to clean up the business. Marilyn and my friend Len Bertin, the *Star*'s science editor, went to see his salesroom and easily discovered the tell-tale microphone hidden behind a framed picture. A tipster in the business had told me about it. The day after my column appeared, the Mayor of Motor City hurriedly left town.

Two others who left town were a pair of up-and-coming young lawyers – Arthur Lundy and Irving Solnik. They were not practising law but had found a more lucrative calling by charging unsuspecting widows outrageous mortgage rates. After my columns appeared exposing the operation, I got an aggrieved phone call from Solnik. "What is it you want?" he asked plaintively.

"I want to put you guys out of business," I told him.

"But what do you really want?" he asked. I repeated myself and finally he hung up. Later, a former employee told me that Solnik had a tape recorder on his phone and expected me to say I wanted money. In my naïveté that thought had not occurred to me. Theirs was one of the million-dollar libel lawsuits that came to nothing. Shortly after my last column about them, the pair moved to upstate New York.

225

I tried to keep a column or more ahead. One day the *Star* killed a column and tried to replace it with a standby. I refused to allow it. "We agreed on five columns a week, not six," I said. "If you kill a column, that's your problem." Later I sneaked a note into a column of short pieces explaining that if any column of mine didn't appear, it was not because I was "on assignment" – a euphemism if ever I heard one – but because somebody upstairs didn't like what I'd written. The brass didn't notice, which suggested that they seldom bothered to read me; the readers did.

My pieces, two columns wide, ran the full length of the right-hand side of the second front page, which dealt with local news. Sometimes, when they tried to put one on the front page, I resisted. "But this is a scoop," Harry Hindmarsh, Jr., the acting managing editor, told me one morning. "You've made news. Every newspaperman wants to be on the front page."

"Not me," I told him.

But, Harry said, this was hot stuff: the fact that a royal commission had been appointed to look into the land scandal in York Township, all because of my columns.

"It deserves the front page. What can we do?"

"What you do is write the main story quoting me, and put it on page 1 under a big headline and illustrate it with photographs of the other columns that started it," I said. Which is what they did.

Himie Koshevoy, who had been lured briefly from Vancouver as city editor, was baffled. "I don't know why you don't want the good columns on page 1," he said.

"Because," I pointed out, "that would suggest that the other columns aren't any good."

A few days later he walked into my office. "You've made your point," he said. "On the subway today I watched the people open their papers. They all skipped page 1 and turned to your column."

I enjoyed my newfound prominence. People were always coming up to ask me if I really was Pierre Berton. Sometimes I was naughty and told them I wasn't. In a Kitchener smoke shop, the proprietor asked me that question. "Who?" I said. "I'm from Poughkeepsie, here for the furniture convention."

"Well, you're his spitting image," he said. "Here's his picture in the paper."

"Are you telling me I look like that sonofabitch?" I asked.

226

He looked again. "No. I see it's not you. Sorry. You're tall and I happen to know he's a little guy."

At this time, 1958, the *Star* was engaged in a contest with the *Telegram* so deadly that the *Tely* had refused to review *Klondike* until just before Christmas, when it was too late to affect Yuletide sales. Sometimes the *Tely* tried to discredit some of my exposés. Once it went so far as to force three young immigrant girls to recant their affidavits to me regarding irregularities in the immigration department. Marilyn and I worked all night interviewing other immigrants and managed to get four more affidavits sworn. That ended the *Tely*'s abortive attempt.

Doug MacFarlane, that paper's managing editor, used to post a daily assessment letter on his bulletin board commenting on its news coverage. More than once he mentioned my column; a spy in the *Tely* always sent it to me. MacFarlane knew this and invariably spelled my name wrong, just to madden me, as he told me long afterward.

The *Tely*'s publisher, John Bassett, tried to hire me for fifty thousand a year. He did it in typical Bassett fashion, hollering into the phone, which I held out from my ear so the staff could hear the offer. This was in total contrast to Honderich's stealthy approach.

"Come on over," Bassett's voice could be heard to say. "Three columns a week and one for *Weekend*!" He was astonished when I told him I wasn't interested, even though I was making less than half his price at the *Star*.

"Why?" he asked.

"Because you'll always want to argue about what I write."

"What's wrong with that? I love to argue. I argue with our Washington guy all the time."

"Yes, I bet you do. Well, I don't need that grief. Arguments take time. Besides, there are too many taboos on your paper."

"*Taboos?*" Bassett shouted. "We don't have taboos. Name one taboo. Go on. Name one!"

"Sure, I'll name one. *Me.*"

"Whaddya mean, *you?*"

"I mean that the *Tely* will never mention my name, even when I make news or win an award."

"I don't believe that," Bassett said, "but I'll look into it right away."

The following day, October 19, 1962, Bassett sent the following memo to Doug MacFarlane, with copies to ten *Tely* columnists:

"The story is that there is an edict at the *Telegram* that Pierre Berton's name is not to be mentioned in the paper. I am told that there is an edict that his television shows cannot be mentioned favourably or unfavourably, and indeed he is to be ignored in every way, shape, or form.

"I want to make it perfectly clear that I strongly denied this story and went on to say that there were no 'taboos' of any kind on the *Telegram*.

"Pierre Berton is a newsworthy figure and an extremely popular and controversial television figure.

"While obviously we do not wish to promote a rival column, nevertheless, when the news justifies mentioning his name, it is to be treated in the same way as anybody else....

"I am sending this memo so there can be no doubt in anybody's mind as to the paper's policy in this matter."

The change was instantaneous. For the next several days it was difficult to find a personal column in the *Tely* that did not mention me.

2

Stranger in town WINNIPEG, April 16, 1962. The celebrity has arrived by jet and the press is waiting. I know what the first question will be; it is the one I used to ask when I worked the hotel beat in Vancouver – the standard question tossed at visiting firemen in every Canadian city except Toronto, where nobody cares: "What do you think of our city?" I know I should respond with the standard answer – that this is the nicest and friendliest city in Canada – but I am suffering from jet lag and feel a little out of sorts, so instead, I tell the truth: I know nothing about Winnipeg – haven't seen it, except from the air.

My frankness is immediately exploited; the TV people hire a limousine and insist on a tour of the town. I curse inwardly and blame the new jet age, which ensures that any traveller arrives at his destination in a state of collapse, a victim of the time-zone changes. As soon as I settle into the limousine's cushions I drop off to sleep. Occasionally I'm shaken awake to examine a typical Winnipeg slum area or the site of the new city hall. I open my eyes, stare fixedly at the object while they take some film, then drop off again. After ninety minutes of this, the TV people give up and deposit me at my hotel, explaining that they will tape

228

the interview later, and that in the meantime I should think carefully about Winnipeg.

All I want to do is catch up on some sleep, but that is not to be. A reporter is hammering on my door, asking me what I think about the budget. He has a crisp, no nonsense air about him, and I notice that he has written down all his questions in advance with small spaces underneath for the answers. I cannot remember anything about the budget except Macpherson's cartoon of the finance minister, Donald Fleming. The reporter looks shocked, and I can see him scribbling MUM ON BUDGET underneath the question.

"In what way do Canadian reading habits differ from U.S. reading habits?" he raps at me.

A slight sense of panic seizes me. I haven't any idea, and he looks pained.

"Well, do Canadians prefer fiction or non-fiction?" he prompts me. Both, I tell him, but maybe, I add, they like non-fiction better; that seems to be the trend these days. In my mind I can see the paragraph in print: "Canadians read more non-fiction than Americans," Pierre Berton declared in Winnipeg today. And that is exactly how it comes out.

"What do you think about sex in books?" asks the reporter, scribbling furiously. "Good or bad?"

This is the "in" question of the era; everybody argues about sex in books, perhaps because they're not getting much any other way. But I know that he's got me. It will be either BERTON LAUDS SEX BOOKS or BERTON URGES BAN ON MODERN NOVELS. Right now I am too weary to fence with him, so I say, simply, that I don't see how sex can be removed from all novels since sex is part of life, isn't it?

He writes it all down, and I get some sleep and then repair to the TV studio to be interviewed on the subject of Winnipeg. The interview is preceded by a film showing me striding about the city, staring at slum dwellings and Massey Medal-winning architecture with a look of fierce concentration in my eyes. Few viewers will realize I was just trying to keep them open. When it comes to talking about Canadian cities I have an ace in the hole that I learned from Ned Pratt, the wild Vancouver architect. With one or two exceptions, all Canadian cities are exactly the same. So I give them my talk on What's Wrong with Toronto using all the approved jargon about Urban Sprawl, Urban Renewal, Green-Belt Zoning, and other buzzwords of the day. Nobody turns a hair.

On the way out to the airport next day I pick up a newspaper and glance at it casually. There it is for all to see:

SEX IN BOOKS OKAY

SAYS PIERRE BERTON

"Sex on Canadian news-stands does no harm if read by children," author and TV personality Pierre Berton said in an interview here Thursday. "Sex is part of life...."

I steel myself for the inevitable flood of angry letters from the blue-stockings of Winnipeg and board the jet for the next stop.

3

Late-night chatter When I returned from the houseboat trip in August 1961, I said good-bye to CHUM. I had written and voiced close to eight thousand capsule comments over the previous three years, not only for the Toronto radio station but also for thirty others that CHUM had brought into the fold. But I had other TV plans in mind. I was still appearing on *Close-Up* and *Front Page Challenge* but needed more time to pursue my newest idea.

Meanwhile, I published my first picture book, *The New City,* with photographs by a young Swiss photographer, Henri Rossier. In the text I attempted to describe the remarkable transformation of Toronto. I had been chronicling these changes in my column and was now able to write that Toronto the Good had become Toronto the Bawdy, the most wide-open town in English-speaking Canada. I used the example of "Cup-cakes" Cassidy, a woman of awesome mammary development, who told me she could do things in Hogtown that wouldn't be allowed south of the border. With half a million immigrants now hived in the city – including 180,000 Italians – the old image of the town existed only in memory. The traditional Toronto Sunday, I wrote, didn't stand a chance; the Old Torontonian was virtually an extinct breed. People were living in apartments downtown; they were demanding better restaurants, more entertainment, and an Open Sunday. I called Toronto "a city in ferment."

The book laid an egg. Torontonians didn't want to read about them-selves. Outsiders didn't want old illusions shattered. "Its principal weakness," wrote the *Montreal Star,* "is that it is all about Toronto." The Winnipeg *Tribune* attacked "the insufferable smugness of the

230

Torontonian." The *Vancouver Sun's* reviewer said the only thing he liked was the passage that said "all Torontonians are gimlet-eyed sharks waiting to bite the pound of flesh from the rest of the country." Had I written that? No, I hadn't – nor anything like it. But it was clear that Toronto was stuck with its old image. When the *Sun's* gossip columnist, Jack Wasserman, came to Toronto to appear as a guest panellist on *Front Page Challenge,* he returned to Vancouver and published a diatribe on Toronto. Gordon Sinclair put him in his place by revealing on radio that Wasserman had spent his spare time looking for a job for his songstress wife – a job, of course, in Toronto.

With my exhausting radio stint behind me, I was exploring the idea of doing the same thing on television – short, pithy comments to fit into a five-minute format. Why was I adding to my workload? The hard fact is that a Canadian journalist, if he is to support a growing family and an expanding house, must use every talent he has. A best-selling author south of the border, or a big-time columnist, or a radio star, or a television panellist could do only that one thing and still make a fortune. In Canada, it is necessary to have several strings to one's bow.

I was no longer poor, but I had six growing children. We needed more bedrooms, more bathrooms, more of everything. I needed a place to write at home, and all this meant more expensive additions. There was more to it than that, of course. As a child of the Great Depression, I worried about the bottom line. What if I died? Would there be enough for Janet? What if I fell sick and couldn't work; how would we live? Anybody raised in the thirties will understand this preoccupation with financial security. In the sixties jobs were plentiful; the good life beckoned. The youth revolution was about to begin – one in which a new generation of boys and girls would give no thought to their financial future, thus creating a generation gap between themselves and their cannier parents. Yet just as Janet was recycling the kitchen vegetable garbage in a compost pile, so I was recycling my own work – putting collections of columns between hard covers and hoping to benefit from what would soon become known in television circles as "spin-offs."

Somebody once said that I had taken more gold out of the Klondike than any prospector. There was some truth in that. One work, *Klondike,* had produced a series of spin-offs ranging from magazine articles to films. I was being called the Great Recycler, and I could not quarrel with the epithet.

In 1961 I proposed to recycle more material into a five-minute television broadcast. I paid for the pilot, titled, like my column, *By Pierre Berton,* and peddled it around until it caught the eye of Steve Krantz, then the top honcho in Canada for Screen Gems, a subsidiary of Columbia Pictures. It didn't occur to me to get any money up front. I was to be co-producer and co-owner and would receive a slice of the net profits. Steve Krantz, whose wife, Judith, wrote pieces for *Maclean's* and would soon become a best-selling novelist, sold the idea to several TV stations and found an Ontario sponsor, Independent Grocers. The show was mildly successful and ran daily for about sixteen weeks. It was not terribly controversial, although when I suggested that Prince Charles marry a black African to prove that the Commonwealth meant something, there was a reaction. In Vancouver, that hotbed of royalists, one local columnist declared: "There are a lot of people in town who are lynch mad at Pierre Berton."

The program clearly made a profit for Screen Gems, but not for me. Profits? There weren't any because of the Hollywood system of creative bookkeeping. When I approached Steve Krantz about this, he simply shrugged and said, "Well, you wanted to own the show." My ego had got the better of my business sense. The company, by contract, had charged one-third of the price to "distribution costs." I had learned a valuable, if expensive, lesson. When dealing with filmmakers, never take a percentage of the net. There never *is* any net.

No matter. My connection with Screen Gems led to a new career. The company was interested enough in the five-minute spots to think of me in broader terms. We talked of several ideas for the coming season, and I realized I would be too busy to continue to handle assignments for *Close-Up.* My last appearance, in June 1962, caused considerable controversy and not a little fury. Near the end of an interview with Lester Pearson, then leader of the Liberal Opposition, I had asked a version of the "Better Dead than Red" question. Would he rather live under Nikita Khrushchev than suffer a nuclear war? His response stirred up a hornet's nest.

It is hard now to recreate the passions of those times. The Red scare had reached its zenith. Almost every organization slightly to the left of centre was smeared with the Red tag. Pat Boone, the popular singer, had announced that if the communists ever took over, he would personally shoot all his children rather than have them live under a Red dictatorship.

When I asked the question, Pearson gave a sensible answer: "Well, I want to do what I can to make that choice unnecessary, but if I have to make it, I would rather live under Mr. Khrushchev than die, and do what I could to throw him and his type out of power."

For this Pearson was assailed as being "soft on Communism," and I was attacked for asking the question in the last ten seconds of the program. I felt uncomfortable about that. I hadn't realized the show was almost over, but of course I should have known; after all, that was my job. I wrote Pearson a note apologizing for throwing him a tough question with only seconds to spare. He responded graciously, saying there was no need to apologize, he understood the nature of the business and was always prepared to take his chances.

Screen Gems had agreed that I would host a late-night talk-and-interview show along the lines that Jack Paar was pioneering in the United States. Herb Sussan, an old pro who had been responsible for NBC's *Wide World of Sport,* was brought in as executive producer. CFTO, the local CTV outlet, bought the concept. The program was to be one hour in length at 11:30 p.m., five nights a week, and would be launched in the fall.

I wanted Ross McLean as my producer. He was an old friend, he understood television, and having departed *Close-Up* the previous year, he was available. Although he had certain weaknesses, he also had undeniable strengths. My outlook was journalistic, his was show business, and so we complemented each other. I was most comfortable in an interview situation that called for probing questions. But I did not believe that a full hour every night could survive on that kind of journalism alone. What was also needed – and Ross could provide this – was witty conversation and big names from the entertainment industry. Until this time, Ross had been the star of his own shows, not in front of the cameras but certainly behind them. That was the CBC style; the corporation did not like to promote its on-camera performers into stardom – a very Canadian attitude. If there was a Cult of Personality, it was to be found among producers like Ross, who picked the guests, wrote the scripts, and turned unknowns into television stars. But now he was working with a man who was not only known but also perfectly capable of writing his own material. We clashed over that from time to time. I let Ross have his way; he clearly knew more about the medium than I did, and I was prepared to learn.

I baulked, however, when he tried to give the program one of those bloodless names – *Tabloid, Close-Up, Telescope, Graphic* – that were so dehumanizing. To the CBC, television hosts were faceless and interchangeable; if one doesn't work, get another. As a result, the programs themselves tended to be devoid of personality. There was tremendous resistance, not only on Ross's part but also from the Canadian executives. Finally, after one of those arguments, Herb Sussan took me aside and said: "Call it *The Pierre Berton Hour* and insist on that title. That way, they can't fire you."

Sussan, a warm and ebullient man, was often driven to desperation by Canadian attitudes. He said to me once, when Screen Gems was trying to sell the show to independent stations: "This is the craziest country! Here I am, an American, involved with a company producing American TV shows, arguing with Canadians that they ought to buy a Canadian show; and here are the Canadians arguing against it. They'd rather have an American-filmed series. Dammit, I ended up sounding like a Canadian nationalist! How can that possibly be?"

How indeed? I would like to think that *The Pierre Berton Hour* was sold entirely on its merits, but the facts, I fear, were different. If it had not been for the 55 percent Canadian content rule, there would have been no show at all.

The statistics of that first year of production exhaust me when I read them. We produced 195 hours of television with 406 different guests, 70 percent of whom were Canadian, and 163 were new faces never seen before on the small screen. There had been nothing like it before in Canada. The CTV network picked up the show after the New Year and moved the time back to 11 p.m., a difficult slot because it was seen opposite the avuncular Earl Cameron reading the CBC news. But we made news ourselves, largely because of the calibre of our guests, who ranged from Lester Pearson to my mother. My own performance as a host was wanting, and I knew it. I was called "a bloody bore," "pompous," "outwardly cold and hard," "gauche, trite, ill at ease and downright inept." Of my first interview with Pearson, then in opposition, Nathan Cohen wrote: "Mr. Pearson did his level best to make Pierre Berton relax last night.... He showed tact and patience, even though his host's mental perspiration made much of the hour a strain...." I couldn't disagree with these assessments. I was not, as Cohen pointed out, "a natural conversationalist," a failing that produced "all kinds of fumbles, hesitations and uncomfortable tensions." I knew I would have to learn the hard way, making an ass of myself at times in front of hundreds of thousands of viewers. It was hard work, and I did not relish it.

The devilish thing about television is that one cannot learn one's craft in private. A TV performer is on display from the very first instant the cameras light up. It is a problem that has existed in no other communications medium. An author is allowed to rewrite, a movie director to re-shoot, but in the kind of television I was doing, there was no second chance. That I survived was a tribute less to myself than to the patience and understanding of a variety of people, notably Ross, who suffered more or less silently through my early fumbling. In the days before the late-night show began, a kind of goofy egotism carried me along. A feeling of confidence is important on TV; it communicates itself to the viewer in some mysterious manner – and vice versa, as Nathan Cohen saw. But confidence is no substitute for technique. It was when I realized the enormous difficulties I faced that I began to lose my confidence; and then every appearance became a torture for me. I knew I was still an amateur. Those first appearances on *Tabloid* and *Close-Up* hadn't been bad; in fact, somebody wrote in the press that I was "the hottest interviewer on television." But later, on both *Close-Up* and my own show, I was simply terrible much of the time. The press noted it, and that only served to reduce my confidence further. All I could do was grit my teeth and bear it, hoping that sooner or later I would learn.

At the outset I found it impossible to concentrate. The ability to *listen* while chaos reigns around you – while the cameras circle about like unblinking vultures, while a man with earphones stabs at you with crossed fingers *(only thirty seconds left!)*, while a disembodied voice in your ear whispers that Camera 2 has gone *ph ttt* this ability is the most difficult of all techniques to absorb. It was some time before I was able to hypnotize myself into a state of concentration and shut off all extraneous noise and movement so that I could give my undivided attention to the one aspect of television that really matters – program content.

I was also criticized, quite correctly, for talking too much and interrupting the guests – "drowning them out," in one critic's phrase. "It's a toss-up which interrupts the conversational trend more effectively, Berton or the commercials," Bob Gardiner wrote in the *Ottawa Citizen*. "The man's presence seems to be a liability unless he learns to shut up."

Slowly, I began to learn my craft, to listen, and not to interrupt, unless the guest was a bloody bore. When Irving Layton or Malcolm Muggeridge or James Baldwin or Farley Mowat was declaiming, I let him talk and forgot my preconceived ideas about moving the program along. I had to learn to relax. This took time, but as the season progressed, so did I. Improvement in this field does not come gradually; it comes in spurts. Suddenly, one day I was far better than I had been the day before.

I was even praised for my next interview with Pearson during the 1963 federal election campaign. "Berton was on his mettle and threw every embarrassing question he could think of," Pat Pearce wrote in the *Montreal Star*. Richard O'Hagan, Pearson's press secretary, told me that Pearson liked being pressed hard; it brought out the best in him, he said. The press agreed; the conventional wisdom was that this was Pearson's finest appearance of the entire campaign. I'm not sure Tommy Douglas, the NDP leader, felt this way. As a known NDP sympathizer, I knew I could not be sycophantic and so pitched him hardballs that took him by surprise, though he held his own. It was the first time in Canada that political leaders had been given an hour on a television show in the midst of a campaign, and it was hailed as a significant and important event, the start of something new, and, in the future, inevitable.

Once the CTV network took us on we began to use music – popular singers and musicians. We also travelled to Vancouver to appease the CTV station there and managed to record five hours of talk one day and two musical hours the next. In New York, we taped sixteen programs in four days. Big-name stars like Woody Allen, Merv Griffin, Rudy Vallee, Al Capp, and Ogden Nash were hustled through in groups of three – Ross's penchant for loading each show with too many guests. I would have preferred a one-on-one discussion.

As a highly eligible bachelor, Ross habitually squired some of the most attractive women in town. I always felt that he treated them more as ornaments than as people, for he changed them as regularly as he changed his ties, wearing each one on his arm like a piece of jewellery but carefully avoiding any entanglement. He liked to decorate the set of *The Pierre Berton Hour* with one or more "talking dolls," as he called them – women whose task it was to sit at my table, look glamorous, and, when called on, contribute to the conversation. I remember encountering one of his sometime companions in London, married by then to Chris

236

Chataway, the long-distance runner who had paced Roger Bannister and John Landy in the four-minute mile spectacular in Vancouver. When I told her I was from Canada she announced that she had once worked for the *Toronto Star* and had also dated Ross McLean. "You belong," I told her, "to the two largest veterans' organizations in the country." She confessed that her experience as Ross's casual date had become frustrating for, she said, he had never so much as tried to kiss her good night.

Ross finally succumbed to Jean Templeton, a pretty comedienne who had been one of the mainstays of *Spring Thaw* as both writer and performer in the days when she was married to another comedian, Dave Broadfoot. Jean came along when we took my talk show to New York. I traded Ross and Jean my suite for a single room, as they had already announced that their impending nuptials would be solemnized at the New York City Hall. Here I spotted what I predicted (rightly, alas) would be an obstacle to a long-lived marriage. Ross was fastidious to a fault. His own apartment in Toronto seemed to have been cosmeticized by *House Beautiful* – not a magazine or a newspaper out of place, and every objet d'art carefully arranged for inspection, rather like Ross's female companions. Jean represented a contrast. Once, in the suite, I remember Ross carefully setting out all her various toiletries in neat rows according to size and shape. Jean entered, took one look at her future husband's handiwork, and with a single, sweeping gesture reduced the entire arrangement to rubble.

When our shows were completed, we repaired to the city hall, Ross in his blazer, Jean in a gorgeous blue outfit with a matching broad-brimmed hat that set off her copper hair, myself as best man, and, as bridesmaid, Ulla Moreland, a model imported from Montreal by Ross to add to the decor of the show. At the city hall we all felt distinctly out of place, like badly dressed visitors to some exotic realm. The hallways were jammed with young Hispanics in gorgeous tuxedos and ruffled shirts of various hues. Their brides-to-be were resplendent in dazzling white lace from neck to ankle. We waited our turn and stood before a civil servant who muttered a few words and sent us quickly on our way. The post-nuptial reception dragged on past midnight, thanks to the presence of Eddie Condon, the world's most famous jazz guitarist and a guest on the show, who refused to leave until the last bottle was drained. Condon was noted for never having taken a solo during all his years with the band. But he was certainly a solo act that night.

237

By this time the show had lost some of its rough edges and was a slicker, if not necessarily a better, production. We were, like all TV shows, fighting for our life. By spring the program was being hailed (by Bob Burgess in the Ottawa *Journal,* among others), as "the best thing on late night television. Controversial, witty, amusing, informative, nostalgic...." Nevertheless, by March, rumours were rife that the network would not renew it the following year because we were not attracting sponsors. Gordon Keeble, the CTV vice-president, told the press that some advertisers were reluctant to be associated with the program's frank treatment of such subjects as "crime, abortion, and the mating customs of the Canadian female."

This was a generation before Oprah, Geraldo, and Shirley. Any program that touched on sex or morals was virtually taboo. But these were among the programs I wanted to do, in addition to such series as "The National Purpose," with guests of the calibre of Bruce Hutchison, Frank Underhill, and André Laurendeau. One of my programs had featured a bisexual male. In another I had talked with two young prostitutes. That brought a "ceaseless twenty-four hours of phone calls," according to Screen Gems. These were subjects that had never been explored on television before, and the sponsors weren't pleased. Then, in May, a program I had taped with Helen Gurley Brown dealing with her best-selling book, *Sex and the Single Girl,* was hoisted by the network and never shown, following complaints from listeners who had heard about it and from some organizations that had not seen it. All this seems fatuous today, but it was a serious matter then. The program was innocuous enough, but something was happening. As Jon Ruddy reported in the *Telegram,* the real reason for CTV's action was not the specific topic but "a growing controversy surrounding the series and Berton himself."

"In the past months," Ruddy reminded his readers, "the show has turned again and again to tender areas of public opinion. Berton has unearthed some disturbing facts about burial costs and customs. He has probed drug addiction, organized crime, penal institutions, abortion, and prostitution, in a manner guaranteed to offend the sensitive, and antagonize all manner of organized groups." The nature of the protests, he wrote, indicated that a religious organization was at work. He was right. As they later publicly boasted, the Catholic Women's League and the Roman Catholic lay association, the Knights of Columbus, were after my scalp. They wanted me off the air and also out of print. In the latter attempt they were remarkably successful.

4

When *The Pierre Berton Hour* went on the air in the fall of 1962, it was *Hoaxing* soon apparent that I would have difficulty continuing to write a daily *the kids* column for the *Star*. That October, Ken Lefolii, who was now editor of *about sex* *Maclean's*, approached me with an offer to write a fortnightly column on the back page of the magazine about anything that struck my fancy. Lefolii's offer would take a tremendous load off my shoulders and allow me to put more time and thought into trying to improve my television technique, which, to put it mildly, needed it. I wrote my last column on November 9. For four years and two months, my name had been familiar to the *Star*'s readers, spelled out in twenty-four-point type at the head of my column, "By Pierre Berton." But not, apparently, to the *Star*'s editors. Five days after I vanished from the paper it turned up in a headline on the entertainment page, spelled "BURTON."

My decision to return to *Maclean's* was a miscalculation of horrific proportions. Four years before I had gone from the magazine world to that of the newspaper and had used the magazine technique to produce a different kind of daily column. When I went back, I tried to use my *Star* techniques, and they just didn't work. As a newspaper columnist I had everything going for me. My main audience was confined to a single city. I could toss in local allusions. I could satirize local events, report on local discoveries, refer to local personalities. Moreover, I needed to have only one or two really sharp columns each week; they were the ones people remembered. I could fill out the week with minor items – nostalgia, humour, food, gardening. At the magazine I had just one column a fortnight, and it always had to be a zinger. I couldn't afford to be less than pertinent, and I had to play on a national stage. My column had to hit people where they lived, be it Campbell River or Conception Bay. There's no doubt that my chores as a nightly television host were interfering with the time I needed to produce such a column for the magazine. I had had such an easy time of it on the *Star* that I thought I could knock off a piece the same way for *Maclean's*. Of course, I couldn't. It took me a long time to get this through my head.

Years later, Allan Fotheringham, in the same space, showed how it could be done.

I was beginning to get the knack of it by April 1963, when I succeeded in persuading Lester Pearson to let me spend election night with him. I remember the scene well: Keith Davey shouting "It's a Newfie sweep!" as the news came in from the Atlantic; Pearson studying the endless stream of teletype messages that eager party workers, wearing "MIKE FOR ME IN '63" badges, put in his lap; Mrs. Pearson, with her corsage of red roses, listening to James Minifie on the CBC trying to assess Social Credit's failure at the polls. "I don't know what caused it," Minifie was saying. "Common sense caused it," said Maryon Pearson, looking firmly at the picture tube.

I was the only reporter allowed in for the entire evening. "Judy got elected!" someone cried, and Pearson grinned. "Truth will prevail," he said, for Judy LaMarsh had been a member of the controversial Truth Squad that tailed the Tories and caught them in exaggerations. When the news of the Social Credit setback in Quebec came in, Pearson looked cheerful. "Maybe it's the best thing about this election," he said. "It sort of restores your faith in the voter. It says the people of Quebec don't want to be steamrollered." But neither did the rest of Canada. Duncan McTavish, a Liberal elder statesman, was burbling, "It looks good"; but Pearson, adding up figures on a small pad, knew otherwise. The West was sticking to John Diefenbaker. "I couldn't make myself into a farmer, Jack," he said good-naturedly, as Jack Pickersgill arrived with his family. By 10:50 p.m. he announced that a clear majority was no longer possible. "Let's turn on the Academy Awards and get down to fundamentals," he said, with just a trace of false heartiness. Nobody budged. A commentator at national Liberal headquarters was claiming that the results would not be known until midnight. O'Hagan told him the service vote could upset at least five seats. "We might just squeak in, at that," Mike Pearson said. "But I'll tell you one thing. This election won't be over for another week. I'd better go down now and tell them that. After that there's nothing more to do except go home and get some sleep." And off he went in his rumpled suit, a genial and easy-going man, and, as it turned out, prime minister of Canada by a narrow squeak.

I needed to do more of this kind of reporting for *Maclean's*. That same month I had squirrelled away a clipping quoting a psychiatrist on the

240

subject of adolescent sex. I decided to use it as an angle in a column expressing my own views. I didn't realize at the time that this was exactly the kind of column the back page required. Alas, the management of Maclean Hunter did not agree.

I called the column "Let's Stop Hoaxing the Kids About Sex." Because of the unholy row it stirred up, I reprint here the gist of it:

> The most recent statistics place the annual total of new outpatients in Ontario psychiatric hospitals at 9,600. Of these an astonishing 4,000 are under the age of sixteen. Commenting on the reasons for this, Dr. Elliott Markson, a psychiatrist who deals with sexual deviates, had this to say:
>
> "Sexual feelings of adolescents are encouraged by the stress on sex in our culture but the official morality of this country is based on postponement. All early sexual experiences for this reason are surreptitious and associated with shame."
>
> Thus did Dr. Markson put his finger on the evil of the Great Twentieth-Century Hoax, whereby every adolescent is taught that sex is the key to everything – but he can't enjoy it for another ten, fifteen or twenty years.
>
> The popular magazines (and I do not wholly exclude this one) have for decades been a party to this hoax. In countless Pollyanna articles and absurd boy-girl fiction they have contributed to the legends that claim that virginity is the greatest prize a girl can bring to the altar, that premarital intercourse can lead only to disaster, and that abstinence is the only policy for unmarried people to follow. None of these statements is necessarily true. Indeed I can think of cases where they are demonstrably false and dangerous. (Kinsey has shown, for instance, that almost half of all American women have enjoyed premarital sex and that few have regretted it.) Yet we continue to be fed these myths.
>
> We had better make the best of the fact that teenage sex is here to stay and that we adults have been helping to build the kind of society in which it flourishes. We have fashioned a world in which "popularity" is the pinnacle to which every youth aspires and then we have managed to equate sexiness

with popularity. And we have sold this package to the kids for straight commercial gain.

For sexual popularity is the foundation on which the great postwar Teen Market has been built. It is the basis of the Going-Steady syndrome – a kind of insurance that young-sters buy to make certain of continued social success through guaranteed dates. What do the ads mean when they urge Sis to *Be the Most Popular Girl in Your Class?* The illustra-tions give the key: they show her being nuzzled by one or more males.

A glance at the score of magazines which live off twelve- and fourteen-year-olds shows what the commercial world is up to. These publications are almost exclusively devoted to the sexual philanderings of adult hero-figures and the on- and-off romances of their teenage counterparts....

With this profitable gibberish being pumped into every child's ear, is it really surprising when teenagers remark on TV (as one did to me) that "sex is the thing to do," when a Toronto Anglican minister states that one quarter of young brides he marries are pregnant (an Edmonton United Church minister tells me it's closer to half with him), or when a California health officer surveys twenty-one schools and reports that teenagers are being seduced by a culture of "fun morality" and that a good many girls consider pregnancy a status symbol?

Yet there seems no likelihood that this state of affairs will change. Unless society does an about-face children are going to be lured into earlier and earlier alliances that are, in effect, mock marriages in which everything is officially condoned save the final moment of consummation. This being true, then surely our attitudes are going to have to change. Having goaded the infants into a state of emotional and romantic frenzy for which intercourse, rather than cold baths, must be the obvious release, we are going to have to accept teenage sex as matter-of-factly as we now accept the other facets of togetherness.

Specifically, I say, society is going to have to accept the fact that premarital sex isn't always a bad thing: what *is* bad is the sense of guilt, shame and sin which keeps young people at arm's length from their parents and in a state of constant emotional tension. Further, we must make much less fuss about virginity and continence and realize that, while they're okay for some people, they are not necessarily okay for all.

The churches ought to be giving a lead in these matters – after all, it was they who made the original fuss about sex. By equating it with wickedness, they rendered it commercially exploitable. It's no accident, as Dr. Markson the psychiatrist has pointed out, that "the incidence of sex problems among ministers' children is very high." A twenty-one-year-old prostitute told me recently that she left home because she was "fascinated by sin." Her parents, both Salvation Army officers, had attacked sex so much they made it sound positively attractive.

It's good news that some churches are facing up to the realities of the new age. E.R. Bagley, an Anglican archdeacon in Toronto, recently wrote that the church should restate its beliefs on sex in recognition of the shifting values among the young. A few days later the Archbishop of Canterbury himself said much the same thing. The Quakers, in a remarkable pamphlet published in Britain, have gone even further:

"The insincerity of the sexual moral code may well be the cause of the widespread contempt of the younger generation for society's rules and inhibitions....

"If Christianity is a true faith there can be no ultimate contradiction between what it demands of us and what in practice works.... We have no hesitation in taking every now and then an empirical approach – to ask, for instance... whether premarital intercourse is necessarily a bad preparation for marriage, whether to have a variety of sexual partners does in fact weaken intimate relations and destroy a community...."

A good many people have been saying all this privately for some time. Few have said it publicly.

When I reached this point in the column I stopped, sat back, and did some thinking. I knew what the response would be: what about your own daughters? You are, in effect, condoning premarital sex. Do you also condone it for them, or are you being a hypocrite? Unless I mentioned my own personal feelings, the column would be a cop-out. And so I continued:

> At this point I fancy I hear a Greek chorus of well-intentioned old women carolling their slogan: "Would you want your daughters, etc...?"
>
> Well, I have several daughters, Mesdames, and I must tell you that this is not a question that haunts my slumber. They are pretty levelheaded girls and if, in a moment of madness or by calculated design, they find themselves bedded with a youth (and I trust it will be a bed and not a car seat) I do not really believe the experience will scar their psyche or destroy their future marriages. Indeed I would rather have them indulge in some good, honest, satisfying sex than be condemned to a decade of whimpering frustration brought on by the appalling North American practice called "petting."
>
> Be that as it may, I pray one thing is clear to them: whatever occurs, they will always have the full sympathy of their parents. They will not be banished into the snowstorm with their little bundle, nor will they be made to suffer shame for acting out, to its ultimate conclusion, the latest Hit Parade ballad or fan-magazine fantasy. Neither will they be condemned to the hell of an incompatible shotgun marriage simply because, for one evening, they decided to learn for themselves what all the adult shouting was about.
>
> As for my sons, I fully expect that by the age of seventeen they will know, from experience, something about life and that when they finally wed they will be wise enough in the ways of the world to make their wives physically content, and tolerant enough, by reason of previous experience, to make their marriages compatible.

It was this personal credo that caused the wave of indignation that swept across the country, with me the target. Here was this dirty old man saying he didn't care if his daughters screwed around – and daring to say it in the pages of a family magazine!

The editors of the family magazine did not utter a squeak about this column. It was passed, copy edited, set into type, and published just as

244

I wrote it. I remember Peter Gzowski, who was then managing editor, passing my office and pausing when I asked him if he thought the column would cause much controversy. Gzowski shook his head. "We got rid of all *those* subscribers some time ago," he said. At *Front Page Challenge* that Monday, Larry Mann, who was hired to warm up the audience, praised the article as good common sense.

It has been my observation that when a traditional institution or belief is about to crumble, its supporters close ranks and fight like mad dogs to preserve it. That explains Joyce Davidson's public pillorying when she remarked on television that Canadians were generally indifferent to the most recent royal tour. I took her side at the time and was mildly pilloried myself. Her sin was not just to say that Canadians were indifferent to royalty but to say it during a guest appearance on *Today,* a morning program on NBC. The furore was so great that the CBC, to its undying shame, buckled under the pressure and dropped Joyce from the program for several days. It would have been better for all concerned, and better journalism, if they had kept her on and exploited the controversy, pro and con. Instead they shut Joyce up. Yet people *were* already becoming indifferent to royal tours and the royal soap opera.

Now, on the very eve of the sexual revolution of the sixties, I had dared to say that premarital sex wasn't necessarily bad, and – worse – that I hoped my daughters, if they indulged, would use a double bed and not a car seat. I cannot begin to describe the absolute howl of rage that reverberated across the land after the column appeared. One of the most vicious letters came from a neighbour who wrote to my wife that she would never allow any of her children to play with ours again. I must say that my own daughters took the controversy with considerable aplomb. Penny, my eldest, came home from high school and said, "Hey, Dad next time you mention me in a column would you let me know in advance?" She had been subjected to some mild badinage and, not having read my piece, had no idea what the fuss was about.

Over this period I was called more nasty names than anyone else in Canada. I was labelled, among other things, a Godless atheist, a sexual pervert, a slug, a dirty, evil old man, a Communist, a pornographer, a brainless scrivener, a wicked influence, a yellow journalist, a subversive, a moron, a nut. A group of Edmontonians wrote: "Here at the University all who read [Berton's] personal views think he is a sexual deviant." The principal of Knox Christian School, Bowmanville, said that my ideas "were more to be feared than nuclear bombs or Communist betrayal." A Kamloops reader urged that I get seven years in the penitentiary for contributing to juvenile delinquency. A Glace Bay reader demanded that *Maclean's* "send this man back with the Doukhobours." A Moose Jaw subscriber said that "no one but the scion of a totally uninhibited jungle ape would hold such views."

I noticed a curious thing about the most extreme mail: the real, deep-dyed, true-blue puritans could not resist using dirty words when they wrote to me. I had observed this phenomenon some months earlier as a result of a remark I had made on *Front Page Challenge*. The guest was a marvellous hoaxer named Alan Abel who appeared in the guise of one Bruce Spencer, allegedly the founder of the Society for Naked Animals, a group determined to put brassieres on cows and jock straps on horses. During the question period, I remarked casually that I saw nothing reprehensible about nudity. I often walked about the house early in the morning, I said, with no clothes on. That also produced a storm of protest, including the inevitable dirty mail from women who insisted on describing me in the nude, genitals and all. It tells something about the state of the nation, then and now, that although this casual remark on TV occurred more than thirty years ago, people still remember it and interviewers want to know if I still walk about the house in the buff.

But this time the fury was more than redoubled. The violence of the response demonstrated that I had scratched a raw nerve in society. A good many, including those who preached sermons attacking me or who launched resolutions against me at public meetings, had clearly misread what I was trying to say, if indeed they read it at all. One wrote that I was leading my readers to believe that "you would even encourage your daughters in taking the first steps that lead to becoming prostitutes." The head of the Ottawa Parent-Teachers Association declared that the author had proclaimed "to the world the unlimited license [he] hoped his own daughters would enjoy with teenagers of the opposite sex." John Rempel, a Toronto architect, said he hoped all my daughters would become pregnant by the age of fifteen.

The more powerful pressure, however, came from the Roman Catholic lay groups, especially the Knights of Columbus and the Catholic Women's League. At its convention in Banff, the league urged members to send written protests to Maclean Hunter. The Knights, at their

246

convention, recommended that all members who subscribed to *Maclean's* cancel their subscriptions. Probably more effective was the solid pressure put on advertisers in the magazine by the Roman Catholic laity, especially those who had commercial clout.

At first I was unaware of the extent of the storm that was building; after all, I had received angry letters before this. The first hint that something was really wrong came when I walked out the front door of the Maclean Hunter building on University Avenue and noticed that Donald Hunter, the vice-president, and several executives were pointedly turning their backs on me. Usually Don Hunter had given me a cheery wave and hello. But not now.

Sometime later I was told that I was not to write any more "sex articles" for the magazine. That did not come from the editor, Ken Lefolii, but from management. My own TV interviews, especially the cancellation of my interview with the author of *Sex and the Single Girl* that same month, had added fuel to the flames leaping around me.

I decided to write a second column quoting some of my critics and answering them. After that Janet and I went up to spend the weekend with Jack and Liz McClelland at their cottage on Lake Joseph in Muskoka. While I was there I received a telephone call from Ken Lefolii to tell me that management had cancelled my column. I told him that I'd written a pretty lively piece replying to my critics that he could have for nothing and could be used as my swan song. "No, you don't understand," he said. "They don't want your name in the magazine." I said okay, I would be in on Monday to pick up my effects from the office. "No," Lefolii said. "They don't want you in the building." I was, in short, a pariah of pariahs.

The word "they," as Lefolii used it, intrigued me. "They," meaning management, had reached down beyond the editor of *Maclean's* and plucked out a staff member without a by-your-leave. Ralph Allen would never have stood for that for a second; nor would Arthur Irwin, or even Blair Fraser. But Lefolii told me he couldn't back me up because the column wasn't working. Now the spirited audience reaction, pro and con, showed that it was working only too well, but he didn't say that. I understood his position; he was caught between a rock and a hard place. He didn't feel he could fight for a columnist who wasn't really earning his keep. But that, surely, was a decision for the editor of the magazine to make, not the business department, and it boded ill for future encounters with the top brass. I told him as much. "If you give in now," I told him, "they'll force you to give in again. You'll be editor in name only."

The pressure on the subscription and advertising departments by the Roman Catholic laity had caused the magazine to cave in. Vincent Kelly, provincial deputy for the Knights, made no bones about it. "This is one example of where we have power," he told the press. "The press is the greatest instrument for distribution of filth in the world today. Little men with dirty minds are trying to foist dirty literature on young minds. The Knights must be ready to fight these evils."

One year later, after another row with management, Ken Lefolii and five other senior staff members, Peter Gzowski, Harry Bruce, Robert Fulford, Barbara Moon, and David Lewis Stein, found they could no longer endure management interference. They walked out, and Lefolii had the grace to call me. "You were right," he said. By then I had a new job as editor-in-chief of the Canadian Centennial Library, Jack McClelland's latest publishing venture, timed for the country's hundredth anniversary. I desperately needed a managing editor I could trust and offered Lefolii the job. He was happy to come to work for me, and I was happy to have him.

Chapter Ten

1

Nineteen sixty-three to that point had certainly not been my best year. The critics hated my TV show. The network refused to renew it. My readers called me a dirty old man. *Maclean's* fired me. It had been a bumpy ride.

As a result, I had nothing to do that summer. I was exhausted, as much by all the controversy as by the nightly hour of conversation. I wanted to get out of town, but I wanted somebody else to pay for it. Salvation came in the bantam form of George Feyer, the puckish, Hungarian-born cartoonist, who was planning to visit the homeland he had not seen since he fled just after the war. He suggested I come with him, and together we offered the *Star* a series of articles from behind the Iron Curtain, written by me, illustrated by George. The paper grabbed it.

George Feyer was one of my closest friends. We shared a sense of wry humour and a common scepticism about the world around us. He was not only one of the best cartoonists in postwar Canada, he was also the fastest. A diminutive figure with a caustic wit, he had a deceptive, little boy's face that had stood him in good stead. Once, he told me, he had disguised himself as a small boy in order to stay out of the army during the German occupation. Later, when the Russians took over, he affected a pronounced limp and again was excused from military service. Alas, he limped for so many years that the limp became real. There was still a hint of it when we set off for Hungary.

George, who was as irrepressible as he was ingenious, drew continually with a felt pen. He drew at parties, often on women's bodies. He drew breasts on their bare backs so they seemed to be coming when they were going. He turned the insides of their elbows into buttocks. He drew elephants with big ears on my two little boys, using their genitals as trunks; they refused to wash them off, reducing their pediatrician to a state of helpless hilarity. If George saw a pair of scissors on any flat surface, he drew a bird, the scissors providing a beak that opened and closed. If he spotted a pepper shaker, he would draw a reclining nude, using the pepper in place of pubic hair. The walls and flats at the CBC's studios were covered with wicked Feyer cartoons; so were all the walls of our children's bedrooms.

He was always irreverent. To announce his wedding to Michaela Fitzsimon, who was twice his size, he sent out a drawing showing a huge bride, with himself a tiny figure, dangling from one of her arms like a briefcase. Women found him endearing, an advantage he pursued with terrier-like determination. If a strange woman spoke to him in an elevator, he would move close and whisper in her ear that he was hard of hearing. After his separation from Michaela, he used his Hungarian sheep dog, Mollie, as a romantic ploy. Women oo-ed and ah-ed over the puli, so shaggy that George insisted she had once been sold as a throw rug in Eaton's carpet department.

STRANGE WOMAN: What a beautiful and interesting dog!
GEORGE: Yes; but she needs a bath and I alone cannot handle that.
S.W.: Could I help?
GEORGE: My apartment is close by. We'll put her in the shower with us.
S.W.: Oh, do you think that would help?
GEORGE: I'm sure of it.
(CURTAIN)

George held no brief for the church, no brief for authority in any form, no brief for prudes and bluenoses, no brief for politicians of any stripe, no brief for bureaucrats. He was incredibly well read. Bertrand Russell was a favourite, and especially his essay "Why I Am Not a Christian."

I joined George in Budapest in July. He had gone ahead to Vienna to rent a Mercedes to drive to his homeland. At the desk of a fancy, if somewhat run-down, hotel, we were handed a thick sheaf of documents to fill in and sign. George baulked. "I left this country to get away from signing documents," he said. "If I have to sign any more I will leave for the Riviera and take my hard currency with me."

There was an immediate reaction: soothing words, and no more red tape. The desk clerk said he would take care of everything, and we were shown immediately to our rooms. The dollar had spoken.

George insisted that I must get a feel for the country. He would introduce me to some typical Hungarian night-life, he said. We would listen to native songs, enjoy the folk-dancing and what he called "the simple entertainment of the people." We drove into the heart of the old city, past sidewalk cafés alive with people; past old turreted buildings reminiscent of the days of Franz Josef; past small, clean garden restaurants

251

from which snatches of violin music emerged; past the grey Danube, coiling lazily beneath faithful copies of ancient bridges destroyed in the war; past rattling streetcars, small, darting Skodas, and lumbering Soviet limousines, copied from long-defunct American models.

This was my third excursion behind the Curtain, and the contrast with the earlier visits was palpable. Moscow had been a puritan society, still devoid of Western influence. East Berlin was unbelievably gloomy and drab. Here, on superficial evidence, I might have been in Vienna. Lovers walked hand in hand in the streets and embraced in the public parks. Prostitutes, though under official ban, lurked in the cafés. Even the advertising had a touch of sex. There was a hunger here for the West, or perhaps for the days of Franz Josef.

"Tell me," one Hungarian asked, "do you still feel you're in Europe?" When I said I did, he replied, "That's the nicest thing you could say to me."

We pulled up in front of the Budapest Tancpalota (dance palace). A sign informed us that this large and spectacular nightclub was full; indeed, a uniformed doorman was turning people away. "Ignore it," George told me. "Just speak English and there'll be no trouble. Recite something. 'The Shooting of Dan McGrew' has an unmistakably rich American sound."

I walked up to the doorman. "A bunch of the boys were whooping it up," I said, "in the Malemute saloon."

He bowed, smiled, and swung open the door, looking more like an archduke than a doorman. "He probably *is* an archduke," George said. "Half the doormen in town are. They have by far the best manners."

On the stage a young woman was singing one of the songs of her people. "My babee no happy!" she crooned. "My babee real sad!"

So we left there and went to the Blue Note. On the stage another young girl was singing: "Allamee! Why not take allamee!"

So we left there and went to the Papacs, where a young, sweatered brunette wriggled past, clinging to a youth in narrow, cuffless trousers. "Let's twist again," she was singing, "like we did last summer."

So we left the Papacs and went on to Old Firenze, where, I pointed out, the band was playing "St. Louis Blues." "True," said George, discomfited, "but they're playing it in Hungarian!"

We gave up that night, but the next evening George insisted we try once more at Sipos, in Buda, across the Danube. "I will even suffer through gypsy music – which, as a Hungarian, I detest – for your sake," he promised.

So we crossed the great bridge with the statue of a phoenix on the superstructure from which, it was said, thirteen Hungarians had once committed suicide as a result of listening to "Gloomy Sunday." We drove under the high cliffs of Buda and finally came to Sipos. Here, at last, was authentic flavour. Gypsy violins and cellos whispered of love. Hungarians quaffed glasses of wine and sang lustily. The place was doing such a roaring business that we were ignored until George shouted, "Can't I have some government assistance?" That brought instant action and served to remind me that every establishment we had visited was owned and operated by the Communist government, though no red flags or pictures of Lenin were visible.

Everybody was singing, and it didn't seem to matter that they were singing different songs. To me, it was all very genuine and native. As the music grew wilder, two Hungarians at a neighbouring table reached across to another table and ate several roses from a vase as a gesture of bonhomie. At last the gypsy violinist caught my eye and advanced upon us. "He will play something typically Hungarian," said George, and he did – sort of. He played "Beautiful Ohio," just for me, but the way he made it sound, it could have been written in Budapest.

A day or so later we decided to make the two-hour drive to the holiday resort of Lake Balaton, which is Hungary's freshwater Riviera. We picked up three university students on the way; they explained that hitchhiking was illegal but that everybody did it. Until 1956 – that date sprang out of every conversation – only party members could own a car. Since the revolution, the new drivers were so proud of their status symbol that they were reluctant to pick up strangers – and certainly not Jews, they added. That was one of three anti-Semitic references made during our brief visit. The almost pathological attitude toward the Jews in a country that had exterminated six hundred thousand remained a fact of life in Hungary. The Jews, a truck driver told me later, hadn't really been exterminated: just the poor ones; the rich got away and were back in business, he claimed.

As the three young men did not speak English, George translated for me. Free elections, they told us, were a farce; the press was useless. They were very curious about the West. They would love to visit New York City, they said, emphasizing the word "visit." They would not want to live there or anywhere else in North America. That was not quite the impression that the Western media had built up about people behind the Curtain. The general impression was that every one of the "slaves" of communism was desperate to escape to freedom. But these young men much preferred Hungary.

Why, I asked through George, wouldn't they want to live in the "Free World"?

"Oh, you Americans work too hard," one of them replied, and the others nodded. Was this the image they had of us – wretched people toiling away, noses to the grindstone?

We dropped them off in the turreted town of Székesfehérvár, a museum-like community with narrow, curving streets, small squares, and baroque buildings – a city, George told me in astonishment, that had been totally obliterated during the war and restored, stone by stone, cornice by cornice. I doubted that we, in postwar Canada, would pay the same homage to the heritage of the past.

We talked about the two images as we drove on through Transdanubia. To these young men, it was *we* who were prisoners – slaves to the Calvinistic work ethic. Politically they weren't free, but under communism they were sure of minimum security for the rest of their lives. They enjoyed a different kind of freedom: to work at a leisurely pace, to lie in the sun, to sit for hours in the sidewalk cafés. No wonder the nightclubs in Budapest were so crowded!

I doubted there were any "workaholics" in this country. The word itself was a North American invention that had more than once been applied to me by the various interviewers who professed to be astonished by my schedule. Was I really a workaholic? I had never considered that what I did was "work." Maybe, I told George, we ought to distinguish between "work" and "toil," an argument I would soon expand in a book called *The Smug Minority*.

I had cause to consider the other part of the Hungarian equation when we arrived at the lakeside resort of Siófok, a town of modern hotels and wriggling masses of human flesh, all a-glisten with suntan oil. As we made our way to our hotel, a small forest of transistor radios all seemed to be playing "Sentimental Journey," but there was nothing sentimental about our reception at the lobby desk. I suddenly felt a vulnerability I had never experienced back home. I had dashed out of Budapest without bringing a single identifying document! Without my passport and papers, I was as naked as the people on the beach – a non-person, a cipher, no doubt an enemy of the state. My hotel reservation was useless. The desk clerk was polite, but firm: no passport, no room. I no longer felt free: any encounter with officialdom, any request that I identify myself, could lead me straight to interrogation.

"You can go without your pants in this country," George told me, "but never without your documents."

We moved on by car and ferry to the Tihany peninsula and found a modern hotel that might have been designed by Le Courbusier himself. I waited while George checked in, saying with a wink and a nudge that he might be entertaining friends later and could they prepare an extra bed? The clerks turned not a hair at this immoral suggestion. We came back at one in the morning to find the place shut tight. George produced a half-bottle of Canadian rye from the car.

"Hold on to this and we'll have no trouble," he said. "In Canada you don't need a passport, but if you stagger in with a bottle you'll get thrown out. Here, it's the opposite. Girls and drunks they let into the rooms. It is the ones who have no papers that have trouble." And sure enough, a cheerful bellboy opened the door and escorted us to the room, where the chambermaid had turned down two beds. Nobody, then or later, asked any questions.

On the way back to Budapest next day, an army truck swerved into our lane, tore the left fender off the Mercedes, and locked itself onto us. Although the road had been empty of people a moment before, a crowd of gesticulating Hungarians quickly gathered; here, a Western car was a rarity, a smashed-up Western car an event. The bystanders began to choose sides and argue as to who was in the wrong. The truck driver and George made long speeches to each other in Magyar. And across the road, behind a frieze of acacias in a small open air restaurant, the inevitable gypsy band was playing.

I often look back on this experience as a bizarre example of bureaucracy gone mad. Officialdom moved in immediately in the form of a policeman, who, of course, demanded documents. I was painfully aware that I had none and so stayed in the background while George climbed on top of the Mercedes and emptied his small suitcase.

"Documents!" George cried. "You want documents? I've got more documents here than I have underwear!"

The crowd, which was growing larger, applauded. The law required

255

TRAFFIC ACCIDENT

everybody witnessing an accident remain at the scene. Several bystanders missed their train as a result, but nobody seemed to mind. Over the next three hours – for that was how long it took to unravel the details of the event – the crowd continued to grow. Nobody left.

The policeman told us we must wait for the traffic division to arrive. More witnesses began to take sides as George and the driver told their stories over and over again to the crowd. After an interminable time, two civilians arrived on motorcycles; although they were not traffic policemen, they did seem to be in authority. One began to direct traffic and motion the watchers back from the highway. When he spoke, they obeyed at once. He was replaced by the second man, who neither smiled nor scowled but whose features bore an impression of authority. The policeman listened carefully to what he had to say.

"Who was he?" I asked George.

"They say he is a member of the secret police," George told me.

"It can't be much of a secret then," I said.

The gypsy violins were still playing when, after an eternity, the traffic squad arrived – a sergeant on a motorcycle and a corporal on another, with a maintenance man in the sidecar. The sergeant began to speak to the truck driver in rapid Hungarian. George was jubilant. "He is giving him

256

absolute blue murder!" George explained. "He is saying: 'You guys, you think you own the road. Do you think you are masters of the highway?'"

Now the corporal and the maintenance man produced tapes and cameras and began to measure and photograph the site. The sergeant shook hands with George, called him "Mr. Feyer," and apologized for the embarrassment. He said he would examine all the evidence before coming to a final conclusion. That took another hour. More documents were asked for and produced as, in the background, the gypsies played on. At this point I began to feel that I had stumbled onto the set of a Lehár operetta.

At last we were told that the entire affair would have to be described in writing with copies in duplicate or triplicate. We were taken to another restaurant that served as a police sub-headquarters a quarter of a mile away. It, too, had a gypsy orchestra, whose violins sang of love and heartbreak while the typewriters clacked. Eventually, we were informed that the accident was not our fault. George was given a document for insurance purposes, signed by the minister of the interior. Everybody shook hands all round. As we left, the crowd of bystanders was as thick as ever, each side grouped near the central figures in the drama – sergeant, corporal, truck driver – and clicking their tongues at the mangled fender. The violins were still sobbing as we drove off.

A few days later we left Budapest and drove toward the Austrian border, first entering a broad no-man's-land fifty kilometres wide, through which travel was restricted. The actual border was a depressing sight. A swath, laced with barbed wire and guarded by machine-guns, had been cut through fields and hedgerows on the Hungarian side. That was the Iron Curtain, naked and ominous.

We drove through two checkpoints and found ourselves once more in the West. Off we went to the car-rental agency with our official document. The man at the desk laughed ruefully when we produced the paper for the insurance company. "They *never* pay!" he told us. "Never in all my years have I collected a cent from the Hungarian government. If you have an accident over there, no matter whose fault it is, you automatically write it off."

2

Comfortable
pews I came back to Canada that summer still virtually unemployed. It was official: CTV would not renew my contract. Screen Gems was hoping to sell a half-hour version of the show to individual stations, but that wasn't a sure thing. *Front Page Challenge* was in summer hiatus, and we weren't yet sure whether the CBC would renew it.

As usual, I had a fallback position. In fact, I had two. CHFI, another Toronto radio station, had offered to use me as a commentator – two five-minute spots each weekday. I accepted. More challenging was a letter I'd received that spring from Ernest Harrison, secretary of the General Board of Religious Education for the Anglican Church of Canada. It surprised me: Harrison was asking me to write a book for the church to use for Lenten reading in 1965. Why, I wondered, would any church ask me to write any kind of book for it? Though I had been raised an Anglican, I had had no contact with the church for twenty years. True, I had occasionally attended the United church in Kleinburg, but only because our children were involved. As a journalist I had rarely mentioned the church, either to attack or to praise it. To put it bluntly, I was, like Joyce Davidson in another context, indifferent to the institution.

I wrote to Harrison that I could not give him an answer until later in the summer. I added that I really didn't know much about the state of the church but would like to talk to him about the project. It wasn't until August that we got together for lunch. By that time I had incurred the wrath of many of Harrison's colleagues because of my final *Maclean's* column. Did the church still want me to write the book? I asked him. He said it certainly did. Why? He told me that the church had entered a period of self-examination, symbolized by the recent Anglican Congress in Toronto. It felt that the views of lay commentators, especially from outside the church, might be of value in promoting discussion. To survive, he felt, the church needed to engage in forthright dialogue with its critics.

I told him that any book I wrote would probably be critical and might well be extremely critical. He didn't flinch. Indeed, when I outlined for him some of my spur-of-the-moment criticisms, I found to my surprise that he agreed with many. He was a pleasant luncheon companion, bespectacled, a little on the plump side, with the light English

258

accent that seemed to be the badge of Anglican ministers from Dawson City to Saint John. His appearance belied his inner convictions, or perhaps his lack of them. Sometime later, when he wrote a book of his own, the Anglicans would disown him.

Now I asked if I might widen the terms of the book and deal with the established Protestant churches in general. He agreed. Suddenly I found myself becoming interested in a project on which I'd had no intention of embarking at the beginning of our meeting. How could I turn down such an intriguing offer? How often does a major institution in society invite and even sponsor criticism of itself? To be honest, there was another wicked little thought lurking in the back of my mind: the idea of writing critically about the very people who had written so critically of me after the notorious *Maclean's* column tickled my fancy. Hadn't the Qu'Appelle Anglican Women's League threatened *Maclean's* with "a concentrated boycott"? In fact, one of its members had stated publicly that I should be shot. The Synod in Algoma had demanded drastic action against me for my "poisonous article." Even my parents' old Yukon friend, Archdeacon Cecil Swanson, had jumped into the fray, arguing simplistically that if I just took a few cold baths I would not write anything more about sex. There was just enough of the small boy left in me to relish the prospect of turning the other cheek – sort of. I told Harrison I would tackle the job, but that I wanted nothing from the church except, possibly, some help with the research. The book, I said, must stand on its own. It would be published by McClelland and Stewart, who would pay me my usual royalty. As it turned out, the church made a good deal of money from the book because Jack McClelland, in a moment of insane generosity, offered the Anglicans a 10-percent royalty for themselves. None of us at the time expected that it would sell more than a few thousand copies.

In the days that followed, the Anglicans were understandably cautious. Harrison and his colleagues made no attempt to let the public know that I had been invited to write the church's Lenten book. The word leaked out via the *Observer,* the respected national monthly of the United Church, and was picked up quickly by the daily press. An acrimonious controversy followed. I doubt that any earlier book had caused such a hullabaloo before it was written or even researched.

Canon Michael Creel, a member of Harrison's board, quickly announced that I had been chosen because I was "an outstanding writer and a man of integrity who can be relied upon to take a strong and balanced view-point." But many church people demurred. The Anglican Diocese of Toronto "protested emphatically" as did those of Calgary and Ottawa, and the Provincial Synod of Rupert's Land. For more than a year the letters columns of the church press were alive with attacks on me and on the book. "I shall not buy it or read it," one typical correspondent wrote. "Pierre Berton will finish us off," another insisted. A third declared that the controversy would harm the prestige of the church. Some church papers mounted editorial attacks. The Rupert's Land *News* called for an "agonizing reappraisal in the Pierre Berton case." So did the *Diocesan Times* of Halifax – even after the book was safely on the press.

Others took a calmer view. "We are neither for nor against Mr. Berton," the *Canadian Churchman* wrote, "because we have not read the book." The Primate of All Canada, head of the Anglican Church in Canada, made a similar comment: "I don't know if I'll approve or not. I won't know until I read it." One correspondent pointed out that the church itself was providing me with much material. "How dare we be so bigoted?" she asked. "Let the book be published, read, and studied, then let them criticize – fairly." With that view, of course, the General Board of Religious Education was in complete agreement.

Meanwhile, Fred Wooding, the church's supervisor of education, backpedalling furiously, announced that my work was not to be con-sidered an official church publication. The so-called Lenten book was downgraded to "a book for Lenten reading." The Lenten book, he declared, was usually written by an authority on theology and was always a serious work on the spiritual implications of Lent. Of course, that wasn't the original idea at all, but we let it pass. "Pierre Berton, as I understand it, has simply been asked to write about the church from a layman's point of view," Wooding said. "This was done with the full knowledge that the author might be critical of the Anglican Church."

I spent the following year squeezing work on the book between radio and TV assignments. By the fall, Screen Gems had succeeded in selling the new half-hour *Pierre Berton Show* to six television stations, including John Bassett's CFTO, and production resumed. The compa-ny's negotiations with the Bassett station had not been helped by the fact that I had written my series on Hungary not for Bassett's own paper but for the hated *Star*. Bassett himself phoned me, more in sor-row than in anger, to explain as subtly as he could the problems posed by any of his people writing for the rival sheet. I could not help remembering his pledge before the Board of Broadcast Governors that if he got the TV licence, the new station would be entirely independent. He would not, he promised solemnly, use one medium to bolster the other. But here he was, making it very clear that if I continued to write for the *Star,* I could kiss CFTO goodbye as an anchor for my program.

The fix seemed to be in for Bassett, making those BBG hearings a farce. He had known from the outset that the gaggle of party bagmen and Tory hangers-on who then dominated the watchdog authority had no intention of handing the plum to anybody but a strong Progressive Conservative supporter. Bassett had been so sure of getting the prize that he had bought the property and paid for plans for his new station on the outskirts of the city even before he got the official nod.

I was more at home with the new half-hour interview format in which I was acting as a journalist and not as a conversationalist. I wasn't completely at ease with the medium, but I was getting closer. As one critic wrote that season, "since he was around for something like fourteen or fifteen months, perhaps it's time we got used to the idea that Pierre Berton may be here to stay." That November I invited Helen Gurley Brown back to Toronto to repeat our banned interview. This time there wasn't a peep of protest.

In between these chores, I did my research for the book, interviewing scores of ministers, social workers, lay people, and others, and poring over more than seventy published works. In addition, I spent a morning each week in discussions with various Anglicans, clergy and laity. These took place in the living room of that remarkable couple, Bill and Betsy Kilbourn. He was a historian, university professor, best-selling author, and reform member of the Toronto city council. She was a devout Anglican who would eventually become an ordained minister over much protest. At one point she was even touted as a bishop, but that, apparently, was too radical for the Anglicans.

At these meetings Ennis took shorthand notes. She also attended a different Anglican service each week and made literal transcriptions of the sermons for me. She told me it was the most boring assignment she had ever endured. Reading her verbatim reports of what the clergy had to say, I could only concur.

I needed a title for the book but couldn't think of an apt one. That August our family visited the Arthur Haileys at their cottage on Kennisis

261

Lake in the Haliburton Highlands where he was working on his third best-seller. When I told him I was at a loss for a title he suggested the word "pew" because of its ecclesiastical context. That required an adjective, and when I explained further what the book was to be about he came up with "comfortable." The following spring I was able to respond in kind. After reading the manuscript on which he had been working, I suggested he call it simply *Hotel*. His publisher, Doubleday, hated it, but Arthur was adamant. It was such a smashing success that when Arthur tried to call his next book "The Surly Bonds of Earth," Doubleday insisted on another one-word title: *Airport*.

The Comfortable Pew was published in the third week of January 1965, generally considered one of the worst months to launch a book. The event was awaited with both anticipation and apprehension. But nobody involved could have foretold the depth of the response.

The Anglican Church had ordered seven thousand copies for its own distribution. Jack McClelland had printed an additional nine thousand for the trade. A first printing of sixteen thousand was very large at that time. My previous average was less than seven thousand. None of us had treated this as a money-making venture; in fact, I had reduced my own royalties and viewed the writing of the book as a kind of spare-time hobby.

Early in the new year, however, it became clear that something unexpected was happening. Jack couldn't keep up with the demand. Additional printings were ordered from high-speed offset presses in Winnipeg. Even before publication another thirty thousand copies were being rushed to Toronto. Jack had insisted on a firm release date, which he announced could not be broken. To his great delight, the *Globe and Mail* broke it. McClelland was a superb publicist who operated on the Hollywood "closed set" principle. If the press thinks something is being kept from them, they break their necks to force the barrier. All across Canada newspapers began to review and write stories about a book that wasn't yet officially available. Reviews are welcome, but it's the news stories, especially controversial ones, that sell books. And my book was making the front pages! The bookstores put it on sale well before publication day. Several newspapers and magazines covered the controversy as they would a war. One periodical featured the topic on its cover and set a record by selling out in three days.

By February, the whole country was talking or writing about the book. Lay groups, women's auxiliaries, and men's church clubs were discussing it. Almost every major radio and television program dealt with it in some way. The CTV program *Telepoll* revealed that 47.6 percent of those who responded said they intended to read it – a phenomenal showing. In February alone, my clipping service dropped 660 news stories, articles, and reviews on my desk. The *Telegram* reviewed the book four times. The Regina *Leader Post,* which did not review many books, reviewed it *eight* times. Scores of ministers wrote to me in delirious gratitude for providing them with easily assembled sermon fodder. The church page ads showed that hundreds of congregations were being exposed to pulpit critiques. Some ministers preached marathon sermons on the subject. One scheduled no fewer than sixteen.

I was called all sorts of names – devil, saint, heretic, prophet. A dazzling array of adjectives was trotted out to describe the book: shallow, superficial, profound, prophetic, hasty, ill-advised, accurate, pretentious, insufferable, incisive, powerful, pompous, ignorant, atheistic. Dr. Ernest Howse, the United Church's moderator, kept insisting, over my objections, that I was a Christian. Vigorous attempts were made to convert me. The Unitarians, Jehovah's Witnesses, Four Square Gospellers, Mormons, Quakers, and Baha'is all bombarded me with pamphlets, tracts, gospels, and weightier tomes, each proclaiming the one and only truth. The country seemed to be crammed with simple souls who honestly believed that a man's whole life, attitudes, and opinions could be transformed – *presto!* – by a few pages of type.

But many who disagreed profoundly with the book's thesis welcomed its publication. "Maybe there's life in the old church yet!" was a typical reaction. In general the established Protestant churches now accepted the book. By and large, the clergy were surprisingly favourable, both in published reviews and in personal correspondence. My theme – that the church was no longer relevant in the modern world – had apparently put into words what many ministers secretly believed.

The bitterest and most violent attacks came from the laity and often from non-churchgoers. The mildest made the point that the book had nothing to say that was new or profound, and that college freshmen had been saying much the same thing for years. "What's all the fuss about?" several reviewers asked. But there clearly *was* a fuss. Obviously the book had struck a nerve, and that ought to have been a matter of concern. It confirmed my earlier view that when an institution is about to crumble, any criticism provokes a violent reaction. Of course my ideas were old hat; I'd held some of them for more than twenty years, which was why I left the church at the age of nineteen. I'd simply put into words what a great many ordinary Canadians were thinking. "Thank you for writing *The Comfortable Pew* in language the man in the street and the woman in the house can understand," one reader wrote. "I only had to look up one word in the dictionary."

The title phrase, with many variations – "comfortable few," "uncomfortable pew," "comfortable view," etc. – went into the language. In February, the official journal of the B.C. Professional Engineers Association even ran an article titled "The Comfortable Slide Rule." In Canada the book sold 170,000 copies.

My agent offered the book to Knopf in New York, who rejected it, claiming that the Canadian references would turn off American readers. Lippincott snapped it up and sold 130,000 copies. The American reviews were kinder than those in Canada, and there was a more enthusiastic reaction. The radical Episcopalian bishop, James Pike, provided every priest in his diocese with a copy. Bishop Gerald Kennedy of the Methodist Church in Los Angeles urged every churchman to read it.

These were frantic months. In between radio commentaries and my own nightly television program, I found myself enmeshed in discussions about the problems of the church – in round-table debates, television panels, interviews, and speeches to university students. I was asked by many ministers to appear as a guest in their pulpits but refused, since I felt it would be hypocritical to deliver a sermon in a setting I had rejected. My schedule for one week in February 1965, just after the book's publication, gives an idea of the exhausting pace to which I willingly subjected myself that month.

I flew to Winnipeg at 9:45 on the morning of February 9 in time to take part in a one-hour discussion of the book at the University of Manitoba. I lunched with a journalist for an hour, then went straight to CJAY-TV for an interview with Bud Sherman, returned to my hotel for a press conference, then boarded a plane for Calgary. The following morning in Calgary I spent two hours at CFCN-TV promoting the book and my TV show and then got back to the Palliser Hotel for a press conference at eleven. That afternoon I taped five half-hour segments of *The Pierre Berton Show,* completing the last one at 6:45. Fifteen minutes later I dined with the Anglican chaplain at the university and then spent the evening on campus discussing the book with the students. I flew to Edmonton the following day for more of the same and then to Vancouver. I was back in Toronto one week after I'd left.

During all that week I was on constant display and scarcely knew a single moment of solitude. Even in waiting rooms, on airplanes, and in taxicabs, I was in continual discussion, answering questions about myself and my work, my book about the church, and my personal views on Gordon Sinclair. The concept of the "personality" was a new one in Canada, and there was little doubt that people wanted to make the most of the experience when they actually encountered one.

I began to get irritated, to feel put upon. The media interviews were more like cross-examinations. My set-tos with university students were even tougher. I was tired and out of sorts and on a couple of occasions snapped back. A year later, when I appeared again on the same programs, plugging another book, I encountered a certain wariness on the part of the hosts. "You're a lot easier-going this year," Colin McLean told me in Edmonton. "You were a real terror last time." Only then did I realize that I'd been a mean interview. I'd taken my irritation out on men and women who were only doing their job, as I did. What had I expected after the publication of a book as contentious as this one? Sugary praise?

The Comfortable Pew produced a spate of spin-offs. Two other books appeared immediately, both taking issue with me. One, entitled *Termites in the Shape of Men: Common Sense Versus Pierre Berton,* was written by an elderly husband and wife team, both members of the United Church. They paid to have it published. I never read the book, but one reviewer wrote that "the view of Berton presented in this book is so passionate it makes everything previously published on him (to use the authors' words) *piffle* " The second book, *Just Think, Mr. Berton (A Little Harder),* was written by an orthodox Christian and journalist, Ted Byfield, later the publisher of *Alberta Report.* I was amused to discover that this book, published also in the United States, appeared on the bookshelves there some time before my own. Potential readers received a detailed answer to my critique before they could read the critique itself – an unfortunate piece of timing that must have baffled them.

Meanwhile, the Roman Catholic Church published its own book, *Brief to the Bishops.* That was followed by a lay critique book, *Objections to Roman Catholicism.* The United Church jumped in with a symposium on the church in the world, to which a good many authors, including myself, contributed. I wrote that "in issues as widely separated as capital punishment, birth control, nuclear armament, racial conflict, business ethics, and sexual revolt, the church has opted out; it has left the job of pioneering, of taking unpopular but far-sighted stands, to the atheists, agnostics, Unitarians, journalists, psychiatrists, sociologists, muckrakers, and politicians." These were the issues of the sixties, the revolutionary era in which old tenets were being thrust aside by a new and aroused generation.

This flood of books was all part of the ferment of the times. You could feel it even as you lived through it. The Anglican Church, emboldened by the success of the *Pew,* immediately commissioned an anthology with the title *The Restless Church,* edited by Bill Kilbourn, to which I also contributed. Ernest Harrison wrote two books, *Let God Go Free* and, later, *A Church Without God.* That was too much for G.B. Snell, Bishop of Toronto, who barred Harrison from preaching or officiating at any service in any church in his diocese, thus reinforcing my point that the church was not listening.

By this time, I think, most Canadians were fed up with all the religious discussion and controversy. Certainly I was. I had done my job. I had, to quote Robert Fulford, "given the church an importance in the mass media it could not have achieved without [me]." Fulford wrote that the book had "made the tensions within the church a matter of public debate. As one clergyman put it, 'it is a kind of healthy trouble the church has gotten us into.'"

But has attendance at the mainstream churches in Canada increased? On the contrary, it has declined. Have the churches become more relevant today than they were in 1965? Perhaps some have. At least the Anglican Church now has a few women ministers, such as Betsy Kilbourn. Certainly some Protestant denominations have, albeit reluctantly, tried to bring homosexuals, whom I had called then the "lepers of our time," into the fold. But, by and large, the mainstream churches have less influence in today's society than they have ever had. The institution was crumbling when I wrote *The Comfortable Pew;* that was the reason for the enormous outcry. If the church had been strong at that time, would anyone really have cared what an unemployed journalist had to say? As for myself, I had had enough. I resolved to call a personal moratorium on interviews, articles, round tables, and television shows about religion. Occasionally somebody calls me to ask my views on the church, or even to appear on a program discussing the subject. I do not rise to the bait. I tell them I have had my say, and that is that.

3

In the midst of all this kerfuffle – in April 1965 – Janet and I decided to adopt a child. Janet had for some time been an active and enthusiastic member of CACY, the Committee for the Adoption of Coloured Youngsters (which might today be called the Committee for the Adoption of Youngsters of Colour!). She made speeches, attended executive meetings, and discussed with me, among others, the problems of children of mixed race that then existed in Ontario. "Mom's out selling babies," the kids used to explain when taking her calls. All sorts of people wanted to adopt a child, but they wanted blond, blue-eyed white babies, not black. (In other provinces, the problem revolved around other colours – yellow or brown.) Finally I said to her, "I cannot, for the life of me, understand how you can sit on the CACY executive if you don't suit your actions to your words. How can you advocate the adoption of black children when you have an all-white family?" To which she replied: "I've just been waiting for you to say that."

We made our decision immediately. After the usual interviews with the Children's Aid Society ("What is your *real* reason for wanting this adoption? Is this a publicity stunt [etc. etc.]?"), our application was accepted and a seven-month-old baby was found in a foster home. We had made no stipulations about age or sex. As we told our interrogators, we liked kids and could afford to add another to our family of four girls and two boys. Now, we learned, we were about to have a fifth daughter.

The day before we planned to visit the adoption centre on Charles Street to pick her up, I received a phone call from a Children's Aid official. "You don't have to take her," she said. The child, I was told, had severe asthma, and because of her infirmity we could opt out. *Opt out?* If this was our birth child, could we opt out? The call angered me. We hadn't asked for a perfect baby; the only stipulation we made was that it be a baby of mixed colour since these children, being neither fish nor fowl, were the hardest to place. I told the social worker we'd be down next day to pick her up. We could hardly wait to see her.

The whole family went. Peggy Anne, now almost four, and the one most likely to have her nose put out of joint if we introduced a rival into the house, was detailed to go with the social worker and bring back the baby. "It's *your* baby," we told her, and she smiled from ear to ear. We waited. Then down the long hallway we could see them coming – the social worker with the little brown bundle in her arms and Peggy Anne clutching the new baby's hand in hers. What a wondering look the new addition gave us! From under that mop of curly black hair, tinged with russet (for she had a white birth mother), two enormous black eyes surveyed us solemnly. We called her Perri because all the other children's names started with P. I wanted to call her Prudence, but the family turned that down flat. "Prudence!" Patsy cried. "Geez, Dad, it's tough enough on the kid to be black in this culture…but *Prudence* – no way!"

In our house, the kids were taught early to fend for themselves. We couldn't spoon-feed them after they were weaned. We simply popped them into a high chair, put a plateful of baby food in front of them, handed them a spoon, and let them go at it. When Perri arrived she was not only asthmatic but she was also unable to sit upright. This was because she had been overindulged and cosseted in a foster home where she had been treated as a doll, not as a human being. Within a week at Kleinburg she was sitting up on her own. The asthma vanished, never to reappear.

She was one smart cookie, this one, with a mind of her own. Once, when she got too obstreperous, I told her to go to her room to quiet down. She looked at me fiercely. "*O-kay,* Idi Amin!" she cried. Well, I thought, at least the child is up on the news.

I often looked at her, this brown, chubby baby with the enormous black eyes and the shock of curly hair, and wondered how she would look when she grew to adulthood. Would she be tall and slender, short and pudgy, plain or pretty? I had a hard time, as many parents do, imagining her as a young woman, going out on a date or walking down the aisle on my arm. That time came soon enough and I will never forget the vision of her when I walked into the room minutes before the ceremony and saw her in her bridal gown – tall, slender, exquisitely beautiful, and, as always, self-possessed. It brought a catch to my throat as my mind went back to the early years: the night she announced she was running away from home and left with her little bag packed, only to return in a few minutes to say that she wasn't going to run away until she'd had her supper; the time on the beach in the Caribbean when I was asked to keep watch on her, a brown little kid in a red bathing suit – only to discover that every little kid on that beach was brown and wore a red bathing suit; or the moment in Jamaica when a motherly black woman stopped us as we walked hand-in-hand down the street and said, simply, "God bless you!" And I, a freethinker, could not resist replying, "He already has."

Because she was adopted, Perri, I think, felt special, though she wasn't quite clear what "adopted" meant. Once when Janet was holding a CACY board meeting at our house and the children were introduced, Perri stuck out her hand in greeting and chirped cheerfully, "I'm adopted." Another time, Betty Kennedy's first husband, Gerhard, offered to take his little daughter, Tracy, and Perri on an outing around town. The two girls sat in the Honeydew restaurant sipping pop through straws, their short legs dangling from the high chairs.

"My, you've got a lovely tan," Perri said to Tracy.

"Not as nice as yours, though," Tracy replied.

"That's because I'm adopted," Perri explained.

At school Perri encountered very little prejudice, perhaps because, after fifteen years, we were all part of the community and she was never thought of as a stranger. Janet knew everybody by name and background, and we had both helped to launch the local Home and School Association. She ran the Explorers' group of young girls for the United Church; I was on the Kleinburg school board. There were incidents, of course, but Perri had a host of friends and siblings, including two big brothers who came to her defence when somebody called her "nigger." An oafish neighbour used to ask if he could brings friends over from the city to view "the little darky girl." Over they'd come to stare at Perri cavorting in our new swimming pool. "See the little pickaninny," he'd say. It was bad enough that he insisted on showing me his interminable collection of home movies about his trip to Banff; now it looked as if he was about to throw Perri a peanut. I had difficulty suppressing an urge to push him into the pool.

When she was eight, I asked her if she ever wondered about her real mother. She shook her head and pointed toward the kitchen. "*That's* my real mother!" she said, and that was that.

Perri arrived when the uproar over *The Comfortable Pew* was at its height. The book critics were going at me, but at least most of the TV

269

columnists had stopped sniping. "I should dearly love to detest Pierre Berton," Lorne Parton wrote in a backhanded compliment in the Vancouver *Province,* "but there is one thing standing in my way. He is one of the most fascinating, talented, and interesting persons in Canada." That was a long leap from the days when I had been labelled awkward – and dull. In the intervening two years I had been learning my craft in front of the viewers. Now I felt at home in the medium – relaxed, confident, professional. But essentially I was a journalist, not a showman, and I was helped by the quality of the guests, who ranged from the eighty-four-year-old confidence man Joseph Weil, better known as the Yellow Kid, to such luminaries as Malcolm X, Mick Jagger, and Liberace.

Screen Gems was remarkably indulgent with me. They wanted very badly to sell the show to a sponsor, which would have meant my appearing in commercials. That I could not do; I was a journalist, not a salesman. An automobile company was on the hook and Herb Sussan tried to explain to me that I would be given wide latitude in my sales pitches. "Why, you could even say: 'Look, I'm a big guy and this compact is too small for me,'" he explained.

"But what if I hated the car?" I asked. That ended the discussion, and the prospective sponsor bowed out.

I alienated another prospect by hosting a heated discussion on the quality of Canadian beer. I felt it had been reduced to the level of pantherpiss by such monopolists as E.P. Taylor, who killed off the good brews in favour of a blander product. Then I had made some sneering remarks about instant coffee, boasting that we drank only the real stuff on the show. That finished off Maxwell House.

The Pierre Berton Show started off with a bang – or at least a near bang. We had taken it to Montreal to satisfy the English-language station, CFCF-TV, which had agreed to carry the show if we would produce some programs using its facilities. A few minutes before our taping began, a bomb threat was phoned to the station. The anonymous caller said my life would be endangered if I went ahead with a program on terrorist and separatist activities in Quebec.

Of course I went ahead, and no bombs exploded. The program was explosive enough, for it featured a young Pierre Trudeau, whom I had met briefly in the 1950s. Almost everything Trudeau said in those days was quotable, as he demonstrated on the show:

270

"It has not been shown how separatism will produce a better engineer or a better artist."

"Quebec is not Algeria, and people who make such comparisons are ignorant of constitutional law."

"I see all nationalism as an appeal to the emotions; I would like to see government based on reason."

"Although the separatists claim they are leftist, they put ethnic ahead of social values, and it is inevitable that the movement will be captured by the rightists, who for years have been identified with nationalism in Quebec."

Trudeau then entered into a dialogue with a young separatist leader, François Lauriault, and wiped the floor with him.

I asked Trudeau if it was true, as the separatists claimed, that President Kennedy would favour a separate state of Quebec. "Why wouldn't he favour it?" Trudeau replied. "It will be a banana republic run by Washington." Lauriault suggested, as the separatists are still suggesting, that there would be better relations with English Canada – such as a common market – after separation. To that Trudeau replied, "Why waste the energies of a whole generation to achieve independence when the first thing you'd do with independence is to try to re-establish the communications and relations we already have?"

This was the kind of content I enjoyed, and I was determined to do more. In its new half-hour format the program was slowly changing from the original lightweight talk show to a harder-hitting interview style. Ross McLean had begun to realize that it was impossible to produce the kind of show he liked without the presence of a live audience, the kind that on the new Johnny Carson *Tonight* show supplied the applause and laughter show-business people, especially comedians and "personalities," must have. In our empty studio, where we produced five shows in less than four days, that was not possible, and, given the subject matter I was intent on pursuing, not desirable. I didn't want my guests to play to an audience; I wanted them to play to me and, perhaps, with the time at their disposal, to reveal things about themselves that would not be possible in a five-minute news clip or before a restless crowd. This metamorphosis was hastened in the fall of 1964 by the arrival of Elsa Franklin.

Ross had left to return to the CBC that summer. Sam Levene, his associate producer, followed shortly after to join a new CBC program to be called *This Hour Has Seven Days*. That left me with an executive producer from Screen Gems in New York, Selig Alkon (who replaced

Herb Sussan), one researcher, one unit manager, and now Elsa, whose title then was "program organizer."

Elsa had had no television experience, but she had flair, common sense, and impeccable taste. I realized she was right for the program when she cornered me at a party and, with her usual bluntness, told me what was wrong with the show. She thought that the best use was not being made of me, that I was often given the wrong guests (stand-up comedians, especially). She thought the show should capitalize on my journalistic ability to home in on a subject rather than on the inconsequential chatter that often marked the hour-long program. Ross, who spent far too much time listening to the critics, had tried to "humanize" me by placing me in comic situations – such as the set of a children's program, where I was belaboured with bags of flour by a man in a clown suit. It didn't work.

I remember suggesting to Elsa one time that I grow a beard since everybody else seemed to be sprouting whiskers. "Never!" she told me. "It's enough that you express controversial opinions. If you want to get away with that sort of thing, do your best to *look* straight. Keep your bow tie; it gives you a vaguely academic look and has become part of your image. Always wear a suit or jacket, a tie, and a crisp shirt. And don't try to change that image: it's what people are comfortable with. Start wearing blue jeans or a straight tie on TV and they'll feel insecure. Wear a beard and weird clothes and they won't take you seriously." She was right, of course. Her motto was: Play to your strengths; don't try to be somebody else. "You're not Johnny Carson, you're *you!*" Until Elsa took over I had not always felt comfortable on the set, even though my technique was improving.

Elsa came to Toronto at the right moment for me, and perhaps for her. She had operated a chain of bookstores in Vancouver and was now handling publicity for Jack McClelland on a freelance basis. She was familiar with the world of journalism, for her husband, Stephen, was a writer for *Weekend* magazine and the winner of that year's Southam Fellowship. She knew the country, having moved from Ottawa to Edmonton to Vancouver to Toronto as Stephen's assignments changed. She was also a graduate of the Lorne Greene Academy of Radio Arts in Toronto and the prestigious Neighborhood Playhouse in New York. She seemed to know everybody. A good background, I thought, for anybody organizing a late-night interview show.

Screens Gems accepted her grudgingly. A totally male-oriented organization, it did not move women into even minor positions of authority. But Elsa took all the authority she could get. By mid-December, she was running the show, doing the work of both Ross and Sam – but without the title.

The company had been searching for a producer, but I had turned all the prospects down. They were earnest young men with CBC backgrounds who saw the show in terms of educational television, with "experts" discussing various high-minded topics. I didn't want inconsequential chatter on my show, but I didn't want academic discussions, either. Our new executive producer was the most controversial and despised man in American television. This was Danny Enright, banished now to Canada because of his leading role in the scandals that had shaken the industry. Danny met his doom when it was learned that he had fixed *Twenty-One,* the hottest quiz program on the tube, by giving out the answers in advance to the contestants, and teaching people like Charles Van Doren how to appear to grapple with the answers. I liked Danny, in spite of this shady background. He knew his business and, best of all, left me alone. He was a small, intense man who always seemed to be on the run from studio to studio. I never saw him remove his raincoat – as crumpled as Columbo's – giving me the impression that he was just passing through. He lived on pills, always wore dark glasses, spoke at high speed but almost in whispers, and made it very clear that he didn't want Elsa on the show.

Our director that season had had a run-in with her in Calgary and complained to Danny that she had overruled him on matters of taste. Until then, nobody had paid any attention to our guests' comfort or mine. The chairs were too small, the audience was badly arranged, the table was a horror, and there was no discreet place for me to put my notes. Elsa had been right, and I told Danny so. I told him I wanted him to get another director and to put Elsa in charge of the program. He baulked. He'd get me a new director, he said, but he still wanted a male producer; if he found one I could live with, would I go along with him? Sure, I said. But I had no intention of living with any of them. A few weeks later, with the search still fruitless, Danny gave in. Elsa became producer of *The Pierre Berton Show* and continued until the end of its long and successful run. After that she produced five more TV programs for me and a couple of her own. She was one of the first woman producers in television, and by her example helped change attitudes in the industry.

I had never encountered anybody like Elsa in television. Nobody had. She wore her jet-black hair down to her shoulders and parted in the middle like a model for a Renaissance painting; that, coupled with her high cheekbones and long, bridgeless nose, accentuated her startling appearance. She might easily have sat for Modigliani. Physically she was a chameleon. In Italy she looked more Italian than the Italians. In Lebanon she passed as Lebanese. In Honolulu, with a hibiscus in her hair she looked half Hawaiian. She even looked a bit Japanese in Tokyo. She dressed with style and flair, affecting enormous earrings, brilliant colours, and an assortment of wild scarves and stoles. Her background was Russian-Jewish, but she had no religion and wanted none. Oddly, her changeable qualities did fail her in Israel, where no one believed she was a Jew.

She knew exactly what she wanted and wasn't afraid to say so. The young men and women who arrived as researchers on the show for a couple of years were clearly in awe of her; she had a tart tongue and didn't suffer fools. Yet they soon discovered that their initial impression was premature. Elsa turned out to be a kindly mother hen to her staff. She looked after them on the trips we made abroad, listened to their problems, and made them feel part of a family. As a result, they worked themselves silly for her. In later days Elsa occupied her airplane time knitting socks and scarves for everybody. No other producer in all of television can top that.

In Hollywood and New York she was treated condescendingly at first, then with respect. She set up a schedule that astonished old TV hands. We could turn out half a dozen shows in an afternoon, with a fifteen-minute break between each. If the schedule ran like clockwork it was the result of Elsa's efficiency and also her knowledge of my strengths and weaknesses as an interviewer.

Danny grew to like and admire her, possibly because during one contentious long-distance call from New York, she simply banged down the phone on him. He was, I think, a bit of a masochist. Certainly he came to enjoy her forthright approach. But it was the fact that she brought the show in on time and always under budget that really impressed him. He would leave us alone for months, knowing that he could depend on Elsa. "I wish I had as little trouble on some of my other shows as I have on yours," he told me.

274

Nonetheless, as a woman producer, Elsa had her problems. When we took the show to New York, the all-male staff of our leased studio refused to take her seriously. "Don't worry, dearie, we'll handle it all," one man told her when she objected to the look of the set.

"No, you won't!" she snapped back.

"Women producers!" he hissed under his breath. When the production meeting ended, he approached Elsa as she walked out. "How's about dinner tonight, sweetheart?" he asked. She withered him with a glance.

More than one American saw her as a sex object, and this was a continual problem in Hollywood. The director of the technical crew, who was staying in the same hotel, actually appeared at her door mother-naked, holding a bottle of champagne. She slammed the door in his face, but next day she treated him exactly as she treated all the other members of the crew.

A woman producer in those days was such an oddity that Elsa made news. In a feature story for the *Telegram,* Cynthia Kelly described her:

"Elsa doesn't sit; she lights like a hummingbird, apparently still, but always in flight. She looks one-third Italian Renaissance, one-third Mona Lisa, and one-third Hayden Street urchin. Her attention span is concentrated, but short-lived. The tame, trite, humdrum, and prosaic bore her. And this is one of the secrets of her success. Variety stimulates her and her main jobs increase, rather than decrease, her vitality."

Having started by promoting one of my books, *Fast, Fast, Fast Relief,* for McClelland and Stewart, she shortly became my agent, manager, and, when we went into production on our own, my business partner. She still is.

4

LONDON, November 19, 1965. On this raw autumn day, Elsa and I are surveying the scene in the lounge of Mayfair's fashionable Westbury Hotel, which has been converted for the day into a temporary TV studio. It is, to the untutored eye, a mess. A ganglion of cables crawls over the floor. A thicket of lights, microphones, and other paraphernalia replaces the tea tables. The cameras are warming up.

Outside, a knot of curious passersby stares into the picture window that is to serve as a backdrop for the nineteen half-hour programs we hope to put on videotape during this week in the United Kingdom. Between now and tea time we will record six programs with the great and the near great, the celebrated and the notorious – a cross-section, we hope, of life in London. Our guests will be steered into the lounge every forty-five minutes according to a split-second schedule that allows for no slip-ups: half an hour for recording; fifteen minutes to get one's breath, adjust make-up, check the lights, and change mental gears. In commercial television, time is money: a few minutes' delay can run into overtime; a missing guest can cost us hundreds of dollars in lost programming.

Our first guest has arrived, but already delay is threatening. She has come in from the country and she is starving for a mixed grill. We hurry her through it and onto the set. She is a psychiatrist named Anne Biezanek, and she is a storm centre of controversy in Britain. A devout Roman Catholic, she has been publicly refused communion by her church because she has opened a birth-control clinic in her home. Handsome, robust, and eloquent, she is psychologically at sea, for her faith has been badly cracked; and this she cannot admit to herself or to me on television.

She clings to the church that has rejected her and stamped her "Sinner," but she cannot tell me why. What she can do is to describe in moving detail the torture of mind and soul she endured when she actively went against the orders of her own priests.

The interview ends; the lights snap off. My next guest is a different kind of fish: young Michael Chaplin, the beatnik son of the great comedian, recently found living on public welfare.

Consternation! We have ten minutes to go and young Chaplin is missing. The scion of the world's greatest show-business success has a job at last, licking envelopes in a publishing firm, and he is afraid to ask the boss for time off. One of our researchers is dispatched to wheedle the boss by phone. Meanwhile a standby guest, an engaging and garrulous London barrow boy, is winkled out of Covent Garden, just in case young Chaplin can't make it.

But Chaplin arrives with seconds to spare, and the barrow boy goes back to hawking violets. The Daily Express is hot on Chaplin's heels, for he has made news again by shaving off his beard and trimming his locks, and they want a picture of the new job-holding suburbanite.

The press must wait, for the tape is rolling. Chaplin is eased into a

276

chair, wired for sound, and we begin to try to discover the reason why he left home and turned Bohemian. It is hard work, for he is shy and hesitant, but it is a fascinating story that emerges in bits and pieces: the old familiar tale of a sensitive second child in a large family with two dominant personalities for parents. He ran from the prison of his Swiss domicile searching for something that was eluding him: searching, in short, for his own identity. Has he found it? Not yet, but then he is only nineteen.

My last question to him produces an intriguing answer. He has not seen his famous father for two years. Are they estranged? No, says Michael, it's just that his father stays at the Savoy when he comes to London, and the Savoy won't let a beatnik in the front door. There is no common ground on which father and son may meet.

Off he goes, back to licking envelopes, with the press in hot pursuit, and into the lounge, punctual to the minute, strides the imposing figure of Nubar Gulbenkian, one of the most engaging men in London as well as one of the richest. (His father, Calouste, was reckoned the richest man in history.) Monocle screwed tightly in place, fresh orchid in buttonhole, Churchillian cigar protruding from beard, the lofty Gulbenkian is a haberdasher's dream and an interviewer's delight. He disdains coffee, asks for and gets a cognac, and begins to talk about the art of living.

Is it true, I inquire, that his father used to order a new eighteen-year-old mistress regularly every year? Oh, quite true, say Gulbenkian, pausing dramatically to flick the ash from his cigar – but on doctor's orders, you understand, my dear fellow, on doctor's orders.

Then he tells the incredible tale of the legal suit his father brought against him because he ordered a cold chicken at his desk and paid for it with the firm's money. His father lost the case and paid out $90,000 in court costs. He could, as Nubar said, afford it.

As Gulbenkian is whisked away in the special taxi that is his London trademark, I greet my next guest – that giant among Methodists, "Soapbox" Soper, now a peer of the realm. He is surely the first Baron ever to appear regularly on a Sunday at Speakers' Corner in Hyde Park.

Tough-minded, witty, and voluble, Soper lets the answers to my questions fall like the blows of a meat-axe. Can Conservatives go to Heaven? I inquire. Just possibly, says Soper – but by a very circuitous route, for "it is quite impossible to have Christianity and Conservatism." No wonder the Labour government elevated him to the peerage.

The minutes tick past. The lights go down as the interview ends. It is stifling hot now, and the air conditioning can run only during the interval because it is too noisy to operate when the cameras and sound are on.

Michael Caine, the newest male movie sensation, comes in wearing an expensive white turtleneck sweater and the Harry Palmer glasses familiar to fans of The Ipcress File.

I had not expected to like this man, for the press clippings depict him as arrogant, shallow, and egotistical. One learns to mistrust Fleet Street. Caine is engaging and frank. The son of a Billingsgate fish porter and a Cockney scrubwoman, he was raised in grinding poverty and now is determined to enjoy his newfound fame and wealth, and he doesn't care who knows it. He has had bad times and, as he loosens up, he starts to talk about them.

He tells a story that Fleet Street has never published – about the terrible time in Paris when, at the nadir of his career, penniless and friendless and half out of his mind, he spent two solid months living in the airport, sleeping on the waiting-room benches, eating at the snack bar, thanks to the charity of the owner, and never able to change his clothes. Who can begrudge him success?

He leaves in a flutter of autograph books. But where is Sarah Miles, my next and final guest? Panic! *The hottest young female star in England has suddenly been taken ill. Quick! Find the barrow boy!*

"Keep calm, guv," says a cheery voice, "I'm here." The barrow boy walks jauntily over to the table, sits down and adjusts his microphone.

"Don't you worry none, guv," he says to me. "I'll put you at your ease."

And then, as the lights go on again, the tape starts to roll, and the floor director makes his little sign, Ted "Monk" Adams, the Cockney King of the Road, begins to talk with the pure accent of the genuine Londoner, and I know instinctively that all is well. For this man is that rarest of all creatures, a television natural. More than anyone who has preceded him to this makeshift studio, he has the gift of the gab. Gift! Ye Gods, he almost springs out of the TV set at you! It is an electrifying and unexpected finish to our first day of assembly-line interviews in London.

Chapter Eleven

1

I look back on the 1960s as the busiest years of my life. *Front Page Challenge* was commanding a huge audience, in spite of the various newspaper critics who thought it had been on long enough. I was now a permanent panellist and yet able to travel with *The Pierre Berton Show,* thanks to the invention of videotape, which allowed us to produce two *Challenge* shows each Monday night. When I headed off to Australia, announcing I would return on Monday morning, two weeks hence, in time for the evening program, Gordon Sinclair bridled.

"You're cutting it too close," he said. "You never know with air travel. You might easily miss two shows, and that's no good." I had every intention, however, of arriving on time, for I had secretly booked my flight to return the day before. Our producer, Don Brown, and I had cooked up a fake telegram to be sent after my departure from Sydney, announcing the plane had been grounded. That Monday night Gordon went on CFRB with an I-told-you-so broadcast. He had warned me, he said, but I hadn't listened. Now they'd have to replace me on *Front Page Challenge* with Charles Templeton. In fact, Don had arranged in advance for me to be the first mystery guest on the show. I hid out during the day and turned up at the studio at the last minute. I had practised a plummy English accent, so far from my normal speaking voice that the panel didn't catch on. They didn't get the story either, which was, I think, my famous trip to Headless Valley. When I was revealed there were gasps and guffaws, especially from Gordon, who took it all with high good humour.

In my days of poverty I had made a rule never to say no to any offer, for I wanted to establish a reputation for availability. Now I found myself involved with all kinds of peripheral activities. I appeared for three nights running at a Yorkville coffee-house, reciting my own poetry and even singing something I'd written. I cut a record for Arc in Toronto, reciting Robert Service. I lifted my best satirical pieces from my three collections of newspaper columns and sent them to Doubleday in New York. They were published there under the title *My War with the Twentieth Century.* I became the voice of a humanoid on a children's animated TV series, *Rocket Robin Hood.* During a Caribbean cruise I wrote lyrics for a projected musical play about the Klondike. I even wrote, but did not publish, a humorous novel. With the CBC's Fletcher

280

Markle and Elsa, I co-wrote outlines for a TV series about sports-car racing to be called *The Glory Hunters,* which was never produced. With Ken Lefolii, Jack McClelland, and artist John Richmond I helped produce a satirical map entitled *The Indefensible Border,* which didn't sell. In fact, few of these projects succeeded.

"You're trying to do too much," Gordon Sinclair said to me one evening as we were being made up for *Front Page Challenge.* "You ought to slow down."

I bridled. "I feel great," I told him. "I'm thriving! I like to keep busy."

He looked at me solemnly. "There are signs," he said mysteriously.

Of course, I knew what he meant. I had developed a facial tic, which I was trying, not very successfully, to ignore. That wasn't easy, for though the twitch came and went, my audience was clearly aware of it; some of them even wrote me letters of sympathy. It was caused not so much by my workload as by the tension involved in keeping my various commitments. As an old newspaperman, I had a horror of missing any deadline – for an article, a script, or a book – and was proud of the fact that I had always been able to deliver on time. There were occasions when I could have been given an extension, but I could never bring myself to ask for one; hence the twitch.

"You ought to relax more," Janet would say to me, but I couldn't do that if there was work to be finished. She was perhaps the most relaxed woman I ever encountered. Deadlines didn't faze her; if she couldn't finish something, she didn't get upset. There was always another day tomorrow. With our brood of children, she was often late for the dentist, for a movie, for a social event, for a meeting with me. I learned to expect it but never quite managed to accept it. I fidgeted until she sailed in, smiling cheerfully, always with an iron-clad excuse.

The twitch bothered me for another reason: my ego was bruised It was a signal to friends and strangers alike that I wasn't quite the relaxed, easy-going TV host that I was trying to portray on the small screen. When I started out in television, I didn't twitch. In those early days, television was a lark. It was only after I was found wanting and then worked seriously to improve my performance that the twitch began to appear. Clearly, I was trying too hard. In the end I gave up trying to control my twitch, and it finally vanished.

I cannot say that this did much to lessen my professional workload or my varied public appearances. I was called upon to appear at every conceivable fête, gala, opening, exhibition, fund-raiser, protest march, and panel discussion. I helped organize money-raising events for the Harold King Farm Foundation and for the Peace Research Institute. I organized a classy evening to raise funds for Stokely Carmichael, the black activist, who appeared on my program. I went to Ottawa with delegations of the Canadian Civil Liberties Association, protesting the latest breach of human rights. When Dorothy Cameron opened an exhibition of erotic art, *Eros '65,* at her Yonge Street gallery, guess who officiated? I made a glowing speech about how romantic love, too long absent from the Canadian scene, had finally come of age in Toronto the Good. "We've come a long way in this city, as a country and as a people, to have a show of this nature," I declared. But not far enough. Two days later the police closed the show, seized seven paintings (which they carried away in brown-paper wrappers in order to protect the morals of passersby), and charged Dorothy with the undue exploitation of sex. She was found guilty and fined $350 or thirty days in jail. I helped raise funds to cover her legal expenses.

In those hectic years I was the subject of a spate of newspaper features and magazine pieces, all of which made much of my capacity for work. Yet almost everything I did I still thought of as play. I did not spend any time on the golf course, nor did I belong to a service club – or any other kind of club. I did what I liked to do. More important, I had a wife who, as a former newspaperwoman, understood that I needed to concentrate on my writing to the exclusion of every household chore. Janet didn't hold a nine-to-five job; she held a seven-to-midnight job running our household. I am mechanically useless. It is all I can do to change a light bulb. I didn't understand the swimming pool's filtration system, or how the furnace worked, or even how the thermostats operated – and I didn't want to. In our marriage we had an unspoken agreement: I would write and broadcast; Janet would handle home and family. I would spend all my time at my typewriter; she would change the typewriter ribbons, a feat quite beyond my abilities.

I had two offices, one at home, where I did my writing, one downtown at Screen Gems, where people could find me and where I worked with Elsa on my television shows. Elsa managed the office, hired the staff, dealt with producers and publishers, handled my publicity, and ran the TV programs. Ennis Halliday (now Ennis Armstrong) fielded all my phone calls with far more diplomacy than I could muster, answered my mail, made my appointments, ran interference for me, and – most important – *knew where everything was*. From time to time other entrepreneurs tried to hire Elsa and also Ennis away. I would have been lost without them. With Janet they kept me free of the hindrances that often plague a freelancer.

Until Elsa arrived, a lot of my time had been taken up reading and replying to typewritten memos and attending interminable meetings, which included everybody on the staff. Ross and Sam Levene were both graduates of the CBC and its bureaucracy. Elsa wasn't. After she took over Sam's office, she discovered a drawerful of memos and threw them all in the wastebasket. "We don't need memos and we don't need meetings," she said. "All we have to do is shout at each other over the transoms."

Now Jack McClelland made me an irresistible offer that found me with a second downtown office, another secretary, and an editorial team. With Canada's one-hundredth anniversary a mere two years away, he was planning to publish a series of low-cost illustrated books dealing with various aspects of the country's first century – a book on art and one on food, a book of history, a book of sports, and several others. He wanted me to plan the series, which would be called the Canadian Centennial Library, and act as editor-in-chief.

"It's easy work," Jack told me. "Won't take too much of your time."

I'd heard that before but took the job anyway, since I hadn't yet learned to say no to offers. I hired a staff, with Ken Lefolii as my managing editor and Frank Newfeld, who had won many awards for book design for M&S, as art director. Since the main M&S offices were far off in the boondocks of East York, I set up a special office for the series in second-floor premises at the corner of Simcoe and Richmond Streets. Jack had taken on *Weekend* magazine as his partner; the idea was that we would produce and publish the series, while *Weekend* would handle advertising and publicity.

Details of this publishing venture, which I called "the most ambitious event in Canadian book publishing history," were announced at a press conference on October 30, 1964. There would be eight books selling at $2.95 each – $3.95 for the deluxe version. We would print one hundred thousand copies of each book with the break-even point at seventy thousand. The first book, *The Making of the Nation,* William Kilbourn's history of the first hundred years, would appear in November 1965. The rest would be shipped bi-monthly until Centennial Year.

Jack, as usual, had underestimated the work involved. The job occupied the best part of my week, for I not only acted as editor but also made myself personally responsible for three of the books. These were an anthology, *Great Canadians* (selected by a committee under the chairmanship of Vincent Massey), *Remember Yesterday,* a picture book covering the century for which I wrote text and captions, and the *Centennial Food Guide,* a history-cum-recipe book, complete with modern colour photography and archival illustrations. This was the first book that Janet and I had worked on together. She was perfect for the task. As a former journalist she understood the importance of lively copy. As a consummate cook she knew what was delectable. She tracked down century-old cookbooks and learned about such out-of-fashion dishes as kromeskies and bread omelet. She combed through the works of Canadian authors, past and present, to put together an anthology of literary passages dealing with food. She tested every one of the 128 recipes herself in her crowded kitchen and then added a few of her own. For an entire winter, we ate not like kings but like early Canadians, until, after about the fiftieth meal, one of the children whose favourite dish was Kraft Dinner asked plaintively, "Hey, Mom? When are we going back to eating *normal?*"

For the next several years and longer, I criss-crossed the city between the two offices – one on Simcoe Street and the other at the corner of Carlton and Church, where Elsa reigned supreme. I had two secretaries now (Ennis stayed with the TV show) and two staffs to ride herd upon.

I suppose that everybody looking back over the milestones of a rich and varied life thinks of himself as the centre of a golden age. But then, all ages are golden when one is young – at least in retrospect. Were the 1950s really the Golden Age of *Maclean's*? Did I play a part in the Golden Age of the *Toronto Star?* And how about the Golden Age of Television? Aging scribes now use the term to describe those early black-and-white days, and that is how I look back on them, nostalgically. Or am I simply basking in the memory of the golden age of my youth? Yet it does seem to me that the Centennial began a Golden Age of Book Publishing in this country. A wave of nationalism, brought on first by our hundredth birthday and second by the huge success of Expo 67, was causing people to examine themselves, their literature, and their past. More than three hundred titles appeared in Centennial Year – everything from a book on indigenous bagpipe music to a history of nineteenth-century building methods. As Bill French, the *Globe and Mail*'s book columnist, wrote, "never before has this country – perhaps any country – embarked on such an extensive program of force-feeding its authors." Every publisher was churning out books to exploit the new awareness, and Jack and I were part of it.

The series was a winner; each book sold more than one hundred thousand copies. I plunged into the mysterious world of mail-order sales, with all the gimmickry that that implied – the free book, the automatic mailings, the negative billing (the subscriber must inform us that he doesn't want the next volume), and the deluxe editions bound in simulated leather, which, I discovered, were cheaper to produce than the ordinary $2.95 editions, even though they sold for a dollar more. Vanity is such that a third of our subscribers wanted them.

By this time Jack had become a close friend and drinking companion as well as partner. He had single-handedly turned the book world upside down in Canada. Before he rocketed onto the scene, it was a fusty, old-fashioned business, which eschewed the kind of publicity stunt that became his trademark. One cannot imagine John Gray of Macmillan's barrelling down Yonge Street with a woman author in a Roman chariot, or dressing up as Santa Claus in a prairie city, trying to give away copies of his latest paperback and daring police to arrest him for peddling goods without a licence.

In the early days, books were launched discreetly in the publisher's office with a few critics and friends sipping sherry. No hard liquor in those rarefied quarters. The book tour, which Margaret Atwood has correctly dubbed the "Kill an Author Tour," was unknown. Some credit this breakthrough to Jacqueline Susann, the best-selling novelist south of the border, but Jack McClelland instituted the phenomenon in Canada just as early. Within a decade the country would be crossed and recrossed each fall by hordes of garrulous authors, haunting the TV and radio studios and the newsrooms, shamelessly plugging their own work.

Jack's credo, "I don't buy books – I buy authors," was the secret of his rise to the top of the publishing heap in Canada. More than any other publisher, he was the writer's friend. As a result, new writers and old flocked to him. Jack stood by his authors, drank with them (vodka, not sherry), held their hands, maintained a long and lively correspondence, got them in and out of trouble, and generally made it fun to be on the M&S list.

His view was long-term. Few publishers, I suspect, would have wanted to court a loss by publishing the early poetry of Leonard Cohen or Irving Layton. Jack did, and in the long run profited. He had an uncanny book sense, which explains the presence of so many of his books on the best-seller lists. He was always prepared to do what every good publisher must do – support a book because he thinks it deserves to be read, even though he knows in advance it will lose money. I've always thought that a publisher who makes too much money is suspect. The essence of great publishing is to damn the accountants and forge full speed ahead. That was Jack; it was publishing that obsessed him, not profit. Yet profit was the acknowledged stamp of success in the old Toronto in which he was raised, and it hurt him to be called a bad businessman. He belonged to the upper-middle echelons of Toronto's WASP society. He knew all the right people. He had gone to the proper schools and had an illustrious war record in the navy behind him. I'm sure that some of his old cronies thought him a failure. He was anything but, and that other world, the cultural world – in which he had one foot – knew it. Jack moved between two levels. On one level was the raffish gang of artists, scribblers, and poets with whom he hobnobbed. On the other were the old Torontonians, among whom his father's prominence as a major Canadian publisher had placed him. He had the affection of the former; he craved the admiration of the latter.

He worked at night, and that brought out the best and the worst in him. After midnight struck, he would sit down at his Dictaphone, a glass of vodka at his elbow, to answer his mail and dictate letters and memoranda. The following morning his superb but long-suffering secretary, Marge Hodgeman, would throw half of it away. She saved him from more than one broken friendship and, I suspect, several expensive libel suits.

He was a perennial hypochondriac, but with good reason, for on several occasions he was felled by a combination of allergies. The merest taste of shellfish would bring on a serious reaction. On a flight from England when he ordered a Bloody Mary, he got a Bloody Caesar instead, and the clam juice almost did him in after the first sip. Nor could he eat anything made of wheat, rye, or other grains – pasta, bread, cake – for he had a gluten allergy. Whisky was taboo; vodka was the tipple of choice.

"I'm near death!" he would often cry, usually as the result of a long session with Smirnoff. Once in New York he insisted that he was doomed.

"I'm running a high fever," he told me one morning. "Please get to the drugstore and find a thermometer. I'm burning up." I took his temperature and found it normal, but Jack would have none of it. "It's broken," he said. "Get another." I complied and again found his temperature normal.

"It's just a hangover," I told him, but Jack refused that diagnosis. Since I wouldn't get a third thermometer, he was forced to grin and bear it.

His was a one-man show. He oversaw everything from the cover design to titles. I tried to call a book of interviews *Voices from the Sixties*. Jack thought it far too weak and insisted on *The Cool, Crazy, Committed World of the Sixties*. I hated it, and when Doubleday took the book in the United States, I reverted to my original. It was a poor seller in both countries.

On one memorable occasion he presented Irving Layton with his first book of poetry. "How do you like it, Irving?" he asked. "Isn't it just great?"

Irving looked at the jacket and scowled. "You've spelled my name wrong," he complained.

Jack looked at the cover carefully, then looked back at Irving. "Picky! Picky!" he said.

If he had a failing, it was his short attention span. He had a habit of launching brilliant projects, then losing interest when something new popped into that agile mind. His short-lived attempt to launch a western division of M&S faded away; so did his plans for a combination book-magazine for children and a new book club called the Preview Book Club, which would allow readers to buy a bound set of printer's proofs in advance of publication. One problem was that like all publishing companies, his was underfunded. On the other hand, his Carleton Library of Canadian classics was a critical and financial success.

The coming Centennial spawned a whole series of other projects, including an abortive business partnership known as Centennial Celebration Consultants. Its board seemed impeccable: Budge Crawley, the Ottawa filmmaker; John C. Parkin, Toronto's leading architect; Jack Dennett, CFRB's top newscaster; Jack McClelland; and me. We were all brought together by Robert Macaulay, a one-time Ontario cabinet minister. What a high-powered group we were! We offered our expertise to municipalities and private companies that were wondering how to celebrate the country's hundredth birthday, but nobody believed such a prominent gang would ever take the time to do the job. And so, though we produced an elegant brochure, held regular meetings, and came up with what we thought were brilliant ideas, it was impossible to convince prospective clients that we were anything but figureheads.

The project was an enormous flop. Ruefully we examined our tiny balance sheet. Here we thought we were on to something; we had spent hours planning centennial celebrations, digging up history and heritage, appearing at municipal councils and private boards, and nobody wanted us! "Oh well," said Macaulay, "it's been a hell of a lot of fun with you guys." And so it had been. With what little money we had left we threw ourselves a party and went on to other things.

For me, other things included a new radio program. "Dialogue" was the brainchild of Charles Templeton, who approached me early in 1966 suggesting that the two of us engage in a daily five-minute argument or discussion on matters of topical interest. He had already talked to CFRB, and they were interested. I grabbed the idea and we went on the air in February.

Charles's plan was that we would always take opposite sides on our daily set-to. I baulked. I told him I had strong opinions on almost everything but didn't want to waste such debating skills as I had sticking up for issues with which I disagreed. We did not resolve the problem until we went on the air. Our first argument was about the Henry Moore sculpture dubbed the Archer, which had just been installed in front of Toronto City Hall. I argued that this work by an internationally famous artist was an ornament to the city. Charles, in the interests of disagreement, took the other side. He didn't believe a word of what he was saying, and that made it easy for me to wipe the floor with him. "Never again!" he said ruefully, as we left the studio.

And so we argued, disagreed, or often agreed with one another, each bringing his personal convictions to "Dialogue." Sometimes, when one of us was out of town, we arranged for a substitute, but that never worked very well. Charles and I were perfectly suited to each other; even though we often disagreed, each respected the other's viewpoint. So we remained friends, even when the discussion grew so hot the microphones sizzled.

We had been friends since the old *Close-Up* days. He was our frequent guest at Christmas dinner, and a good one, since he gave a convincing performance as Joseph in the annual nativity play the children staged. He was, and is, one of the most remarkable men I've known.

288

He could have been another Billy Graham, but, in truth, he could turn his hand to almost anything in the communications world. Honderich hired him (against my advice, I blush to reveal) to run the op-ed page of the *Star*. He learned the job overnight and was quickly promoted to managing editor. He left the paper to run for the provincial Liberal leadership and came within a whisker of getting it on the basis of a real stem-winder of a speech. Much to their later regret, the federal Liberal Mafia thwarted him.

He went on to become head of news and public affairs for the CTV network. Then *Maclean's* offered him a job as editor-in-chief and he took it, only to find his new office being torn apart shortly after his arrival. The space he had been assigned was six inches bigger than that of the publisher! This kind of picayune one-upmanship, so typical of the Maclean Hunter company, continued. Charles refused to brook interference from the business side and quit. Nothing daunted, he began writing novels that proved best-sellers as well as hosting a couple of television shows. He also continued to invent everything from board games to children's toys. He is, among other things, a first-rate draughtsman and an artist of quality, who, in his teens, produced a regular sports cartoon for the old *Globe*. He holds a raft of patents, but his interests are largely confined to the inventive process rather than marketing. His penthouse is crammed with all sorts of devices that he has conceived but rarely bothered to take any further.

Charles and I thus began a broadcasting relationship that was to last for fourteen years. I rose at seven each morning, skimmed the morning paper, then phoned Charles (if he hadn't already phoned me). It took us less than thirty seconds to settle on a subject. An hour later we met at the studio, sat down at the microphone, and, with scarcely a word to each other, started in. Charles had an Irish temper but never used it on me. I once called him a redneck and saw him bristle. It was a cheap shot and provoked the closest he ever came to exploding. We often differed, especially, I remember, about movie censorship. I was opposed to all censorship and could not understand why magazines, newspapers, books, TV, and radio were free of a censor board, while movies had to be screened and chopped up in advance. Charles's hands were tied on this one, I think, because he was a close friend of Don Sims, a former broadcaster who had become chief censor for Ontario. The two had known each other since their days in the Youth for Christ movement, and Charles was always loyal to his friends. Once, standing at a bar beside McKenzie Porter, then a *Telegram* columnist, who was in his cups and sneering at me, Charles shook a fist in his face and told him that if he said one more word against me, he'd flatten him. Porter shut up. The next day the two of us were again going after each other, exchanging verbal blows almost as wicked as the ones that had been threatened the night before. But that's show business and it's also friendship.

2

Nature It may well be asked – and indeed it has been asked more than once –
Boy if I ever had time to lie back and smell the roses. As a matter of fact, I did – literally. In the summers when I had a season free from television and a month off from radio, I spent hours in the garden. When Janet and I first moved to the country, I announced, in my innocence, that I would have nothing whatsoever to do with the land. But living close to the soil as we did, with the rich, black fields on every side being tilled and seeded, we could not long resist the urge to create. A tree became as sacred as a wayside shrine after I had planted one or two; topsoil became more precious than any treasure; compost, the subject of endless comic essays, took on a truly noble quality.

Thanks to Janet, who could not stand to waste anything, we threw nothing away that could be returned to the black earth. Dead leaves and old grass cuttings, the discarded tops of frost-killed annuals, kitchen refuse, lumps of old sod, the carcasses of small animals and rats – all of these we piled in a corner of the lot and covered with earth, to be turned over regularly until they assumed the consistency of mush and could be spread out to renew a tired plot. Long before blue boxes came into style, we were conserving. When I began, I did not know a hyacinth from a tuberose. I learned by trial and error, like a Sunday painter – planting a clump of shrubbery one season and digging it up and moving it the next. Every gardener is a forward-looker, seeing his handiwork not as it is but as it will be. When I planted a small whip of locust or a maple sapling, I saw it as a sturdy tree a dozen years hence. In the late fall when I looked out on my borders, I saw not a strip of black loam, empty of growth, but a garden ablaze with April's scarlet. For I knew that, beneath the soil, row on row lay the plump bulbs of the Red Emperor,

290

and that within each bulb was a tiny green miniature of the tulip that would burst forth in Technicolor when the snow fled.

In the long winter nights, I literally dreamed of blue sheets of *Scilla siberica*. I could scarcely wait to see the flowers of the new, and to me unknown, tulips I'd planted the autumn before, after poring through the bulb catalogues. As an amateur I had often planted seeds and seedlings too close together, but I soon learned to plant them farther apart and to bide my time. When you work with the soil you come to realize that patience is a virtue.

In the warm spring evenings we would pack the family into the car and drive the back-concession roads. Yellow is surely the colour of early spring, and on these jaunts we would see the dandelions in their legions starting up from the moist earth and buttering the meadows. The awakening willows, genuflecting before the May breezes, were already clothed in a mist of catkins. The very warblers, nesting in orchard and thicket, were dappled with the protective hues of forsythia and daffodil. In the cedar groves, the first wild flowers burst forth in various shades of citron, sulphur, apricot, and gold.

Every year at this season we drove with the kids along a sideroad and stopped at a small swamp, where, concealed from the speed-blinded sports-car set, lay a cool glen with a gurgle of water at its base and a mosaic of marsh marigolds. I know of no more luxuriant sight in mid-May than these golden flowers. But now the swamp is gone, filled in by an unthinking, uncaring developer, and the marsh marigolds are gone with it.

I knew nothing of wild flowers, of course, in those early days, even though my father collected, pressed, and mounted them in the Yukon. But you cannot live among the woods and meadows without learning something – otherwise why bother to flee from the city? For years we used to stop at a secret bank where wild strawberries grew so thick and with berries so plump that we could spot them glimmering redly from our car. They too have gone. In the untrammelled meadows beneath the dying elms we spotted the delicate adder's-tongue with their mottled leaves poking up from the dry grasses. And we would watch, with ill-concealed expectancy, the progress of the heart-shaped leaves of the violets on the edge of the cedar copses. At last, with a shout of delight, one or other of the children would be rewarded by the glitter of pale blue and lavender, sparkling like jewelled pinpoints almost everywhere on the dark rim of the forest. I pointed out to the older children that there were some fifty varieties of violet to be found in the woodlands of Eastern North America. Pamela, my Number Two daughter, was the best student. Eventually she went to work for the Federation of Ontario Naturalists.

Because of my Depression background I am part pinch-penny, part profligate, and so is Janet. But bottom line or no bottom line, when it came to our property, cost was no object. While she was scouring the shops for cheap cuts of meat and taking advantage of cut-rate sales, I was throwing caution aside to buy new species; when the moraine and sunset locusts, both patented plants, and thus expensive, came on the market, I simply had to have a few. I brought in bulldozers to create two ponds, complete with pink, yellow, and white water lilies, and also the sacred Egyptian lotus. I never bothered to ask the price. And yet we were the last on our block, as they say, to switch our record collection from the old 78s to the new 33 1/3s, the last to buy a tape deck with a new selection of cassettes to play on it, the last to put in twin speakers. As I write this, we still haven't got around to buying a CD player or CD discs to go with it. On the other hand, I've thought nothing of picking out a few mugho pines and some Japanese dwarf maples to set off the huge rocks I bought from the Acton quarry, and, at great expense, put near the entrance to the house.

Life in the country, in fact, was our salvation. Before we lived outside the city we were at odds with the elements. Snow and rain had been my foes, but I soon learned to welcome both. There have been summers when I have prayed for rain. In the city, where plots are small, one can afford to water with a hose. In the country there is too much space, and you learn to leave the watering to nature. For me, there is no sweeter music than the rumble of thunder on a hot summer's eve, and when the small rivulets of water stream across the cracked and weathered surface of the soil, like tears on an old man's cheeks, the heart leaps. Some people, I suspect, would be unnerved by the utter silence of a country midnight – the absolute absence of brake squeal, for instance. We cannot pop into a supermarket, for there is none handy; nor is there a neighbour just over the fence. There are no fences, only a rolling expanse of pastureland dotted with trees. But there is also a valley and a river winding through it and a clump of pointed cedars and a wild orchard. And when these turn chalk white, as they do each winter after a snowfall, and the ghost of a mist rises through them, soft as a maiden's breath, I would not trade the country for the fanciest penthouse in town.

It was this pastoral presence, surely, that sustained me through the ups and downs of the sixties. For I could always escape to the serenity of the countryside when trouble knocked on my office door. I sometimes view my career, in retrospect, as a roadway fraught with obstacles – a pothole here, a barrier there – but interspersed with smooth patches, down which I can glide unencumbered. If 1963 had had its share of potholes, 1966 was remarkably gentle. The critics were kind, even enthusiastic, about the television interviews, some of which I published in book form. Of course, I put only the good ones in the book: my interview with Lee Harvey Oswald's incredibly awful mother; Malcolm X's half hour with me – the last interview he ever gave; Lenny Bruce's interview, also his last; and a session with Maureen Murphy, a young civil rights worker fighting for voter registration among blacks in the American South.

I included these last two in the book because both had given me trouble. Screen Gems didn't want me near Lenny Bruce because, they insisted, he was a wild, crazy comedian who would use foul language on air. He didn't; I found him a quiet, deeply troubled performer, totally obsessed by the law, who talked sensibly, even fervently, about his attempts to fight the obscenity charges against him. He had turned down a thousand dollars to appear on a CBC show, opting instead for an unbroken half hour with me. Maureen Murphy was one of several guests through whom I tried to tell the story of the civil rights battle below the Mason-Dixon line. It was a considerable shock to me when the Windsor television station refused to air the program for fear of offending its Detroit viewers.

By now the program was reasonably well known in American entertainment circles. We were offering something few other North American programs were able to provide – a chance to talk for half an hour and know that nothing would be cut out. Norman Thomas, head of the U.S. Socialist Party, said that a U.S. network would cut the talk part to a seven-minute sound bite and insist on following it with a juggling act. Henry Fonda, who rarely gave interviews, told me he'd agreed to come on the show because his agent ordered him to do it. It was, he told him, the best exposure he could have.

My relations with Screen Gems had always been informal. Once a year Lloyd Burns, the company's Canadian-born vice-president, would come up from New York and we'd settle my contract over a drink. I had gone to the *Star* without a contract and accepted the first offer Honderich made me. I'd gone back to *Maclean's* on the strength of a handshake. I'd spent a full year doing radio commentaries and hadn't collected enough to break even. My first five-minute TV show for Screen Gems hadn't earned me a nickel; in my arrogance and my naïveté I had tried to handle all business arrangements myself. Now, in my forties, I came to my senses. My New York literary agent, Willis Wing, found me a good lawyer, John Fernbach, who agreed to run interference for me. This resulted in the following dialogue when Lloyd Burns called me from New York:

LLOYD: Pierre, I'll be in town next week and I'm looking forward to getting together with you. By the way, it's contract time, and we can settle the details over a drink.

ME: Hey, Lloyd, I'd love to have a drink, but let's not spoil it talking business. Let's leave that to the legal people.

LLOYD: Well, sure, our legal department is working on the document right now.

ME: That's great, Lloyd. I'll have my lawyer in New York call them and work it out. You and I don't need to bother ourselves with business details. That's what lawyers are for.

LLOYD: Uh. *What* lawyer? You don't need a lawyer. Our people can handle all that.

ME: Great, Lloyd. You tell your people to handle it with my lawyer. I'm looking forward to seeing you up here.

John Fernbach negotiated an iron-clad agreement in which Screen Gems contracted to produce thirty-six weeks of *The Pierre Berton Show* annually. One year later the standard television year was reduced to twenty-eight weeks. As a result of the new contract, I was paid for eight weeks of shows that were never produced. That was the way it would be for as long as *The Pierre Berton Show* stayed on the air. There was a delicious irony here. I had started out with Screen Gems working for nothing, while they took a profit. Now they were paying me for not working at all.

Fernbach achieved a few other perks, one of which ensured that I would always travel first class when the show moved out of Toronto.

One day, coming up from New York, I ran into Lloyd Burns at the airport heading for Toronto in the same aircraft. Screen Gems put him back with the peasants in Economy. I moved into First Class and drank champagne.

I thought about that and concluded that if for the first half of my life I had been grossly underpaid, I would strive to be grossly overpaid during the second half.

Only one thing frustrated me, and that had nothing to do with money. I could not discuss matters of day-to-day political interest because the program wasn't live. It was "bicycled" about so that my Fonda interview might be shown on a Monday in Toronto and ten days later in Calgary. I really wanted to be on the network, live, and so I approached Doug Nixon, then in charge of programming, and suggested that the CBC might be interested in carrying the show. He asked for an outline. I gave him much more. Elsa and I produced a thick booklet describing the current show and how it would be changed for the better if it ran live on the CBC. I took a sample of my interviews and showed him how they would be more pertinent if we could discuss what was going on that day or that week. I then made a one-hour tape to give him the flavour of a program. I don't think he ever got around to viewing it.

Weeks went by, then months; no word from Nixon, no flicker of interest from anybody at the corporation. More than six months later I ran into Nixon at the Toronto airport and made so bold as to ask him what had happened. He looked baffled at first, then remembered. It was clear he hadn't bothered to read my prospectus or look at the tape. He promised, however, to set up a meeting with half a dozen key people to discuss the matter. He named a date – at nine in the morning – in a screening room in the old "Kremlin," the CBC's executive headquarters on Jarvis Street. I arrived early, and waited, and waited, and waited. Finally, one minor official turned up. Nobody else came, not Nixon – not anyone. And that was the last I ever heard of the matter.

In one way I was relieved. I knew that if the corporation took the show, half a dozen sticky fingers would want to change it. There would be endless meetings and endless memos. Elsa Franklin had become a superb producer, but would the CBC accept a woman from the outside? Probably not. Yet much of the show's success depended on Elsa, who chose subjects that interested me. She and her staff preceded me to places like Hollywood and London, so that when I arrived there would be a list of prospective guests waiting for me. I'd cut some out and okay others, but usually went along with Elsa, who was also a brilliant publicist.

Whenever we made news, Elsa alerted her contacts in the media. Pierre Trudeau appeared again on the show to declare that there should be no special status for Quebec in the future. Pierre Bourgault, then a young separatist, warned that his group, Le Rassemblement pour l'indépendance nationale, would not hesitate to sink a ship in the St. Lawrence Seaway as a bargaining chip in the coming struggle with Ottawa. Marshall McLuhan announced that colour television would bring a craving for hotter and spicier foods, and that more and more people would work at home because of new communication devices. The arrival of the FAX machine suggests he was right on target; so does the craze for Thai cuisine.

The program was also ahead of the times. In September 1966 Mrs. Jacqueline Lucie told how she was beaten unconscious and subjected to brutal handling at several publicly supported institutions for emotionally disturbed children in Ontario and Quebec but had received no psychiatric treatment. A few weeks later I produced three other women who spoke frankly about similar conditions, and three ex-staff members who confirmed, in essence, what had been revealed. The next day I interviewed three experts about the system and what was wrong with it. They blamed the hospitals and the churches that ran them, providing dates and details of irregularities. Looking back, it seems incredible that there was little public protest, and certainly no commission of inquiry as there would be today. But it's not true to say, as some have said, that these medieval conditions were not known to the public or the media.

The following year we made major headlines as a result of the appearance on the show of the secretary of state, Judy LaMarsh, the minister responsible for the CBC. The fuss began as the result of my question about conditions at the *Front Page Challenge* studio. I told Judy that the CBC must be really short of money if it couldn't afford a better home for the show than an old automobile salesroom full of chipped furniture. To this Judy replied: "Well, quite frankly, I think there is some rotten management in many places in the CBC and with a little better management there will be money at least for necessary things."

Oddly enough, neither Elsa nor I picked up this remark. It didn't occur to either of us that this was an extraordinary statement for a cabinet minister to make. *We* all knew there was rotten management in the CBC. The quote, to us, was old stuff.

That was a serious misjudgement on my part, and also on Judy's. Here she was, the overseer of the CBC, by inference damning its president. There was an immediate public reaction – much greater than there had been after my interview with Mrs. Lucie – and an even bigger one in the media. There was consternation among the corporation's top brass. Alphonse Ouimet, the president, and eight directors shot off an angry "profoundly distressed" letter, demanding that Judy supply proof of what she'd said. Judy, hanging tough, called the letter "arrogant." Less than a month later, Ouimet quit. But the run-down studio was never improved.

By this time the country had entered the period we now call the sixties, which did not really begin until 1964-65 and persisted into the early seventies. More and more the subject matter of my program dealt with the issues of the day – Quebec separatism, the civil rights movement in the United States, the war in Vietnam, the youth movement, the beginnings of the women's struggle, the generation gap. We took our cameras to the burgeoning Yorkville district, then the hotbed of hippie nonconformity and the centre of the coffee-house culture. We did several programs with groups of young people discussing and arguing the issues of the day – not just civil rights and war but also the need to legalize marijuana. I myself failed to understand why tobacco could be legal while grass was banned. "Let the kids have their own Nirvana," I said in one of the many speeches I made that year. That was heresy, but nobody paid much attention. I did not know until long afterwards that my own kids were trying to grow the weed in the woods below our house. They were not very good gardeners, however; it was far too dark among the cedars for anything as exotic as cannabis to flourish.

Most of the time my outrageous statements went unreported because they weren't covered by the press. I was fond of declaring, for instance, that I wouldn't want my daughter to marry a movie censor because if certain films corrupted the viewer, then the censor who had to screen them must be the worst kind of sex maniac. One day in Thornhill, a young reporter happened to be in the audience, and suddenly I made the front pages for a statement I'd been making for years. News is that which gets reported.

Meanwhile, Elsa and I had been having our own controversy with

Bassett's CFTO, which did not run the program until 11:40 p.m. How could I attract an audience at that hour, after forty minutes of news, sports, and weather? Screen Gems agreed and turned to CHCH, the lively Hamilton station, which was prepared to run the program twice – at seven o'clock and again at eleven. CHCH quickly discovered that they not only got a new audience early in the evening but also increased my late-night ratings. Wives who watched the early show were urging their husbands to tune in on the repeat.

In September 1966, with our CFTO contract at an end, we took the show to Manhattan to pick up some celebrities for our new launch at CHCH. What a strange week that was! First there was the odd performance of Joan Fontaine, the star of *Rebecca*. After she was booked, Elsa called her to remind her that this being television, she would need make-up. Fontaine said that she'd do her own. But when she appeared at the studio, fifteen minutes before the interview was slated to begin, a look of dismay and panic distorted those lovely features. "Oh no! No!" she cried. "It's television!" She turned on her heel and literally ran off down Broadway, with two of our researchers trailing after her until she vanished into the crowd at Forty-second Street. Did she really think it was radio? Or had something else disturbed her? I never knew.

We taped, as usual, eighteen programs in New York – six on each of three days. I was now insisting on two days' rest between tapings – one day in which to prepare the programs and another to relax. On our last taping day, our first guest was to be David Merrick, the brilliant but controversial Broadway producer, whom *Time* had just dubbed "the Abominable Showman." Naturally, my first question dealt with the *Time* article, and Merrick's response to it. But Merrick bristled. "I'm not going to sit here for this!" he cried, and flung out of the studio.

At the end of the day, with all the programs in the can, Elsa got an unexpected phone call from Merrick. It was all a mistake, he claimed, unchivalrously blaming his secretary. He wanted to return and complete the interview, even offering to pay overtime for the crew to stay. She told him it was impossible, whereupon he offered to come up to Toronto. "Fine," she said. "I'll send you a ticket." But he insisted on paying his own way. As this was our seasonal opening, we held a press party at the end of that day. Merrick attended, had a few drinks, talked jovially to everybody, and was the last to leave. Meanwhile he had his lawyers send us a letter pointing out that we could not show the original tape with him walking off. Being Merrick, he had been careful not to sign his contract in advance.

None of these guests impressed me as much as did a young Inuit girl, Mary Carpenter, whose father I had met during my Northern tour for *Maclean's*. She was perhaps the very first Inuk to talk frankly and emotionally about attitudes towards aborigines in general and the class system in Inuvik in particular. There, the whites got the privileges and the Inuit got none. Mary was a born shit-disturber, hard-hitting, emotional, and not popular with the white establishment of the Mackenzie Delta. In one moving sequence, she told how, after a public meeting at which she spoke out, a white woman asked "why wasn't I grateful for all the white people had done." At that point she had slapped Mary's face. As Mary was telling the story she broke down, reached for her handkerchief, and, at the memory of that humiliation, dissolved into tears. I brought in a commercial and returned to remark that it was important for us all to know such things. The program caused a mild sensation. Pat Pearce in the *Montreal Star* wrote that "more than all the pictures of the North's frozen lands, of sleds and sewers and shanties, Mary Carpenter's sobs made us instinctually aware of the people of our world – of the pride in them, of the hurt." It was, I think, the first time any Inuk had been depicted not wearing the stereotypical ear-to-ear grin. As for Mary, she appeared later with the children on our annual Christmas show. By then she had become a member of our extended family – as she still is.

All that fall Elsa had been making arrangements to take the show to Prague. William Havelka, the enterprising public relations chief for the proposed Czech Pavilion at Expo, offered to let us put onto tape, unedited, uncensored, and uncut, half a dozen interviews with members of the Czech political, artistic, and economic establishment. Havelka told me I could interview anybody I liked and ask anything I wanted to ask. I must say I was astonished at the offer, which was unprecedented. But it was genuine, as we found when we arrived in Prague with three enormous mobile trailers that had driven all the way from London because Czech TV was incompatible with our own.

The idea of a communist nation employing a P.R. man struck me as nutty, but the Czechs were clearly out to change their image. In fact, everybody in Prague talked about the "change," almost as if discussing a religious cataclysm. The word seemed to dominate every conversation.

Events tended to be dated "before the change" and after. It had started in the late fifties after Khrushchev's revelations about Stalin, and had gathered steam after 1962 when the Czech government began to encourage Western tourists. Before that, I was told, life had been stultifying.

Prague was remarkably Western – though not as Western as Hungary. The big establishments took the American Express card. Heinz ketchup graced the café tables, and you could rent a late-model U-Drive. Marika Robert, who had been born and schooled in Slovakia and who came along as a freelance researcher, was astonished to find that old friends were no longer fearful of coming to our hotel for a drink. "It's unbelievable," she said. Clearly, there was a thaw of sorts.

The country's Western patina made it difficult to remember that every business, from the great Skoda works to the smallest antique store, had been nationalized. In the government nightclubs young people in tight pants danced politely to modern music. Their hair was shaggy, their trousers purple, their stockings patterned, but they did not react as a Western crowd would. Reacting, I discovered, was banned, along with new dances – the Frug and the Watusi. Discotheques were outlawed; so was the striptease. But, as everywhere in the world, including Canada, youth was beginning to rebel, even sneaking in a few new dances between the waltzes and the fox-trots.

In Canada, young people were showing their nonconformity by becoming atheists. In Prague, where atheism was the official creed, they rebelled by becoming Catholics. I asked one woman if Czech youth felt, as many of ours did, that their teachers and parents had sold out. "Yes," she said. "That's it. You see, they are asking awkward questions about the Stalinist period. They want to know why we suffered it. How could it have been like that? Why did we go along with it? And these, of course, are questions that cannot be answered." Clearly something was in the air. Another revolution? I thought it possible.

As we always did when we visited a foreign country, Elsa and I planned an open forum with a group of students ranging in age from nineteen to twenty-five. This would be the first ever held behind the Iron Curtain for Western TV. To my discomfiture, they all wanted to talk about Canadian hockey, a subject I know very little about. They knew all the names of the players and all the team standings, of which I was ignorant. They must have thought I was a peculiar kind of Canadian – a blockhead who hardly knew what the blue line was.

300

"Stan Mikita, he's our favourite because he's a Czech," a young fifth-year economics student told me.

"No, no," I said indulgently, "I wasn't talking about the Czech team."

"Stan Mikita plays for the Chicago Black Hawks," another youth told me, sounding a bit like a Grade 3 teacher correcting an especially obtuse pupil.

That ended the hockey discussion. But the conversation was so good we extended it to a second half hour under the title "What Do Czech Students Want?" The answer was inescapable: *Freedom*. That would be a long time coming.

3

PRAGUE, January 1967. The Communist Establishment is throwing us a party. All the Czechs here, with one notable exception, are trusted, high-status party members, well off by Czech standards – smartly dressed in good broadcloth shirts with French cuffs, suits of contemporary cut, and Western-style slip-on shoes. All speak English well. As favoured comrades all have been abroad not once but many times. Membership has its privileges.

Party time in Prague

Here they are, each securely positioned near the top of his or her profession, all well over the age of fifty, enjoying the fruits of their various struggles, some of which go back to the Hitler days. I am fascinated to observe them as they sip their vodka or Scotch, chatting easily and arguing volubly, as old friends can, and making small and large talk with Elsa, our two researchers Barbara Black and Marika Robert, and me.

Our host, Adolf Hoffmeister, is a writer and artist of stature – portly, sixty-ish, heavily moustached. His apartment, surely one of the most luxurious in the city, is adorned by works of art, mostly avant garde, dating back to the 1920s. He has lived in this flat continuously for fifty-six years except for a brief wartime span when it was occupied by a Gestapo officer.

Hoffmeister began as a left-wing caricaturist. He talks easily of his friendship with Dali, Cocteau, and Sartre. His guest book contains such names as Picasso, Steinbeck, and Chagall. John Grierson, late of the National Film Board, is a personal friend, and he is intimate with the animation of the board's Norman McLaren, whom he considers a genius.

I mention Marshall McLuhan to him and he pulls The Gutenberg Galaxy *from a shelf. "That man comes out with the most outrageous things," he says. "I tangled with him at the P.E.N. convention in New York. Somebody had to stand up for the writers."*

Elsa is deep in conversation with Dr. Vladimir Kadlac, director of Prague's school of economics, who is close to the top of the Communist Party hierarchy and one of the handful of iconoclastic thinkers who hope to set their country on a new course. Kadlac has at last conceded that the profit motive and the free market are no longer incompatible with Marxism, an attitude that would have been considered treasonous a few years earlier. Now he wants to know why we allow Americans to own so much of Canada. He just can't understand why the Canadian nationalists don't take over.

Professor Edward Goldstucker, the world's greatest expert on Franz Kafka, is talking to Barbara, who wrote her university thesis on Kafka's The Trial. *He promises to take her on a tour of Kafka shrines. After spending four years in a Stalinist prison for high treason, Goldstucker has been mysteriously restored by the new regime. He doesn't know, or won't say, why he was imprisoned or why he was so suddenly released.*

He tells us that an immense number of Western books are now in translation in his country. I ask him about J.D. Salinger and his face lights up. "The Catcher in the Rye *is the Bible of the university generation," he tells us. And Canadian writers? Yes, he knows of Mazo de la Roche, whom he thinks of, wrongly, as French Canadian. Stephen Leacock, too. But he has not heard of Morley Callaghan.*

Otto Klicka, deputy minister of foreign affairs, is in an adjoining room talking in Czech with Marika. A small, balding, courteous man, he is the most hard-line Communist present. He praises China, which he has just visited; it holds the key to the future, he says; it will emerge as the major power in the world.

The party moves on. Hoffmeister, napkin tucked into collar, carves an enormous ham as the pilsner flows. The talk turns to the government's new economic experiment mixing Marxist principles with a market-driven economy. Will it work? Kadlac admits he doesn't know. "It will take five or ten years," he says, sounding like a child playing with a new toy.

Everybody is obviously waiting for someone. There is an air of suppressed anticipation: "He said he'd come…" "He's working late…" "Perhaps you should go downstairs and see; they lock the doors at ten…."

302

Suddenly, there's a knock. The buzz of conversation ceases, and a tall, flamboyant figure, bearded and bespectacled, enters, eyes twinkling.

This is Jan Werich, the great actor-satirist, who acquired the status of national monument in the1930s when he and his partner were the Wayne and Shuster of pre-Hitler Prague. He is an oddity – a self-confessed individualist in a Marxist state. "I am not a member of the Communist Party," he exclaims. "I am not a member of any religion. I am not even a Boy Scout. I am not a joiner."

He laments the decline of satire in his country. He says it isn't as much fun as it was when criticism of the Establishment was even harder to pull off than now. He specializes in double-meanings – in saying things without actually saying them. In North America, says Werich, real satire is impossible because you can say anything you want directly – there is no opportunity to develop the wicked innuendos that convulse audiences here. I think of Spring Thaw's *mild spoofs on Canadian foibles, and have to agree.*

The party progresses. Hoffmeister is pouring Czech champagne. Dr. Vladimir Stepanek, the polished diplomat, who is deputy commissioner of the Czech exhibition at Expo 67, points to an adjoining room where voices are rising and clashing in Czech. "They're arguing politics," he says. I find that odd. Arguing politics in a communist country? "Marxism," Dr. Stepanek explains. "They're arguing Marxism." And so they are – about whether Marxism is keeping abreast of the times or whether it needs a new set of ideals, about the direction in which the country is going, about old ideas and new ideas, freedom and the lack of it – in short, about the kind of things we argue in our own system.

Such an argument would still not be possible outside the confines of such a private gathering. But things are clearly on the move here. Are they moving too fast? That is one of the arguments being thrashed out in the room next door. Some think so; others think that change is still too sluggish.

When I return to Toronto, Lubor J. Zink of the Telegram, *a former Czech who is slightly to the right of Vlad the Impaler, lambastes me for my political naïveté. Nothing has changed in Czechoslovakia, he insists; the old gang is keeping the lid on. Yet it will soon be clear that, if anything, I have underestimated the changes bubbling beneath the surface – changes that are moving too fast, and alarming the country's Soviet masters. Shortly, some of those who talked so ingenuously about newfound freedoms will be throwing Molotov cocktails at Russian tanks as the Curtain is clamped down with a bang.*

4

The Centennial Year was upon us – twelve months of nationalistic whoop-de-doo, whose centrepiece was the great exposition in Montreal. It was also the year my mother died in Vancouver at the age of eighty-nine. I could only feel relief at her passing, for she spent her last months in a nursing home, unable even to recognize my sister, Lucy, on whom the burden fell most heavily.

She had been failing for the past couple of years, and sometimes her mind played tricks on her. I remember once, when she stayed with us in Kleinburg, the look of dismay that crossed her face when I said I was heading off to bed with Janet. "Oh no, Pierre," she said. "No. No. You go on home and wait till you're married." The following morning she was her old self.

Now she was gone, another link with the Victorian age cut. She was born in 1878, in the gaslight era, before the CPR was built, when telephones and typewriters were futuristic devices, and sex was never discussed. She once told me that as a young girl she had believed grown women were solid from waist to ankle. The word "legs" was taboo – even when referring to those on the dining-room table. Yet she was in no way Victorian. She had gone to the far-off Yukon just after the turn of the century looking for adventure, for she was a member of an adventurous family. Her elder sister had gone to Paris to paint on the famous Left Bank, the younger to the North West Territories as an Anglican nun. They live today in my own genes, this unconventional trio whose father, Phillips Thompson, was the first Marxian journalist in Canada – a theosophist, a single-taxer, a nonconformist, and a man who dared to demand that the streetcars be allowed to run on Sunday in Toronto. It was my mother who took me to my first CCF meeting in Vancouver when I was fourteen. I was an R.B. Bennett Tory in those days, like my father. The mining camps and the newspaper business helped radicalize me, but I suspect that the genes also contributed.

I miss her to this day. We were always close, but grew closer when we worked together on her book. To the world, especially the confined

world of a small Northern village, she presented a strait-laced image –
singing in the choir, carrying the flag for the Imperial Order Daughters
of the Empire, and pretending to vote Conservative, though I knew she
favoured the Liberal side in Dawson. (After all, my father was a bene-
ficiary of Tory patronage.) In private, she had a keen sense of the
ridiculous. She cast a sardonic eye over the world around her. She was
passionately in love with my father; my earliest memories are of her
sitting on his knee with her arms around his neck. But I also remember
her nudging me when a military parade went by. "Look at your father,"
she whispered. And there he was, Tory imperialist, a soldier of the
king, standing stiff as a ramrod, knuckles at trouser seams. "He can't
resist it," she said once. "Anytime he sees an officer in uniform, his
eyes light up." But she said it lovingly.

She hated old age. When we planned a party in her honour she always
chided us. "Don't invite any old people for me," she'd say. "I don't want
them around me. Invite a lot of young people; they help keep me alive."
She loved to read stories to the children, or, in many cases, to make them
up – stories about kids in the Yukon and their dogs. They still remember
her for that. I thought of these things in Vancouver as she went to her
rest, her ashes interred in a small plot next to the man she loved.

Meanwhile, the country was caught up in an orgy of self-discovery.
The Centennial Library was so successful that Jack immediately launched
two more mail-order series. Ken Lefolii left and I brought Les Hannon
back from England to replace him. He had been managing editor at
Maclean's after me. I was now in charge of the company's entire illustrated books division, which turned out a variety of volumes, ranging
from *The Taming of the Canadian West* to *Remember Expo*.

Of my five visits to Expo 67 that summer, the opening day was the
most emotional. Having managed a business trip to Montreal, I stood
on the Expo grounds and watched as the band played and the balloons
rose in their thousands over the island site. I tried to fight back the tears
in my eyes and failed. My friend the witty Bill Forbes, who ran one of
Maclean Hunter's trade magazines, stood with me, and I saw that his
eyes were damp, too. It was a glorious moment; all over the country
Canadians were congratulating themselves for launching – against considerable opposition – what was already being hailed as one of the best
world's fairs of all time. It was impossible at that moment not to sense
the feeling in the crowd. *We did it!* – Francophones and Anglophones

305

working in harness. Was this the beginning of something – or the end? I asked myself. In those days there was scarcely any talk of "sovereignty," that bittersweet word that for Canadians has its own special spin. Here, on St. Helen's Island, with Moshe Safdie's innovative Habitat in the background and Buckminster Fuller's geodesic dome not far away, the future seemed as bright as the fireworks bursting over our heads.

This was a historic moment, and we all knew it. But it is not always easy to recognize such a moment, even when you're an eyewitness. Only in retrospect do certain events take on a significance they didn't seem to have at the time. As a writer who records the past, I have tried to see the present in terms of the future – tried to understand how the historians of the next era will look upon my own times. It was a question I asked myself at the United Nations that first day in 1947, at Jack Kennedy's nomination in Los Angeles, and, of course, in Korea, especially in Seoul on that dark night when machine-gun fire rattled through the empty streets. *Savour this while you can,* I tell myself; this is history.

That well-travelled novelist Somerset Maugham once wrote that he found it difficult to recognize and enjoy a genuinely romantic moment when it crept up on him. He had, he said, known only three such instances in his life. Once, on the deck of a launch moving down a Chinese river, with the moon emerging from the clouds, he had felt it; this, he had told himself, is romance! Ever since reading Maugham's comments I have tried to cherish the moment, as I did at Expo, as I did driving on the autobahn through East Germany to Berlin. "Someday we'll laugh about all this," my friend Harry Filion once remarked to me in jest, as we sweated on a ten-mile route march during officers' training in 1943. As he predicted, we did have many laughs together over the years.

Yes, and many tears, too. In those days I had a game that I played with myself, which always made the grass seem greener and the sky bluer. I tried to think of myself as an old man looking back on certain moments with nostalgia. Here, at Expo, I caught a glimpse of myself seen through the inverted telescope of the future, standing with Bill, my throat choked up, as the flags waved and the strains of "O Canada" floated over the island. What a day, I thought, to be here, at this memorable moment, in the very prime of life, drinking in an experience that can never be repeated!

I use this technique on certain family occasions that seem memorable only when I see them as I might, looking back, some decades in the future. Then the picnic along the river, and the scent of hot dogs sizzling on the fire, and the sight of our children, laughing and scampering about on the bank, become special. I lie back and enjoy it, freezing it for an instant or so, like a video picture with the Pause button pressed. And then I know that I have caught the moment forever and will, from time to time, be able to return to it and enjoy it, even though, sadly, I can never repeat it. And I also know why it is that parents weep at weddings.

I had already planned to take the entire family to Expo that summer. Our eldest daughter, Penny, now nineteen, was working there, having learned French in Switzerland. During a documentary that I made in 1966 with Ross McLean for CTV, I learned that the big fair would include a marina so that a family could arrive by boat and live right in the heart of the big show. That seemed to be the obvious course for us. Janet liked the prospect. "The little ones can have a nap every afternoon without leaving the park," she said.

"Never mind the little kids," I told her. "It's you and me who'll need the nap."

In July we leased a twenty-six-foot Pacemaker and set off by way of Kingston and the Rideau Canal for Montreal. At my suggestion, Janet had taken the entire Power Squadron course, which I passed up, being too busy. That made her the expert, but since I had appointed myself captain, that didn't do too much good. Most of the time her advice went unheeded, which explains why we were stopped for speeding in the Rideau lakes and given a sharp lecture. "You're flying the Power Squadron flag," the policeman reminded us. "Surely you know better than to race through cottage country making waves."

Expo was in sharp contrast to the New York World's Fair of 1964-65, which I had covered for the *Star* as a freelancer. At Flushing Meadow, the vaunted American individualism was apparent; that fair was lively, raucous, often tawdry, sometimes awe inspiring. Anarchy reigned; bad taste competed with high art for the consumer's dollar. At Montreal, the Canadian Way was supreme; even the sound was controlled by a decibel counter. Our passion for order and control was to be seen in everything, from the triangular motif of the street furniture, to the washroom signs, to the repetitive image of Michael Snow's *Walking Woman*. Here the serenity of the Northern hinterland had been superimposed on an international carnival.

When we left Expo we decided to return not via the Ottawa and the

Rideau but by the St. Lawrence Seaway. That meant an interminable wait at one of the big locks because of a submarine's priority. By the time we entered the lock, dusk was falling. On emerging we had no idea where the nearest marina was located. "Follow me!" cried a man in a small boat, and we blundered along in his wake. His craft drew only a few feet of water and so escaped the rocks that lay only a few feet below the surface. We didn't. I could hear them scraping away below.

We found a marina on the American side. The next morning we tried to head back along the Seaway. But something was terribly wrong. The boat was lurching and failing to respond to the tiller. As the gates of the big Eisenhower Lock opened and a flurry of small craft moved in, I found that our own boat was slipping into the lock sideways. A doom-like voice shouted at us over a loudspeaker: "Get control of that boat!" But I could not control it. Fortunately, people on a nearby craft seized one of the boathooks brandished by the children, and we tied up alongside.

"Mom, there's water all over the floor of the toilet," Peggy Anne shouted.

"It's not the toilet; it's called the head," responded the newest graduate of the Power Squadron course.

"Well, there's a lot of water on the floor."

"I wish you kids wouldn't slosh so much!"

But it was soon clear something was wrong. Peter and I opened the hatch to check the motor and were shocked to discover jets of water erupting through empty holes where bolts had attached the outboard motors to the hull. Peter started stuffing Kleenex into these holes, to no effect. I got out the dipstick, broke it into four pieces, and jammed them in. Meanwhile, Janet was getting the smaller children into their life-jackets and hoisting them aboard the adjoining craft.

An official, arriving to find out what the fuss was all about, stood on the edge of the lock and peered down at us. I explained that we were sinking.

"You can't sink in the lock," he warned. "That's forbidden. You'll have to wait and sink outside." I couldn't believe my ears. The gates were closed; our boat, listing heavily to starboard, was trapped. Luckily, the holes remained plugged, and in spite of its crazy list, the Pacemaker stayed afloat.

Janet was lifting children over the side. Suddenly she noticed that one was missing. "Where's Perri?" she called out in panic, looking about for our three-year-old.

"She's in the kitchen," Pamela told her, and so she was. With everybody too busy to oversee her, the child had constructed a ladder of two chairs and climbed to the topmost shelf of the galley, where, as she well knew, the jelly doughnuts were kept. There she was, stuffing as many into her mouth as possible.

Later, when I described our accident to friends, they remarked that we must have been in a panic when the boat started to sink. "Not Perri," I told them proudly.

The gates opened and we lurched out of the lock, the other craft keeping the widest possible distance from us. We phoned the leasing company, invoked the deductible clause in our contract, dropped the boat at the nearest marina, picked up our station wagon, and drove home.

I paid another visit to Montreal that summer, somewhat reluctantly, to receive an award from the Canadian Authors' Association. To my considerable embarrassment, they had decided to name me Man of the Century. I was trapped! If I declined the offer they would be insulted and would call me a snob. If I accepted it, the country would guffaw. There were so many obvious candidates for the title, living and dead, but I wasn't one. I wasn't even Author of the Century – that could have been Stephen Leacock, Morley Callaghan, W.O. Mitchell, Gabrielle Roy, Roger Lemelin, Donald Creighton, or many others. Not me. But the deed was done, the announcement made, and so I gave in gracefully, and accompanied by Jack McClelland took my seat at the head table.

The dinner dragged on; business was conducted, announcements were read. The chairman said a few words about the country's one-hundredth birthday, but refrained from mentioning me. Finally, as the applause died down, he turned to his audience and said, "Well, that just about winds everything up, and I must say I think it's been a very worthwhile event." Chairs were being scraped back when a man detached himself from a nearby table, plucked at the chairman's sleeve, and whispered something in his ear.

"Ah!" he said shamefacedly, rising once more. "I'd completely forgotten the Man of the Century!" He produced a plaque (or was it a scroll? I haven't kept it). I accepted with a brief and, I hope, graceful speech. And that was that – not the high point of our anniversary year.

Neither was my venture into musical comedy. I had, during an earlier

Caribbean cruise, whiled away my time writing lyrics for a musical play based on a true story about a Klondike miner who buys, or rather rents for the winter, a dance-hall girl for her weight in gold. I had hoped, vainly, that the CBC would do something with it. Then, in the winter of 1966-67, Mavor Moore approached me about the Charlottetown Festival in the coming season. I told him about the lyrics and suggested he try to find a librettist and a composer to work with me. I should never have sung those lyrics to Mavor, using the corny tunes that were in my head when I composed them. Mavor professed to like the music, and when the search for a librettist failed, persuaded me to write the entire production.

It was, of course, a disaster, in spite of the mandatory standing ovation it received opening night. I was too busy at the time to be there but determined to get down to Charlottetown as soon as feasible. The critics, to put it mildly, were not enthusiastic. Nathan Cohen wrote that it was "an outstandingly turgid and lifeless concoction." Of course, up to that point I thought I had produced a masterpiece; I always do until somebody, usually an editor, sets me straight. A writer has to believe in his own work; if he doesn't, it shows, and the audience senses his insecurity. Every time I finish a book I think it's the best thing I've ever done. That's why editors are an absolute necessity. Only after an outsider takes a hard look do I understand the flaws. Harold Town once told me, on air, that he was a better painter than Picasso. He had to believe that, he said, or his own work would suffer. I understood this completely.

But no one edited *Paradise Hill.* Nobody said: "It stinks. Fix it." Time was too short and Mavor badly needed the show, no matter how flawed it was. When I saw it on the stage in Charlottetown, I realized how much work it needed, and how right Cohen had been. It needed a different librettist and a good composer. In my own arrogance I had thought I could do it all alone, and there was no one to tell me otherwise. Indeed, I had been encouraged to forge ahead. Maybe it could have been fixed – maybe; but there was no chance for that now because the production was frozen. Major musicals are taken on tour and rewritten almost nightly; the festival didn't work that way. Worse, I hadn't been able to attend rehearsals. I put the script away along with my abortive novel. I could have spent the rest of my life rewriting *Paradise Hill,* but I preferred to move along to something else.

I also found myself involved in my own community's Centennial plans.

310

The entire country was on a summer-long binge, as every town, village, and hamlet set out to mark the nation's birthday in its own fashion. Bands played; fireworks lit the sky; Old-Tyme activities prospered; pageants were re-enacted, historic buildings restored, medals awarded, old landmarks renewed, worthy citizens honoured. Quite clearly, I realized, the communities wanted to arrange their own Centennial celebrations; that was another reason why our consulting firm failed. Every civic body wanted to put its own stamp on our national birthday without any help from outsiders. Kleinburg was no exception.

When I first moved to the country, I remember Norval Bonisteel, the photo editor of *Maclean's,* remarking that I'd soon find myself involved in a host of community activities.

I bridled. "Not me," I told him. "No way. I'm keeping out of all that." But then I had also announced that I wouldn't cut a single blade of grass on my property. I would leave it as wild as I found it.

"You'll soon find out that you can't cut yourself off from the community," Bonnie said, and he was right. I was not only cutting several acres of lawn but I was also going to several meetings a month. Janet, of course, had joined everything as soon as we moved in. I expected that. At university she had belonged to a dozen clubs, from the Musical Society to the Student Christian Movement. But, I told myself, I wasn't a joiner. As a newspaperman I had covered enough of clubland not to want any part of it – or so I thought. Yet now I was on the local school board, the Home and School Association, the parents' group of the Boy Scouts, the Kleinburg and Area Ratepayers Association, and a political committee to keep the township green, which helped elect two councillors. And in 1967 my wife and I found ourselves members of the newly founded Kleinburg Centennial Committee.

Small towns do that to you. When Vic Ryder suggested that the community re-enact the traditional Binder Twine Night in September as a Centennial project, I was all for it. From the 1890s until the Depression, Charlie Shaw, the local tinsmith, had entertained the village when the hired men poured into town to buy binder twine to tie up the sheaves of winter wheat. There was music, dancing, frivolity. Now it would come alive again, a piece of the past renewed for the Centennial. It appealed, of course, to my sense of history.

So there we were on a bright September Saturday, parading about the main street, Janet in a billowing nineties dress and a Victorian hat,

311

I in a nineteenth-century cutaway and a grey topper. And having taken the plunge, we were caught. The festival was so popular we couldn't drop it. Ever since then, on the first Saturday after Labour Day, with forty thousand people on the main street, you will find me, topper and all, hosting the Binder Twine Queen Contest, in which local ladies compete by chopping wood, hammering nails, shucking corn, flipping pancakes, milking a prize cow, and indulging in other old-fashioned womanly skills.

Meanwhile, another television show, *Under Attack,* invented for Screen Gems by the ingenious Elsa Franklin, went on the air that fall with me as host and Elsa as producer. The program was just what the title suggested: a prominent public figure was put on the hot seat in a university setting to be quizzed (we hoped mercilessly) by a panel of three students, and later by the full student audience. We were, in short, putting the generation gap on tape and exploiting a source that TV had not really scrutinized. We had learned on our travels that young people are natural material for television. Curiously, except for a few specifically oriented "youth" programs, very little use had been made of the potential of this questing, irreverent, and uninhibited section of the population.

When I put my book of interviews together I realized how much of my own show had been devoted to the subject of youth. Some of our most successful programs had featured panels of young people. They were the true amateurs of the medium in the best sense, being completely unself-conscious. The result was often unexpected and exciting.

Under Attack taught me a good deal about adult and youth behaviour. The smartest grown-ups were those who didn't allow themselves to get riled under the kids' questioning. Yet there was almost always one moment when the guest became visibly annoyed, even though we had been assured that each one welcomed tough questions. On the other hand, the college students weren't very good inquisitors. They often failed to pursue a point; their facts were sometimes open to challenge; and they tended to get off the track. They had one priceless quality, however – commitment. Their questions came from the gut. They became personally involved, often emotional. They could be mean, sneaky, even offensive. They booed, hissed, groaned aloud, stamped their feet, shouted down their quarry, and sometimes attacked one another instead of the guest. In short, these encounters made excellent television.

We did our best to prepare our human targets. Old pros like David

312

*In 1973, the CBC rebuilt the CPR using the old Kettle
Valley line and a restored locomotive, circa 1885.*

Mary Carpenter, the Inuit girl from Sachs Harbour, was sponsored for two years at the University of Western Ontario by two professors who had seen my television interview with her, Oscar Langtvet, (right) and Peter Sims.

Eric Basciano, foster son.

Perri Berton, adopted daughter

Whenever we travelled we tried to replace the darkened studio with something livelier and more representative. In Italy Elsa and the crew worked above the tiled rooftops of Rome. In Hollywood, I interviewed Lily Tomlin against the background of a hotel garden. (Below) In London, we were on display in the Westbury Hotel's lounge, where broadcasting star David Frost drew a crowd of curious onlookers and fans.

Radio station CKEY lured Charles Templeton and me from CFRB by promising to double the money and launch a massive promotional campaign. This billboard was part of it.

Every May for thirty-five years, Janet and I have spent a weekend at Point Pelee National Park looking for birds. Here we are searching for the elusive prothonotary warbler. Eventually, after slogging through this swamp, we tracked down our quarry.

Canada Day, 1977. With separatism growing in Quebec, the Canadian government sent celebrity families around the country to preside over an orgy of national feeling. Alas, our own part in the show almost came to a tragic end when our plane made a forced landing on an Alberta highway. The kids took it in their stride and the next day we marched in Vancouver's Canada Day parade with the mayor, Jack Volrich.

In the People's Republic of China, Jack McClelland and I were given the
VIP treatment, which included our own interpreter, Mr. Yu, shown at far right.

Below: *When you're made an honorary Indian chief in Canada, you know you've
arrived. Here I am on the Blood Reserve, Alberta, with other celebrities, including
the former president of the CPR and an ex-commissioner of the RCMP.*

In the Beaufort Sea in 1988 I landed by helicopter on the deck of a working oil rig—
all in the interests of publicizing my new (and biggest) book, The Arctic Grail.

Below: *A CBC photograph used to promote the 35th anniversary of*
Front Page Challenge.

Each September, the second Saturday in the month finds me on the streets of Kleinburg, costumed, with Janet, for the annual Binder Twine Festival, where she helps in the information booth and I help run the Binder Twine Queen Contest.

Susskind, the TV producer, and Al Capp, the creator of the *Li'l Abner* comic strip, took it in their stride. Capp was tougher than his attackers. If they got personal, he got personal right back – told them to wipe their noses or get a wet nurse. They liked that. When a guest made a telling point they cheered him, but if he evaded the question, as Phil Gaglardi, a B.C. cabinet minister, did, they rose to their feet and booed him unmercifully.

Under Attack was not a public-affairs show in the traditional sense. It was an emotional show. When it worked, it involved both participants and audiences viscerally. At its best, it wasn't a TV show at all; it was a happening. But it was not immune to the prevailing Canadian prudery. When Capp needled his attackers by kidding them about masturbation, that dreadful word was beeped out by Screen Gems at the request of stations that were terrified of losing their licences if it went out over the airwaves. Elsa and I fought to retain it but lost the battle. Was that only a quarter-century ago? It seems now like the Dark Ages.

We took *Under Attack* to various campuses in Ontario and Quebec, fitting it in with our regular TV chores. I coached the three-student panel before each show, explaining how to follow up questions with supplementaries and urging them to be as tough as possible. It was on one of these programs that Gilles Gregoire, an independent M.P. from Quebec, announced that his province would become a separate nation by 1970. Pierre Trudeau, who appeared that fall in Ottawa, complained bitterly that the show didn't go the way he had expected. "I was brought to Carleton not to talk politics in general, but to defend myself against other French Canadians before an English-speaking audience," he declared.

Nathaniel Branden, the spokesman and lover of the right-wing novelist Ayn Rand, was outraged by his treatment at the Ryerson Institute of Technology in Toronto. The students hissed and booed him as his choler rose. "Why are you so afraid of us?" asked Sally York, one of the panellists. Branden insisted that he wasn't afraid. "Then why are your knuckles so white?" she countered. "Why are you trembling?"

Branden exploded. He charged that she was engaged in a "psychological attack," became increasingly agitated, and suddenly rose to his feet. "I'm not going on with this!" he shouted. "I've been brought here under false pretenses." He was, of course, used to the sycophantic, one-on-one discussions that passed for probing debate on some American channels. He hadn't been ready for the unpredictable. Now he tried to tear off the microphone that had been securely planted under his shirt. That meant he had to pull off his tie and then try to unbutton his shirt and unclasp the instrument. This ineffectual striptease brought a chorus of catcalls. Both Elsa and I had told our director, David Ruskin, that no matter what happened on the program, he must never, under any circumstances, stop the tape, and so Ruskin continued to record the spectacle. Now, with his microphone finally removed, Branden tried to continue the discussion; with no microphone available, he strode across the stage and seized one from the panel's table. "You're stealing my mike!" cried one of the students, to general laughter and applause.

Branden walked off, but I continued the discussion without him, using the panel as well as the general audience. I could hear our guest in a heated discussion with Elsa behind the scenes. "I shall use every legal means in my power to prevent this program going on the air," he was shouting. Unlike the cannier David Merrick, however, he had already signed a contract. With the program continuing, he realized he had to salvage something. He worked out a deal with Elsa: if she agreed to delete the scene where he walked out, he would go on with the program, answering questions from the audience but not the panel. I think now we should have refused. Still, as it was aired, it was a pretty entertaining show.

We went to Hollywood again that fall and also to New York, returning with thirty-six half hours. After that I was off to Ottawa to cover the Tory leadership convention that dumped Diefenbaker and elected Robert Stanfield. There I managed to get one of the few scoops possible by sneaking the results of the first ballot to the viewing audience before they were officially released or known. In this case, it was proof of the old adage in journalism: it's who you know that counts, not what you know. My old friend Bob Macaulay, late of Centennial Celebration Consultants, was a delegate as well as a Tory backroom boy. I stayed close to his seat during the balloting and when it ended asked him if he could get the results in advance. He did, and I scored a clean beat for the CTV network (with Charles Templeton as anchor man). I left the interviewing of the obvious delegates to others and instead tracked down the youngest delegate in the convention hall, a startlingly sophisticated fourteen-year-old who listed abortion, contraception, and the drinking laws as being in need of immediate reform. That interview made news, to the discomfiture of the more mossbacked Tories in Ottawa.

That winter Elsa had to schedule and produce both *Under Attack*

314

and *The Pierre Berton Show* and dovetail our trips abroad into my own crowded program. I needed to be in Toronto every other Monday for *Front Page Challenge* and also for "Dialogue." Charles and I sometimes managed to tape a few shows ahead, but as we preferred to be topical, we both had to be on hand as much as possible. We used substitute guests only when it was absolutely necessary. At the same time I was gathering material for another book, *The Smug Minority,* scheduled for publication early in 1968.

I thought of my mother again that fall. "We gave you your health," she had told me more than once. It was, she insisted, the secret of my success. As a child I had lots of nourishing food to keep up my energy levels: tomato juice, squeezed by hand from hothouse tomatoes (you couldn't grow them outdoors in the Yukon climate); Scott's Emulsion by the daily spoonful, in the winter absence of sunlight; homemade bread; no fat pork, little butter, and, of course, very little junk food, for there wasn't much of that available; lots of outdoor living; and long hikes with my father. No doubt she was right; I must have got my energy from somewhere. Considering my schedule that fall, I needed it.

In one three-week period I taped twenty-two half-hour interviews in Toronto, Rome, and Tokyo, six *Front Page Challenge*s at home, and two *Under Attack* programs in Montreal. Rome was a problem because the Italian TV staff virtually ignored Elsa. The crew did not want to work for a woman. The idea of a female running everything, especially on a television show, baffled and dismayed them. She had to battle hard to get them to heed her instructions.

It was worse in Tokyo. The Japanese crew flatly refused to believe that Elsa even worked on the show. As far as they were concerned, she was invisible. It was decided that our peripatetic executive producer Dan Enright, who had dropped by on his way to Australia, would direct the show from the booth while Elsa acted as floor director in the studio. The TV people also refused to believe that we could do eight shows in one afternoon. Nobody ever had. After much haggling they settled for six, and, of course, we finished with time to spare. At that point, they announced we could do eight after all. Alas, it was too late.

The shows ran like clockwork. The Japanese guests all arrived on time, perhaps because they were being paid. We did not usually pay interview guests, but in Japan we bowed to custom. Elsa had learned that all TV stations followed an agreed scale of payments, discreetly described as car allowances and therefore tax free. Payment was based on status. Everybody, from the prime minister down, received a stipend in an exquisite envelope. If a politician lost his seat, his status decreased and, therefore, his fee. Our guests never mentioned money. They knew it was coming, and we had no choice in the matter. The rate had been set long before we came to Tokyo.

We had a deal with Alitalia to fly us around the world in return for a credit on the show, and so the staff flew back to Toronto from Japan the long way, via Rome. I took a shortcut across the Pacific through Vancouver, arriving in Toronto in time for *Front Page Challenge*. The next day the staff met me in Montreal for *Under Attack*. It all sounds exhausting, I know, but I sleep well on airplanes, and the exotic nature of these journeys – the Piazza Navona one day, the Ginza the next – stimulated and renewed me; that, and my parents' gift of good health.

5

Challenging the puritan ethic   *The Smug Minority,* on which I had been working in fits and starts that summer and fall, might have been called *Son of The Comfortable Pew.* It wasn't a book about religion; it was about the state of Canadian society and constituted a critique of the smug establishment that I felt was ruining the country. The success of its predecessor had stimulated the New Democratic Party to ask me to tackle the job. I agreed to write a book with the party's help but under the same conditions that the church had accepted. It would stand by itself as a trade publication, royalties to be paid to me by the publisher. The only assistance the NDP would provide would be a series of weekly discussions with people chosen by the party and by myself. I spent more than a year on the book, reading widely and discussing the subject matter at our weekly meetings. The NDP is not mentioned. I was dealing with social rather than political issues.

Although my critics would certainly not understand, *The Smug Minority* remains, for me, one of my most satisfying books. It was written at the height of the sixties – the decade of the generation gap, the drug culture, the radical youth movement, and the attack on the establishment. It is very much of its time.

The attitude of the adult world toward the new youth culture disturbed me. To a very large extent we had made enemies of our children and they of us. We forget now that young people, especially those who flouted establishment styles of dress and personal appearance, became the subject of adult repression and, yes, adult hatred. In schools, youths who wore their hair long were disciplined and sometimes expelled. Young women in miniskirts were sent home with a reprimand, or worse – even though private school uniforms included skirts that reached no lower than mid-thigh. In more than one case young men were forcibly shorn of their locks. My teenaged daughter Patsy was sent home from high school on a hot day for daring to wear a dress with a bare midriff. That angered me. What on earth did her choice of fashion have to do with her education? I enrolled her in a free school at Everdale, from which, I believe, she benefited greatly. Indeed, she met her future husband there.

The new hippie movement was causing fury and dismay among the adult establishment, for it threatened the well-ordered and rigid way of life that had been the norm until the sixties. The world was clearly changing; the puritan ethic was losing ground, but the smug members of the establishment were closing their eyes to this revolution. Although women's place was still said to be in the home, so many were working that one million children were being farmed out to relatives and friends. Yet society still refused to consider the establishment of day-care centres. A woman who took a job or left the care of her family to others was considered by many to be a menace to society.

Five million Canadians were living in a state of poverty – a scandalous situation that has worsened over the years. Automation was already threatening to reduce the workforce, but we were still refusing to spread the work around by shortening the workweek. Newspapers were insisting that productivity could easily be increased if only Canadians would work harder. These were among some of the problems I dealt with in the book, some of which have a resonance for the present. My targets included the financial establishments, the Canadian Manufacturers' Association, the various Chambers of Commerce, and the press. That helps to explain the reaction that followed.

The book was published in February 1968 to an absolute howl of rage, especially from the reviewers in the business press. The *Calgary Herald* reported that it had received "probably the worst critical drubbing in the daily press of any volume published in this country in a hundred years." The *Windsor Star* called it "one of the most controversial volumes ever written in Canada." That astonished me. *Controversial?* I had thought

I was writing the obvious, and some critics thought so, too, attacking me because, they said, there was nothing new in the book. Then why the fuss? As Jack Hutchison wrote in the *Toronto Star,* "it's hard to tell which the reviewers hate more: Pierre or his book." Clearly it was open season on Berton. The attacks were often personal. "To expect the public to get indignant about this kind of stuff in 1968 is just too much," John Curran wrote in the *Telegram.* "This is a big soft lad telling the little kids that teachers drink and smoke, and that babies don't really grow on cabbage stalks." In the Ontario legislature, Elmer Sopha, a Liberal, rose to attack me as "a flatulent blatherer." A few critics, fortunately those I respected, such as Robert Fulford and Douglas Fisher, praised the work. The *Star Weekly* published three excerpts. My U.S. agent sold *The Smug Minority* to Doubleday, and I basked in a *New York Times* review that called it "this absorbing book."

Jack McClelland had liked the book so much that, in a burst of enthusiasm and with an eye to publicity, he announced the biggest advance printing in Canadian publishing – one hundred thousand copies. That may be why the impression grew that the book was a financial flop. It was anything but, although sales did not reach the hundred thousand mark. Jack never expected they would; he had a built-in break-even point that showed he would make money after about forty thousand sales. The book sold more than seventy thousand copies, an enormous figure in those days and one that had been exceeded only by sales of *The Comfortable Pew.*

Nonetheless, the press continued to report that the book was a financial failure. It was said that its publication had nearly bankrupted McClelland and Stewart, that I had been forced to buy up half the printing so the book would not be remaindered. McClelland was said to have fifty thousand copies hidden away in his basement. Actually, *The Smug Minority* was one of his biggest financial successes that year.

Quite clearly, I had baffled and confused everybody, including the critic of the *Canadian Statesman* at Bowmanville, who first denounced the book and then announced he had changed his mind and actually liked it.

Who, I thought, can ask for anything more?

Chapter Twelve

1

National dreaming

2

Life begins at fifty

3

Good morning, Maestro

4

Oh, Canada

5

A mere potboiler

6

Bruner's folly

1

Life is a series of turning points, and I have had my share. My first came at the age of nineteen, when I chucked my science courses and decided to become a journalist. The second came at twenty-six, when I left the West Coast and headed for Toronto. The third saw me quit *Maclean's* at the age of thirty-eight and move to the *Star.* The fourth came at forty-three, when I became a full-fledged freelancer in print, radio, and television.

Now, at the age of forty-eight, I was about to make another change. By 1968 my name was on the jackets of seventeen Canadian books, ranging from *The Big Sell* to *Remember Yesterday.* Yet I did not feel fulfilled. By this time Jack McClelland had promoted me to editor-in-chief of his publishing firm, a spurious title since he was the real editor; I was only a traffic manager. But I could not rid myself of a sense of unease. Apart from *Klondike,* I hadn't written anything I felt was really lasting.

I had known what I should do ever since *Klondike* was published. I should produce another odyssey involving the movement of large numbers of people through time and space. I had learned the technique when I put the history of the great stampede together. I had even chosen my next subject: the story of the building of the country's first transcontinental railway. It had everything – a huge cast of larger-than-life characters, a major political scandal, an engineering feat of immense complexity, a prairie revolution, and, most important, the stitching together of the new nation from sea to sea.

But journalism, radio, and television were my bread and butter. They left little time for a major work about a great national endeavour. Finally, in 1967 I decided to take the plunge. I already had a part-time research assistant, Norman Kelly, a doctoral candidate in history, scouring the archives for me. Early in 1968, I told Jack that I could not handle my duties as editor and also produce the kind of book I wanted to write. He reluctantly agreed.

That was the year that Pierre Elliott Trudeau became leader of the Liberal Party. I gave each of the eight leadership candidates a half hour on my television show to talk about themselves. The questions were personal, not political: *Can you assess yourself objectively? What do you think are your weaknesses and strengths? Why do you believe you're the best? How badly do you want to be prime minister?* No one else was asking this sort of thing.

320

Douglas Fisher and Harry Crowe, in their syndicated column, assessed the results: the most uncomfortable candidate was Allan MacEachen; the biggest surprise was the candour of Paul Hellyer; John Turner was the "likeable, self-needling, gutsy fellow some of us have known privately"; Mitchell Sharp was plain, simple, and pleasant but "somehow a bit faded"; Joe Greene was the "most consciously partisan"; Robert Winters was "like a feature in *Fortune*"; Paul Martin was "hard surfaced, like a shell, and somehow small, like the head of a pin." And Trudeau? "It is easier to imagine him in a Shaw play, even in a Noel Coward comedy, than in this cast...one senses the witty malice of an exceptionally good intellect."

I covered the convention for television and early in the proceedings spotted Margaret Murray, the salty B.C. weekly editor. We were old friends, having split more than one bottle of rum together in 1947, when she was the editor of the *Alaska Highway News* in Fort St. John and I was heading for Headless Valley. She cheerfully agreed to be interviewed and provided me with the quote of the week when she peered at Trudeau and asked, "Is that fella strung right?"

"That fella" was the focus of the entire convention. A scrum of media hawks surrounded him wherever he went. His women supporters were the prettiest, his campaign was the liveliest – his eventual victory certain.

My contract with CFRB gave me a month off each summer. The TV show went into repeats. With my job for Jack abandoned, I now had a good chunk of free time to work on the book. My annual income was cut in half, for I had also quit as host of *Under Attack* (Fred Davis took over the job). I wasn't gambling that the CPR book would make money; I didn't expect it would. But I had made my choice.

It wasn't the best time to quit two jobs and take on a costly and time-consuming piece of research with the expectation of nothing but a mod est profit. My expanding family was becoming more expensive. I had two daughters at university and five more offspring waiting to be educated. The house at Kleinburg was bursting at the seams. There was no longer room in the dining alcove for everybody to sit at the table. The kitchen wasn't much bigger than a closet. The smaller children were stacked like cordwood in bunk beds. We would have to expand, even if we didn't yet have baseboards in the living room.

I spent much of the spring and summer sharing the research chores with Norman Kelly. Fortunately, the Public Archives in Ottawa were

321

open all night to serious researchers. To my astonishment, John A. Macdonald's original handwritten correspondence was available to me. I had to decipher his scrawl, which was difficult but not as bad as the cramped hand of George Stephen, the railway president. Macdonald refused to use a typewriter when he wrote to personal friends, and I cursed him for it, little knowing that one day I would spurn a word processor. It was a relief to find that the Van Horne letterbooks had been transcribed in typescript.

It was obvious that I could not start the book at the point when the first rail was laid. I would have to go back to the original dream of a transcontinental line of steel. I would have to look at the story of the surveyors and understand the place of railways in pre-Confederation Canada. It would be both a political and a social history, not only of railways but also of the new nation. I would have to get to know the players in the drama as well as I knew my friends. I would have to read the newspapers for a period of sixteen years – from the *Globe* of Toronto to the *Inland Sentinel* of Yale, B.C. Norm Kelly and I divided this work.

In short, I would have to give myself a university course in mid-nineteenth-century history. I had majored in history at the University of British Columbia but had skipped most of my classes in order to work on the university paper. In one exam, which consisted entirely of true-or-false questions, I had simply tossed a coin, figuring that 50–50 odds were quite acceptable. Indeed they were: my mark was exactly 50 percent. Now, to learn about the history of my own country with no real professional background, I would have to start from scratch. Writing non-fiction is a learning process as well as an earning process. When I plunged into *The Mysterious North* I had to give myself a course in geology to understand the glacial age that had transformed the face of the North. Future books – on the Arctic, on war, on politics and economic depression – would require crash courses like the ones I'd tried to avoid in my college years. I could no longer toss a coin. I had to soak up the knowledge exactly as I would for an examination. I had graduated from university with a variety of journalistic skills, but I was woefully uneducated. My real education didn't begin until I started writing narrative history.

I became a literary detective, searching for hidden treasures that no one else had unearthed, such as the unpublished reminiscences of Tom Wilson, the horse wrangler who worked for Major A.B. "Hells Bells"

Rogers, and the diary of Robert Rylatt, who served two dreadful years as a member of the Howse Pass survey gang. I became obsessed by small details. What was the facial hair fashion in the 1880s? Who exactly *was* George McMullen, the villain of the Pacific Scandal, and what did he look like? What was the most popular family card game on the continent?

This emphasis on minutiae got critical jabs after the work was published from newspaper reviewers who thought I'd made a lot of it up. After all, this kind of book was new to Canada. How did Berton know it was misty on a certain day, one asked. Of course, the state of the weather is one of the easiest facts to unearth: everybody talks or writes about it; the newspapers report it. Another took me to task for describing the mood of the House of Commons at the start of the railway debate. But that debate was fully covered by the press, which also described the mood. And how could I possibly know that the governor general, Lord Dufferin, felt a little embarrassed at having to read the Speech from the Throne a second time in French? I knew because His Excellency had said as much in a letter to a friend that I had read and noted.

Many of my friends and colleagues were baffled at my choice of subject, as my mother had been perplexed when I told her I was going to write about the gold rush. Why would I want to write about the CPR, which sounded like pretty dull stuff? Morley Callaghan was one of these; he later wrote me a graceful and rueful note of apology. Like so many others, he had thought of the prospective book as a kind of company history, rather like *Steel of Empire,* written in the thirties by John Murray Gibbon, a CPR public relations man, or perhaps like Harold Innis's brilliant, trail-blazing, but virtually unreadable work, whose footnotes took up as much space as the text. But I saw the building of the railway as *the* great epic story in our history. Every nation has one – usually a civil war, a revolution, or a bloody victory. But this, our sem inal epic, was a unique historical adventure – not a struggle of brother against brother but of man against nature. Our history has been remarkably free of the bitter bloodletting that has stained so many nations. Our major battles have been against the environment. That would be my sub-theme.

Meanwhile, I had my television program to consider. In addition to interviews with the celebrities of my time – Lucille Ball and Phil Spector, Petula Clark and Steve Allen, Carol Burnett and Gypsy Rose Lee – I wanted something meatier. After all, the country was in ferment; a new generation was in conflict with the old. That same summer of 1968, June Callwood was arrested for creating a disturbance in the Yorkville coffee-house district. She had been listening to a group of young people trying to explain that the police had just beaten up the wrong man. An officer tried to hustle her away. When she didn't move fast enough, she was thrown into a paddy wagon and trundled off to jail. It was said that the disturbance was impeding traffic – a heinous crime in Toronto. (The police were opposed to sidewalk cafés because they believed that the wine-sippers would tumble drunkenly off their chairs and into the roadway, thus "impeding traffic.") I testified for June at her trial, where she was quickly acquitted. Through her own kids she had become involved with the Digger House for wayward youngsters, and this incident completed the politicizing process.

The country was ready, I thought, for a five-program series entitled "Shame of the Prisons," dealing with life behind bars. I interviewed criminologists, ex-convicts, and sociologists who called Canada's prison policy "one of the most backward in the world." Eyewitnesses described "bucket cells," homosexual rape, and suicide inside prison walls. Dr. Raymond Boyer, the McGill scientist implicated in the Gouzenko spy revelations, spoke for the first time about the appalling conditions in Montreal's notorious St. Vincent de Paul penitentiary. I urged my viewers to write to Solicitor General George McIlraith, demanding changes in the system. Five hundred did so and received a standard reply so mealymouthed that I described it publicly as "misleading to the point of being dishonest."

That series ran in November. I started to work at once on another five-parter about what I called "the coming Indian revolution in Canada." The purpose was to expose injustices committed against the original peoples and to make it clear that they were justifiably angry at the lack of concern over the conditions they were forced to endure. I devoted one program to the revelation – new to me, and shocking – that in the church and residential schools Indian children were punished and even beaten when they tried to speak their own language. Dr. Howard Adams, a native-born professor at the University of Saskatchewan, predicted violence. Surprisingly, two decades went by before it broke out at Oka. This program brought me a greater response than anything I had yet done on television, but I doubt that it changed much. Years later, when the mainstream media began, at last, to reveal the scandal of the Indian schools, people expressed surprise that they hadn't known about it earlier. But, of course, they could have. Predictably, the establishment responded to my revelations with a sneer. Father J.E.Y. Lévesque, director of the Oblate Indian and Eskimo Council, dismissed my program as a "cockfight sensation." But the sad fact is that many of the problems that aroused those natives who appeared with me on television have not been resolved to this day.

In February 1969, Screen Gems gave a banquet to mark my one-thousandth program. I made a short speech, not about the past but about the future of the medium. I forecast that within a few years, new specialty channels would be nibbling away at the mass audience, as had happened a decade before when the big mass magazines folded. It took a bit longer than I expected to come true.

I had a free month that summer to get a draft of my book written. In July I had the phone taken out, much to Janet's dismay. But I wanted no interruptions. In fact, I told my friends and colleagues that I was leaving for a month in Mexico. Instead, I stayed home and wrote like a madman. The subject consumed me, occupied all my waking hours and even my dreams. I could scarcely wait to get to my typewriter each morning. I worked through lunch – nothing more than soup and a sandwich – joined the family for a brief afternoon swim, took time out for dinner, then pounded away until midnight. I loved every minute of it.

Some writers claim to hate the process of writing. I don't. I had been studying my subject and thinking about it morning, noon, and night for two years. I looked forward to the day when I could put the first sheet of paper in my machine the way children look forward to Christmas. Now that day had arrived. This is always a memorable moment. Here at my side is a box of 8 1/2-by-11-inch manuscript paper – hundreds of empty pages, waiting for me. Some will be crumpled and tossed aside; some will be marked with scribbles, defaced with blacked-out sentences and marginal queries. But, in the end, hidden in this monstrous pile, a book lies waiting. Sculptors, I know, feel the same way when they visualize the human features hidden in a block of marble.

But I could not begin until I was ready, until my research was sorted, annotated, and bound in legal-size loose-leaf folders, until my index cards were filled out and organized into a working plan, until every source had been uncovered. I often forgot where I was. In my mind, I was living in the past, standing, perhaps, with one-eyed Jim Hill on the bald, snow-swept prairie on a hazy day in February 1870, watching the vague outline of a dog team coming south bearing Donald A. Smith of the Hudson's Bay Company – the first meeting of the two men who eventually started the railway to the Pacific. It was a scene, I later wrote, that deserved to be preserved on a wide screen; in my writing I was always influenced by the movies.

I can always tell when a tale is ready to be told by my own sense of joy at the feeling of finally getting it on paper. A good story virtually writes itself; a bad one, or a badly researched one, fights you every step of the way. The story of the building of the Pacific railway literally poured from my Smith-Corona. I reached the age of forty-nine that July, and I was bursting with energy and ambition. By working all day and every day, from morning to midnight, I got a first draft on paper in a little more than three weeks. A first draft, of course, is a long way from a book, but the back of the work was broken on those long midsummer days.

I was about a week into the draft when I realized that my ambition to tell the story in a single volume had to be revised; it would require two. The second, I knew, would be called *The Last Spike,* a phrase made memorable by E.J. Pratt in his epic poem. The title of the first volume, however, required some thought. When a phrase popped out from my own writing – *the national dream* – I knew I'd found it. Oddly, it appears only in the first draft.

That fall, *The Pierre Berton Show* flung its net wide, visiting both Australia and Berlin. I took the manuscript of *The National Dream* with me, scribbling revisions as we travelled. In between trips, I worked my way through the story again and again. I saw it as a series of highly visual scenes. If I could not envisage any of these scenes, I did more research in order to describe them in detail. I engaged Michael Bliss, who taught history at the University of Toronto, to vet the manuscript, and made many of the changes he suggested. At last I turned the work over to Jack McClelland and started immediately on the second volume.

The Australian junket had not sat well with the women on my staff. Elsa was taken aback by the Aussie attitude toward the female sex, which she described as Neanderthal. That was one reason why we decided on another five-part series, this one about the women's movement, then in its infancy. It was so young, in fact, that the phrase "Women's Lib" was not yet part of the argot of the day. I called our series "The New Suffragettes" and declared, at the outset, that just as the great issue of the sixties had been the black movement, so the great issue of the seventies would be the women's struggle. Few males took this prediction seriously.

I did not pretend to be objective – none of this "on the other hand" nonsense that waters down so many documentaries. After all, male chauvinists had had their say for centuries. It was time to give the women activists a platform. We deliberately chose the most outspoken among them.

A furious and predictable reaction followed, mostly from the male TV critics. In the *Star,* Patrick Scott described the series as "pretty funny stuff, though probably not intentional, provided you can stomach the steady parade of women whining about getting paid less than men for doing the same jobs (in which case, why don't they quit?)." Frank Penn, in the *Ottawa Citizen,* took umbrage because I had equated the women's situation in North America with that of the blacks – a comparison that was to be made often enough in the years that followed. One female columnist joined the attack, professing to be astonished that I had "lent my ears to these maladjusted, prattling harpies." It is a measure of the enormous revolution that has taken place since that none of these comments would be considered politically correct or acceptable today. Long before the end of the seventies, Women's Lib ceased to be a joke, and nobody on TV was complaining about women "whining" over unequal pay.

All of that was background, however, to the phenomenon of *The National Dream,* which was published in September 1970 and was soon setting records. Almost overnight I became a celebrity of a different kind – not a "personality" but a distinguished author, hoisted into the pantheon of Canadian icons by the tidal wave of nationalism that had swept the country following the Centennial Year.

Yet, looking back on that autumn today, I realize that the arrival of Eric Basciano on his sixteenth birthday was an event of more enduring significance. The truant officer brought him (at the suggestion of Dr. Peter Granger, the local Scoutmaster) – a slim, darkly handsome youth who was on the outs with his family. Could we take him for a day or so? Of course we could. A foster home, we were told, awaited him, but that fell through. Instead, he stayed with us and, though he kept his name, became part of the family. The time would come when he would graduate with honours from the University of Western Ontario. Now, here he was, with the hastily arranged birthday cake on the table – sixteen candles blazing away – saying very little. Sometime later, when he was as much a part of the family as Peter or Penny, he told me that the reason he hadn't spoken on that first night was that he had never celebrated a birthday before, and he didn't trust himself to say a word. This I could understand.

With Eric's arrival, Janet and I were the parents of eight children, ranging in age from six to twenty-two years. A good many people mistook us for Roman Catholics, partly because of the family size and partly because of my French-sounding name. But the children were planned. After each youngest grew out of diapers, Janet could be heard to say, "Oh, I really miss having a little baby in the house!" So we proceeded to have another baby.

Fortunate children! They lived in the country and with nature, surrounded by acres of forest and open fields. They lived in the same house (albeit an expanding one) for all their formative years – and with the same set of parents. They all had their own rooms. They went to a country school where they mixed with children from every economic walk of life. And they weren't so far from a big city that they could not enjoy its benefits.

Benefits, yes, and also fear. It was this drive into Toronto, especially at night, that concerned and worried us both. As they grew out of childhood, received their driver's licences, and borrowed the family car, we were haunted by the possibility of an accident. Janet had difficulty sleeping until they reached home. I slept, but the possibility of a dreadful tragedy haunted my dreams. Would our Elysian existence in the rolling countryside turn into a nightmare? We had blithely chosen to be exurbanites and had thrived. But would there be a reckoning? There were times when I felt that sooner or later the scales must balance. Maybe we had been a little too lucky. Surely, some nameless horror lurked in the dark future. I had coasted along through life, letting the slings and arrows bounce off me. But this was an eventuality I could not bear, for it was something over which I had no control. Every parent, I think, has such fears. When Casey Frayne was killed on his motorcycle, heading back to Queen's, I felt a knife in my heart. Hit by a drunken driver! He had no chance. When we hugged his parents at the funeral, it was as if we were hugging one of our own, knowing, at the

328

same time, that no gestures from us could relieve the torture they were going through. Would one of ours be next? The question remained unspoken, but it could be seen in our eyes and in the eyes of the other parents who wept with their friends.

I am not usually given to emotional speeches, even on those rare occasions when I have been asked to give a eulogy in a hushed chapel for an old crony – Ross McLean, John Clare. And yet I find it difficult to refer to my children in public. I remember, when researching *The Royal Family,* reading about that gruff old sailor George V, who would almost break down when mentioning his family during a formal address. I am the same; my voice goes husky and falters, and sometimes, on the public platform or on television, my eyes glisten when I talk about my eight children and their mother. It is something I cannot control. Probably I shouldn't try.

2

The National Dream was my eighteenth book. I had just turned fifty *Life begins* when it reached the bookstores. How could I know that the main body *at fifty* of my work lay ahead of me? Over the next two decades or so I would produce eighteen more books, of which thirteen would be books of narrative history. I had found my métier. Eventually people would begin to think of me as a writer/historian, though I made no claim to the latter. In spite of my university courses, I wasn't a historian by academic training. I preferred to be called simply "writer," an honourable enough name. And when strangers came up to me on the street to say "I love your books," instead of "I watch you on TV," I felt fulfilled.

I was praised now for telling Canadians about their past. People began to buttonhole me on the street to thank me for being "a true Canadian," whatever that means. A great many concluded that I was engaged in a personal crusade to enlighten the masses on the virtues of being a Canuck. Halfway through this present book I was introduced on the stage of a Vancouver theatre as "a national icon." But when I asked my hotel desk clerk for a spare room key, he demanded identification.

"But I'm a national icon," I told him.

"I'm from Jamaica," he said.

In fact, I have never thought of myself as a crusader intent on bringing history to the masses. I simply found that I thoroughly enjoyed telling this kind of tale, and since I had entered a barren literary field waiting to be ploughed, I decided to seize the territory for myself.

The National Dream received unqualified praise from those critics who reviewed it. Some ignored it, thinking, apparently, that it was just another potboiler. *Time's* Canadian edition, which reviewed most major works, was silent. The most influential review came from John Bassett in the *Telegram;* he said the book should be in every Canadian schoolroom. The academic community was grudging, but the fact that its members noticed it, reviewed it, and took it seriously was enough for me.

The scholars, of course, said there was nothing new in the book. I puzzled over that, since I knew I had uncovered all sorts of material that had never before seen print. It took me some time to realize that they meant there was no new analysis of the railway's significance, there were no startling revelations that could change our attitudes. I was more interested in telling a story. The analysis I kept hidden beneath the surface; it's there for anybody who looks for it, but I didn't intend to slow the narrative with great gobs of postulating.

The professors who reviewed the book had one curious complaint, which amused me. They said that I had made it difficult for scholars to read because I had insisted on documenting my sources at the back and not throughout the text. Too bad; I wrote the book for the ordinary reader, who, like me, is often bedevilled by tiny numbers sprinkled about the pages. Let the scholars do a little work! The source for almost every line was listed at the back. They could look them up, if they weren't too lazy. Barbara Tuchman, a respected American historian, used the same technique.

These natterings didn't affect the ordinary readers, who began to buy the book in astonishing numbers. Jack McClelland had announced a first printing of ten thousand, a huge quantity for a hardcover selling at $9.95, a fat price in those days (*The Smug Minority* was priced at $2.95). Jack was so jubilant that he insisted on having a cake the size of a pool table and covered with ten thousand candles made for the launch. Every restaurant in town, including the CPR's own Royal York, turned him down. Jack finally found his man in Pierre Moreau, the smiling maître d' of Les Cavaliers on Church Street. A former French Resistance fighter, Moreau wasn't afraid of anything, and certainly not a cake. As the media gathered for drinks and speeches, the monstrous confection was trundled in and the candles lit. The result was spectacular. The ten

330

thousand blazing candles created a firestorm on the same principle as the one that occurred when the RAF bombed Hamburg in the Second World War. I can still hear the flames roaring to a crescendo before Pierre produced a fire extinguisher and doused the conflagration, ruining Jack's cake but creating a sensation that could not go unreported.

The sales of *The National Dream* reached fifty thousand by Christmas, and the book continued to lead the best-seller list all the next year until it was finally displaced by its sequel, *The Last Spike*. At that time I had no competition in the field of narrative history. There was no such tradition in Canada as there was in the United States and Britain. The story of the country had been left largely in the hands of the history professors. Now people were saying, in effect, "My God, we do have a history, after all!" My mail proved it.

Jack and I now embarked on a massive campaign to publicize both books. Perhaps we didn't need it, but we weren't taking any chances. No amount of publicity will persuade a single reader to buy a book he doesn't want to read. Publicity tours – Jack's invention – were designed not to sell the product but to tell the public the product exists. The most difficult problem a writer faces is to make people, even friends, aware that he has actually written something. Even after I've done an exhausting publicity tour, old acquaintances come up to ask, "How come you haven't got a book out this year?"

Elsa Franklin, who handled all the publicity for my books (as she still does), had devised a tour to end all tours. Jack and I would cross the nation, hosting all-Canadian breakfasts in CPR hotels along the line. The aperitif would be a Last Spike Cocktail, made of champagne spiked with cognac and flavoured with curaçao and orange bitters. The breakfast would include buckwheat pancakes with maple syrup, Winnipeg goldeye, New Brunswick fiddleheads, and wild blackberry pie – all very Canadian. At the end of the tour, Jack announced he'd never eat another goldeye as long as he lived. The press had a wonderful time but later begged us not to repeat the experience; the Last Spike Cocktail had ruined the working day for most.

A marathon series of interviews resulted. I had, of course, worked both sides of the microphone for years and understood an unspoken etiquette that amateurs don't know about. The interviewer plugs the book; his guest gives him a lively show in return. "We'll get to your book later," was generally the opening gambit (it had been mine), "but

331

first, we'd like you to explain your views on movie censorship." The amateurs did not always understand this. "I came here to talk about my book, not about abortion," they'd say, and "Aren't you going to hold up the book?" It is better manners to help the host disguise the fact that he is about to run an unashamed commercial for your work. The really strident amateurs turn every innocuous question into a plug ("That's an interesting question. As I say in my book…"). Betty Friedan was one of these; she managed to work a reference to *The Feminine Mystique* into every response. On my tour with *The Last Spike,* I was happy with a brief mention of the book and a glimpse of the jacket. Actually, I got more because both *The Comfortable Pew* and *The National Dream* had already become phrases in the language. Is this my gift to posterity? Two phrases enshrined in the common tongue? I can, as they say in Hollywood, live with that.

By the time Jack and I reached Victoria, I was wrung out. This is my last marathon author's tour, I told Jack. In the future I would do no more than two cities at a time. At Bolen's bookstore I was subjected to a mob scene unlike any I'd known. A mass of people, every one waving a copy of *The Last Spike,* descended on me and began shoving their books in my face. I signed blindly, as fast as I could. Others were thrusting before me scraps of paper, backs of cheque books, menus, even matchbooks, but I could not accommodate them. I scribbled at top speed and in half an hour somehow managed to get my scrawl into four hundred books. I look back now on that scene with nostalgia. Today there are so many Canadian books published and therefore so many authors on the road, if I sign seventy-five books, I'm content. Sometimes I long for another mob like the one in Victoria, but the literary scene has changed since then, and for the better.

I had planned a quartet of books dealing with the opening of Western Canada, beginning in 1870 with *The National Dream* and ending in 1914 with the fourth book, covering the immigration wave that settled the prairies after the railway was built. That would make *Klondike* Book Number 3. Jack, who had once wanted me to shorten it, now asked me to lengthen it. More material had surfaced by then, and I had no trouble adding twenty-five thousand words, with an introduction that set it all in context. At the same time, Jack's brilliant art director, Frank Newfeld, and I produced a picture book entitled *The Great Railway.* Both this and the new edition of *Klondike* were published in 1972 and enjoyed phenomenal sales. That October I had four books on the best-seller list. *The National Dream* had been on the list for 104 weeks, *The Last Spike* for 54. Now, *Klondike* zoomed up to Number 1; the picture book stood in sixth place. That record has never been exceeded, and, I suspect, never will be.

A year or so later I received the supreme accolade – I was made an Indian chief. On the Blood Reserve in Alberta, they daubed my face with paint and I smoked the pipe of peace as the drums pounded away. The Commissioner of the RCMP, W.L. Higgitt, who was also being rewarded with an eagle-feather headdress, turned to me and in a dead-pan voice whispered, "We must be prepared to sell our lives as dearly as possible!"

I was installed as Honorary Chief Big Plume. The CPR's chairman, Buck Crump, who was being honoured too, leaned toward me. "Big *what*?" he asked, raising an eyebrow. I prefer to believe the title had to do with the power of my pen.

After *The Last Spike* won me my third Governor General's Award, a consensus developed at the CBC that my two books should form the basis for a television miniseries. The drama department was anxious to produce, but I baulked; I wasn't crazy about the way they'd handled Mazo de la Roche's *Jalna*. Fortunately, Lister Sinclair, who was then head of the Arts and Sciences Division, wanted to do it. I preferred to work with him. The two of us sat down one weekend and plotted a series of eight one-hour drama-documentaries, to be called *The National Dream*. The CBC bought the idea, but at that very moment Lister was elevated to vice-president of the corporation and moved to Ottawa. Jim Murray, his second-in-command, took over, and for the next two years I was deeply involved as historical consultant and narrator.

Now interdepartmental jealousy raised its head. I'd rebuffed the drama people in favour of a documentary unit. Would *The National Dream* be a drama or a documentary? It was decided (not by me) that it would be both, a composite animal like a cattalo, half of one, half of the other. And half *meant* half – *exactly* half. The drama department kept a sharp eye on the process to make sure the dramatic parts never exceeded the allowable 50 percent. That led to some absurd compromises in which the drama and documentary sections were actually timed to make sure that one did not encroach upon the other. ("We'll have to cut these last lines of dialogue – it would put us over the 50 percent.")

My role was to make sure the series was historically accurate. I had no difficulty there because the two writers, Timothy "Tiff" Findley and his partner, Bill Whitehead, were people whom I admired. Tiff wrote the drama, Bill the documentary, including my own on-camera remarks, which I revised and edited to suit my personal style.

It was a formidable undertaking. Jim Murray and I crossed the country twice, the first year to pick out locations for me, the second to film my portions of the series. He had hired a light plane to fly over southern Alberta, seeking an abandoned track that could do duty as a section of the newly built CPR line. He found one outside Brooks. The old line was torn up; then a crew, composed half of actors and half of railway navvies, rebuilt it according to 1880 specifications. The old Kettle Valley railway in south-central British Columbia, complete with trestles and shattered tunnels, did duty for the Fraser Canyon section, now so built up it couldn't be used. Fortunately, a trestle falling down looks like a trestle half built. They played their part in the more spectacular aspects of the construction period. A ninety-one-year-old double-headed steam locomotive was resurrected, rebuilt, and shipped to Brooks by flatcar for the series.

The main problem facing Jim and his director, Eric Till, was to keep the sights and sounds of modern Canada out of the picture. It was necessary for me to appear on camera at the Rogers Pass to describe its discovery by Major A.B. Rogers. But how? The CPR no longer ran through the pass, but the Trans-Canada Highway did. Enormous diesel trucks roared by every thirty seconds, drowning out my commentary as I stood among the spruce trees with the snow-capped mountains at my back. It meant that my narration had to be broken into short segments. Over and over again I would have to stop in mid-sentence while another truck zoomed past. It was nerve-racking, but after a full day of fits and starts we got the necessary ninety seconds on film. There is no hint in the final footage that I am standing a couple of feet from the highway, virtually surrounded by automobiles, trucks, and gawking tourists.

On the Precambrian Shield in January, we faced an equally difficult problem. My job was to stand on the main line on the shore of Lake Superior and describe the country through which the troops were dispatched to fight Riel in 1885. The temperature had dropped to minus 54 degrees Fahrenheit – so cold that at several points I found I could not move my lips and had to be revived with mugs of hot coffee. Just as I thawed out, the camera froze. By the time it was warmed up, the sound equipment stopped working. At last we were ready. I started to say my piece, pointing out at the frozen lake – the exact spot where the soldiers had crossed on foot between gaps in the unfinished line. At that very moment we heard the rumble of a freight train just around the bend, and all of us – narrator, sound man, lighting crew, and director – scrambled to get off the tracks. In the end, however, the job was done, on time and on budget, and the result was one of the CBC's greatest successes, so popular that it has been sold to more than a dozen countries, from Ireland to Saudi Arabia (but not to the United States, where PBS found it "too Canadian" for *Masterpiece Theater*). The BBC cut the eight hours to six and arrogantly decided to use one of its own people as narrator – Robert McKenzie, an expatriate Canadian academic with a plummy mid-Atlantic accent. That I could not stomach. Instead, I flew over at my own expense and did the job for scale.

Meanwhile, Jack suggested that I abridge the two books and publish them as a single paperback, illustrated with colour stills from the TV production. That sold a record 175,000 copies. The royalties went to pay for the addition to our house, which was needed more than ever because of the arrival of our eighth child.

I spent the best part of that year hacking away at my other child – the literary one. I had cut it by two-thirds for the picture book; now I cut it in half for the paperback. When I sold it as a single volume to Knopf in New York, under the title of *The Impossible Railway,* I cut it again, this time by one-third. Some writers cannot bear to cut their stuff; after all, it is their baby. It has never given me pause. In fact, I rather enjoy slashing away at my own prose like an explorer with a machete, chopping his way through the encroaching jungle.

By the end of 1973, when all these abridgements were complete, I was heartily sick of the story. Twenty years and more than a dozen major books later, I am still introduced at luncheon clubs as the man who wrote *The National Dream.* I now understand J.B. Priestley's frustration when, at a literary luncheon in Toronto in the early fifties, he was introduced solely as the author of *The Good Companions.* An indignant Priestley remarked that he had written other and better works since. Then, without giving his prepared speech, he sat down. I don't feel as strongly as Priestley. Every mention is, after all, a boost. But I have not

335

re-read *The National Dream* or *The Last Spike* since 1973, and I doubt
that I ever will.

3

Good MEXICO CITY, March 20, 1971. I am strolling down the Reforma with
morning, David Alfaro Siqueiros, the greatest living painter in Mexico, a small,
Maestro slim figure in a brown fedora who wants to show me his latest work. I
tower over him, but I know I am in the presence of a giant. He is surely
the best-known and best-loved figure in the city. Everybody seems to
know him, and as people pass by they raise their hats. "Good morning,
Maestro," they say, and sometimes they stop him. "It is a pleasure,
Maestro," they tell him; always "maestro."

Siqueiros turns to me. "Is not too bad a country, eh," he asks, "when
the artists and not the generals are called maestro!"

He loves his country, though he has reason enough to loathe it. He
has been jailed fifteen times for his opinions, exiled thrice, and has seen
his work defaced, slashed, white-washed over, and destroyed. In 1967,
after he had personally taken out advertisements in the local press supporting the student revolution, one of his greatest works was torn to bits
by a gang of thugs.

But he carries on, this last living member of the great triumvirate of
Mexican revolutionary muralists that includes Diego Rivera and José
Clemente Orozco. Few other artists have painted with so much passion
and engendered so much controversy as these three.

"Come," says Siqueiros, "you must see my polyform. I wish to show
it to you myself."

I have heard of this remarkable work – a mural so large it must
occupy its own building, the Siqueiros Cultural Polyform, not yet finished. It covers forty-eight thousand square feet, the most gargantuan
mural in the world – three times as large as Michelangelo's work in the
Sistine Chapel. I am dying to see it, but I am not prepared for the spectacle that assaults me when, after climbing the three flights of stairs (the
elevators are not yet working), we burst upon Siqueiros's masterpiece.

The effect is staggering. I reel back. Around me, above me, below
me, an explosion of colour reaches out for me. This is not a traditional flat piece of work. The mural is three-dimensional; it seems to move

336

toward me and back again. To get this effect, Siqueiros has made use of every kind of coating – automobile paint, plastic, silicone, aluminum, steel.

It is called The March of Civilization in Latin America *and it has already been six years in the making. Siqueiros produced all the preliminary sketches while serving a six-year jail sentence. Sixty helpers – artists, architects, painters, sculptors – have worked under him to produce this extraordinary piece of art.*

The artist cannot stay still. He leaps about, running from vantage point to vantage point. "Look at it from here!" he cries, then, moving on, "now from here!" He loves his work, loves to take people to look at it, revels in his creation. "Isn't it a gas?" he seems to say, and I am reminded of my friend Harold Town, who always used those words when contemplating his latest canvas.

"A mural," Siqueiros tells me, "should flow continuously. It should always be dynamic; never static. Here, come here: look out there. More mural on the outside!" For indeed, every square inch inside and outside the polyform is thick with texture.

He is seventy-six years old now, and he still works twelve to fifteen hours a day in his monstrous studio, the size of an airplane hangar, in Cuernavaca. It is there that pieces of his work are produced to be shipped to Mexico City.

"An artist," Siqueiros explains to me, "cannot stand aside. One must be involved." No ivory tower for him: he has been a labour leader, writer, editor, teacher, and soldier as well as a painter. In the Spanish Civil War he was a colonel commanding a brigade. And always, from the beginning, he has been a revolutionary, opposing over the years the former revolutionaries who, having been seduced by power, now opt for the status quo.

He insists on taking me on a tour of the city to show me more of his works. One, commissioned sixteen years ago, is still unfinished because the building is falling down. But no building that contains a Siqueiros work can be allowed to topple. It is now being repaired, he tells me; when construction is done, he will finish it.

"Good morning, Maestro," says a young man, lifting his hat as we pass. Siqueiros lifts his fedora in return.

We repair to a bar for a tequila or two, and there Siqueiros talks of his years in jail.

337

"One good thing, you know," he says, "they allow your wife to visit. It is called by the inmates 'Going to New York.' We shave and dress up in our best that day.

"A bad thing," he adds, "is that one must always carry a knife. A knife I always carried. They'll murder you for a hundred pesos."

A strange country, I think. The president puts him in jail and then, when a new work of his is opened, the same president helps cut the ribbon and is photographed gripping the jailbird's hand.

What an interview he will make, he and the others we have selected: Ivan Illich, the Roman Catholic priest who wants to get rid of all formal education; Isela Vega, the movie actress who flouts convention by refusing to marry her lover and demands women's rights in a machismo society; and, of course, the students, talking politics.

Do I really believe the Mexican government will countenance open interviews with these people – rebels all? Why am I astonished when the owner of the television station we've hired to produce our shows casually remarks, at the last moment, that a censor will sit beside us in the studio? Nor will they allow any tape to be released until the censor has looked at it to make sure it carries no "adverse political comment."

The station owner seems equally astonished when I tell him that I cannot allow any censorship. It can be resolved easily, he says; just don't ask any political questions and everything will be all right! I explain that that will be impossible, especially as I've planned a round-table with about a dozen students – I want to ask them what they think of the Mexican government.

He blanches. Students! Only a few years before, the students rioted against the government. The police and army killed three hundred of them. Why must I interview students? Recently, he points out, I did a program with Patrick Dennis, the author of Auntie Mame. Why can't I just do shows like that?

These are supposed to be our final shows of the season. I'm meeting my family in Acapulco for a holiday. Elsa is off to Zihuatanejo. The staff is scattering. If we cancel, we'll have to reorganize and produce six more half hours back home at additional cost.

I call Dan Enright in New York to explain.

"You can't do any shows in Mexico?" he asks. "Not any?"

"I won't do them," I explain.

He pauses. Then: "Well, if you can't, you can't. Don't worry. We'll

338

*pick them up when you get back. Meanwhile, have a good holiday." This
from Danny, the hard-driving, budget-conscious executive, the man who
fixed the big quiz show. I like him better now.*

*On my return, the Mexican ambassador phones me from Ottawa. The
press has been on to him, and he's upset. We haven't given Mexico a
good image, he says. He wants me to come back, and he guarantees that
we can do any subject of our own choosing without interference.*

No censorship?

*None, he says. "You can do what you want!" But then he adds, "Of
course, we'll want to put somebody on the program in every case to
give our side of the story."*

*Nobody, I tell him, has ever asked for that – not even in Prague. And
I'm not going to start now. The Canadian public will not meet David
Alfaro Siqueiros after all. It is our loss – and Mexico's.*

4

On a November morning in 1971, Charles Templeton and I found ourselves standing in front of the White House in Washington, trying to
persuade some minor official to accept the longest telegram in the world.

*Oh,
Canada*

We had moved "Dialogue" the previous year from CFRB to CKEY,
a station that offered us double our fees if we'd come. They also offered
Charles the regular morning newscast. It was on one of these newscasts
– Thursday, October 28, 1971 – that Charles had reported on the U.S.
plan to set off a test nuclear blast on the Aleutian island of Amchitka,
uncomfortably close to Canadian shores. Charles added that he and I
intended to send a telegram of protest to President Richard Nixon and
suggested that every listener should have a chance to put in his two
cents' worth. For two cents we'd add their names to the telegram. The
newscast was barely over before a man parked his car outside the station, walked into the newsroom, and handed his business card and a
dollar to the girl at the front desk.

By ten that morning, when "Dialogue" went on the air, we were able
to outline the idea. The cost would come to more than five cents a name,
and so we suggested individual contributions of a dime, the extra money
to be spent to buy time on an all-news station and others in Washington
to which senators and congressmen habitually listened. Four stations

turned us down. In those times it was considered almost communistic to deplore nuclear testing. Three others agreed to carry our message.

CKEY was swamped with names, money, and offers to help. Pensioners sent in dimes; children sent pennies. One woman endorsed her baby bonus cheque to the campaign so we might include the names of her offspring. A family of Japanese Canadians whose relatives had died at Hiroshima turned up with a donation. By night time, when the switchboard closed, volunteers manning the phones had logged ten thousand names, and that was only the beginning.

By the time the story reached the media, we had 26,000 names. Within a week we had collected 112,000 paid signatures.

We would have to go to Washington to deliver the message in person – if we could get one of Nixon's people to accept it. The Canadian government, whose help we solicited, wanted nothing to do with that. In neither Ottawa nor Washington could we reach a press aide or a ranking official. In the words of Harvey Clarke, CKEY's P.R. man, "they ran and hid." The Trudeau government was playing it safe.

It took days of negotiating with Washington consultants, senatorial assistants, even Henry Kissinger's secretary before somebody grudgingly agreed to receive the protest. At eleven o'clock on the morning of Thursday, November 4, Charles and I turned up pushing a wheelbarrow containing the longest telegram ever sent anywhere – 224,000 names on rolls of yellow paper that, tied together, would have reached for almost a mile. There we stood at the entrance to the White House executive office building, and there we met the president's counsel, a balding young man with an impassive face and rimless spectacles. I felt a little foolish. We had entered into the scheme in good faith – both of us angered by what a foreign power was proposing to do off Canada's west coast. Now it looked like a cheap publicity stunt, and the irony was that here in blasé Washington, nobody really cared. I don't recall that a single member of the media was present.

Yes, the bland young lawyer assured us, the president would certainly be informed of the monstrous telegram. Off he went, trundling our wheelbarrow, but we were not allowed to follow. We trusted him to deliver the massive message. He was a presidential aide, wasn't he? The next time I became aware of him, his picture was on the front pages of the newspapers and covers of news magazines.

His name, as it turned out, was John Dean.

We never found out whether Nixon ever saw or heard of our protest. But certainly the editors of the new tabloid newspaper in Toronto, successor to the defunct *Telegram,* were aware of the prediction we made on New Year's Day, 1972. We declared flatly that the Toronto *Sun* would be dead within months, if not weeks. We had failed to grasp the huge changes that were taking place in Toronto. The subway city was ripe for a sassy newspaper to reflect the growing sassy spirit of a big chunk of the population. The paper never let us forget this look into the clouded crystal ball. On successive anniversaries they made a point of mentioning it and once even asked us to turn up at a *Sun* event to eat roast crow. I was out of town with my TV show, but Charles gamely appeared and gnawed on a drumstick.

Meanwhile, *The Pierre Berton Show* was running into more censorship, this time in Lebanon.

In Beirut, the government wanted to control what I and my guests had to say. We had gone there to balance our coverage in Israel, where to my regret the one man I really wanted to talk to had turned me down. General Moshe Dayan, I was informed, was far too busy to come from Jerusalem to Tel Aviv to talk to me. But not too busy to toast an attractive woman in champagne that evening at one of Tel Aviv's livelier cafés, not far from our hotel. I watched from a nearby table but did not speak to him. She was a stunning creature; there was no way I could compete with her.

In Lebanon, as in Mexico, we were assured in advance that there was no such thing as censorship in the country. We planned, as we always did, a round-table discussion with university students, but after we made the program we found we were not allowed to export the videotape. There was no official explanation. Later I was told there had been objections to remarks from some of the students about the absence of real democracy in the country.

What to do? The discussion had been live, and on our tight budget I didn't want to lose any more shows. Luckily for us, our announcer, Bernard Cowan, had been taking photographs throughout the program to use in publicity. Talk about overkill! He had shot scores of photos showing every one of the students in action – long shots, medium shots, and close-ups. We were able to smuggle out both the film and an audio tape of the entire program. In Toronto, Elsa had the pictures blown up to poster size and mounted on a camera stand. We then shot the stills as we would a television show, matching recorded comments to the individuals. The result was remarkable; one forgot that the entire half hour was made up of stills.

These were heady days in which to be a Canadian, enjoying the wave of nationalism that washed over the country in the wake of the Centennial Year. As Christina McCall Newman wrote in *Maclean's,* "the need for a show of independence has taken hold of the Canadian psyche in a way that four or five years ago nobody would have believed possible." Yet this phenomenon had escaped the closeted mandarins of Ottawa, who, she said, felt that the new enthusiasm was "at best a bore and at worst an irritant."

In 1969 I had lunched with Peter Newman, then the editor of the *Toronto Star,* at the King Edward Hotel and listened while he enthusiastically outlined a new organization to be called the Committee for an Independent Canada. It was backed mainly with Walter Gordon's money and was to have a strong influence on government policy, even though the *Financial Times* referred to its inaugural meeting as "an orgy of nationalistic nonsense." I remember being part of a delegation from the committee that met with Trudeau and Herb Gray, his designated hitter on the nationalism field. Gray was certainly enthusiastic, Trudeau jaundiced. But, in spite of the Ottawa mandarins, the politicians, and the business press, the country was in ferment. Phrases like "Canadian content" and "Canadian culture" were tossed about like tennis balls. Looking back on those times, it seems to me that I was spending a disproportionate number of hours flying to Ottawa as a member of various delegations trying to convince those in command that it was time Canadians stood on their own feet.

In April 1970, forty-six of us, all members of our union, the Association of Canadian Television and Radio Artists, chartered a plane at our own expense and flew to the capital to express to the CRTC our concern about the future of Canadian television. The cream of the broadcasting world turned up at the airport at 6:30 a.m., even though some of them hadn't finished work until past midnight. After the plane took off, the irrepressible Farley Mowat asked the flight attendant if it was possible to get a drink at such an hour. She looked at him as if he were some sort of strange, furry creature seeking a jungle waterhole. "Well," she said, hesitantly, "I suppose so," and poured him a stiff vodka.

342

"I'll second that!" cried Hugh Garner. As a result he missed the entire meeting, having been packed off to the hospital suffering from something very close to the D.T.'s. He remained in confinement for several days. Mowat, however, was none the worse for wear.

At the hearing, at which Fred Davis was spokesman, I put in a brief of my own. "The tragedy today," I said, "is that our Canadian broadcasting philosophy… has become an American broadcasting philosophy, which sees the medium simply as an extension of the market place.… The Canadian broadcasting philosophy has to be bound up with the Canadian dream and the Canadian dream is the dream of an independent nation in North America…a nation with its own mythology, its own heroes, its own songs, its own character, and its own idiom."

Brave words! But in hindsight, they weren't very effective. Most of the private broadcasters at the hearings were interested only in being awarded a licence to make money. Their lobby group, the Canadian Association of Broadcasters, firmly resisted all attempts to increase the Canadian content rules – a bit of myopia that caused a furious John Bassett to pull his Ottawa and Toronto stations out of the CAB.

On the flight back, Betty Kennedy, Lorraine Thomson (then on the staff of *Front Page Challenge*), and I discussed the need for an all-Canadian awards evening to celebrate excellence in the broadcasting industry. Thus were conceived the ACTRA Awards, symbolized by the irreverent overweight nude statuette quickly dubbed Nellie (with the belly). What we wanted was only a handful of awards presented during a lively and informal evening that, in the Canadian fashion, would not take itself too seriously. "This is not the greatest moment of your life," I said when I opened the first of these dinners at the Park Plaza. "Remember, it's only an award, for Christ's sake." In contrast to the other award nights, there was no solemn academy invented to give status to the evening. Moreover, we insisted that the presenters write their own speeches and say whatever came into their heads. That caused Brian Doherty, founder of the Shaw Festival, to speak for forty-five minutes, resisting every effort by myself and the band to play him or drag him off the podium. But the evening was saved by Bill Mitchell with a hilarious and irreverent address that the best Hollywood gag writer couldn't have equalled.

It was as warm and lively a family night as I have ever attended – and it was ours. Everybody knew everybody else; there was no television, so we didn't have to rush through dinner; people kidded themselves and the medium. Everybody had a good time, but it couldn't last that way. Soon the CBC was televising the entire production from coast to coast. Recipients began thanking their mothers for bringing them into the world, and God for helping them win. The example of the American-style awards night was too strong. By the time the ACTRA Awards ended, fifteen years later, professional writers were composing set speeches for the presenters to read, and everybody was demanding an award for his or her category. The CTV network began to whine that the whole thing was a CBC plot to discredit it, since the corporation snagged most of the Nellies. That caused Ron Haggart, in his *Star* column, to suggest an award for the most crassly commercial use of television – an award, he said, that CTV would win hands down.

At last the broadcasting industry took over and created a copycat "Academy of Television Arts and Sciences." What spontaneity remained quickly vanished; a sober statuette replaced the Nellie; and there were so many awards that it took three evenings to present them all. As in Alice's caucus-race, everybody won, so everybody must have a prize. The CBC continued – surprise! – to dominate the awards; the recipients continued to sob out their heartfelt thanks to everybody from their agents to their baby-sitters and to announce that "this is the greatest moment of my life." Today, watered down like cheap mining stock, the awards have lost their exclusiveness and their lustre. They did, however, serve one of our original purposes: they made the name of the ACTRA union known across the country.

Meanwhile, with the nationalistic fervour at its height, Jack McClelland announced that he would sell his firm, probably to an American book publisher. That caused a dreadful outcry. The company, at the suggestion of Elsa Franklin, had been calling itself *The Canadian Publishers*. Now that imprint was about to be hawked to the highest Yankee bidder. Here was an anomaly. Thanks to the new nationalism, authors like me were making a good thing from our work, while the big chains, Coles, Smith's, and Classic, were raking in the profits. But best-sellers weren't enough to balance the losses from the small, if worthy, works that Jack was gambling on. His own enthusiasm and philosophy had put him in a Catch-22 position. As a confirmed nationalist and one of the founders of the Committee for an Independent Canada, he had already jettisoned many of his American connections, at considerable cost.

344

Jack's nationalism was killing him. As the leading Canadian publisher and the leading Canadian nationalist, he had to publish admirable
books that he knew in advance would lose money. He'd even started
a Western division in Calgary (I was a director) as a sop to growing
complaints that the country was dominated by "Eastern interests."

Fortunately, the growing national feeling had persuaded the Ontario
government that books were a part of culture. A royal commission chaired
by Richard Rohmer, himself a novelist, rushed out a preliminary report
recommending that M&S receive a low-interest loan of one million
dollars. Three watchdog members of the Ontario Development Corporation joined the M&S board along with Margaret Laurence, Elsa Franklin,
and me. For the moment, Jack had gained a reprieve.

The country was in love with itself. Ever since the Centennial, people
had discovered an interest in their origins, fuelled partly by the growing separatist movement in Quebec. The production of *The National
Dream* in 1973 received one of the highest ratings in the CBC's history. An interest in the Canadian past also sparked a new interest in the
symbols of the past. My own commitment to the preservation movement represented a complete about-turn. When I first arrived in Toronto,
I couldn't have cared less about saving old buildings. I was a disciple
of the new, a slavish fan of the International Style; I thought Victorian
houses were ugly monstrosities that ought to be levelled for new and
modern structures of glass and steel. I do not know exactly when my
attitudes began to change, but I think the books of narrative history had a
lot to do with it. Turreted edifices that had once appalled me now began
to look quaint, and then beautiful. I began to look up at the second storeys
of old city business blocks and marvel at the workmanship.

I was one of those who fought to prevent the destruction of Fort York
and the Romanesque city hall in Toronto. In 1972, as a member of the
Union Station Committee I found myself making an impassioned plea
to the city council to save one of the most magnificent and symbolic
buildings in town. I remember looking directly into the faces of the council members and giving a warning: "You may think that people will
soon forget this act of vandalism. But I'm here to tell you now that I
will not forget and that I will be here in the future to remind the public
of your guilt." After our delegation had its say, two members changed
their votes and the station was saved by a whisker.

In 1973, Bob Phillips, a long-time Ottawa mandarin, dropped into my office and asked if I would join another new organization, the Heritage Canada Foundation. The prime minister, he said, was inviting me. Who can resist a call from the prime minister? Actually, I was pretty sure he knew very little about it and that the list of governors had been drawn up by the civil service, with the usual assortment of Canadian content: somebody from every province and territory, including three or four women and a native Indian, a lawyer or two, an architect or two, a politician, a couple of local archivists, and two or three businessmen of impeccable qualifications, such as Hart McDougall of the Bank of Montreal, who became chairman. And me, of course, wearing my railway historian's hat.

Even as we all sat down in Ottawa to discuss our mandate – how to save important buildings – one of the most significant mansions was being trashed in Montreal. It had been the home of the CPR's general manager, William Cornelius Van Horne, the star of *The Last Spike*. As a member of the English-speaking establishment, he no longer had any standing in French Canada. One Laval professor, in fact, was quoted as calling Van Horne a union buster whose home was therefore of no consequence. This very Canadian attitude – that the memory of only "nice" people ought to be preserved – grated on me. As I wrote at the time, if we saved only the homes of the saints, there would be, perhaps, three left in all Canada to commemorate our past, and the birthplace of Maurice Duplessis would not be among them.

But in 1973, even the Parliament Buildings were not sacrosanct. The government had actually considered demolishing the venerable East Block in favour of a modern glass-and-steel office building. The public was only then beginning to wake up to the fact that the texture of the past was worth preserving. The politicians, as usual, were hopelessly behind. "Our job," I told a heritage meeting in Vancouver, "is to make heritage preservation acceptable; after that we must try to make it popular; finally, we must make it fashionable." Though we had some bitter losses, I think that over the years we have succeeded.

That same year, The Writers' Union of Canada was formed under the chairmanship of Margaret Laurence. At an early meeting, the membership committee voted 12 to 3 to limit the organization to novelists and short-story writers in order to "keep out amateurs and dilettantes" and also because, the committee insisted, only novelists made a cultural contribution. The feeling was that if the definition of the group was

346

too wide, nobody would benefit. I was flabbergasted. Didn't anyone understand the purpose of a union – that in numbers there is strength?

"A pressure group has to exert pressure," I said. "If fiction writers and poets think that they alone can exert pressure on entrenched publishers and libraries, they are living in cloud-cuckoo-land. They can't do it alone. The only way is to get as many authors who are actively writing books as possible into the organization." I added that I was really arguing against my own interests because if the original motion was passed, I could go home, be absolved of all further meetings, and get on with my own work, which was writing non-fiction. But the membership saw the light and included the rest of us.

There was a sense of giddy enthusiasm over our new venture in those early days. We felt, correctly, I think, that we were taking part in a historic moment. The union was launched just as the literary renaissance in Canada was picking up steam. Its membership has since grown to almost a thousand professional authors, each of whom has written at least one successful trade book. Its influence has been immeasurable.

There were some memorable moments at our annual conventions. Few will forget the morning we picketed Coles Bookstore in Ottawa because the company insisted on allowing American publishers to dump Canadian-written books on the Canadian market at fire-sale prices. "Coles' Law is Coleslaw," read Graeme Gibson's placard. We won that battle.

There was also Project Porno, an ingenious plan to publish a book of pornography. We felt it would sell so many copies to inhibited Canadians that the union's coffers would overflow with royalty profits. But nobody really wanted his or her name on a pornographic story – too autobiographical, perhaps. Only one member submitted a manuscript to Project Porno. It was called *Bear,* and to everyone's surprise it won a Governor General's Award for fiction for its author, Marian Engel.

It was because of the union's pressure on the government that money became available for the kind of Kill an Author Tour that few publishers could afford. Today, as each Yuletide approaches, scores of garrulous authors criss-cross the nation, peddling their books. We meet each other in airports, hotel lobbies, and broadcasting stations, lining up like hogs in a slaughterhouse, waiting our turn and playing the old game of scratching the backs of the talk-show hosts. It may be that the tour has become self-defeating, and that the public as well as the broadcasters have become weary of this ceaseless book plugging on the airwaves.

Somehow I doubt it. One still hears the lament that there is no such thing as a true Canadian culture. Yet, looking back on that autumn afternoon in 1973 when we formed what Margaret Laurence called "the tribe," it is clear that we were helping to preside over an institution that has had considerable influence in the post-centennial years. I'm glad that I was a part of it.

5

A mere "Pierre!" a woman shrieked at me as she was about to enter the elevator
potboiler at CKEY. "Pierre Trudeau!"

I stood my ground. "I'm the other one," I explained.

"Robert Stanfield!" she cried in triumph. The elevator doors closed on me, like a curtain falling at the end of a play, leaving her still on the main floor, looking a bit baffled.

There's no use pretending that I didn't enjoy the notoriety. Anyway, it came with the territory. I had already learned I couldn't dispense with my bow tie without causing comment. It was part of my persona – slightly kooky, perhaps, and not in style, but also faintly scholarly.

The critics no longer bothered me. I was called everything from "the Captain Marvel of the Canadian Communications field" (*Montreal Star*) to a "self-appointed national scold" (Montreal *Gazette*). I expected to be torn apart from time to time. "Don't read the reviews," Jack McClelland advised me. "*Measure* them!" He was dead right, as I soon learned. The day after a particularly vicious critique appeared in one of the Toronto papers, a chance acquaintance approached me to extend congratulations. "Wow, did you see all that space the *Star* gave your book? You must feel really good about that!" I certainly felt good about the remark. More than once I was called "a professional controversialist" in the press. I have never set out to be controversial; I have simply said what I thought.

I accepted the perks, responsibilities, and burdens that went with the territory. I marched with the Ban the Bombers. I sat at a table on Yonge Street and asked people to sign a petition attacking police brutality. I prepared a brief for the CRTC charging that the CBC was guilty of promoting separatism by running two networks, in two languages, without any cross-fertilization. All of this took time, and time is a writer's most precious asset. I was trying to put together the fourth

348

book in my quartet on the opening of Western Canada and had even hired a student to do some research. But I couldn't find a focus for the story and put it aside for the moment – a moment that did not come for another ten years.

Instead I looked about for another subject – something simpler, more evocative. I didn't find it; it found me. It really began in 1971 when I had been appointed historical consultant on an ambitious international project – the establishment of a gold rush park straddling the coastal mountains that separate the Alaska Panhandle from Canada and encompassing both the Chilkoot and White Pass trails. That summer I climbed the Chilkoot with a party of Canadian and American experts. In lieu of a fee I was given permission to bring along two of my children, Pamela, twenty-one, and Peter, sixteen. It was for us a marvellous adventure. I had, of course, described the famous pass as it was in the gold rush days, but I had never seen it. Now a helicopter from Skagway dropped us not far from the first canyon on the trail that led up the slopes from the abandoned seaport of Dyea.

We climbed into the clouds and back into history. All around us, undisturbed, lay the artifacts of 1898 – women's pink slippers, old axes and A-frames, tattered gunnysacks, tools, boots, rotting packsacks, and miles of tangled cable that had once been used to haul supplies on an overhead line from the base of the pass to the summit. When we reached the rocky ledge known as the Scales, where the professional packers had weighed their loads (and doubled their prices), we were soaking wet, for we had been climbing through a heavy mist and our rainwear had made us sweat so profusely we had to wring out and change our clothes. Ahead of us rose the thirty-five-degree slope up which that long line of gold seekers, bent double by the weight of their sixty-pound packs, had struggled not once but as many as fifty times in order to haul their mandatory ton of goods over the mountains. As we resumed our climb, rendered difficult by huge boulders and slippery shale, I realized that we were walking in my father's footsteps. He had come this way almost three-quarters of a century earlier. Was any of the paraphernalia strewn along the way and abandoned by weary climbers his? I still had his letters to his mother, written in a tiny, cramped hand with a hard pencil. I wondered how I could make use of them.

Randall Iredale, the Vancouver architect who had been enlisted to prepare a feasibility study on the proposed park, had hired Skip Burns, an outfitter from Juneau, to help us over the heights. Skip was a romantic Southerner, in love with the Yukon, in love with the idea of the gold rush, and much in love with his fiancée, a slim girl of twenty-two who hoisted a man's load over the mountains. They would be married in the most romantic setting of all – the little log church on the shores of Lake Bennett, built by the gold seekers and long abandoned. Standing on the summit of the famous pass, on which seventy feet of snow fell each winter, and looking down at the round little crater lakes beneath us, I came to a sudden decision. I told Skip that I had decided to take my family down the Yukon waterway from Lake Bennett to Dawson the following year. His eyes lit up. He wouldn't miss that for the world, he said, and offered then and there to supply boats and boatmen at cost.

Thus was born my next book, *Drifting Home,* out of an impulsive remark. I had not intended to write a book. I simply thought of the excursion as another family holiday. It had become almost an annual ritual that we would all go away for two weeks to some exotic spot – to the beaches of the Caribbean, the pyramids of Mexico, the Gulf Islands of British Columbia. In 1972, I decided, we would make our way by rubber raft downriver to my home town.

Janet enthusiastically agreed, even though the burden of the journey would fall on her. She was and is a great cook. I have said more than once that I married her because we both like our beef rare. She knew that our river voyage would stand or fall on the quality of the cuisine and that there was no way any of us would agree to subsist on the kind of dried provender that most outfitters supply. Because there are no grocery stores along the way, she and Pamela spent the winter working out a fortnight of menus for fifteen people (Skip's crew and our family). The food for each day was packed individually into fourteen carefully labelled cardboard cartons. It was a monumental undertaking, and I do not know of anybody else who could have done it. We were prepared to eat like kings on that trip, and we did eat like kings, though not quite as Janet and Pamela had planned.

The boxes of food arrived by train at the Bennett station along the White Pass company's narrow-gauge railway. We packed it all into our rubber Zodiacs and set off. The following day the mountainous waves on the Windy Arm of Tagish Lake engulfed the cartons, turning the cardboard to mush and ruining much of the winter's work. We still had our food, but it was pot luck for the rest of the journey.

350

I kept fourteen-year-old Paul beside me in the boat, bundled up and protected from the angry waves by a waterproof slicker. He was still recovering from a second bout of open-heart surgery, and his doctor had not wanted him to take part in our family adventure. Janet and I had no intention of leaving him behind; that would have been unthinkable. We were both convinced (rightly, as it turned out) that he'd have a better chance of recuperating in the open air with his family around him. I'm sure the doctor thought of our journey as a hazardous undertaking – a kind of Grand Canyon adventure. But with that one exception, the river and the lakes are benign. I saw no point in telling him about Windy Arm, where so many boats had capsized during the gold rush. As it was, the family was drenched – all except Paul.

Now, as the other children wrung out their wet clothes and changed into dry ones, Paul announced that he was hungry. He was always hungry – a good sign in a boy who has just had major surgery. My mind went back to that earlier open-heart operation – an operation so new at the time that his chances were only 50–50. He was always a feisty kid, and when I went in to see him in Intensive Care, with all those tubes sticking out of him, he remained feisty. "They're feeding me through my feet," he told me. I asked if he was hungry. "Not in my feet," he replied. But he was hungry the following day, and when the nurse asked him what he'd like – some Jell-O, perhaps? A little gruel? – "I'd like a BLT," said Paul.

The nurse looked baffled. "Bacon, lettuce, and tomato sandwich," I explained. She was rendered briefly speechless by this bold request. Finally she said, "Well, if that boy wants a BLT, then that's what he shall have!" Paul, fortified by bacon and tomato, bounced back quickly on that occasion and now, seven years later, with the open-heart technique improved, he bounced back again. Today he's the father of two and stills eats BLTs for breakfast.

We filmed the trip in 8mm and I showed the movie in the fall of 1972 on my own program. Jack McClelland saw the show and urged me to write a book about the experience. I demurred. I doubted that I had enough material and was certain the critics would write, "Now Berton wants to tell us what he did on his summer holidays." But Jack was insistent.

Besides my own memories, I had Patsy's lively log of the journey, the old steamboat charts of the thirties that I'd copied from the Yukon

Archives, and my father's letters to his mother. I thought the book might work if I wrote it on three levels: looking back to my father's journey down these same waters, then to 1925, when my parents had taken Lucy and me down the river in a poling boat, and finally, to the present journey. The book would move through time and space – part history, part geography, part nostalgia, part memoir.

I wrote *Drifting Home* in the spring of 1973 in a rented villa on the Portuguese Algarve coast. The difficulties that faced me were mechanical ones brought on by my quirky insistence on using one model of typewriter, and one model only – my Smith-Corona portable electric (one of the staff assignments on the TV show was to track down such a typewriter in every city we visited). Because Portugal operates on European voltage, my travel agent arranged for a transformer to be flown from Lisbon to be ready for me when we reached the Algarve. And there it was in our rented villa when I arrived.

I could hardly wait to get started, for I had been writing *Drifting Home* in my head during the flight across the Atlantic. I prepared to plug in the device so that the 220-volt current would be magically converted to my typewriter's 110. I sat down at my machine with Patsy's log, the steamboat charts, and my father's letters by my side, and plugged it in.

It blew up. Literally.

By that, I mean that great tongues of flame issued from the carriage, while a cloud of smoke enveloped me. I was not hurt, but dreadfully depressed. I had planned to get a first draft of the book on paper, giving me time on my return to rewrite it for publication the following fall. Now that would be impossible. My typewriter – the only one I felt comfortable with – was a charred ruin.

The real estate agent in the Algarve sympathized. She said she had a typewriter I could borrow for the two-week stay. I was grateful but suspicious. What kind of a typewriter? When she returned with the machine, my heart sank. My God, it was a Hermes Baby, an eight-pound midget, brother to the one I'd carried about in my big pack during my four years in the Canadian army and later in Korea. I loathed everything about it, but what could I do? Lie in the sun for the next fortnight? That, it occurs to me now, would have been a sensible and healthy course. But I was too wound up for that. The new book was already running through my head. I had to get it onto paper, and so I gritted my teeth and began to clack away on the wretched Hermes, even though my fingers were too big for the keys, thereby worsening my already limited two-finger typing skills.

Drifting Home is my shortest book. I managed to get a draft on paper in two weeks, working away each morning, relaxing each afternoon. The results were indecipherable to anyone but me, but when I got home, I translated it (thanks to another Smith-Corona) into a final draft.

The book surprised me by outselling almost everything on the market that fall. At three autographings in Calgary, I signed, in one afternoon, twelve hundred copies. The critics tended to carp. Several, including *Time*'s, dismissed it as "a mere potboiler." One reviewer, true to prediction, wrote that "Berton has decided to tell us how he spent his summer holidays." Yet today I am constantly told that this is my best book. The reason, perhaps, is that it is the most personal. It is still in print and still selling.

I too tended to think of *Drifting Home* as a potboiler. I wanted to do something more substantial, something with weight that hadn't been done before. But what? As an old movie buff I had once rushed to see *The Far Country,* which allegedly dealt with the Klondike gold rush. I was bitterly disappointed and irked, too, that it had badly distorted the story of the stampede, turning it into another shoot-'em-up Western, complete with the usual cattle drive and James Stewart in white cowboy hat and gun belt. Everything was wrong about that picture, just as everything was wrong with Cecil B. DeMille's *North West Mounted Police,* made on a Hollywood back lot, and *Canadian Pacific,* with another white-hatted cowboy, Randolph Scott, running the CPR.

I had my subject: a look at how Hollywood movies had distorted the Canadian image. I would steep myself in research for what I was convinced would be a better and more significant work than *Drifting Home.* My new assistant, Barbara Sears, herself a movie buff and former film archivist, would find the films and set up the projectors for me and get the scripts or synopses for those that had vanished. Out of that I would produce a magnum opus.

It didn't work out that way. *Hollywood's Canada* was not the raving success I had expected. Film buffs liked it, but my regular audience was not interested. I now think it needed a lighter touch; I took the subject far too seriously. But even so I doubt that it would have been a best-seller. *Drifting Home* outsold it five to one, and that doesn't include the many paperbacks and foreign sales. An author can never assess his own work and probably shouldn't try.

6

The Global Television network was the brainchild of a hotshot salesman named Al Bruner, a man of considerable ambition who had been a joke in the television industry until July 1972, when the CRTC gave him a licence to establish a third network in Ontario. A few months later he walked into my office, a likeable, pudgy broadcaster, boiling over with enthusiasm.

"I came to dialogue with you," he said, briefly removing the cigar from his cheek. Bruner always talked in the argot of his trade. He was trying to persuade everybody, including me, that there was room for another TV outlet in Toronto. Did we really need it? Toronto already had six, with seven more leaking across the border. But Bruner was irrepressible. He would dispense with the traditional network of individual stations and, instead, buy shelf space through a grid of transmitters from a single broadcasting source. He was convinced he could lure back the advertising lost to Buffalo, and, with only eight minutes of commercial time an hour instead of the standard twelve, attract viewers. A decade earlier, his plan had looked like pure science fiction. By April 1973, with two Anik satellites in orbit, it would be feasible.

So here he was, explaining, with great enthusiasm, how he planned to buy more than twenty new programs from independent producers – including Elsa and me.

"You guys can do anything you want," he said. "I'm giving you a free hand. You produce me a show; I'll buy it unseen. I've got faith."

It was a tempting offer, and it came at the right moment. My television show was in its eleventh year. When it ended in March 1973, we had produced 1,650 half-hour programs in addition to the original 160 full hours. We were now seen on twenty-two Canadian channels. We were identified as "the program that comes to you from the major capitals of the world" – twenty-three cities in a dozen countries. I felt that I'd seen about as much of the world as I needed, that I didn't care if I visited another museum, temple, synagogue, cathedral, or nightclub. It had been a hectic, maddening, exhilarating, exhausting period, but now

354

I wanted out, wanted to stay home, wanted a less demanding schedule, wanted more time with my family and more time to write my books – especially books of narrative history. The bug had bitten me as a result of *The National Dream,* and the bite had gone deep.

I wanted to do something different. By now I had interviewed most of the prominent figures of my times – poets and politicians, tycoons and troublemakers, fanatics, rock stars, crusaders, novelists, movie greats – celebrities all.

I could look back on some memorable moments. There was, for instance, my encounter with John Creasey, the world's most prolific author. This cheerful Englishman thought nothing of turning out twenty-two mystery novels *a year.* When I met him in the London Westbury Hotel, he had written more than four hundred and fifty novels. We talked a bit about how he got his ideas and I noticed him looking closely at my shirt. "Most shirt buttons have four holes," he said. "I notice yours have only three. Now suppose a corpse is found grasping a three-holed button? That could easily be the start of a mystery novel." After we had finished, Creasey sat quietly in the lobby; he had a couple of hours to wait for his train, while I conducted other interviews. At the end of the day he was still there, scribbling away on a notepad. What was he writing? "Oh, I'm working on the novel about the shirt with three-holed buttons," he told me, jovially.

I remember interviewing Malcolm X, the black activist, in Toronto. He had just broken with his leader, Elijah Muhammad; that and a recent trip to the Middle East had affected him profoundly. He seemed to me to be two men – a fiery orator on the platform but a quiet-spoken, moderate, and reasonable man in private. The break with the Muslims seemed to me to have changed him, but I had no way of confirming that because a month later an assassin's bullet ended his career.

And then there was Sugar Ray Robinson, perhaps the greatest prizefighter, pound for pound, in the history of boxing, who was so troubled by claustrophobia that he refused to take the elevator to my makeshift studio on the roof of the Hyatt in Los Angeles. He ran up the entire seventeen storeys, took his seat at my table, and replied to my questions – not the slightest bit winded by his long climb.

I had met them all, everybody from the secretary of the British Flat Earth Society to the Maharishi Mahesh Yogi. I encountered some as they scrambled up the slippery ladder – Mary Quant, Bruce Lee, Anne

Murray – and others as they tumbled back down – Dick Haymes, Diana Dors, Busby Berkeley. I talked to the forgotten pop heroes. Who now remembers Murray the K, Screaming Lord Sutch, or Mr. Fish? Most important, I talked to those men and women who, by their actions or opinions, helped to delineate my times: Jesse Jackson, Jerry Rubin, Abby Hoffman, Germaine Greer, Alger Hiss, René Lévesque, Daniel Cohn-Bendit.

Most were voluble and forthcoming, partly because one of Elsa's staff interviewed them in advance to make sure they weren't the type to clam up in front of the cameras. Once in a while we boobed. Terry Southern, who was best known for co-authoring an early pornographic novel, *Lollipop,* and for working on the script of Stanley Kubrick's *Dr. Strangelove,* appeared to be asleep when I interviewed him. He replied to my questions in monosyllables and I thought at one point he would pass out in front of the cameras.

Stan Getz, the acclaimed jazz saxophonist, was no better. He, too, was quite clearly stoned. The opening encounter went something like this:

ME: Stan, I guess you must have had some interesting experiences doing one-night stands, travelling with the band on the bus and playing a new gig every night. Tell me, what was the craziest night you ever spent on the road?

GETZ: Yeah, well, you know, man, it was like, cool, you know, yeah, kinda cool.

At this point I realized I was stuck with this guest for a full hour. To this day, I have no idea how I got through it.

Eddie Condon, the jazz guitarist who had overstayed Ross McLean's wedding party, arrived in our Toronto studio considerably the worse for wear. The night before, Richard Gehman, the freelance writer (known as "the Typewriter" because he was constantly at work on a dozen articles, each in its own typewriter), and I had taken him out pub-crawling. By midnight, when none of us was feeling any pain, Condon stumbled on the stairs of the old Four Seasons Hotel on Jarvis Street and bashed in his face. Gehman and I rushed him to Wellesley Hospital for treatment. Dick, who was working on a book about Condon, was certain he was going to die and began to sob openly in the hall of the emergency ward in the belief that he had killed his friend. But Condon recovered,

356

arrived at our studio the following morning, and proceeded to lie flat on the floor of the make-up room, where arriving guests stepped gingerly across his body. We woke him for the show, which started off something like this:

ME: Eddie, there's a question I've always wanted to ask you, though I'm sure it's been asked before. It is this: How come, in all your years with your own band, you never took a solo?
EDDIE: Well, y'see, it was farnster 'n' raxpid to validash the resporsful frnst.

Well, we lost that one. Budget or no budget, it couldn't be broadcast.

And I will not soon forget my interview with the great Jack Dempsey. I could not take my eyes off his huge hands, the knuckles scarred and battered by scores of bouts. It seemed to me, in this case, that the hands told the story, and so I asked our director, a new man named Merle, if he'd got lots of shots of Dempsey's hands.

"You want hands?" said Merle. "You shoulda told me. I didn't know you wanted hands."

I thought Elsa would lose her cool, but we kept our heads and did not strangle him. Our next guest was the buxom Jayne Mansfield. When I ran a bit of the tape I noticed that Merle rarely showed her most prominent features but concentrated entirely on her hands.

"But you said you *wanted* hands," he said reproachfully. What could I do? Other guests were waiting. If I put Merle out of business with a well-placed Dempsey-like blow, we couldn't do the show. But close shots of the Mansfield *hands?*

Merle did not stay with us very long after that.

The television interview, especially the kind I did – a full half hour without any editing – was an entirely new form of communication. In the very early days when I worked on *Close-Up,* we were all disciples of Mike Wallace, whose hard-hitting and often embarrassing encounters with the famous and the infamous were the talk of the medium. Wallace went for the jugular and we tried to ape him, with varying results. But you can't be a tough guy five nights a week. The audience requires a change of pace. With some exceptions I tried to establish a rapport with my guests. This was especially true of actresses unaccustomed to playing themselves, who were often skittish and sometimes plain terrified.

357

In these cases a TV interview resembles a seduction. The interviewer becomes a con man whose job is both to keep his quarry at ease and to boost his confidence, rather like a snake-oil salesman convincing the mark that he's his best friend.

We usually produced six half hours a day out of town (sometimes as many as eight), with only a fifteen-minute interlude between each one. In that time I had to change my jacket, shirt, and tie in order to preserve the illusion that we weren't churning out programs like baloney. That left me with five minutes to establish an affinity with absolute strangers so they would feel at ease when the camera lights winked on. In my off hours I screened their films, went to see their plays, skimmed through their books so that I could tell them how extraordinary they were. That was not hard since I was interested in talking to extraordinary people – ones whom I genuinely admired and liked. A good television interview should provide more than information and entertainment; it should, above all, be revelatory. As a TV host I had an advantage over print or radio journalists because the camera provided an extra dimension to our encounters. There is no such thing as "dead air" in a TV interview. The long pauses in which the camera moves in to examine the features of the subject are sometimes more important than mere words. I remember asking Lucille Ball whether it was difficult for her to continue with *I Love Lucy* when the man who played her husband was, in real life, writing finis to their marriage. In the long pause that followed, a variety of emotions played across her face. I waited. Finally, she said, "Yes. It was difficult. Very." But she had already answered my question with that long silence.

Except for the handful who became close friends, I never really knew my guests. Some I cannot even remember. Somebody asked me not long ago about my interview with Deborah Kerr. I didn't recall I'd done it. That is the way with television: you meet the most interesting people, but oh, so briefly! They are ushered in minutes before the lights go up. I do my con man act to settle them down. "Hurry!" cries the producer. Valuable seconds are ticking away – valuable for me because the schedule is always tight, valuable for my guests because people who appear on TV are always in a rush.

The lights go on. The camera begins to record our encounter. We appear on the screen as old friends, calling each other by our first names as if we dine together every other week. As the interviews progress, they become eager to discuss the most intimate details of their lives – their lost loves, their sessions with their analysts, their hopes, dreams, fears, suspicions. Then the camera's red light winks off and they vanish into the twilight. "Hurry!" the press agent calls; a limousine awaits at the studio entrance, its engine purring, its door already ajar. We murmur our swift goodbyes, vow to meet again, and vanish from each other's sight. "Hurry!" somebody else calls. Another guest, whom I have scarcely met, is being led to the set. The lights go up, I switch mental gears, and another encounter begins.

There were some guests I would have liked to know better, such as John D. MacDonald, my favourite mystery writer, author of the Travis McGee stories. That was not possible. We were like two ships passing in the night. He had come to New York, he told me over a drink in the Algonquin bar, for two reasons, "First, to appear on your show, and second, to personally serve a writ in a damage suit against the president of American Express." His credit card had been accidentally cancelled, causing him great embarrassment in a tony restaurant. He could hardly wait, he chuckled, to see the look on the credit card mogul's face when he walked into his office with the writ. We got along famously, but when the interview ended he departed for Miami and I for Toronto. I never did learn how the suit turned out.

Television interviews are a form of play acting. We stare into each other's eyes, my guest and I, establishing an artificial intimacy. Although we seem to be talking to one another, we are really playing to an unseen gallery. I must conquer my natural shyness to fit into the role of the all-knowledgeable, incisive journalist. The man or woman in the guest seat has a personal part to perform: witty conversationalist, dedicated do-gooder, hard-hitting opinion-maker, candid commentator, big-time star. We are playing "let's pretend" like the characters in *The Secret World of Og,* but without costumes, unless you count a bow tie or a pair of faded blue jeans.

Television intrudes on our lives, confusing everybody. The face on the screen becomes eerily familiar. When people pass me on the street I often catch a look of confusion on their features. They know me, but they can't place me. "Hi there!" they say, unsure of who I am, but certain they've encountered me somewhere before. But where? At a party? A luncheon? A business meeting? I can see the puzzlement in their eyes. But then I am never sure who *they* are, either. They have greeted me with a familiar "Hi there!" Is it possible that they are old and valued friends whom I've forgotten? Have I unwittingly snubbed a former acquaintance? Or are they simply members of that unseen audience, trying to figure out, in passing, where they saw me last?

The number of continuing acquaintances I made as a result of a decade of television could be numbered on two hands. The most enduring were the unknowns: Mary Carpenter, the Inuit girl from Sachs Harbour; Suzanne Moss, a cerebral palsy victim whom I helped with a book; Monk Adams, the London barrow boy. There were also a few professionals, more or less in my own field, whose company I enjoyed: Dick "the Typewriter" Gehman, the engaging writer; Al Capp, the comic strip genius; Alan Abel, the professional hoaxer; Jim Moran, the New York publicist; Art Buchwald.

I was never under any illusion about why the program continued on the air; if it hadn't been for the CRTC and its insistence on the 55-percent content rule, there would have been no *Pierre Berton Show.* As I wrote at the time, without that rule some Canadian TV stations would not even have bothered to report the news. On two occasions when I interviewed the prime minister, more than one station baulked because I promised Pearson we'd do the show without intrusive "messages"; they hated to lose the revenue. Even when we offered them that program without fee there were complaints. "I can't figure out this cockamamie country," Herb Sussan exclaimed the first time this occurred. "Imagine what would happen in the U.S. if a station got an exclusive hour with the president. Why, there'd be dancing in the streets!"

On the other hand, in those days I'd been able to tackle subjects in greater depth than interviewers below the border, especially in those week-long series into various topics ranging from women's liberation to the plight of the aboriginals, and, most recently, the trials of the new wave of immigrants I called "The Bewildered Canadians." These had been watershed years, and I had tried to reflect my times through the voices of those most intimately involved.

Now the times were changing again, and it behooved me to make a change of my own. Al Bruner had given me the impetus. I told Screen Gems that it would be my last year. Danny Enright expressed dismay but, of course, had no intention of cancelling a lucrative show. It became *The Fred Davis Show* and after that *The Larry Solway Show.* Nobody is indispensable.

Elsa and I had the summer and fall to come up with a program for the new Global network, which Bruner was planning to launch in January 1974. Actually, we came up with two and he went for both. The first, *My Country,* would make use of my story-telling abilities, sharpened over several years on *The Pierre Berton Show.* It was a simple proposition. I would appear on a specially designed set and, with a few artifacts and pictures, ad-lib from a set of notes the liveliest stories we could dig up from the past. There was no dearth of these: they ranged from the tragic tale of the lost Franklin expedition to the story of Mina Hubbard's pioneer race across Labrador at the turn of the century. We produced fifty-two. Most were then virtually unknown to our audience. Since that time, a remarkable number have become the subjects of full-length books. Indeed, I produced two anthologies of my own, rewriting the best of the lot.

The second program was *The Great Debate,* a no-holds-barred debate between two public figures on a subject of national or international importance, staged before a live audience in a studio theatre in Yorkville. It lasted an hour – partly formal debate, partly ad-lib discussion, partly audience participation. Some of the topics we covered during the eight years of the program's life give an insight into what people were talking about in the seventies: *Resolved,* that the monarchy should be abandoned; that all women should have the right to abortion; that nuclear reactors are necessary; that prostitution should be legalized; that Israel should recognize the PLO; that living together before marriage is a dangerous experience; that modern churches discriminate against women; that the traditional family unit is outdated; that bisexuality is normal; that sex education should begin in Grade 1.

Some of these subjects sound old hat today, but several had not then been debated on TV. Geraldo and Oprah were still in the future. We were able to lure to Toronto public figures who would not generally have taken the time to come: William F. Buckley, Jr., Ralph Nader, Benjamin Spock, Germaine Greer, Edward Teller, Ann Landers. Besides these there was a host of Canadian notables. It was remarkable, to me at least, how few really understood the art of parliamentary debate, apparently a lost art in North America. The English were better at it; the best, not surprisingly, was a team of students from the Oxford Union, who were cheerfully prepared to take any side we offered them.

Global was launched on time to a blast of fanfare. Bruner had managed the remarkable feat of putting twenty-three new and original shows on the air, all but one Canadian. Most were produced on a shoestring but were, as the critics pronounced, a welcome change from the usual fare. The only clunker was Global's own production *Anything Goes,* a copy-cat late-night talk show starring an American second banana named Norm Crosby.

Bruner was ecstatic. "I came out of show business," he kept reminding everybody. "I'm a producer. I felt all the frustrations of not being able to get on the tube. Programming is what it's all about. You're dog-gone right that the office of the president is concerned with programming. The rest is just incidental, just mechanics."

It was all too good to be true. The programs were lively, but they didn't pay the bills. Inexpensive as they were, they still cost too much. Bruner was never concerned about the budget. When Elsa or I asked him for something for the program, we got it, even when his own people told him he couldn't afford it. Like Jack McClelland, he put the product first, the profits second.

There were other problems. Cable TV was in its infancy, but most of Bruner's viewers could get Global only on cable, which cost them money. His worst move, however, was his decision to go on air in mid-season. Viewing patterns were set by that time, and, worse, advertising budgets had already been made up. Yet Bruner couldn't wait until the following fall – overhead was already eating into his revenue. It takes time for any new program to attract viewers, and he had twenty-three to worry about. His early ratings were so small they couldn't be measured.

I had learned something about the "cheque in the mail" syndrome from my brief, unfortunate experience as a producer of my own radio show. Now I sensed trouble. Payments slowed and finally stopped. Global owed us more than fifty thousand dollars but was evading our attempts to collect. Our offices were in the Lord Simcoe Hotel. I called in Ennis and told her to go up to the Global headquarters in North York and insist on getting *something*. She was away for the rest of the day but finally returned with a cheque for twenty-five thousand. I told her to deposit it at once.

The following day, Global went bankrupt. There were long faces at the creditors' meeting when it was realized we'd be lucky to get ten cents on the dollar. Yet so valuable was the Toronto franchise that other broadcasters were lining up to buy it cheap. Bruner, of course, was

362

finished; he lost everything, including his house. The successful bidders got Global free of debt, which meant the rest of us could whistle for our money. The new boss was Al Slaight, whom I had known when he was in charge of programming at CHUM. Bruner, in his enthusiasm, had contracted for one run only of *The Great Debate*. I told Slaight he could have the entire first season of re-runs for a fee equal to what we were owed. It was a bargain for both of us. We were off the hook; he had a summer of programs at very low cost.

That June Global announced its fall schedule. Fifteen of the new shows that Bruner had so triumphantly launched were gone. The survivors included *My Country* and *The Great Debate*. In place of the discarded programs, Global would run three hours of movies every night and maintain the bulk of its mandatory Canadian content with two hours of nightly news. Thus did Al Bruner's vision fade quietly away.

Chapter Thirteen

1

We look back on the sixties as a decade of turmoil, of causes lost and won, of social upheaval, of draft dodgers, and of a new understanding of human values. But social change rarely fits neatly into prescribed periods. In Canada, the restless era we call "the sixties" would carry over into the early seventies.

We imported from the United States two sixties controversies that had little to do with Canada – the furore over the Vietnam War and the confrontations in the South. Young Canadian activists seemed more concerned with the plight of American blacks than they were about the appalling conditions facing Canadian Indians. In this country the issues in which I was involved – censorship, civil liberties, heritage preservation, native rights, and, above all, nationalism (including the Quebec variety) – did not reach their height after until the sixties ended.

I made a great many speeches in the seventies. I was by this time as glib a public speaker as any politician, almost as glib, in fact, as my "Dialogue" adversary, the eloquent Charles Templeton, who acted as the whetstone on which I honed my technique. At times I became a rabble rouser. I remember once turning up at a United church on Edmonton's south side to exhort an audience of three hundred to organize a protest march and picket the Alberta legislature, which was trying to frustrate a native land rights claim.

I became a joiner of activist committees – everything from the Save the Crystal Gardens Committee in Victoria to the Canadian Committee for the Scientific Investigation of the Paranormal, which might be called the "We Don't Believe in Ghosts Committee."

I went to Niagara Falls as a member of the Canadian Civil Liberties Association to protest an unconscionable raid by fifty-three policemen, allegedly searching for drugs in a Fort Erie motel. These searches were typical of the decade. The slightest suspicion that anyone was using marijuana drove the police to a furious defence of the status quo. At the Landmark Motor Inn, this huge force of blue coats frisked 115 patrons, including 36 young women and girls, in what Alan Borovoy, the CCLA counsel, called "an exercise in gratuitous voyeurism." I remember Judy LaMarsh exclaiming to the protest meeting, "Why did the police think that each woman was carrying drugs in her natural orifices?" But under the federal Narcotics Control Act, the police had the right to enter any

366

public place without a warrant if they merely suspected that drugs were present, and the same law allowed them to search anybody on a whim. "It's time to change this silly, old-fashioned, outdated, monstrous law," I said, working myself up to high dudgeon. I then presented a resolution demanding an independent public inquiry into the affair. Of course, there was nothing of the kind.

I was even more horrified by the government's implementation of the archaic War Measures Act in the so-called October Crisis in Quebec, which touched off the decade. The following morning on "Dialogue," Charles Templeton insisted that we must "trust Trudeau." After all, the prime minister had warned of an "apprehended insurrection," and, Charles declared, we were duty bound to take his word for that. I refused to go along. The next day Charles reversed himself and agreed that the government was using a blunderbuss to swat a mosquito. But at a party that evening everybody except me thought we ought to trust the prime minister. The government kept hinting that there were secrets it couldn't reveal at the time and that the whole story would soon come out. That, as it developed, was hokum.

Later, when tempers had cooled and the arrogance of the government's action became clear, I seconded a motion at a Civil Liberties meeting demanding a royal commission inquiry. Whose homes had been searched? Who had been jailed without charge and without the age-old right of habeas corpus? Many of those were thrown into jail in the dark of the night simply because they were political opponents of the party in power. As I said at the meeting, "I don't like charging people with belonging to an organization that they didn't even know was illegal when they went to jail." Of course, there never was an inquiry, nor has there ever been any believable explanation as to why the War Measures Act needed to be invoked.

What was bothering me during this period was the use of arbitrary power by the establishment to choke off debate, to ride roughshod over the rights of ordinary citizens, be they native or non-native, to withhold essential information, and to stifle creativity. Here was my old paper, the Toronto Star, going through one of its periods of solemn-faced morality, urging that motion picture censorship be tightened, and naming two horrible examples of turpitude, A Clockwork Orange and The Godfather. When I wrote to the paper saying I didn't want any group of civil servants telling me or my family what we should see on the screen, I was attacked through a barrage of furious letters upholding the principle of movie censorship. People must be "protected against certain subversive or blasphemous or immoral influences," I was told; if some brake were not put on freedom of expression, society would surely degenerate. I fought back in print. "A society," I wrote, "truly degenerates in direct ratio to the number of censors a country suffers."

It seems ludicrous now that Canada's largest and most liberal paper would be citing Stanley Kubrick's trend-setting film and Francis Ford Coppola's brilliant saga to demand stronger censorship. But my own experience with controversial views about sex and religion had taught me, as I wrote, that "yesterday's blasphemy becomes today's cant; last week's heresy becomes this week's orthodoxy."

I had myself put money into one film that was mangled by the Ontario Censor Board. This was Alan King's *A Married Couple,* in which a cinema verité technique was used to explore the domestic life of two people. The censor, O.J. Silverthorne (whom I always referred to as "Silvershears"), was appalled at the number of four-letter words used by the pair during their domestic arguments. There were about thirty – a small enough number in these days of cinematic frankness. The censor wanted to reduce the number to about a dozen, and King now found himself bartering dirty words like a rug salesman in an Algerian souk. When he pleaded to be allowed to keep a couple of F-words, Silvershears would offer one more F-word if he'd drop two S-words. But he stonewalled when King pleaded for a C-word. "That's an insult to women!" Silvershears cried. In the end King was allowed twenty of the wicked words. "Presumably," I wrote in *Toronto Life,* "the audience would not be depraved by this number. But how did Mr. Silvershears, or anybody else, know what that number would be?"

We were not yet a closed society in the Silly Seventies, and not really in danger from that kind of authoritarianism, but a remarkable number of people failed to remember or understand the bit about eternal vigilance being the price of liberty. I had, of course, been able to see personal liberty reined in and often stamped upon, from Mexico to Moscow. In 1976 I was about to witness the process from yet another point of view when the Canadian government arranged for Jack and Elizabeth McClelland, Janet and me to visit the People's Republic of China. No F-words for the Reds – and that was the least of their restrictions.

2

The culture shock began in Tokyo the moment we boarded the airline *The land* of the People's Republic. We had just come zooming across the Pacific *of Mao* on a jet whose flight attendants seemed to have been worked over by Max Factor, Vidal Sassoon, and Edith Head. Now we handed our boarding passes to a young woman who wore her straight black hair chopped short and dressed in a loose blouse and shapeless pantaloons. There was no hint of make-up and nothing bourgeois like a brooch, ring, or barrette in evidence. And this was the way it was for the next fortnight in the puritan world of Mao Tse-tung (the new spelling had not yet been adopted). In all that time we did not see so much as a wedding ring.

Ahead of us, the vast bulk of Mao's personal fiefdom loomed out of the murk. Below us was Shanghai, vying with Tokyo for the title of world's most populous city. An hour later we reached Peking. These vast human hives were almost as dark as the far side of the moon – scarcely a glimmer of neon and none of the fairy-tale glitter of Toronto or Montreal at night. On the long ride to our hotel we saw no other private cars, only hordes of bicycles silently slipping through the dark.

Like all tourists at that time, the four of us were treated as VIPs, assigned to first-class hotels reserved exclusively for foreigners, and trundled about in private cars with guides and interpreters – from the Ming tombs to the Great Wall, from agricultural commune to ivory factory – on a schedule so packed that it made us dizzy.

The Chinese had come as close as anyone to devising a classless society. If there was a bourgeoisie, it was composed of "tourists" like ourselves, enjoying brief, intense periods of luxury in an ocean of austerity. We were whisked through customs with the briefest of formalities, given the best seats at the theatres, fed meals that few Chinese could afford, and followed everywhere by curious crowds. When Liz McClelland stopped on the street to change a film in her camera, no fewer than two hundred people crowded around to gawk. "Now I know how the queen feels during a royal tour," Janet remarked.

The first thing that hit us was the ubiquity of Mao. His gigantic portrait stared impassively from a hundred vantage points. His monumental effigy – in bronze, stone, concrete, marble – dominated the portals of public buildings. His poems were reproduced in his own calligraphy on gigantic scrolls. And his "thoughts," fashioned in huge characters of

369

white plastic on brilliant backgrounds of Chinese red, appeared at every important intersection, as well as on the walls of hotels, hospitals, schools, airports, and every other public structure of prominence. The jungle of signs and billboards that once gave cities like Shanghai a special flavour had been extirpated. Mao's words and Mao's likeness stood alone.

Was he loved, I wondered, as the late premier, Chou En-lai, was loved? More venerated than loved, I thought. I had seen the photographs of Chou's recent lying-in-state produced on billboards about the city; such an expression of personal grief I would never have believed possible. Here were scenes of his people filing past the body, tears coursing down their cheeks, expressions of genuine distress distorting their features. No rent-a-crowd could have produced such visible anguish. Chou was human, Mao a god.

The Chinese we met quoted Mao in conversation as fundamentalists in our world would quote the Old Testament. Within a few days we found ourselves lapsing into the jargon, saying "Chairman Mao" even to ourselves, while phrases like the "Great Proletarian Cultural Revolution" tripped easily off our tongues. It was impossible to escape Mao's philosophy because it dominated everything we experienced, even to the children's musical performances.

In Shanghai we watched a group of brightly costumed eight-year-olds perform a spirited dance with great precision and aplomb. An interpreter gave us the jawbreaking title: *Dance to Beat Back Right Deviationist Trends to Reverse Correct Verdict.* It was, in short, an attack on the three villains of modern China, Liu-Shao-ch'i, Lin Piao, and most recent and greatest villain of all, Teng Hsiao-p'ing (now known as Deng Xiaoping). Who could have believed then that this wizened old man, a former party vice-chairman who was condemned for turning the land of Mao from the path of righteousness, would end up at the top of the political heap?

We finally saw one children's playlet that seemed entirely non-political. Here were tiny moppets dressed like honey-bees, buzzing around a huge hive, singing and dancing. A large bear entered, and I had visions of a Chinese version of Goldilocks. But when the bees danced away it soon became clear that the bear had an evil purpose, sneaking off with the honey the bees had worked so hard to produce. It slowly dawned on me exactly who the bear was supposed to represent. Just to make it clear, one of the bees uttered a moral: "We'll not rely on others... The great bear is not powerful if we dare to wage a struggle against him." During our stay we heard more than one reference to "the bear" and Mao's dictum that the Chinese must not depend on others.

The only billboards I saw that did not refer to Mao carried pictures of the Canadian doctor Norman Bethune. His picture and his books were sold in every bookstore. In the schoolrooms we watched children colouring his likeness. "You are here because of Bethune," we were told by one of our embassy's people. Everywhere we went, specially coloured posters with Chinese characters greeted us with the phrase, "Welcome friends of the home town of Dr. Norman Bethune." It made us feel slightly uncomfortable, but, as Jack McClelland pointed out, it wasn't entirely inaccurate since his summer cottage in Muskoka was only a few miles from the Bethune birthplace at Gravenhurst.

Many of the Chinese we met who headed communes, factories, hospitals, and other institutions were women. Here, we learned quickly, the female of the species was no longer a sex object. In fact, sex seemed to be the missing ingredient in the Chinese mix. The country was so earnest, so evangelistic, so puritanical, that after a few days we longed for just one sidelong feminine glance, one slit skirt, one advertising sign featuring a beckoning model.

Music, played incessantly from hidden speakers in the rice paddies and cow barns of the communes, was strictly political. There were no love songs in the Chinese version of the Top Fifty. Every form of art – painting, literature, opera – was harnessed to the service of Mao's version of Marxism. China had no time for detective stories, abstract painting, or lyric poetry. When I asked a writer in Shanghai whether he wrote any love poetry, he looked baffled. Political poetry, he said; nobody in China writes love poetry.

In the beautifully executed illustrations on the posters, every single person – from tractor driver to farmer – was shown smiling toothily. There was something very familiar about these paintings of smiling people. Where had I seen such pictures before? Suddenly I had the answer: they looked exactly liked the old magazine ads showing happy customers holding bottles of Labatt's 50.

One scene at the university in Peking stands out in my mind. We were being guided through an interminable information display designed to demonstrate Mao's new educational policy following the Cultural

Revolution. Our guide stopped before a photograph of a venerable Chinese. This was Feng Yu-lan, who had devoted his life to the study of Confucius. But since the Cultural Revolution, Confucius had been under bitter attack because, the young people were being told, he had wanted to preserve the status of the old "feudal" society. Our guide praised the old scholar because he had seen the error of his ways, recanted, and denounced Confucius and everything his philosophy stood for. But as I listened to the guide's enthusiastic words I could feel only sadness at the spectacle of this eighty-two-year-old scholar admitting to the public (if not to himself) that his entire career had been, in effect, a dreadful waste. China had its own Galileos.

There was a good deal of talk about the Cultural Revolution. One of our guides had taken part as a Red Guard, dashing from town to town, proclaiming Mao's revealed truth, harbouring no doubts. He was a dedicated evangelist, and as he talked about the acceptance of "correct" attitudes and the long exercises in self-criticism at the evening meetings, I was reminded of Charles Templeton's days in the evangelical movement in Toronto in the 1940s. Charles told me his world, too, revolved around endless prayer meetings and religious discussions. All forms of worldliness – dances, movies, make-up, personal adornment – were totally rejected.

It struck me then that all the things in Western life that we profess to loathe, but secretly love – commercialism, sexual freedom, the hard sell, personal ambition, cut-throat competition, lust for fame, materialism – had no place in Mao's society. The Chinese admire Bethune because of his absolute selflessness. It was a word one heard constantly in China. Mao's thoughts on the gigantic posters exalted the Calvinistic work ethic. The lack of adornment and the shapeless, dun-coloured clothing were a defence against the sins of the flesh; premarital sex carried an unbearable social stigma; extra-marital sex was punishable by law (but birth control was encouraged). Tipping, happily, was impossible in China and theft rare.

It is, I know, a dreadful confession to make, but I found myself missing the tinsel commercialism of the West. Chinese cities were even more austere than Toronto was in 1947. If you could have widened Hogtown's main streets, replaced all private automobiles with bicycles, done away with every commercial billboard, neon sign, and brand name, and then have placed biblical quotations in gigantic letters at every major intersection, you'd have had a Canadian approximation of Peking as I saw it then.

The Chinese were touchingly proud of all this and had developed a stock routine for showing off their country to visitors. For all of our stay we were subjected to earnest lectures, fuelled by a torrent of statistics. These took place in draughty rooms where the upholstered sofas and armchairs (with lace doilies on the backs) were arranged in a hollow square, and the low tables held tea, cigarettes, pencil, and paper. We were expected to take notes, to ply our hosts with questions (which often brought ponderous answers running for more than half an hour), and to offer criticism of what we had heard and seen.

We were too polite to criticize. We were there to learn and not to carp. Besides, how could we criticize a country that, after centuries of decadence and corruption, was trying to put into practice all the copybook maxims we had learned at our mothers' knees? The mass of the people might or might not be as deliriously happy as the Labatt's-style posters suggested, but they were clearly better off than at any time in their long history. They might not be "free" in the Western sense, since they could no more question the orthodoxy of Chairman Mao than a fifteenth-century European could have safely questioned the doctrines of the church. But at least they were free of starvation, endemic disease, the horrors of the opium trade, and the humiliation visited upon them by centuries of foreign and domestic exploitation. We thought about that, too, as we boarded the train in Shanghai for the day voyage that would take us to the shrine of that other Chinese deity, the Canadian doctor Norman Bethune.

3

EN ROUTE BY TRAIN FROM SHANGHAI TO SHIHKIACHWANG, Mr. Yu
June 1976. "Tell me about your literary circle," Mr. Yu says, as he picks with his chopsticks at his crispy fish, pickled duck, and beef with lotus root.

We are crossing the great North China Plain, heading for the little community that has become a shrine to Dr. Norman Bethune. Hidden speakers leak out the Chinese equivalent of Muzak – the theme song from a popular movie, significantly but awkwardly titled "Breaking with New Ideas." Through the window the countryside unwinds in fascinating

373

detail, like – well, like a Chinese scroll: little walled villages, bare-legged peasants in broad straw hats, bicycles, army trucks, water buffalo and camels hauling loads of cabbages, firewood, old machinery, straw, pottery, and sacking.

My literary circle? *Do I belong to a literary circle? Does anyone? The phrase grates on my ear. I suppose I could tell him about picketing the Coles bookstore, but I don't think that's what he wants. Or maybe the Stephen Leacock dinner where, at my prodding, Farley Mowat raised his kilt and mooned the audience. Or the Montreal Book Fair, where one member (female) of our literary circle leapt, mother-naked, into the Hotel Bonaventure's pool, and another member (me) engaged in fisticuffs with an obstreperous novelist.*

"Your literary circle," says the thirty-six-year-old Yu Shao-jung, looking at me over his spectacles, "what is it that you discuss?" He is the official translator assigned to us VIPs; he has been with us throughout our tour, first in Peking (Great Wall, Forbidden City, Peking Duck Restaurant), then in Shanghai (ivory factory, collective farm, bicycle factory, theatrical performance, "typical" school). He is insatiably curious about life in Canada. How do I spend my day? How do I go about writing a book? What exactly is a Gallup Poll? He writes down the answers in a small notebook. "Not just for me," he explains. "It will, of course, help to make me a better interpreter; one must understand each country, you see, but I must also share my knowledge with my comrades at the tourist office."

Now he wants to know what goes on within my literary circle. I look across at Jack and note the ghost of a smile on his lips.

"Well," I finally tell the eager Mr. Yu, "mainly, I guess, we talk about money. You know – how the publishers are screwing us with lousy contracts, how the agents are taking too much, how nobody is spending enough on publicity, how the libraries are stiffing us by making more on fines than we do on royalties. That sort of thing."

Mr. Yu looks startled. What has he been expecting – an analysis of Proust? I decide not to tell him about Project Porno.

"Money," says Mr. Yu to himself. "You talk about money." He does not change expression, nor is there even a hint of censure in his voice, yet I feel slightly soiled. How crass we must seem to him, how vulgar! Yes, and how obscenely free.

Mr. Yu's job is to explain the new China to us – a land where all

374

citizens, no matter what their stations, must spend at least sixty days a year doing manual labour among the ordinary people. This, Mr. Yu tells us, is Mao's plan to forestall the growth of an intellectual and bureaucratic class. It is, of course, foredoomed, as it would be in Canada. I contemplate, not without a certain grim amusement, the spectacle of the Honourable Judd Buchanan picking rice with the Indians of Northern Ontario, or Bryce Mackasey carrying the mail through snow and sleet for two months.

Mr. Yu explains that this is the result of the Great Proletarian Cultural Revolution. His talk is peppered with such phrases and always with the same adjectives. Mao's leadership is always "Chairman Mao's wise leadership"; Mao's essay on Bethune is always "Chairman Mao's brilliant essay"; and when Mr. Yu talks about the people of the Third World, it is always in terms of "the just struggle of the Third World peoples for independence."

Who is it that Mr. Yu calls to mind? Not a person, I decide, but a type: the enthusiastic, proselytizing, born-again Christian fundamentalist. Chairman Mao is his personal saviour; Marxism is his religion. There is something engaging about this serious, bespectacled young man – his earnestness, his faith, his pride in his country, his asceticism. No frivolities for Mr. Yu. No detective stories, no pop music, no hanging around. Such things do not belong in the new China. He refers at one point to "the responsible person" back at the tourist office. "Your boss?" I ask. He winces. There are no bosses in China.

He is baffled by our negative reaction to one of his few Western heroes, President Richard Nixon. Nixon, he keeps saying, was a great man and a great statesman; how could his people reject him? Jack looks hard at him. "Mr. Yu," he says, "what you've got to understand is that Nixon was a fucking thief!" Mr Yu's eyes open wide. His eyebrows shoot up. He looks distinctly uncomfortable and embarrassed, not, I realize, because Jack has damned Nixon as a thief but because, in this society of puritans, he has dared to use the F-word.

When we reach Shihkiachwang, a responsible person takes us in hand. Perhaps, he says, we would care to lay a wreath at the memorial to the saintly Norman Bethune. Of course we would; where can we buy one? "We will prepare everything," we are told. I envisage a modest garland of the kind sold at home on Poppy Day, but when we reach the cemetery an astonishing creation is trundled out, fashioned entirely of plastic flowers and standing a full five feet on its tripod. It costs a mere five dollars – a steal at the price, I think.

A scroll is produced along with a brush and ink, and we are asked to inscribe an appropriate message. Then all four of us stagger off through the drenching rain to be photographed with the gargantuan wreath in front of Bethune's tomb. Once the ceremony is over, we rush for the shelter of our car, but Liz McClelland, who has forgotten her camera, insists on going back to get a picture of the tomb and also of the remarkable wreath. Off she trots through the rain to the sacred spot.

She is almost too late. Even as she arrives, the frugal Chinese are spiriting away the floral offering – back to the storeroom to await the arrival of the next group of Canadian VIPs.

We return to Shanghai and then move on to Kwangchow in the south, enduring each morning and afternoon the same endless indoctrinations. At the end of ten days our tour ends, and we are ready to board the train to the border. The responsible person in Kwangchow hosts a Cantonese banquet in our honour, with so much Chinese brandy laid on that Mr. Yu accidentally wets his pants and succumbs.

The next day we take the train to Shumchun and walk to the border point. Mr. Yu walks with us, promising to visit us if he ever comes to Canada. Then we say goodbye and enter the strangely raucous world of the West. The first thing I see are three dogs lying in the shade of the railway station. For the past two weeks we haven't seen a single canine. Now they seem to be everywhere. "I guess they eat them," Jack remarks.

A gaggle of vendors, hawking souvenirs, crowds around us as we leave the railway station at Kowloon. A moment later a professional beggar extends a hand. Now the real culture shock begins. An unaccustomed jungle of overlapping signs, brilliant with neon, advertises everything from Kentucky Fried Chicken to topless bars. Our taxi crawls through an infuriating snarl of traffic to our hotel. The lobby, jammed with people and ringed with shops, is like a dark and colourful cave. We traipse to the bar and utter a kind of collective sigh.

"I feel like a kid who has just been let out of school for the summer holidays," I say.

Jack McClelland studies his double extra-dry vodka martini reflectively.

"Sunday school," he says, and gulps it down.

4

By the early spring of 1977, the Canadian government was in a panic. *Patriot* René Lévesque had smothered Robert Bourassa's Liberals to win a *games* provincial election handily. His Parti Québécois was committed to a form of separatism he called "sovereignty association," whatever that meant. A referendum on that subject was in the cards.

That explains why, a week before Canada Day, Janet and I and three of our children were on a private jet heading for Edmonton. The government, heeding the advice of a hastily called conference of writers (including me), had decided to celebrate the country's birthday in a big way, not only with a television spectacular on Parliament Hill but also in every community in the land. Celebrities such as King Clancy, Foster Hewitt, Al Waxman, Bruno Gerussi, and I would be whisked about with our families to join the celebrations from Dawson City to Corner Brook. So here we were, aboard a twin-engine Rockwell Turbo Commander, about to complete the first leg of a journey that would take us beyond Edmonton to Vancouver, Fort Smith, Yellowknife, and Dawson, all at government expense.

Peter, now about to turn twenty-two, sat up front with Bob Crone, the pilot, and Bob's son, Dave. These were old friends; Bob had been with me in Egypt as a CBC cameraman and in Monte Carlo to film my interview with Robert Service. Peggy Anne, sixteen, and Perri, thirteen, sat in the back with Janet and me. Paul, eighteen, had driven across the country with a friend and was waiting to meet us in Edmonton.

We were about ten miles out of Edmonton airport when I heard Dave Crone say, "We have a problem." At that moment a Klaxon blared in the cabin. Suddenly the engines stopped. Dave was calling "Mayday!" into the microphone as we slid soundlessly through the sky at sixty-five hundred feet. For a moment none of us broke that eerie silence. Then Peter turned back to us. "It looks like lights out," he said, without a trace of panic.

I took off my glasses, a gesture that terrified the two girls.

"I'll never see Paul again," cried Perri.

"I don't want to die," said Peggy Anne.

"You haven't time to die," said her always practical mother. "Just put your head between your knees."

The plane had run out of fuel and was losing altitude rapidly. Below

377

us the countryside seemed littered with obstacles – telephone poles, high wire fences, herds of cattle. In order to be able to control the plane Bob needed speed, and so went into a steep dive. As if this wasn't enough, he had trouble getting the landing gear down. Finally, by dint of shaking the plane, he freed the wheel that was stuck and turned his attention to the problem of landing in one piece. He had decided to put her down on a grassy field when Peter quietly pointed out that a provincial highway wasn't far away. Bob headed for it. "We may get bumped up a bit," I warned the girls, but in fact Bob made a perfect three-point landing on the road. I looked out the window as we came to a stop and noticed that an approaching car had suddenly pulled off the highway in our path.

It all happened so quickly that Janet and I, concerned about the children, hadn't had time to feel fear. Nor was the situation new to me. I'd been in tight spots in the Nahanni, in Korea, and over the Andes. But as we climbed down the ladder, I felt a little shaky in the knees. Peter turned to me. "There's a little bit of vodka left in your bottle, Dad," he said. Back the two of us clambered into the plane and had a couple of swallows together. I must say I was proud of him.

The rest of the Canada Week odyssey was uneventful. Paul met us for a late supper in Edmonton, and the next day we flew on to Vancouver to march with the mayor in a parade down Granville Street, feeling more than a little embarrassed at this public display. I made one of my nationalistic speeches, arguing (in vain) that if the government wanted to keep the country together, it ought to subsidize, through Air Canada, cross-fertilization tours for young people to visit parts of Canada away from home. In the North we attended a series of celebratory barbecues, where I did my best to be inspiring. There were complaints about the cost of the tour, and I was accused (by Allan Fotheringham, of all people) of insisting on a fat fee for taking part in a patriotic exercise. I'd done it for no fee, of course; a free trip to my old home town with my family was perk enough.

The wave of national feeling that characterized the early years of the decade reached its climax in Quebec when René Lévesque's government put its notorious Bill 101 into effect. Now all advertising signs had to be exclusively in French, even, as I noted, in bookstores that sold only books written in English. This, I thought, is ridiculous. At a meeting of The Writers' Union, I announced dramatically that I was

378

prepared to go to Montreal, post an English circular in a bookstore, and, if necessary, go to jail for breaking the law. Boos and catcalls in the Montreal French-language media greeted this statement. In November 1978, Lévesque appeared at a press conference in Toronto to which I had secured credentials as a radio reporter. As soon as questions were called for, I had my hand up to ask the Quebec premier if he didn't think the new law was silly when it applied to books written in English.

"I've been expecting you," he said genially, and then announced that the government had come up with a "fresh interpretation" of Bill 101 that would allow English bookstores to use signs in the language of their customers. With that, my vision of rotting in a Quebec dungeon vanished. But it was no more than half a victory. Quebec was embarked on a path that could only be described as totalitarian, no matter how many excuses were made for it.

Nationalism in that era was not confined to French Canada. It had its counterpart in the rest of the country. The new interest in history, the concern for the physical environment made it clear that some people were beginning to care, and then to care fervently, about the kind of country they were fashioning. There was more emphasis on the need for Canadian "heroes" – larger-than-life figures to compete with the Davy Crocketts and Eddie Rickenbackers south of the border. This had not been the Canadian style in the past, especially among the academics. One leading historian, Jack Granatstein, took issue with me on the subject in a piece in the *Globe and Mail,* claiming that my most recent book, *My Country,* was itself "a collection of studies that aims to create Canadian heroes, Davy Crockett style." Had the professor read my book? I doubted it. When people praise me, as they still do, for creating heroes from the past, they really mean celebrities. The sports pages have long turned scoundrels into paragons simply because of their athletic prowess. Frankly, it is more fun to write about villains than about heroes. *My Country* contains eighteen stories, only seven of which deal with men I would describe as heroic. Five are villains of the deepest dye, and the rest are the ones I really enjoy describing – flawed or tragic figures, failures, or eccentrics. Granatstein also charged me with the most terrible of all crimes in the field of historical writing – "consciously making my work interesting."

"Well, professor," I wrote in a letter to the *Globe and Mail,* "I sure as hell don't consciously make it dull."

This new concern was one of the reasons the government had funded Heritage Canada as a private charitable organization. By 1978, when I became chairman of its board of governors, the public had begun to care about the fate of some of the country's historic buildings, from the Crystal Gardens in Victoria to the façades of Barrington Street in Halifax. More and more I found the heritage movement occupying my time and resources. We had a new executive director, Jacques Dalibard, a Belgian-born architect, who told me that *City of Gold* had been a powerful influence on him in his days with Parks Canada. It had, indeed, convinced him that the department should start a project to restore much of Dawson City. I basked in the knowledge that this film, like *Klondike,* had made a tangible difference in the town whose history it celebrated.

It was Dalibard, too, who conceived the imaginative Main Street program, which, in a decade, was to help renew the face of small-town Canada by revitalizing the downtown core of more than one hundred communities, from Whitehorse in the Yukon to St. John's, Newfoundland. This didn't happen a moment too soon. Years before at *Maclean's,* we had hailed the newest postwar phenomenon, the shopping centre, a retailing revolution spawned by the burgeoning suburbs. It was an enthusiastic article, as most were in those days. Now, however, the heritage movement saw the shopping centre as a villain that was sucking the lifeblood from the central core of hundreds of communities. The new shopping centres on the outskirts of town were devoid of individuality; if you entered one, you entered all. But the Main Streets had their own character, and it was on this texture of the past that the new program focused. I found myself talking to community groups about the need for business to form a local improvement association, to upgrade window displays, to hold major events on the main streets, and to refurbish and restore the fading historical faces of the town's best-known structures – in short, to beat the shopping centres by stealing their ideas.

By the decade's end, this unpaid work was taking about a third of my time. I enjoyed every moment of it – well, almost every moment. At one point I made the supreme sacrifice by carrying out a national tour of Rotary Clubs to explain the need to save something from the past. This forced me to eat luncheon-club food. I cannot soon forget those indigestible clumps of chopped meat, smothered in plastic gravy, that took my mind back to my Dawson childhood, when horse-drawn liveries polluted the streets.

380

I was not always terribly diplomatic. "You'll never be a politician," Jacques Dalibard told me when, in Perth, I publicly criticized the city council for its initial coolness to the heritage movement. Fortunately, I wasn't running for anything. When Guelph allowed the destruction of its splendid Confederation Life building, I said that its main street now looked like a mouthful of teeth with two missing. Calgary, I announced, "looked like it was built yesterday, and is likely to crumble tomorrow. There's no texture of the past, no sense of its generations of citizens." Edmonton's downtown, I said, had been rendered so lifeless by the big suburban shopping centres that it was now impossible to get a cup of coffee on the main street after five o'clock. In rebuttal, some local booster searched about and actually discovered one spot where coffee was available after six.

We were always up against entrenched ideas. It was a hard job trying to convince the Vancouver Parks Board that a one-block park could be more than a patch of scuffed grass bracketed by two goalposts. That was the fate in store for Parksite 19 in the West End. At least five fine heritage buildings stood on the site, all scheduled for demolition. Jacques and I worked to persuade the board that a different kind of urban park – a heritage park – could be created by saving several of the houses on the perimeter, removing the lanes and backyards, and landscaping the new space. It was a hard struggle, but in the end the board met us more than half way.

My biggest and most controversial contribution to the heritage movement was my attempt to make the second Monday in February a holiday to be known as Heritage Day. In this Calvinist land, I discovered, we have fewer national holidays than any other Western nation. But the business establishment was absolutely opposed. The country, it was said, couldn't afford to let the workers take a single day off in the long drought between New Year's Day and Easter. That objection came from a group who regularly decamped to Florida or Hawaii during the February blahs. My board wasn't unanimously enthusiastic, either. The idea, some said, wouldn't float; we'd lose the campaign. That, I tried to explain, didn't matter. It was the fact that we were *calling* for a holiday that mattered. We needed to get people talking about heritage: "We need something startling to shake the nation from its lethargy." So what if people took the day off to go skiing? The media would use the excuse to talk about heritage. In fact, on the second Monday in February they still do, even though Heritage Day is still a working day. I know, because years after I have left Heritage Canada, I still get phone calls from radio stations and newspapers asking about the proposed holiday and about what it would stand for.

5

During my decade with Heritage Canada, I managed to publish nine books of varying quality. The most successful was the one I liked the least – the one that Professor Granatstein had condemned for reviving Canadian heroes. *My Country* was a lazy writer's book, written entirely from research done for the TV program of the same name. The title, I think, helped sell the book at the height of the country's love affair with itself. But research done for a casual half-hour talk on television isn't research for a book that aspires to have historical value.

It was a quickie. I admit unashamedly that I wrote it because it was easy and the money was good. I was still paying for the education of six of my eight children and also for the most recent addition to the house, which had expanded from its original 1,450 square feet to an eventual 6,500. It was now as much a motel as a home, and we still didn't have a garage. That space had to serve as a bedroom for one of the kids.

I wrote most of *My Country* during a family vacation in Jamaica, working away on my portable each morning and relaxing with the family after lunch. Elsa and I had produced fifty-two stories for television under the *My Country* banner. I chose eighteen for the book. In spite of my reservations, the book was a success, both in hardcover and later in mass-market paper. Three of the stories – "The Franklin Mystery," "Bloody Sunday in Vancouver," and "Blondin Walks Niagara's Gorge" – sparked my interest in the Arctic, the Great Depression, and the Falls – all subjects I later tackled in much greater depth.

One of the stories, "The Search for Gun-an-noot," also resulted in the only successful libel action against me, one that I was quick to settle out of court. Gun-an-noot, a Kispiox of the Carrier tribe in central British Columbia, was charged in 1905 with the murders of two men. Apparently falsely accused, he evaded capture for thirteen years, regularly visiting his wife and siring five children in a community where no

382

one would betray him. He finally gave himself up and was acquitted in a Vancouver courtroom, a celebrated case of justice perverted.

In my story I had written that one of Gun-an-noot's sons, David, had a criminal record. I was wrong. A libel notice quickly arrived from a lawyer in the Queen Charlotte Islands. I went straight to Stewart, B.C., to meet with David Gun-an-noot, now an old man. There was no doubt that I was in error, and McClelland and Stewart quickly settled for about ten thousand dollars, of which I paid half.

I got on well with David Gun-an-noot. In the winter of his life he wanted, at last, to reveal the story his mother had told him half a century before when she swore him to secrecy. What was the secret? That his father really *had* done it – killed both men after a series of insults and taunts directed at him! I revised the story to include this startling footnote to history.

One tale I'd told on television that didn't make the book was the story of the birth and exploitation of the Dionne quintuplets. I was fourteen when they were born in 1934. During all my teenage years they made headlines. The Dionnes were part of the cultural baggage I carried from the thirties. In fact, I had their story on my list of possible books that also included *The Promised Land* and *Niagara*.

I wanted to write a story that sprang out of my own time, and with Barbara Sears's help I plunged into the research. Neither the three surviving Quints nor their parents would see me. I couldn't blame them, for they had been interviewed to exhaustion and wanted nothing more to do with the media. But there were other sources. Here my television image helped me. People seemed as curious to see me in person as I was to see them.

When I took the idea to my publisher, no one applauded wildly. Anna Porter, Jack's editor-in-chief, was a recent arrival in Canada and knew next to nothing about the Dionnes. Jack himself was lukewarm. But, remembering the groans from almost everybody who heard I was doing a book on the CPR, I ignored the reaction. Jack, of course, agreed to do the book, but I got nowhere with my U.S. publisher, Alfred Knopf. Alfred himself was dead; so was Harold Strauss, my editor there. Random House had taken over the firm, and none of the young editors seemed enthusiastic about publishing a story about a forty-year-old phenomenon. But Evan Thomas at Norton, the son of one of my heroes, Norman Thomas, the U.S. socialist leader, was.

I had originally intended the book to be a kind of social history of the thirties, but the quintuplets' story was so compelling that I eventually cut twenty thousand words of background from the manuscript, leaving just enough to give the flavour of the times without impeding the breakneck progress of the narrative.

To the surprise of many, the book was a hit. The *Toronto Star* gave it the best kind of plug when it said that "it reads like a novel." The *New York Times Magazine* ran a long excerpt. The woods, it turned out, were full of Dionne aficionados; in fact, there was even a catalogue available listing Dionne collectibles. The book sold close to one hundred thousand copies in the United States and Canada and went into two paperback editions.

The success of *My Country* convinced me that I should prepare a second anthology of tales from the past, but with deeper research. All would deal with some aspect of the Canadian frontier. I did not use my television research but turned the task over to Barbara Sears, who dug into the primary sources. As a result, five of the seven stories contained material not hitherto published. In several cases the new research altered the thrust of the narrative. I was happier with *The Wild Frontier* than I had been with *My Country,* but quite clearly the public preferred the latter, as my royalty statements – the only true indication of a book's success – made clear. I think, in this case, the title *My Country* appealed to Canadian nationalism. After all, the frontier was old stuff.

Now I wanted to write something on a broader scale – a slice of history that would provide not only a lively narrative but also something about the country and its past. I remember Lister Sinclair's asking me one day if I found writing was getting easier for me or harder. I thought about that and replied: "I'm trying to make it harder." The Dionne story, though it was a joy to write, hadn't given me much opportunity to stretch the technique I had developed in *Klondike* and the railway histories. I called Barbara Sears and asked, "How would you like to dig into the War of 1812?" She was enthusiastic. If she had not been, I would not have done it, but we both saw possibilities in the subject. It would tell something of how the war was fought on the frontier; it would examine the differences between the British, the Americans, and ourselves; and it would say something about war itself, for this was a bloody conflict that nobody won.

Once again I would be telling a story in which large numbers of people moved through time and space – from Lake Huron to Brussels –

and it would involve the troops of three countries, not to mention the politicians and civilians. It would also be the story of the first stirrings of the new country, the beginning of a national identity, and the great conflict that helped define the nation. I could not contain my enthusiasm as Barbara and I talked it over at lunch. I wanted to get to my typewriter immediately, but I knew that long months of hard slogging lay ahead as I tried to make sense of the piles of documents that Barbara would photocopy for me.

As I read these documents – letters, military histories, transcripts of courts-martial, first-person memoirs – it became clear that once again I would have to split the narrative into two books. As the research progressed, I came to realize that the first book, *The Invasion of Canada,* would, to a large extent, be about Indians and the white man's treatment of them. It would be framed by two battles – the opening battle of Tippecanoe, where white Americans had massacred a mixed community of natives, and the closing battle of 1812 at Frenchtown, when Indians, in revenge, massacred whites. The second volume would cover the war in 1813 and 1814, and the diplomatic efforts to end it.

The underlying theme was obvious: this was, perhaps, the stupidest and most inept of all wars, fought with no purpose and with no sensible outcome – and fought badly by comic opera leaders on both sides who, in some cases, verged on the imbecilic. I did not have to state that theme; it was inherent in almost every page. There were few Davy Crockett types in this bloody conflict. (Indeed, we now know that Crockett wasn't the saint that John Wayne and Disney made him out to be.) The closest, I suppose, was Isaac Brock, whose dash up the heights of Queenston was certainly heroic, but also unnecessary and foolish. I did not call him a fool in the book; until I tackled *The Great Depression,* I preferred to let the narrative speak for itself – my *Maclean's* training, perhaps. But Brock was certainly asking for it. The real hero of this tragic conflict was Tecumseh.

Early on I was surprised to discover that nobody had written a book about the war of the kind I was contemplating – seeing the events from the Canadian point of view. Most important, the role of the Indians in the early stages of the war had been badly neglected. Yet without them, Upper Canada might have become an American state.

All this apparently baffled Colonel Charles Stacey, the Canadian Army historian, who wrote, a little petulantly, that "Berton doesn't tell us why he has written a book about the War of 1812." I should have thought that was obvious. No other Canadian, including Stacey, had done so. Stacey also wrote, ruefully, that the book seemed to be full of Indians. Sometimes reviews tell more about the reviewers than they suspect.

I took the second draft of the first volume to Jamaica, again on a family holiday, working in the mornings while leaving the afternoons open for family outings.

I have a continuing problem with typewriters. I learned the two-finger process during my newspaper days and have never been able to avoid hammering hard on keys that need a gentler touch. As a result my type-writers suffer continually from metal fatigue. Since Smith-Corona no longer makes my electric portable model, and since I cannot think prop-erly on a substitute (or so I tell myself), I live in terror that I may have to quit writing if I cannot lay my hands on another one. That explains why I now own four Smith-Corona portables and why two are always in the repair shop. I took only one machine to Jamaica, and, of course, the inevitable happened. I banged on it so hard that the *h* character snapped off. Now I learned that there are, on the average page, more than eighty *h*'s – a useful letter that appears regularly in *the, they, that, them, this, him, her, his, who, when, where,* and *why.* Worse, I was deal-ing with the leading American general and future president, William Henry Harrison. What could I do? Stop writing? Try to find another Hermes Baby? Commit suicide? None of the above. I simply carried on, typing away without the letter *h.* At the end of each page of typescript I pencilled in the missing letters, with the result that the manuscript seemed to be covered with fly specks.

That slowed me down slightly, which was probably a good thing.

I was not happy with the early chapters. The narrative wasn't work-ing properly. After about seventy pages I found myself switching to the present tense. It was not a conscious decision, but suddenly I found the story becoming more immediate. Events of those long-ago days jumped out from the pages, or so it seemed to me. By and large, I think it worked; certainly the results in sales and critical acceptance supported me. One American reviewer got his rhetorical terms mixed up when, to my delight, he described the book as having been written in the first person; it's always a pleasure when a critic makes a boo-boo.

It was soon obvious that the second volume, *Flames Across the Border,* would be longer than the first. Jack McClelland tried hard to persuade

386

me, in a long letter dictated as usual in the middle of the night, to write a trilogy. "This is undoubtedly the most important letter I have ever written," he began portentously. No doubt he believed it, but I could not help suspecting a commercial, as well as an editorial, reason behind his plea. I could not, however, see any sensible way of breaking up the narrative further. Instead, to Jack's dismay, I cut out twenty-five thousand words. It sold well in Canada, poorly in the United States (where the myth of an American victory is still a part of American folklore). As usual, I got better reviews south of the border, where several critics remarked, not without astonishment, that I had been remarkably fair to the American side. That surprised and pleased me; I may have been writing as a nationalist, but never as a chauvinist.

I did not want to commit myself immediately to another work of this magnitude and complexity, though I did toy with the story of the Rebellion of 1837. Barbara demurred; she didn't want to dig her way through any more handwritten documents for a while. Besides, she disliked William Lyon Mackenzie intensely. He was, by all accounts, a nasty piece of goods, albeit an authentic Canadian hero, raised to that pantheon with the help of his doting grandson, William Lyon Mackenzie King.

So I took a breather. My work on the country's past and the relationship of the colonial Canadians with their revolutionary cousins south of the border had been the subject of a host of after-dinner speeches. One day, while I was driving into town and going over one of these speeches in my mind, a light bulb went off above my head, as it used to do in the old *Mutt and Jeff* comics I had devoured as a child. Why not adapt the same material to a small book about the Canadian identity? The result was *Why We Act Like Canadians*.

I had difficulty with that book. I couldn't seem to relax with it, it sounded far too pretentious. Then I recalled Tom Wolfe's story about the writer's block he had suffered when he tried to write an article for *Esquire*. His editor suggested he write the piece as he would a letter home. It worked, and the famous Wolfe style, aped so badly by so many budding writers, was born. That gave me the key to my book. I would write it as a series of letters to an American friend, trying to explain the nutty people we are. I called the friend Sam – a rather corny device, I think now, but the book itself worked and became a commercial hit. People sent it to their American friends, who hated it, thinking

I was putting them down. Canadians wrote me weird letters, thinking I was putting *them* down. I didn't intend to say that Canadians were better than Americans, as my American correspondents thought, or that Americans were better than Canadians, as some of my Canadian readers believed, just that we are two different kinds of people inhabiting the same continent. Our language and dress may be the same, but our history, our geography, and our ethnic make-up are all quite different. This was not well understood when I began writing about my country, but it has recently come to be recognized. Certainly it has been a major theme in my books of narrative history since *Klondike*. Maybe that even helped a bit. But it would have been a lot simpler to understand the differences if Wolfe had lost the Battle of the Plains of Abraham and we had all been brought up to speak French – a piece of heresy I have occasionally uttered in public, to almost universal condemnation.

Chapter Fourteen

1

Age and decay

2

Birthday boy

3

Goodbye, Gordon

4

Low budget

5

The C-Beast

6

Playing fair

1

By the eighties I began to be haunted by a growing feeling that things were winding down. In that decade, *The Great Debate* came to an end, the Committee for an Independent Canada closed down, Gordon Sinclair died, "Dialogue" went off the air, I retired from Heritage Canada, Jack McClelland sold his publishing company, and my own life almost came to a full stop.

Nineteen-eighty was the year of the first Quebec referendum. Like most English-speaking Canadians, I was on the "No" side. I thought, and still think, that the loss of Quebec would mean the end of Canada. British Columbia, always a maverick province, would either opt for independence or try to join the United States. The Atlantic provinces, or some of them, would also try to become American. The moot question was whether or not the Americans would accept them.

Canada was swiftly becoming Americanized anyway. My belief was that we might still end up with a country called Canada – but that it would be *de facto,* if not *de jure,* an American state. We were pretending to be an independent nation in spite of the Americanization of our economy, our politics, and our culture. If Quebec left, wouldn't we be prepared to pretend a little bit more?

In April 1980 I was asked by a committee made up largely of old Liberal hangers-on to come to Quebec City to speak on behalf of the No's. I hesitated. I was an outsider, a hated Central Canadian from Toronto. What business had I, a man who could speak only college French, in coming to the heart of French Canada to tell the people how to vote? But then I told myself, this is my country, too – *all* of it. We are not yet a foreign nation. And so I went and did my bit, speaking almost entirely to the converted, and making very little impact on the results. Pierre Trudeau, of course, did. He had been re-elected to the accompaniment of the usual chorus of television commentators – Patrick Watson, Iona Campagnolo, David Lewis, Robert Bourassa, and me. I cannot recall what I said on this CTV election night broadcast. I was not in the CBC's grace and favour, having broken a taboo live on camera at one of the leadership conventions. I thought it uncommonly silly, after each of the speeches, to find CBC pundits rushing to buttonhole the speaker's closest colleagues – the very men who had written the speech that had just been delivered. "What did you think of the speech?" they'd ask, as if they didn't know. That falls into the same category as the infamous "How do you feel?" question, which is still used by incompetent TV interviewers: *Mrs. Blodgett, your husband has just killed himself with a carving knife after dispatching two of your children. How do you feel about that?* Did the CBC people expect the speechwriters to say that their work was an unmitigated disaster? Of course, they all said the speech was one of the best they'd ever heard. I thought this both pointless and hilarious and said so on air. Later, Barbara Frum, who hosted our little group of commentators, told me she'd had a dressing-down from the top brass and been given definite instructions to put a cork in it. The corporation always did lack a sense of humour.

The Great Debate ended the following year. We'd had a good run; eight years is a long time for any program to remain on the air. But it had not been easy. Global Television was prepared to continue, but it was up to us, not them, to get financial backing. That we'd managed to do, though I don't think any of the backers made money, except for the usual tax loss. We had had to cut back to keep the program alive. I longed to get into the debate myself, especially on contentious issues on which I held strong opinions. But my job was to remain strictly neutral, making sure I asked both sides the same number of hard questions. That was a Herculean effort. I pleaded with Elsa to be allowed to take part in just one debate – just *one!* – using Charles Templeton as moderator in my place. She would have none of it.

I was, at this time, playing a minor role in the CBC's adaptation of *I Married the Klondike*. It was not a happy experience. The script, written by a recently arrived Englishman, was, I thought, way off base. The writer had no sense of the way people talked in those days, no feeling for the flavour of the North. It was insipid, conventional, boring. Elsa thought so too. When we arrived at the next production meeting, we both assumed that everybody else would agree that it was a bad job. "I guess we all know this series needs a major fix," I told the meeting, in my innocence. Then I saw the look of shock on their faces. *They thought the script was great!*

"It's *not* great," I said. "But I'll tell you what I'm prepared to do. I'll take the weekend and try to fix it so it sounds authentic. I don't want a fee; I just don't want to see a bad script televised."

More shock! Peter Kelly, the executive producer, pronounced himself appalled that I would interfere with the work of another writer. It would, he said, be an insult. I thought the script was an insult. At that point, Peter made a remark that has stayed with me all these years. "Look," he said, *"I've never had a failure."*

Never a failure? How then did he measure success? I'd had plenty of failures, but forbore to say so.

I made several suggestions about the structure, some of which were followed. The dialogue, alas, was virtually unchanged. The CBC drama department played it safe. The director was Peter's choice, not mine – somebody who could be counted on to follow orders and not make waves. I tried to convince Peter that the great Canadian actor R.H. Thomson, who played my father, should wear a beard. Most men had, in those days, and my father was no exception. But Peter said, "I can't ask him to grow a beard. He doesn't do that sort of thing." A couple of years later I ran into Thomson and told him the story. "Of course I would have worn a beard," he said, "but nobody asked me." He added, "I thought of calling you about that script. I wish now I had." He'd had trouble, understandably, making his character sound real.

In the middle of the production, one of the unions went on strike and the whole program was hoisted for the better part of a year. A set for Klondike City – Lousetown, the red-light district across the river from Dawson – had been built at Kleinburg, not far from where we lived. Thanks to the work stoppage, the cabins, sidewalks, and everything else weathered nicely over the winter. Meanwhile, in Dawson, Parks Canada was restoring the buildings that would appear in the background of the film when the principals were flown to the Yukon. This produced an odd effect: the newly built Lousetown at Kleinburg looked remarkably authentic; some viewers thought it was the real thing. But the refurbished buildings in Dawson, spanking new in their fresh paint, looked like a film set.

The three-part miniseries got a cool critical reception when it was finally aired. Canadian Press damned it as "beautiful to look at but ponderous because of a wobbly script." It was later peddled to the Disney Channel, so perhaps Peter Kelly could count it as one of his unbroken string of successes. The CBC, at this point, had contracted to produce only the first half of the book, being content to wait and film the second half if the response was positive. Needless to say, it was never produced.

By this time outspoken nationalism was on the wane. In August 1981 the Committee for an Independent Canada breathed its last, announcing that it had done its job and was no longer needed. That wasn't true, but the "me" generation of the eighties was more interested in profit than patriotism. The first chairman, Jack McClelland, chosen because he had no political affiliations, was now too occupied trying to keep his company alive. Claude Ryan, a later chairman, had become a Quebec politician. Only Mel Hurtig – feisty and dedicated, from Alberta of all places – seemed to have the energy required, but he was taken up with a competitive project, an all-Canadian encyclopedia that threatened to sink him financially. And Walter Gordon, the quintessential Canadian nationalist, had put more time and money into the project than he could afford. We had all put our money where our mouths were. I had contributed five thousand dollars to fund a CIC telethon at the opening of CITY, the lively new television station in Toronto. I figured it was well spent.

I believe we had had some effect in pushing the Trudeau government toward a more nationalistic policy. When sixty of us had gone to Ottawa in 1969 to present our briefs to the prime minister and other party leaders, Trudeau listened politely and soothed us with words of encouragement, but I, who was there and said not a word, didn't think his heart was in it. He was not a nationalist by our definition. How could he be? As a world traveller, he had seen what narrow nationalism could do in its extreme form. He had seen it at its best and at its worst in his own province. Nonetheless, Herb Gray, then a minister without portfolio and a strong nationalist, was at Trudeau's elbow. It was he who later prepared a study of foreign ownership, one factor in the National Energy Program, which drew cries of outrage from Alberta.

I was still spending a good deal of time in the capital because of my work with Heritage Canada, which would be ten years old in 1983 – my final year as chairman. I planned an ambitious annual general meeting to mark our tenth birthday and quickly learned the art of raising money from various government departments – so effectively that we actually had some left over when the bills came in. No doubt we should have given some of it back, but of course, we did nothing of the sort.

My "image," to use that horrible TV word, was softening. The media insisted on referring to me as an "icon," an embarrassing term, suggesting that, if not dead, I was certainly old and ineffective. I remembered telling Gordon Sinclair that he, who had once been a highly controversial public figure, could by then get away with anything. He grudgingly agreed. Now I was moving into the same category.

I was an Officer of the Order of Canada and would soon be raised to Companion, the highest level in that status-conscious institution. (I make no apology; I long ago decided to accept any award offered me as long as I wasn't required to make a speech.) One wall of the house was rendered colourful by the silken hoods that had come free with some dozen honorary degrees. And though I no longer had a talk show on television, I was turning up on most of the others, from Wayne and Shuster to Peter Gzowski. The critics were reporting that Gzowski's late-night audience ratings were abysmal, but I did not find that true. The night I cut my finger almost in half trying, in my clumsy way, to demonstrate a Cuisinart food processor, every man, woman, and child in the country seemed to be watching and tittering. The affair even made the pages of the *National Lampoon,* which, I believe, thought-fully presented me as a typical Canadian bungler.

Some critics looking back nostalgically on my old show were now praising it. Even Dennis Braithwaite wrote that the CBC should have chosen me to run its late-night program and referred to me as "the sine qua non of talk show hostmanship." I was startled. Was this really me? I immediately wrote to Braithwaite: "What have I done to deserve this, Dennis? I was happier when you attacked me as inept, gauche, jejune, bumbling, and ineffective." He replied in kind. By writing to him in jest I had given him a free column – something every scrivener prays for. It was the least I could do.

2

Birthday   YORK CENTRAL HOSPITAL, *July 12, 1983. Today is my birthday, but*
boy   *I am not exactly celebrating. I am lying on my back in a hand-cranked bed in a semiprivate ward, with an IV needle in my arm and an oxygen mask on my face, contemplating, for the first time, my own mortality. A curtain separates me from an elderly male, groaning in an adjoining bed. His wife is with him, struggling to feel wanted. Would he like his pillow plumped up? He answers with a groan. A drink of water? Another groan. Something to eat? A long groan. Later his family arrives from out of town – nieces and nephews who keep telling him how wonderful he looks. A groan escapes him after each one of these lies. In a grisly sort of way it helps keep my mind off my own problems.*

394

My doctor has just left after totally unnerving me. "What's this lump here?" he asks, poking at my clavicle.

"Just part of my collarbone," I tell him.

"Then how come there's not one on the other side?" he asks, triumphantly. Panic! He's right! "Could be a lymph gland," he says briskly. "We're going to have to take you off the heparin so your blood won't be too thin when we operate."

Operate? That's not what I'm here for. I'm here because I don't have pneumonia after all. I've got a pulmonary embolism; my lungs are full of blood clots. On the x-ray screen they look like Japanese bonsai trees. But now all the talk about embolism is set aside. I've got the Big-C in the lymph glands! They haven't said that, of course, but they're talking like undertakers and have scheduled "exploratory surgery" for the day after tomorrow. The man next to me is still groaning and I feel like groaning too. Many happy returns.

Out comes the IV: they've got to get my blood back to normal. If the cancer doesn't doom me, the thickening blood may do the job. I lie on my back, contemplating the future, or the lack of it. Every morning Janet arrives with a glass of fresh-squeezed orange juice, bless her! I drink it greedily – the condemned man enjoying one last swallow. Other members of the family pop in and out bearing gifts – sushi, fettuccine Alfredo, roast beef with Yorkshire pudding, egg rolls, fried rice, Peking duck – anything to stave off the hospital cuisine. If I go out, I intend to leave with a full stomach, and none of that slop they cook up below.

I spend a sleepless night mentally trying to put my affairs in order. Is there enough in the kitty for Janet, who will certainly outlive me by half a century? Do I need to hand out a power of attorney? What's happened to the key to the safety-deposit box? Have my forward-averaging annuities run out? But what really concerns me is the new book, The Promised Land, *the voluminous research for which lies beside my typewriter at home, waiting to be digested into deathless prose. I've finally figured out how to put it together. I know how it will start and how it will end: those scenes are flashing through my mind like clips made for a Hollywood trailer. In between I have assembled a lively cast of rogues, heroes, and eccentrics. Once again I can hardly wait to get to my typewriter, but now I'm here in this white jail, too weak to hammer down a single key, mourning a work that will never see the light of day. It's too soon, I tell myself, as half a dozen movie scenes take shape in my mind:*

"I'm too young to die, Maw." Hell, I've just turned sixty-three. I'm practically a kid. Too goddamn young.

A small voice whispers: "You're feeling sorry for yourself. That's not your style. Stop brooding; you're not dead yet. You don't even know what that lump is. You've been in tight corners before. You're a survivor and you're an optimist. Remember when the critics said you'd never make it on television? Remember your first mike fright? You endured, didn't you? So lose the self-pity."

With that I decide to stop worrying, turn off my brain, and get some sleep. I wake in the morning, watch daytime TV, and think myself better off than the miserable people on the tube who spout a litany of woe. They sound a bit like me, but their diseases are far more mysterious and incurable, and their married life is pure hell. I turn my mind to my new book, working out passages in my head. By the time the doctor digs into my clavicle and comes up with a benign cyst, I'm running on a full tank.

Even my transfer to Intensive Care fails to bother me, though it seems to bother everybody else. My doctor and neighbour, Peter Granger, explains that he's merely shielding me from a media invasion. The papers have caught on to my condition, which, of course, they get wrong. They're demanding an interview – undoubtedly the basis for a coming obit. Peter puts them off.

There's also the matter of using a new and dangerous drug, streptokinase, which, I am told, will turn me into a hemophiliac for at least twenty-four hours as it blasts away at the clots in my lungs. I cheerfully sign a form absolving the hospital of all responsibility and listen carefully as a medical expert explains that if I fall out of bed when the drug is in me, I'm done for. Also, he says, if I have to use the john I must be accompanied by two nurses. I tell him that's the greatest recipe for constipation I've ever heard. He doesn't laugh.

The drug works. The clots vanish. I'm out of Intensive Care. Visitors are again allowed. Jack McClelland arrives. He's come from another hospital and must go back within the prescribed time. I want to talk to him about my new book. He feigns interest, consults his watch, and tells me he's due back in stir within the hour. Off he goes and has a hell of a time getting out of York Central because he's wearing a hospital wristband himself.

It's time for me to go home, too, but no intern can release me. I can't bear another night here. I threaten to walk out anyway, and who's going to stop me? Somebody relents and promises I can leave as soon as Janet arrives with the car. On the way into the house, she tries to take my arm. I shake her off; I don't want to be treated as an invalid. Hell, I'm not an old party yet! The Beatles' refrain runs through my head: "Will you still need me, will you still feed me. When I'm sixty-four?" I hum the tune, feeling good, and think of Ringo Starr as I head to my office where my little typewriter awaits me.

3

That same year "Dialogue" went off the air after four years on CFRB and ten more on CKEY. That was a nervous station. It had once been CFRB's closest competitor for the mainstream audience but, unlike its rival, was a captive of the ratings. The management panicked and changed the program format almost every time a new rating study appeared. CFRB sailed blithely on, always at the top, resisting the latest fashions and providing solid entertainment with which its listeners were comfortable. But when CKEY's rating fluctuated – *consternation!*

Goodbye, Gordon

The station's ratings went up and down, but numbers for "Dialogue" stayed high. We had scored some notable coups. On one occasion, to demonstrate the flaws in airport security, Charles had easily circumvented watchful eyes and entered the departure area through an unlocked door. That done, he walked out onto the runway and boarded an aircraft being readied for flight. He chatted cheerfully with the cleaners, then returned to broadcast his adventures. Needless to say, airport security was tightened. On another occasion we were able, quite easily, to secure the supposedly sacrosanct income tax returns of four prominent citizens. That caused a furore. The tax department claimed that our discovery was a fluke – nothing more. We immediately announced that we would get a copy of Joe Clark's income tax return. We got it, and sent it to the tax department. We did not, of course, broadcast the details. My only memory is that Joe Clark wasn't making a hell of a lot of money. That broadcast won us an ACTRA Nellie.

Not long after these triumphs, I suggested to Charles that since our contract had less than a year to run we should renegotiate well before the deadline. Thus, before the station went into another panic, we were able to sign a five-year, ironclad deal with a built-in yearly increase of 10 percent.

After the next disastrous rating book was published, showing a serious drop in CKEY's audience – but not ours – Doug Trowell, the station's manager, suggested we all have lunch.

"He wants to change things because of the ratings," Charles said. "That probably means they want to dump 'Dialogue.'"

I reminded him of our contract.

"Oh, well," said Charles, "we shouldn't be too hard on them. I don't think it would be fair to hold them to it."

Pause.

"Charles," I reminded him gently, "it's *Maclean Hunter!*"

It was true. The same company that had interfered so much when he tried to edit *Maclean's* and had bowed to pressure in my case now owned CKEY.

Charles looked hard at me. "I'd forgotten!" he said. "Let's squeeze the bastards!"

At lunch, Doug Trowell was Mr. Geniality.

"Well, fellas," he said. "We've had a great run. Now we're going to throw out the old format. The times demand it. We're no longer going to be Talk Radio. We're going to be Music Radio."

He paused to sense our reaction. We said nothing.

"So," he went on, "we'll naturally keep you on until the end of the year. I guess that's about it."

He made it sound as if he was distributing free Popsicles to deserving but obsolete followers.

"Doug," said Charles quietly (but I could see a small gleam in his eye), "you forget we're contracted until 1983."

"Oh, well," Doug said. "I mean, you're not going to hold us to that, surely. Not with the big change."

"Well, we are," said Charles.

"I'll have our lawyers look into it," said Doug.

But his lawyer told him that ours was the tightest contract he'd ever seen, and so Charles and I continued to argue with one another, morning after morning, until June of 1983.

Some months after "Dialogue" ended, Charles asked me, hypothetically, if I would do the show again, were it offered to us.

"Not for a million dollars," I said. "How about you?"

398

"Not for two million," he replied. We were both tired of rising before seven each morning, rushing through the paper, driving to the station, and spouting off instant opinions on the topic of the day. "Dialogue" was stimulating, but it was also confining. We both wanted something more leisurely.

Charles had plenty to occupy him. He was writing books – successful ones, such as *The Kidnapping of the President* – and he was still inventing things. Some of these inventions he had patented; others, which he thought up independently, he found had already been patented. Once, I recall, he told me about an ingenious new device he'd thought of that would reach down to the roots of trees and shrubs to water them in the subsoil.

"I have one," I told him. "It's called a Ross Root Feeder."

He looked crestfallen but continued to patent a wide variety of inventions, some of which actually made money, like his successful "warm teddy bear," which miraculously heated up like a hot water bottle. This was the era of the trivia craze, touched off by the phenomenal success of Trivial Pursuit. Charles invented a different kind of trivia game, which he called Tour de Force, and asked me to help him with it. We played it together, adapted it, and sold it to a game company. It was mildly successful; our profits reached six figures. But there is no substitute for being first.

Now I found myself with time on my hands. I no longer had my own radio show or television program. I had retired from Heritage Canada, and *Front Page Challenge* was slowly being cut back from thirty-nine programs a year to eighteen. Outlet or no outlet, I found I could not keep quiet about events of the day that concerned me. And so I blew off steam in the letters column of the newspapers. I wrote so many letters to the press announcing that I was shocked and appalled that Gary Lautens, in his *Star* column, suggested that all the paper had to do was to keep me mad enough and they'd have me free of charge five days a week.

Example: (February 25, 1984) "To the Editor of the *Globe and Mail*. Sir: In the matter of the Dome stadium, is it too much to ask that others be consulted before their money is spent?... You can bet your sweet bippy that whatever the estimated cost of the Dome is reckoned at today, it's going to be three times as much before the grand opening. Where's the money coming from?..." For that I was mildly admonished by two of my friends, Trent Frayne and Scott Young, who wrote sports columns.

After all, the refrain went, what did I know about sports? Didn't I care that baseball fans had to sit out in the wind and the rain? Three times as much money indeed! Alas and alack. The final reckoning, for which the taxpayers were billed, was three times more than my wildest predictions.

Gordon Sinclair died that spring of 1984. He had by then achieved the status of Lovable Old Coot, the eccentric uncle who is indulged by his family. His career was amazing, and very un-Canadian. He had been front and centre on the national stage since the thirties, when the *Star* sent him off to foreign climes. The books that emerged from those exotic journeys were all phenomenal best-sellers.

There was a time when Gordon was called every name under the sun, when thousands professed to believe the canard that he had never been anywhere and made it all up. Fortunately, he had kept his passports and was able to prove that libel a lie. But his personal flamboyance, his adoption of unpopular causes (he referred to fluoridated water as rat poison), his publicly acknowledged interest in money – his own and others' – and his atheism, also publicly expressed, had brought him a peck of trouble. Now he was dead, and the city and the nation mourned his passing. "Colourful" was the word obituaries used. How we longed for a few colourful personalities to match the hordes below the border!

In his own way, as I well knew, Gordon was a Canadian nationalist. He had stayed in the country and made it, a poor boy from Cabbagetown, with little education but a flair for the dramatic. In his later years he could do no wrong. I remember once when *Front Page Challenge* travelled to Calgary, the panel was invited to lunch by the Women's Canadian Club and called upon, one by one, to say a few words. Betty Kennedy rose to say how nice it was to be back in a community she considered a second home town. Fred Davis talked briefly and enthusiastically about the warm hospitality of the Stampede city. I spoke about the time I had spent in Calgary during my wartime officer's training at Currie Barracks. Then Gordon rose and here, verbatim, is what he said:

"I was sitting down in the bar here last night with Lorraine Thomson and I couldn't help overhearing a conversation at the next table about the current recession. The guy was saying: 'You know, I'm in the furniture business and I'm losing my ass.' The girl replied: 'Well, I'm in the ass business and I'm losing my furniture!'"

With that Gordon took his seat. There was a brief moment of silence from the blue-rinse set, followed by an explosion of laughter and applause.

400

Oh, that devil Gordon, wouldn't you just know?

"Gordon," I whispered, "you're the only one here who could get away with that."

"You think so?" He looked pleased.

He was a sensitive man, hiding behind a mask of indifference. The attacks on him over the years hurt and sometimes crushed him. But he never let on. Of course, around income tax time he was almost impossible to talk to. Most of all he loved *Front Page Challenge*. It had given him back the national audience he had once had as a footloose traveller, dominating the front pages. There were times when his adventures constituted the only cheerful news in a black depression. He really cared about the show. He was always a team player, quite prepared to make a fool of himself if he thought it would help. He didn't try to cultivate an image – didn't need to. He was the same off-camera as on – himself, warts and all. I once chided him for getting his facts wrong during one of his radio diatribes. "But that's *me!*" said Gordon. "Sure I get things wrong. That's *me!*"

We wondered how the program could continue without him. To many he *was* the show. But Allan Fotheringham replaced him, and it continued. Gordon's health in later years had made it difficult for us to travel. Now we travelled all the time, taking the program across the country from Kelowna to St. John's, Newfoundland – helping local charities raise funds. The CBC saw this, correctly, as a useful public relations gesture. We attracted overflow crowds in local theatres and school gymnasiums, so popular that the tickets handed out on a first-come basis were often scalped for a good price by young entrepreneurs. I remember well the night that hundreds of Saskatchewan farm families drove miles through a blinding blizzard to see us perform in Regina.

For years the TV reporters had predicted our imminent demise. When Gordon died in 1984, *Front Page Challenge* had been on the air for twenty-seven seasons. By then the predictions had ceased. The show seemed impervious, perhaps because, like "Hockey Night in Canada," it was a Canadian institution. It had eleven more years to go (the CBC finally dropped it in the spring of 1995), and we now had Jack Webster along with the acerb Fotheringham. But it was never quite the same without Gordon.

4

I was not off the small screen for very long. By 1985, Elsa and I were producing a drama series, *Heritage Theatre*. This was an odd business. The series was produced by CHCH-TV in Hamilton, which paid for it. But it ran on the CBC.

We produced it very cheaply – had to, because CHCH operated on a shoestring. *Heritage Theatre* consisted of twenty-six half-hour dramas about the Canadian past – true stories that had action, tension, strong characters, and, when we could fit it in, the requisite amount of sex. We had little trouble finding these stories; some were dramatized from our *My Country* series, others were new – to us and to our audience. They ranged from the story of a nineteenth-century surgeon who hid the fact that she was a woman to that of Cariboo Cameron, the prospector who buried his wife four times.

The budget forced us to run a tight ship – no fancy offices, no stretch limousines, simple sets, a short production period, and a small cast of distinguished actors. Lister Sinclair wrote the scripts; I acted as story editor and on-camera narrator; as producer, Elsa oversaw everything. Lister's mandate was a tough one: to produce a half-hour play every week. Not only that, he was restricted by the tight budget to no more than six principal actors and three extras.

Over the next hectic year we managed to get the job done. Lister would write a script, I would work it over, and then Lister would rewrite it – all in a week. Although Elsa had corralled some of the best performers in the country – Frances Hyland, Eric House, R.H. Thomson, Bruno Gerussi, Gordon Pinsent, Fiona Reed, Graham Greene – we could rarely pay more than union scale. But as jobs were scarce in those days, we had no trouble getting the people we wanted. Lister had to confine each drama to nine scenes. We shot the first three in the morning, the next three in the afternoon. The rest were shot the following morning, and that afternoon we mounted the second drama. Our director, Nigel Napier Andrews, had worked in soap opera and knew how to cut corners.

Each show was budgeted at twenty-five thousand dollars, a laughable figure that few believed possible. The people at Telefilm, the government agency that helped us out, were convinced it couldn't be done at that price. They boosted the ante to thirty thousand a show, a sum we

402

cheerfully accepted. We were determined to use the funds carefully. "Great Heavens!" Sean Mulcahy exclaimed when Elsa climbed into the truck that took us to Hamilton, "a producer riding in a truck! No limousine? You must be putting all the money on the screen." Which, of course, we were. The sets, built at the studio, were simple, unconventional, even surrealistic. I thought they gave the production a certain style, but one critic wrote that they looked like the backgrounds for an SCTV skit. Well, if they were good enough for the hottest comedy show around, why not for something more serious? Why not scrimp when the financial squeeze is on? I was convinced that certain productions don't always need a cast of thousands, or realistic and expensive sets. The CBC produces excellent dramas at high cost, but there's also room, in these fragmented days, for the kind of experimentation in which we were indulging. I learned a lot from this production, such as that TV drama doesn't always have to cost a quarter-million dollars a half hour, and that with some imagination and ingenuity, the job can be done even when budgets are tight.

Actually CHCH, having got some of its costs back from Telefilm, made a profit selling several runs of the series to the corporation, which showed them at weird hours. I don't believe CHCH ever did run them; management changed and the tapes of *Heritage Theatre* lay gathering dust in their storeroom as they went on to other things.

For most of our careers in private television, Elsa and I have had to cut corners while trying to produce quality shows. Make them cheap or don't make them at all – that's been the rule. I remember once, on *The Pierre Berton Show,* interviewing Doug Leiterman, a longtime CBC producer and one of the leading lights of *This Hour Has Seven Days.* I asked him after the show what he thought our budget was. He looked around with a practised eye and came up with a ballpark figure. "I'd say you might bring it in for five thou," he told me. I was surprised; that was our exact budget for a week. Only then did I realize that Leiterman meant five thousand a *show* – not for a strip of five.

Certainly, in the early days of television, the corporation played fast and loose with the taxpayers' money. In the belief that no foreigner would appear on a Canadian show without a hefty stipend – a typical example of our lack of self-assurance – CBC producers paid extraordinary and unnecessary fees to visiting firemen. *Front Page Challenge's* outlay on the outrageous Lady Docker was not uncommon. Once, on the anniversary of the Dieppe raid, Ross McLean sent me with a crew to New York to film a ten-minute interview with the former war correspondent Quentin Reynolds. Over a drink at the end of the interview, he exclaimed over the generosity of the CBC. "Boy, do you Canadians pay handsomely," he said. "I would have walked over and done a ten-minute spot for you for a quarter of the price." These overpayments, I think, reflected the Canadian inferiority complex. The unstated excuse was: We've got to pay these international personalities big money. Otherwise, why would they deign to come on our show?

In 1987, a group of Northern Ontario stations asked us to come up with an inexpensive program to fit the Canadian content requirements. This resulted in a half-hour documentary series, *The Secret of My Success* – profiles of Canadians who had made it and who could give advice on how to climb the slippery ladder. Looking over the list now, I see that of the thirty men and women we featured no fewer than fifteen were either immigrants or the offspring of immigrants – people like Linda Lundstrom, Sam Sniderman, Frank Stronach, Ed Mirvish, Murray Koffler, Anna Porter, Adrienne Clarkson, Ben Wicks, and others. What would the country do without them? They have helped save us from the dead hand of the WASPs. Some day I should like to do another series devoted entirely to people like Moses Znaimer, Garth Drabinsky, or Issy Sharp, who have given this lacklustre land a little flair. None of them would have been welcome in any exclusive Toronto watering hole in the days when I first arrived.

I enjoyed grappling with the problems posed by tightly budgeted TV shows, but I enjoyed my main vocation more. For me, television had been an attractive and well-paid sideline that took care of the bills (I was about to take on another radio series called "The Canadian Achievers"), but the planning, researching, and writing of books had given me more satisfaction. While Elsa and I were planning *Heritage Theatre* we also produced, with the help of Barbara Sears and the great designer Frank Newfeld, a really magnificent picture book about the gold rush. *The Klondike Quest,* with a new text by me, sold for fifty dollars a copy and won for Frank a coveted New York Graphic Society award. To keep the price down Jack McClelland had ordered fifty thousand copies. For many, however, the price was still too high. Jack sold twenty-five thousand but had to remainder the rest at a loss. I hate to think that any venture of mine might have pushed him to the brink of insolvency, for that

404

was where he was headed. The cost of *Klondike Quest* was only part of the creeping paralysis immobilizing an ambitious but underfunded publishing firm. Jack was in a strait-jacket, unable to put into practice many of the plans he had for his company; most of his time was taken up trying to ward off creditors and struggling to raise funds.

He had stepped back from day-to-day operations, which is why he, and indeed almost everybody else, was unaware that M&S was about to publish a novel, *Masquerade,* that I'd written under a pseudonym. This was a series of short stories linked together because they centred around a brothel that specialized in arranging elaborate fantasies for its clients. I wrote it as an experiment, attempting a totally different literary style, which nobody recognized. Elsa arranged a press party at which three young women appeared, all claiming to be the author, "Lisa Kroniuk." The high point was a panel based on *To Tell the Truth,* with Paul Soles as moderator and Dinah Christie, Bill Kilbourn, and me as panellists. When Paul said "will the real Lisa Kroniuk please stand up," all the women stayed put. There was a buzz of curiosity. Nobody in the room except Elsa – not even Jack – was in on the secret. Finally, I stood up, and there was a gasp. It was the most elaborate practical joke in which I've ever been involved. I'm glad to say that it didn't cost the beleaguered company any money, for the book sold thirty-five hundred copies, made a small profit, was trashed by the critics, and has since become a collector's item.

At the end of 1985, Jack, with a sigh of relief and no little chagrin, sold the company to Avie Bennett, a successful real estate entrepreneur and an enthusiastic and generous supporter of the National Ballet of Canada. "It ain't over till it's over," said Jack, in a characteristic press statement, "and it's over for me as a publisher."

It was a fortunate move for Avie, who got out of the real estate business at the very peak of the market. The profits he made on the sale of shopping centres helped balance the continuing losses he suffered as a book publisher. "I now realize that Jack wasn't as bad a businessman as everybody claimed he was," he was heard to remark, a little ruefully. But, of course, like Jack, Avie didn't get into the publishing business to make a killing. After rescuing members of his family from a devastating bankruptcy, he was looking for something more challenging and found it in publishing. He was an unusual sort of businessman, for his political ideas were left of centre. His wife, Beverley, was a strong

NDP-er, and one son was married to the granddaughter of the Reverend Charles Gordon (a.k.a. Ralph Connor, the novelist), a close friend of the CCF's founder, J.S. Woodsworth. Now, as head of the most prominent publishing firm in English Canada, Avie found he had more in common with his new friends in the writing community than with those who had once been part of his hard-nosed business circle.

Avie's arrival on the literary scene was providential, for it saved M&S from certain oblivion. Previous governments had been more than sympathetic to book publishers; but we had now entered the Mulroney years, and the honeymoon was over. The day was not far off when the Tories would tax books for the first time – the much-hated GST.

I'd had two brief, but revealing, encounters with Mulroney before he ascended to the heights. I remember his stopping at our table in Montreal's Ritz Bar and offering to buy Elsa and me a drink, which we cheerfully accepted after a long day of book promotion. His contempt for Trudeau during our conversation was visceral, but he flatly denied having any further personal political ambitions. None at all. Wouldn't consider it. He was through with politics after his defeat for the party leadership by Joe Clark. Then, having convinced us that his glory days were over, he departed, leaving me with the check.

He was, of course, already planning his comeback. I ran into him sometime in 1983, the year he returned to the fray, knocking Clark out of the box. It was on an Air Canada flight out of Vancouver. He spotted me sitting across from him in First Class and looked guilty. "They didn't have any room for us in Economy," he said hastily, explaining why he wasn't rubbing shoulders with the peasants. I told him his secret was safe with me. When I recalled our earlier conversation, he merely shrugged: *Well, you know, that's politics.* A provincial election was in the offing in British Columbia, and Mulroney told me confidentially that all signs definitely pointed to a shoo-in for the NDP. I had learned to take his prognostications with a shaker of salt, which was prudent, because when the results were tallied, Social Credit swept the province.

Now it was time to get my teeth into something more suited to my talents than fiction. I'd enjoyed writing about the War of 1812 because I've always loved military history. Four years in the army, especially the part as an instructor at the Royal Military College, had taught me something about how battles are fought. All my life I had heard stories about the battle for Vimy Ridge, the big Canadian victory in the Great War. Five earlier writers had already ploughed the same furrow, but, after reading their books, I was convinced there was room for another, different kind of narrative. It would, as usual, be a monumental task, studying war diaries, personal letters, and journals scattered in archives and attics from Nova Scotia to British Columbia. Great War veterans did not like to talk about that most hideous of all wars, but they had written about it so that their grandchildren would understand what they'd gone through. Barbara Sears tracked down thirty of these personal memoirs, the work of ordinary soldiers who had squirrelled them away, unread and unpublished. She and I were also able to interview eighty survivors, many of whom, sadly, did not live to read the finished book.

Vimy is my shortest book of narrative history, but writing it presented just as difficult a problem as the longer works. I had no idea how to start it dramatically until Jan Tyrwhitt, my editor, picked up a phrase from the middle of the book about the explosion of guns that began the battle. "In all of history," I had written, "no human ears had ever been assaulted by the intensity of sound produced by the artillery barrage...." At her suggestion, I moved my description of the opening assault to the beginning of the book. After that I was able to explain the hows and whys of *Vimy* before returning to the battle.

The book is more than the story of one battle. It is also the story of a young nation, just emerging from the wilderness, whose citizen soldiers showed the adaptability and ingenuity needed to achieve a victory that had been denied to others. *Vimy* is about the spirit of the frontier and how the children of that frontier rose to the occasion.

In spite of the book's popularity, there were some who were both shocked and angered by my final assessment. "Was it worth it?" I asked. "Was it worth the loss of thousands of limbs and eyes and the deaths of five thousand young Canadians...to provide a young and growing nation with a proud and enduring myth?

"Was it worth it? The answer, of course, is *no*."

That final sentence riled some readers who had been fed from childhood on the myth of the War to End Wars and on the glory, the glamour, and the gallantry of what had once been portrayed as a great crusade. How dare I say that Vimy wasn't worth it? No soldier wants to be told that his feats of valour were fruitless; no mother wants to hear that her son died for no good purpose.

On the monuments you can still read those reassuring phrases – *They Did Not Die in Vain.... Their Names Liveth Forever* – both suggestive of the gnawing suspicion that the Great War *had* been fought in vain and that its victims would soon be forgotten. A nation must be convinced that its young men fought cleanly and with high moral purpose; that is the basis for all wartime propaganda. But when the purpose becomes unclear, as it did in Vietnam, and the men are no longer seen as saints or heroes, the country suffers a trauma.

Five years after *Vimy* was published, a new controversy exploded regarding the Second World War when the CBC aired its documentary *The Valour and the Horror*. The suggestion that the mass bombing of German cities was not only counterproductive but also inhuman was seen as heresy by the major veterans' organizations, who thought that the honour of their members had been besmirched. All wars are immoral, a truth the propagandists do their best to conceal. All of us who lived through the war years can remember how jubilant we were when we learned that Hamburg and Dresden had been obliterated. Now we were being told that the gallant boys in blue – and indeed all of us – had been party to mass murder, and for no good reason. *Vimy* was published when only a handful of Great War veterans were still alive, and so the controversy was muted. Had the book appeared a generation or so earlier, I really think I might have been lynched for that final assessment. But the battle was already fading from memory when the book appeared in 1986. The CBC optioned it for a television miniseries but dropped the project in favour of a similar one about Dieppe. How Canadian, I thought, to prefer the story of a defeat to that of a victory.

Even while I was writing *Vimy,* Barbara Sears was doing some preliminary digging into the sources for my next book. *Vimy* had been a backbreaker; just untangling a minute-by-minute history of the battle had proved exhausting. I wanted something easier, perhaps along the lines of *My Country* – a series of short essays on some aspect of the past. Over a plate of sushi, Barbara and I tossed around ideas and hit upon a book of short profiles of various Arctic explorers searching for the North West Passage and the North Pole. It seemed the perfect subject, and a simple one – nothing too demanding, nothing more than a series of lively character sketches. And we wouldn't have to deal again with John Franklin. I'd devoted a chapter to him in *My Country*.

In retrospect, that all seems terribly naïve. One should never try to cut corners. How on earth could anybody tell any tale about the exploration of the Canadian Arctic and leave Franklin out? What I had in mind was another superficial book – something I could knock off in a few months. In the end, I came to my senses. I soon realized that the story of the lost Franklin expedition and the ten-year search for it must stand at the core of any study of nineteenth-century polar exploration. Bit by bit, as I dug into the backgrounds of the various explorers, my horizons began to expand and I became as obsessed with the dominant puzzle of Arctic exploration as the early explorers had been. Why, after years of devastating hardships – starvation, cold, and, worst of all, boredom – had they kept returning to the frozen world? The book began to change shape as I sought answers to that puzzle and as I came across new characters of whom I'd known nothing, and wanted to know everything.

Out of this quest emerged my longest book, *The Arctic Grail*. On the surface it's a seamless narrative covering the major attempts to find the Passage and the Pole. But below the surface it's a story about the class system in England and the folly of trying to transfer one's environment to foreign climes. I had started out believing that I had an easy story to write. It turned out to be another backbreaker, the most challenging and exhausting of my career. Not long before this I had suffered a serious attack of tendonitis in my arm as a result of leaning over my desk, scribbling notes and annotating my research. Charles Templeton had told me how he had escaped similar problems by putting his typewriter on a slant. My son Peter, now an architect, redesigned my office at home, inventing a desk in which *everything* was on a slant. I have not suffered from tendonitis since.

The Arctic Grail was published in the fall of 1988 and as usual did well in Canada. In the United States the reviews were enthusiastic and numerous, from *Newsweek* to *People* to the front page of the *New York Times Book Review* magazine, but the book did not break any sales records. It is, I think, my best book of narrative history, although I still have a soft spot in my heart for *Klondike*. When it was finally finished, Barbara Sears remarked that I looked "bloody awful," but I felt rewarded.

I wrote it while serving as vice-chair of The Writers' Union, succeeding to the chair the following year. The union's rise marked a new attitude to books and authors in Canada. In spite of this, most daily newspapers had been neglecting the writing community. Books were making news, but the news didn't get published. Most book pages, when they existed at all, were wretched. There were few qualified literary critics in Canada. We had many distinguished women writers, but books by women were getting less attention than they deserved, perhaps because most reviewers were men.

I decided, with my usual cockiness, that during my term of office I would change all that. The newspapers were always taking surveys and publishing the results. Why not turn the tables and publish a survey of newspaper book pages? So we undertook a six-month survey at the height of the Christmas book season, measuring the amount of space given to news and reviews on the book pages of each of thirty papers. As I wrote in a press release, "it is our belief that book reviews and book news now deserve the kind of attention that entertainment, sports, fashions, and travel receive...."

There is nobody more sensitive than a newspaper editor who finds himself under the gun. Our survey caused a howl of protest, especially from papers like the *Ottawa Citizen, Toronto Star,* and *Globe and Mail,* who learned to their chagrin that the little Kingston *Whig-Standard* had come first in our rating system. All sorts of excuses were offered: our methodology was faulty, our system of weighting newspapers by circulation was skewed, and so on. The fact that we had discovered that books written by women were reviewed less often than books written by men was given short shrift. The following year, in response to this criticism, we did a second survey using different criteria. Once again the Kingston *Whig-Standard* won out over the larger papers.

Meanwhile I had crossed the country speaking to newspaper and book-page editors. They listened politely and in some cases made changes. I cannot say how successful this campaign was. Certainly more attention is paid now to books and to news about books and authors than in 1989. But it may well be that all this would have happened without the union's lobbying. It is quite possible that so many books are now being published and sold, and so many bookstores carry them, that the press, a little tardily, has had to recognize their existence.

410

5

SECHELT, B.C., August 18, 1989. We are mooching for coho aboard *The*
Hal Straight's boat off the Sunshine Coast – Straight, Hans (his handy- *C-Beast*
man), Jack Webster, and me. We are telling – well, not lies about the old
days, but tales that have ripened over the years like wine. We have four
lines out, and there are already several freshly gutted coho salmon in
the cooler.

Straight is reminiscing about the day Sid Godber, having just switched
jobs from the Vancouver Province *to the* Sun, *got his great wartime scoop.*
Sid was looking out into the harbour when a Liberty Ship, the Greenhill
Park, *blew sky high, shaking the waterfront and sending showers of*
debris into the harbour. Sid rushed to the phone with an eyewitness story
– good for a page 1 byline – but forgot he'd changed jobs. The rewrite
man, who got the story, didn't utter a peep, and so the Province *got the*
Sun's *scoop.*

"It's not the same today," Straight is saying. "The fun's gone out of
the business. Remember Little Miss No-Nose?" I certainly do. The child's
nose had been bitten off by a dog and the Province *had raised a fund*
to send her east for an operation. They thought they had an exclusive
picture of the child emerging from the hospital, but Straight copied the
picture. He had an artist paint a doll in the tot's arms to make the photo
look different, ran it in the first edition, and beat his hated rival.

"That was straight thievery," I tell him.

"Everybody stole pictures in those days," he reminds us.

Suddenly one of the reels emits a high-pitched whine.

"It's yours! Grab it! Grab it!" Straight shouts to Webster. "Don't lose
it, for Christ's sake. Let it run. Let it run!"

Webster grabs the rod from its holder, but the line has already gone
slack. "Reel it in! Reel it in!" Straight cries. He is like a heavyweight
trainer giving advice to his boxer. "For God's sake, keep it tight!" he
shouts to Webster, but it is too late; the fish is gone.

"You lost it, goddamn it!" Straight exclaims. Webster looks abashed,
like a naughty boy who has committed an unpardonable sin. After more
than seventy years of fishing in these waters, the one-time managing
editor of the Vancouver Sun *still hates to lose a fish.*

"You're a great TV personality, Webster," Straight says sarcastically,
"but you got a lot to learn about coho."

411

We get to reminiscing about the time he and I and Hans and Harry Filion each had a fish on the line. "I never saw Harry scramble so fast," Straight says. "He held on, though. That fish went under two boats, but the big man landed his fish."

We sit silently, sipping our beer, thinking about Harry.

"The world's drollest man," I say, and Straight nods.

"Old Harry," he says. "Too bad he didn't live to see Vicki triumph. How proud he'd have been."

"He was always proud of her," I remind him. "You know she met Michel Gabereau at our place? We were having a benefit for some charity – Voice of Women, I think – and he was part of the entertainment – an assistant lion tamer at the time, if you can believe."

"Well, I can believe it," Straight says. "Remember when you and he faked a picture of the mayor in hospital? Harry was a great photographer. They don't make them like Harry any more."

"There hasn't been a columnist in this town could touch Jack Scott," says Webster.

"Scott sure had a way with words," Straight says. "The piece he wrote when he and his family were dragging a trailer across North America and he got caught in traffic in New York? Where are the Scotts today? Did you see him before he died?"

"He didn't want to see anybody," I tell him.

Suddenly my reel speaks up and I lunge for the rod.

"Let it go!" Straight shouts. I let it run until the fish, now a quarter of a mile from the boat, turns and heads back. Before the line can go slack, I reel it in.

Straight is on his feet, giving advice and instructions, searching for the net as the fish and I struggle.

"Keep the tip up!" he shouts. "Don't let it drop! That's it. Bring him in."

We can see the salmon leaping in the water, trying to break the line as it comes close to the boat.

"Don't let it get under the boat!" Straight cries. "Keep it away from the motor. You know how clever they are. That's it. Now! *Keep the tip under water.* Under the water, *I said. And walk him in."*

I walk slowly backward, pulling the coho along until Straight can get a net under it. "You did all right," he tells me as the fish wriggles on the deck and Hans clubs it. I bask in the ultimate accolade.

"I taught him all he knows," Straight says to Webster, "and I don't

only mean about fishing. We drank a lot of rye in my kitchen tearing the paper apart, worrying about how to make up a page, crop a picture, and sell a story with big type."

"The good old days," says Webster, who took my place after I left the business.

"Do you know what I've discovered after all this time?" says Hal Straight. "I've discovered that none of that meant a damn. Headlines, make-up, pictures are fine, but what people buy a paper for is the stories. If you've got good writers and good stories, you'll get readers. The rest is window dressing."

"Well, you got a lot of good stories," Webster tells him.

"Yes, we did," says Straight. "We sure did."

Suddenly his own reel starts to sing. "I'll take this one," he announces, and with an agility I can scarcely credit, he leaps to his feet and neatly lands his fish.

A passing boat gives a hail. "How'd ya do, Hal?"

"Not too good," Straight calls, poker-faced. "This isn't much of a spot. Try over at Sangster."

The boat moves off, leaving us to land our limit. We head back for Secret Cove, and I watch the big man slowly making his way up the dock. How many fish, I wonder, has he landed in the last seventy-odd years since he first ventured out onto these waters with his father? It doesn't matter. "Every time I reel one in, it's just like the first time," he tells me. "It makes me young again." He looks tired, but his face shines with excitement.

"It's been a wonderful day," he says. "I'm glad now you came out."

Me, too. He had phoned a fortnight before our outing to tell me not to bother. "I don't think I can make it," he said. "The Sea Beast has got me." But I had come anyway, and for a time I had seen him again as I had known him fifty years before, when we were both young in that golden age of newspapering.

"It's been a wonderful day," Hal Straight says again. He pauses and looks back over the ocean, the little waves glittering in the light of the dying sun.

"This has been the most wonderful day of my life!" says Hal Straight.

A few months later, I fly out to visit him for the last time. He has spent the better part of a day on the long-distance phone to Florida, trying to buy a new boat to go fishing – a boat he can never use. Now he lies, whitened and suddenly shrivelled, gasping, on his bed. The next day he is gone. The C-Beast has won, as it always does.

6

Playing fair

"Where do you get your ideas?" people ask. The question baffles me. The subjects I choose seem obvious to me. Vimy, the War of 1812, the CPR are all in the public domain. The titles are obvious, too. When one writes a book about the Great Depression, the title ought to be just that. I was criticized by several reviewers for choosing such an obvious title for the second volume of my CPR story, but *The Last Spike* seems to me the best possible title, since it explains in three words what the book is about. I've had my share of goofy titles, such as *Just Add Water and Stir,* a collection of newspaper columns that sold better than those that followed, possibly because the customers thought they were getting a cookbook. When you're not dealing with humour but with "true facts," you do well to play fair with your readers.

The Great Depression seemed to be the proper title. I had spent my teenage years in that decade. The book was written just as another depression was beginning and so had a resonance for our own times. It seemed to me that we were facing similar problems without learning from earlier experience. Many people remarked that I had dropped my usual objectivity and written an angry book. To that, I plead guilty. I couldn't hide my feelings about those days. *The Great Depression* is about what happens to a country when it is faced with an economic crisis. Fear takes hold. Human rights go into the trash can. Children are allowed to starve because the governments say they can't afford to feed them. Unemployment increases as public projects are cut. The poor are berated for not working hard enough, for being lazy, for trying to cheat the taxpayers. Immigration slows to a trickle, and those newcomers who slip in are reviled for taking the jobs of good Canadians. Refugees hammer at our doors and are turned back. Social progress comes to a standstill. Scapegoats are discovered and tagged as subversives. New political parties spring up, promising panaceas. Extremists on both the left and the right offer easy solutions. Crime is on the rise – or, at least, that's what the public believes.

Though the parallels were not exact, I experienced a sense of déjà vu as I dug into the story of the Hungry Thirties. We have fewer soup kitchens today, but we do have the scandal of the food banks. The social services the Depression bequeathed us are being nibbled away. Again, it is the children who suffer most and the poor who take the blame, while immigrants, who are the real entrepreneurs in WASPland, are being kept out. The new scapegoats are the teenagers, once again feared by an adult world whose only solution is to lengthen prison terms and put children on trial as if they were grown-ups.

By the time I set out in the autumn of 1990 to promote *The Great Depression,* I was deep into a new work, and, as usual, heartily sick of talking about the old one. I was full of my research on Niagara Falls but was under orders from Elsa not to talk about it. Why plug a book that nobody can buy yet? "Don't even mention Niagara," she warned. "Don't waste one valuable minute! Talk about the Depression and *only* the Depression!"

I had to go back and re-read my own words so I wouldn't make an ass of myself on camera. I had banished much of the detail of the Depression from my memory. The brain has room for just so many facts. I skimmed the book again and wrote out some typical questions for those talk-show hosts who hadn't read it, thus saving both of us from looking stupid.

But I really wanted to talk about *Niagara,* a book I'd planned to write a quarter of a century before and had quite forgotten. I realized, after some preliminary fiddling, that the story had everything. It was really a kind of social history, ranging from the development of photography to the discovery of alternating current – the heroic age of invention that produced a variety of new products, from Carborundum to Shredded Wheat. The whole story of the continent's fads and fashions revolved around the Falls, from the change in wedding rituals to the invention of the tourist trade, not to mention public power and private pollution.

It was an international story, and yet I could not find an American publisher. The comments irritated me. There was too much Canadian material, I was told, even though there was more about the American side of the Falls than our own. I am still baffled by this parochial attitude. Fortunately, I have never depended on sales below the border.

Meanwhile, a packaging firm offered me a fee to produce for them a picture book on the four seasons in Canada. I told them there was only one season that counted in this country, and that was winter. I said I would both write and edit such a book but wanted total control. After some hemming and hawing, they agreed. Picture books are fun to do and this one more than most because it would be a personal book about my own experiences with winter, enhanced by André Gallant's stunning photographs, Barbara Sears's archival research, and Andrew Smith's art direction. Elsa would act as co-ordinator. It served as a much-needed break between my hard slogging on *Niagara* and the equally difficult book I was planning to follow *Winter.* That, too, would be a narrative history, but a different kind of narrative history for me – more personal, more subjective, and more informal, a look at the last half of the twentieth century as I had witnessed it, suffered it, and lived it; a book not about the dead past, but a book about my own period – about my times.

This is it. And I'm already at work on the next one.

416

Epilogue

I am writing these words on a Smith-Corona electric portable, a model identical to the one that blew up in Portugal and to the one that dropped its *h*'s in Jamaica, when I tried to write about William Henry Harrison. In a sense, this old and obsolete machine symbolizes my stubborn resistance to the twenty-first century, which is almost upon us. I am a child of the twentieth, but my own children tend to think of me as an Old Fogy, who refuses to climb aboard the communications network and join the computer age. They look on me now as I once looked on those of my aging colleagues who wrote their pieces in longhand.

I am painfully aware that I am no longer With It, as I once thought I was. I can sing all the lyrics of every popular song written in the thirties and forties, from "Barnacle Bill the Sailor" to "Sweet and Lovely," but I cannot relate to the MuchMusic channel on television. Sinatra, *si;* Peter Gabriel, *no.* I have tried to come to terms with my VCR, but when I try to record a classic movie, all I get is the next day's soap opera. There was a time when I did my best to interview all the stars in the heavens, but the other day I had to ask who Garth Brooks was. My times are accelerating so fast that the world has started to pass me by.

I ask myself, does it really matter? In some cases, it does. Attitudes are changing so swiftly that I cannot keep up with them, and in certain cases I don't care to. Everything changes, yes; but in some ways, nothing changes. I am irritated, for one thing, by the new intolerance that goes under the vague buzz-phrase "political correctness." There was a time when I was disturbed by the old intolerance of the Canadian Establishment. Those bigots have been silenced, more or less; but in their place we are experiencing others with a new kind of myopia. It is proper that people should lean over backward in trying to assuage the guilt of the centuries, but not at the expense of the historical record, and certainly not at the expense of other segments of society. Should I resign from the Alexander Mackenzie Trail Association because that estimable explorer did not always act like a twentieth-century liberal? Should I

417

play down the aboriginal savagery (but not the white savagery) in the War of 1812 so that everybody can feel better? Should I clap my hands in glee because my union, in which every writer is supposed to be equal, decides to support a conference in which some members are excluded because of the colour of their skin?

This rankles. If the excluded skins had been black, brown, or yellow, The Writers' Union of Canada would never have condoned such a conference, nor devoted some of its funds to support it. But the skins were white, and so it was thought perfectly proper to bar white writers from the sessions of Writing Through Race, held in Vancouver in the spring of 1994.

The conference was a good idea, long overdue. It was proper that writers of colour should get together to discuss mutual concerns and that the union should help. But the union's strength is that it does not discriminate. Anybody who has written a book in the trade can enjoy all the privileges of membership. No professional writer is excluded. But a short time before the conference, I realized for the first time that in this union-supported and union-financed conference, whites were to be treated differently.

The union's council had no trouble, apparently, in rationalizing its decision to spend union dues in a reverse form of racial discrimination. Indeed, our chair, Myrna Kostash, tried to defend it in the *Globe and Mail,* pirouetting around the real issue, making it sound as if those of us who opposed the exclusionary nature of the affair were really opposed to the idea of the conference itself. In short, by inference, we were the real racists.

That word was not used until the morning before the union's annual general meeting in May, when a panel discussion was held at Ryerson University to discuss the matter. There, to my astonishment, speaker after speaker rose to support the exclusion of white writers from the proceedings and to dissociate themselves from any suggestion that writers of colour might themselves be discriminating. A shroud of white guilt hung over the proceedings. "I honour you!" cried Libby Scheier, a poet, addressing the people on the panel, only one of whom was white. "I *honour* you!"

I rose at last to speak and to say that when some members of our union were denied entrance to a union-sponsored conference, there was only one word for it. I was interrupted by boos, hisses, and catcalls. As I concluded, a Jamaican member of the panel leapt to her feet. "I've fuck-ing well had enough of this racist shit!" she shouted, and stomped off.

I was crushed. I have been called every name over the past half-century—from card-carrying Communist to Antichrist – but this was the first time I had been called a racist. It hurt. I left the meeting that morn-ing, returned to my downtown office, and skipped the afternoon ses-sion. Am I out of it? I asked myself. Has the world passed me by? Have I missed something? Am I, a white liberal, part of a dying breed? I can't work a computer. I don't really know much about Garth Brooks. Is my stubborn attitude just another sign that I am no longer With It? Are the principles by which I was raised and have espoused all my life out of date?

The pendulum has swung wildly out of control, I thought. Almost fifty years earlier in *Maclean's* I had reported on the discrimination against Japanese Canadians in British Columbia. Later, in the *Star,* I'd written about discrimination against blacks in Ontario. I found it ironic that the organizer of the conference was himself a Japanese Canadian and most of the invitees of colour were black.

It was a minor incident, but it suggested how swiftly the times were changing. In bending over backward to demonstrate our tolerance we are in danger of executing a pratfall. Not long ago I used the term "WASP" in a newspaper column and was attacked (by a WASP) for sneering at a visible minority.

The twentieth century, it seemed to me, had already ended – five years before its time. The postwar world with all its promise was as dead as the Trudeaumania I witnessed at the Liberal leadership con-vention in 1968. Nationalism, too, is dead or dying, to be replaced by a narrow provincialism. People are more concerned about the lack of jobs and the deficit, for which Trudeau and his party are partly to blame. It has become popular to blame him for the spendthrift policies that threaten to beggar the nation. But he looks good when compared with his successor, who thought he had to explain why he was travelling First Class on Air Canada. After his election, Brian Mulroney went first class all the way, to the country's cost.

The end of the Cold War changed everything. For years we were taught and were willing to look at the world in terms of black and white, although my own experiences in Prague and Budapest suggest-ed it was closer to grey. You can no longer tell the good guys from the bad guys, even in the new Hollywood Westerns. Is Boris Yeltsin a hero or a villain?

How quickly nationalism takes new forms and how quickly did the federal state seem old-fashioned! The camaraderie between the two founding nations that I saw and marvelled at in Expo year has dissipated. Over the past decade I have witnessed and sometimes fought against the Americanization and also the Balkanization of this country. When I flew to Edmonton at Mel Hurtig's request to speak out against free trade, the premier, Don Getty, attacked me publicly as an interloper, not welcome in his province. What kind of a country is this when its citizens treat each other as foreign invaders?

Would *The National Dream* be as big a best-seller if it were published today rather than in 1970? Somehow I doubt it. Bands of steel no longer bind us. What have we got to boast about, with the CBC on the ropes and medicare up for grabs? What is today's National Dream? The Americanization of the country goes on apace, led by the very broadcasting corporation invented to prevent it. Television productions (such as *Butterbox Babies*) use the American courtroom techniques and language, making a mockery of their Canadian setting. As I well know, the Dionne quintuplets were saved when Gordon Sinclair had fresh mother's milk rushed to Callander. But the Canadian producers of *Million Dollar Babies,* with an eye to U.S. sales, apparently felt it necessary to give credit for that generous act to the Americans, thus making Canadians look like heartless slowpokes. As for Gordon Sinclair, he was eliminated from the story entirely and replaced by a fictitious New York sob sister. We have few enough authentic characters in our background and cannot afford to trade the liveliest of them to the Yanks for a mess of pottage.

One reason why history is written is to let future generations profit from the mistakes of the past. When I wrote *The Great Depression,* I could not conceal my disgust with those leaders who failed to face up to the greatest economic crisis of our time. I was equally disgusted to realize that nobody had learned much. The Great Depression was not solved by erecting provincial barriers, cutting people off relief, and balancing the budget. It was solved for us by the spending spree and the full employment that, miraculously, accompanied the start of the Second World War.

I dug into the Depression story just as a new economic crisis was

420

looming, searching out significant quotes from Depression leaders. (*We must pause and consider before embarking on enterprises calling for the expenditure of large sums of money.* R.B. Bennett, 1931) But as I set out on my promotional tour I saw little evidence that attitudes had changed. We have always spent big in boom times when the country is riding high, and cut back in bad times, inverting the theories of John Maynard Keynes.

A historian lives on two levels: the past keeps crowding in on the present. I remember living twelve hours a day and longer in the Public Archives in Ottawa, unravelling the handwritten letters of Charles Tupper, Lord Dufferin, and John A. himself and leafing through the brittle pages of the newspapers of the 1880s. At day's end I felt that I was actually living in the past. The pen scrawls of the men and women I'd been recording, the headlines, and also the advertisements of the previous century did not entirely vanish when I left the building and strolled past the ancient stonework of the East Block.

At the time of the first Quebec referendum I was obsessed with an earlier struggle for Canada. I was struggling with the complicated epic of the War of 1812 while René Lévesque was struggling to do what American armies could not do – tear the nation apart. When Lévesque went down to defeat in 1985, I was with Franklin in the Arctic. And when Preston Manning's Reform Party was on the rise, I was, in my mind, climbing down the slippery cliffs below Niagara Falls.

Even as the debate in The Writers' Union continued, I had one foot in the past, writing in *Winter* about the snobbism of the nineteenth-century snowshoe clubs, which wouldn't let the natives join them on their tramps, though the Indians had actually invented the snowshoe. If membership had its privileges, discrimination had its ironies.

The debate in The Writers' Union was hoisted for a year to allow tempers to cool. I was actually writing a few paragraphs about the union that week for this book. I hope by the time it is published the problem will have been resolved and I will be spared further catcalls.

But then, my career has been a roller-coaster ride all the way, and I cannot pretend that I haven't enjoyed it. I've loved every minute – the ups, the downs, the victories, the defeats, the laurels, and the booby prizes. There's never been a dull moment, partly, I suspect, because I have never shrunk from controversy. In fact, a voice inside me whispers that I revel in it, like a mischievous small boy throwing snowballs at a top hat. Jacques Dalibard was undoubtedly right when he told me I'd make a bad politician. Certainly I could never support any cause in which I did not believe.

Life is a series of accidental opportunities, and I've had my share. If I hadn't talked the *Vancouver Sun* into letting me investigate the Nahanni country in 1947, I'd never have written the piece that led to a job at *Maclean's*. If Maclean Hunter hadn't got stubborn, I would never have become a columnist for the *Toronto Star.* If I hadn't written that infuriating article about kids and sex, I wouldn't have been let free to write *The Comfortable Pew.* Was that a good thing? I'm not sure; there were, perhaps, better books to occupy me.

I do know that if I hadn't driven out to Kleinburg on that spring day in 1948, my life would have been distinctly different. I look out now over the valley that Janet and I first saw and loved, and I feel a sense of timelessness. Nature, unlike technology, is slow to change. How green my valley looks! It is lusher now than it was in those early days when we were young. Then the far slopes were bare of trees and the sere acreage on which we settled was naked pastureland, unrelieved by foliage, unbroken by the ponds and hillocks we have built over the years. The house we put up in fits and starts is now screened from the roadway by the digging and planting of forty years. For almost half a century we have rejoiced in "our own space," to use that baffling new expression. The grandchildren – twelve of them, now – jump from family cars when they arrive for the weekend and hit the ground running. There is almost unlimited room to race about, far from the narrow traffic-clogged city streets.

If we hadn't made that mad decision to buy the lot, would I have stayed in the country, or would I have opted for a career south of the border? Who's to say? If I'd hustled the old *Life* magazine or the *Saturday Evening Post* – both of them eventually driven out of business by television – I might have become an American magazine writer. But I'm not a hustler, at least in that sense. I've never gone after a job; I've waited for the jobs to come after me. I slipped into television almost by osmosis, thanks to radio; and I sneaked into radio, thanks to my friendship with Lister Sinclair. I've never taken a job I didn't enjoy, which explains why I don't sell deodorants or cornflakes on the tube. I push my own books shamelessly because I'm proud of them. My friend Jack Webster once needled me on his television show, in

422

that thick Scots burr that is as much a trademark as my bow tie. "So you're here to plug another book," he said.

"Well, it's all my own work," I explained. "I sure as hell don't plug stoves from Wosk's." Webster, the TV spokesman for Wosk's in Vancouver, grinned and changed the subject.

A former newsman once called me with a promise of "the most money you've ever had in your life." The discussion ended when he mentioned a make of Japanese car. I wish I could have taken that lucrative assignment, but it simply wasn't my bag. To be fair, I didn't need the money. If the cupboard had been bare I might cheerfully have peddled swampland in Florida.

Writers rarely retire. Certainly I don't intend to. The great body of my work – all my narrative histories save *Klondike* – has been accomplished since the age of fifty, when most adult males have started to look ahead to unlimited days on the golf course, beach, or easy chair. None of these mature books has been greeted with unadulterated praise. Every one has had its share of harsh reviews, some from critics I admire. That is probably a good thing. An author is not at his best when he writes with a swelled head. Interviewers are always telling me I could publish the telephone book and it would sell under my name. That, thank God, is a fantasy. Every fall season finds me on the road, waxing garrulous about my latest creation. As with the movies, you're only as good as your last book, a truth that keeps us writers honest.

The public, not the critics, decide in the end what is worthwhile and what isn't. *The Last Spike,* to quote one example, survived the worst single review I've ever received. Some writers claim they never read reviews, but I find that hard to swallow. I read them all avidly, agreeing smugly with the praise, fulminating over the derision. It's part of the fun, and it's also part of the pain. But if we never knew the pain, how would we recognize the fun?

I've had it all – disdain, scorn, ridicule, contempt, respect, flattery, veneration, and esteem. One learns to disregard it and get on with the job. We've all had low moments in this business; if I've had fewer than most, it's because I've never set my sights impossibly high. I've attempted to be a good professional writer, not a great one, trying as best I can to understand my times by studying the past. When life occasionally turns troublesome, as it did in the spring of '94 when a young activist shrieked that I was a racist, I dig into my Hold-basket, where

I can always find solace in a letter written a few months before by a seven-year-old boy in Delta, B.C.

"Dear Mr. Berton," he wrote. "You are a real good writer. The Secret World of Og is the best book I've ever read in my whole life."

Somehow that kind of support makes it all worthwhile.

Index

429

Guayaquil, Ecuador, 38
Guelph, Ont., 381
Guggenheim Museum (New York), 165
Gulbenkian, Calouste, 277
Gulbenkian, Nubar, 277
GUM (department store, Moscow), 183, 185
Gun-an-noot, 382-83
Gun-an-noot, David, 383
Gutenberg Galaxy, The, 302
Gzowski, Peter, 245, 248, 394

Habitat (Montreal), 306
Hadden, Brit, 16
Haganah, 50
Haggart, Ron, 156, 344
Haig-Brown, Roderick, 40
Hailey, Arthur, 41; and family, 261-62
Halifax, N.S., 100
Halifax *Diocesan Times,* 260
Halliday, Ennis (later Ennis Armstrong), 169-70, 222,
    261, 282-83, 284, 362
Hambleton, Jean (Mrs. Ronald Hambleton), 52
Hambleton, Ronald, 52, 57
Hamilton, Frank, 43-44
Hamilton, Ont., 171, 172, 402-3
Han River, 73
Hannon, Leslie, 94, 305
Hans (handyman), 411-12
"Happy Gang, The" (CBC radio), 95
"Happy Valley" (Kleinburg, Ont.), 52-57
Hardinge, Lord, 101
Harold King Farm, 173; Foundation, 282
Harrison, Ernest, 258-59, 266
Harrison, William Henry, 386
Harron, Don (pseud. Charlie Farquharson), 121
Hart, Harvey, 139
Hastings, Ont., 213
Havelka, William, 299
Haymes, Dick, 356
Headless Valley, 96, 280
Hefner, Hugh, 173
Hellyer, Paul, 321
Hemingway, Ernest, 152
Hepburn, Mitchell, 26
Herbert, Bill, 67, 68
Heritage Canada Foundation, 346, 380, 393; Main
    Street program, 380-81
Heritage Day, 381-82
heritage movement, 380
Heritage Theatre, 402-3
Hewitt, Foster, 41, 377
Higgins, Marguerite, 74
Higgitt, W.L., 333
High River Times, 34
Hijiyama Park (Hiroshima), 204

Hill, James J. (Jim), 325
Hindmarsh, H.C., 152-53
Hindmarsh, Harry, Jr., 226
Hiroshima, 203-5; Castle, 205
Hiss, Alger, 356
History, Canadian, 49, 322, 329-30; popular, 49, 115;
    narrative, 124, 331, 355; social, 415
"Hockey Night in Canada," 51, 401
Hodgeman, Marge, 286
Hodgins, Dorothy, 17-18
Hoffer, Abram, 92
Hoffman, Abby, 356
Hoffmeister, Adolf, 301-3
Hogg, Ruth, 110
Hogtown, *see* Toronto
Hollywood, 192, 275
Hollywood's Canada, 353-54
Home-Made Banners, 40
Honderich, Beland, 149, 153-56, 158, 159-61, 171,
    198, 289, 294
Honey Harbour, Ont., 210
Hope, Bob, 64
Horn, Johnny, 39
Hotel, 262
Hotels:
    Adlon (East Berlin), 208
    Biltmore (Los Angeles), 188-89
    Biltmore (New York), 21
    Europa (Moscow), 186
    Fairview (Dawson), 116
    Four Seasons (Jarvis Street, Toronto), 356
    Hyatt (Los Angeles), 355
    Imperial (Tokyo), 67, 198
    King Edward (Toronto), 342
    Kootje (Seoul), 76
    Landmark Motor Inn (Fort Erie, Ont.), 366
    Lord Nelson (Halifax), 100
    Lord Simcoe (Toronto), 154, 362
    Marinouchi (Tokyo), 67
    Occidental (Dawson), 218
    Palliser (Calgary), 264
    Park Plaza (Toronto), 51, 139, 144, 343
    Plaza (New York), 164
    Royal York (Toronto), 163, 208, 330
    Savoy (London), 277
    Ukraine (Moscow), 182-83
    Westbury (London), 275, 355
Houde, Camillien, 153
House, Eric, 402
Howdy Doody, 88
Howse, Dr. Ernest, 263
Hubbard, Mina, 361
Humber River, 51-53, 107-10
Humber Summit, Ont., 52, 55, 108
Hungary, 250-57, 300

431

432

435

437

Templeton, Charles, 132, 134, 147, 280, 288-90, 314, 315, 339-41, 366, 367, 372, 391, 397-99, 409
Templeton, Jean, 237
Teng Hsiao-p'ing [Deng Xiaoping], 370
Termites in the Shape of Men: Common Sense Versus Pierre Berton, 265
This Hour Has Seven Days, 271, 403
Thistletown, Ont., 52, 108
Thomas, Evan, 383
Thomas, Norman, 293, 383
Thompson, Jack, 74
Thompson, Phillips, 304
Thomson, Lorraine, 144, 343, 400
Thomson, R.H., 392, 402
Thomson, Tom, 107
Tihany peninsula, 255
Till, Eric, 334
Time, 16, 298, 330, 353
Tippecanoe, battle of, 385
Toad River, B.C., 216
Today (NBC TV), 245
Tokyo, 66-67, 198-201, 315-16
Tonight Show (TV), 271
Tonks, Allan, 171
Tonks, Chris, 171
Top of the World Highway, 217-18
Toronto, Ont., 6-8, 23, 25, 54, 95, 107-8, 162-63, 222, 230-31, 282, 286, 354; Centre Island, 8; High Park, 8; Kingsway, 58; city halls, 163-65, 288, 345; Anglican Diocese of, 260
Toronto Harbour Commissioners, 162
Toronto Life, 368
Toronto Press Club, 155
Toronto Public Library, 152; Boys and Girls House, 175
Toronto Star, 17, 24, 27-28, 143, 149, 152-53, 154-57, 159-60, 182, 187, 189, 198, 210, 211, 212-13, 222, 223, 226-227, 237, 239, 250, 260-61, 294, 307, 318, 327, 342, 344, 367, 384, 399, 400, 410, 422
Toronto *Sun*, 341
Toronto *Telegram*, 26, 27-28, 40, 171, 227-28, 238, 263, 275, 290, 303, 318, 330, 341
Toronto Transportation Commission, 7
Tories, *see* Conservatives
To Tell the Truth (TV program), 137, 405
Tour de Force (trivia game), 399
Town, Harold, 310, 337
Trans-Canada Highway, 334
transcontinental railway, building of, 323, 326
Trent Canal, 211-14
Trent-Severn waterway, 210-15
Troberg, Walter, 219
Trowell, Doug, 398
Troyer, Warner, 142

Trudeau, Pierre Elliott, 270-71, 296, 313, 321, 342, 367, 390, 393, 406, 419; government of, 340
Truman, Harry, 82
Truscott, Stephen, 166
Truth Squad, 240
Tuchman, Barbara, 330
Tupper, Charles, 421
Turner, John, 321
Tweedsmuir Park (British Columbia), 146
Twelve O'Clock High (movie), 70
Twenty-One (TV program), 273
Typewriters:
    Underwood, 59
    Hermes Baby, 68, 352-53
    Smith-Corona, 326, 352, 353, 386, 417
Tyrwhitt, Janice, 47, 407

Ubyssey, 50
Under Attack (Screen Gems TV), 312-14, 315, 316, 321
Underhill, Frank, 238
Union Station (Toronto), 209; Committee, 345
Unitarians, 263
United Church of Canada, 265-66
United Nations, 19, 75, 76, 82; General Assembly, 18-21, 189; Security Council, 21; Korean War forces, 66, 70, 72, 84-85; Civilian Assistance Command, 76
United States, 19, 30, 70, 71, 81, 82, 105-6, 137-38, 387, 390, 409, 415; culture, 184; South, 366
University Avenue (Toronto), 8, 208
University of British Columbia, 13, 50, 322
University of Manitoba, 264
University of Toronto, 47, 116; Victoria College, 9
University of Western Ontario, 328
Unter den Linden (East Berlin), 209
UPI (United Press International), 189

Vallee, Rudy, 236
Valour and the Horror, The (CBC TV), 408
Vancouver, 6, 23, 98, 232, 236, 264, 378; Parks Board, 381
Vancouver *News-Herald*, 22, 162
Vancouver *Province*, 269, 411
Vancouver Sun, 22, 98, 131, 142, 154, 162, 222, 231, 411, 422
Van Doran, Charles, 273
Van Horne, William Cornelius, 49, 346
Vanishing Point, The, 93
Vaughan, Sarah, 183, 184
Vega, Isela, 338
Verdi, Lieut. Col. Joe, 74, 76
Victoria, B.C., 9, 332
Vietnam War, 72, 80, 366, 408
Vimy, 97, 407-8

439

440

Why everybody hates Berton

Everyone hates Pierre Berton. In fact,
...way you can separate sophisticated pe...
...s by *how much* they hate Pierre B...
...hat's because Berton is the most
...n journalist in this country's h...
...cessful, in fact, that...
...ses.

...us it is th...
...elevision...
...ve disapp...
...ay, there...
...k the fifth...
...has bee...
...11. That'...
...0 p.m.. as...
...gree to the...
...epeat the sh...

...nel 11 swe...
...s just to as...
...ver. a fact...
...rton as C...
...

U.S. would hurt our culture: Berto

VANCOUVER (CP) — Americans
...their cultural ex-...

award winner told 250
Council of Canadians din
day night that four distir...

Berton demolishe:

**THE PROMISED LAND: Settling the
West 1896-1914 by Pierre Berton; pp.
388; McClelland and Stewart; $24.95.**

By Bill Peterson
of the Star-Phoenix

...e who would have us be-
...trigue were confined
...er while Cana-

with a character in The Sting th
man of the cloth.
Of Barr and his type Berton
"Their credentials seem imped
their dreams and visions bold .
later does it begin to dawn on

2   THE WINNIPEG SUN, Tues

Berton: Use 'em or else

Old buildings our heritage

By JEFFREY SLUSKY
Sun Staff Writer

Use them or lose both them
...and the past — that was a

Calls Burton series "cockfight sensation"

When Pierre Burton
opened his five-part TV
series on Canadian Indian
...oblems, he said he want—
...to make people "a little
...angry."

...e did. But at least one
...Council, son was more than "a
4, Ont. e bit angry."

...ther J. E. Y. Levaque,
...ter of the Oblate

Canada as disgruntle
grateful, and irrat
and to disregard as
existent the constr
and valuable wo
many hundreds of
Canadians in schools
pitals, social cen
friendship centre
across the country, on
off the reserves."

The former Oblate
...school directo

SOPHA ROASTS SHULMAN AND BERTON AS LITERARY PHONIES

Outspoken MPP Elmer
Sopha (L, Sudbury) thinks
two of Canada's best known
authors are phonies.
Last night he pinned the
title on Dr. Morton Shul-
man and Pierre Berton.
Dr. Shulman. fired last
year as Metro chief coroner
and now New Democratic
Party member for High
Park, wrote Anyone Can
Make A Million, a book explaining how to make mon-
ey on the stock...

Mr. Sopha said the book
is a swindle and should be
withdrawn.
The left-leaning Mr. Ber-
ton — "St. Pierre Berton,"
Mr. Sopha called him —
recently wrote The Smug
Minority, a viewpoint on
the Canadian establish-
ment.
The Liberal MPP called
Mr. Berton a flatulent blad-
der of phonism...

ways preaching against
U.S. domination of the Canadian economy.
Sir John A. MacDonald,
he said, would have called
such advice treason.

SUGGESTION

Mr. Sopha suggested Dr.
Shulman withdraw the book
from circulation and buy
space in the...

at the same time was on
television bemoaning the
fact Toronto restaurants
serve only half-a-dozen hors
d'oeuvres . . . who was pic-
tured sitting in his Kleinburg home sitting in his Oriental robe and drinking
mulled wines.
Mr. Berton, he said
...